Things with a History

HÉCTOR HOYOS

Things with a History

TRANSCULTURAL MATERIALISM AND
THE LITERATURES OF EXTRACTION
IN CONTEMPORARY LATIN AMERICA

Columbia University Press
New York

Columbia University Press
Publishers Since 1893
New York   Chichester, West Sussex
cup.columbia.edu
Copyright © 2019 Columbia University Press
All rights reserved

Cataloging-in-Publication Data is available from the Library of Congress
ISBN 978-0-231-19304-7 (cloth)—ISBN 978-0-231-19305-4 (pbk.)—
ISBN 978-0-231-55012-3 (e-book)
LCCN: 2019011892

Cover image: © A. Baraya. *Proyecto Herbario de Plantas Artificicales.* 2013.

Cover design: Lisa Hamm

—¿Qué le dijo la tortillera al filósofo?

—...

—*No hay masa ya.*

Contents

List of Illustrations ix
Acknowledgments xi

Introduction: A Tale of Two Materialisms   1

PART ONE

Objects

Chapter One: Raw Stuff Disavowed   41

Chapter Two: Of Rocks and Particles   67

Chapter Three: Corpse Narratives as Literary History   105

PART TWO

Assemblages

Chapter Four: Politics and Praxis of Hyperfetishism   143

Chapter Five: Digitalia from the Margins   171

Conclusions: Extractivism Estranged   199

Notes   231
Bibliography   273
Index   289

Illustrations

FIGURE 1.1   Workers and extracted rubber in the Amazon basin   44
FIGURE 1.2   Diego Rivera, Palacio Nacional, Mexico City, 1949   61
FIGURE 1.3   Vik Muniz, *Sigmund Freud*, 1997   61
FIGURE 1.4   Vik Muniz, *Action Photo I, after Hans Namuth*, 1997   62
FIGURE 2.1   *Reloj del sur*, Plaza Murillo, La Paz   70
FIGURE 2.2   Cover of César Aira's *El té de Dios*, 2010   91
FIGURE 3.1   Giuseppe Arcimboldo, *The Cook*, 1570   134
FIGURE 4.1   Tombstone of José Asunción Silva and Elvira Silva, Bogotá   154
FIGURE 4.2   Daniela Rossell, *Untitled (Ricas y Famosas)*, 2002   166
FIGURE 4.3   Daniela Rossell, *Untitled (Ricas y Famosas)*, 1999   167
FIGURE 4.4   Daniela Rossell, *Untitled (Ricas y Famosas)*, 1999   169
FIGURE 5.1   John Gerrard, *Solar Reserve (Tonopah, Nevada)*, 2014   190
FIGURE 5.2   John Gerrard, *Solar Reserve (Tonopah, Nevada)*, 2015   191
FIGURE 5.3   John Gerrard, *Farm (Pryor Creek, Oklahoma)*, 2015   192
FIGURE 5.4   Kim Steele, *Facebook Server Farm*, 2013   194
FIGURE 6.1   Carolina Caycedo, *YUMA, or the Land of Friends*, 2014   215

Acknowledgments

While the materialist inklings of this book are my sole responsibility, an assemblage of hospitable institutions and bighearted people made them possible. The former include, decisively, a 2012–13 Internal Faculty Fellowship at the Stanford Humanities Center; a spring 2014 Deutscher Akademischer Austausch Dienst (DAAD) Faculty Research Visit Grant at Freie Universität (FU), Berlin; and an Alexander von Humboldt Foundation Research Fellowship for Experienced Researchers for the summers of 2015 and 2016, also at FU. I am appreciative of fellow travelers and mentors in Iberian and Latin American Cultures (ILAC), the Division of Literatures, Cultures, and Languages (DLCL), the Center for Latin American Studies (CLAS), Modern Thought and Literature (MTL), and Science, Technology and Society (STS), among other provinces of Stanford's acronym heaven and alphabet soup. The latter include, unwaveringly, Dan Edelstein, Lanier Anderson, Debra Satz, Sepp Gumbrecht, Joachim Küpper, and Susanne Zepp. Intellectual sustenance—*un caldo de cultivo*—was provided by *materia*, the research group on Latin Americanist and comparative postanthropocentrisms at Stanford, as well as its co-chairs, guest speakers, regular participants, and cognate courses.

Since 2013, I have presented on sections of this book by invitation of esteemed colleagues and graduate research groups at Urbana-Champaign, Bern, Complutense, Javeriana, Duke, Yale, Copenhagen, Harvard, Instituto Cervantes in Tokyo, Brown, Tulane, Köln, Utah, Northwestern, Santa Cruz, Princeton, Pontificia Universidad Católica del Perú, Universidad de Santiago de Chile, Paris 8, Berkeley, Penn State, and Konstanz. A ruefully incomplete list of interlocutors includes Ximena Briceño (to whom this book is indebted in more ways than one), Ericka Beckman, Florencia Garramuño, Bruno Bosteels, Aníbal González, Patricia Valderrama, Richard Rosa, Nancy Armstrong, Mariano Siskind, Michelle Clayton, Idelber Avelar, Thomas Mullaney, Carlos Rincón (†), Alejandro Quin, José Luis Villacañas, Ellen Spielmann, Valeria de los Ríos, Matías Ayala, Jorge Coronado, Fred Turner, Otavio Leonidio Ribero, Gabriella Nouzeilles, Javier Guerrero, Julio Premat, Gabriel Giorgi, Lea Pao, Natalia Brizuela, Ewa Domańska, Eduardo Halfon, Álvaro Fernández Bravo, David Stentiford, María del Rosario Acosta, Virginia Walbot, David Damrosch, Ignacio Sánchez Prado, Antonio José Ponte, Rodolfo Dirzo, Mario Bellatin, Camilo Malagón, Bonnie Honig, María Evany Nascimento, Vicky Googasian, Craig Epplin, Eric Santner, Bill Brown, Dierdra Reber, Anna Castillo, Jacques Lezra, Orlando Bentancor, Marisol de la Cadena, Donna Haraway, and the formidable Francine Masiello.

Sections of this volume have appeared elsewhere in modified form. Part of the introduction appeared as "A Tale of Two Materialisms," *Novel: A Forum on Fiction* 51, no. 1 (May 2018): 101–16; to appear in translation as "Historia de dos materialismos," in the forthcoming *Naturaleza, literatura y modernidad en América Latina*, edited by Jeffrey Cedeño for Fondo de Cultura Económica, Chile. A portion of chapter 1 appeared as "Materia prima e historia en *Muñecas*," *Cuadernos de literatura* 40 (2016): 453–64; translated as "History and Raw Material in *Muñecas*," *Review: Literature and Art of the Americas* 96 (Spring 2018). Excerpts from chapter 3 will appear as "Bolaño: Solar Anus of World Literature," in *The Wiley Blackwell Companion to World Literature*, vol. 5, edited by Venkat Mani (in production); and appeared as "Corpse Narratives and the Teleology of World Literary History," *Journal of World Literature* 2 (2017): 63–79, edited by Nora Catelli, Annalisa Mirizio, and Marta Puxan-Oliva. Passages from chapter 5 appeared as "The Tell-Tale Computer: Obsolescence and Nostalgia in Chile after Alejandro Zambra," in *Technology, Literature, and Digital Culture in Latin America*, edited by Matthew Bush and Tania Gentic (New York: Routledge, 2015), 109–24. Pages from the concluding section appeared as "Global Supply Chain Literature vs. Extractivism," in *Re-Mapping World Literature*, edited by Gesine Müller, Jorge Locane, and Benjamin Loy (Berlin: De Gruyter, 2018), 33–44. A word of thanks goes to the rights holders and editors.

For their keen eye, I am grateful to Philip Leventhal and to the anonymous readers at Columbia University Press. Romina Wainberg and Patric Di Dio Di Marco kindly assisted in preparing the manuscript for publication, as did Michael Rendón. Cristian Soler provided additional image editing.

My greatest debt is to family and friends in California, Bogotá, Medellín, and Berlin for keeping things scattered and life collected while the present study was taking shape.

I dedicate this book to my students.

Things with a History

Introduction

A Tale of Two Materialisms

Things are not made to last anymore.

This phrase, whose utterance seems to have outlived the very items it laments, is now commonplace. When, one wonders, were things made to last? Is the golden standard, say, vacuum cleaners from before offshore outsourcing took hold in the 1990s, or cars from before the oil crisis of 1974, or, farther back in time, preindustrial, handmade shoes from the 1700s? In an entirely different order of magnitude, there is the Venus of Willendorf, dated some twenty-five to twenty-eight centuries ago. Now *that* was "made" to last! But perhaps the saying implies a more modest timescale: a lifetime. It speaks to the discomfort people experience, in their own brief stint as living beings on this earth, upon realizing that objects that might resist the passing of time succumb to it all the same. This casual utterance conjures many complex, interrelated matters. As the examples suggest, things that do not last may bear witness to changes in labor relations or in geopolitics; to the relative transience of human flesh when compared to more robust materials, such as limestone; to mortality itself. I have chosen this introductory vignette because it shows language trying to come to terms with material transformation.

The present volume is interested in more elaborate expressions than sayings—namely, in works of fiction and other cognate works of art that face similar challenges. I focus on a region and on a period, Latin America after 1989. In recent years, there has been a seismic transformation in our rapport to objects. To point to just a few examples of this shift, prior to roughly 1989 there was no consolidated World Wide Web or widespread mobile phones, let alone smartphones; there was no buzz about an "internet of things" or "3-D printing"; the trade in digital-age commodities (like lithium from Bolivia for batteries) was much smaller; the market for global luxury brands was more modest; more poor people around the world were getting their nourishment from industrial food-supply chains; an increasing number of better-off, "food-conscious" enclaves were abandoning those networks here and there; the Amazonian rainforest was larger; and there were smaller amounts of waste everywhere. The cumulative effect of these gradual transformations, which have picked up speed lately, suggests that we are currently undergoing a shift in a long-prevailing material paradigm. If one could imagine a long-standing, unwritten pact between humans and nonhumans, as of late we would be in the process of rewriting it. Take the awe and shock implicit in "things are not made to last anymore" and multiply it in many directions, some of the things in question being technological and others less so, some manufactured and some not, some organic and some inorganic, and you may appreciate the conjuncture that literature currently faces.

Things with a History shows that contemporary Latin American fiction not only reflects this transformation; it enriches our understanding of it and challenges the status quo that underwrites it. Once in motion, material change can have its own dynamic, and ecological transformation its own force. Capital may not fully control these new flows, but it quickly adapts to them and learns to profit from them, finding renewed occasions for inequality—hence my allusion to a status quo in a context that is, like climate change, essentially unstable. As my previous monograph showed, Latin American literary and cultural interrogation of globalization—the accelerated, uneven flow of people and things—make the region a privileged site at which to theorize our times.[1] In this book, I formulate the notion of *transcultural materialism*. While not exclusive to Latin America, the phenomenon has taken shape there, at the intersection of intellectual and literary history. I characterize it throughout the volume, focusing on its more recent stages. Transcultural materialism shares with other materialisms—Lucretian, mechanical, dialectical, and so forth—a fundamental orientation toward bodies instead of souls, tangible affairs instead of speculative notions. At their most basic, all materialisms oppose idealism; they claim that matter is all there is.

Several traits distinguish the transcultural variant. For one, it is an intellectual praxis rather than a philosophical doctrine. Its raison d'être is the *critique* of extractivism, in the two senses of study and opposition. Extractivism, simply put, is exploitation of nature and labor. Economists use the term to describe an economic model that revolves around extracting natural resources and selling them on the world market. It's the default strategy for Latin American economies; it's also one that practically forecloses the possibility of ever catching up with those nations that truly reap the benefits of added value. (Think of rubber trees coming back to the Amazon, priced at a premium, as truck tires.) I favor an expansive use of the term.[2] Crucially, I find that extractivism traverses economics, nature, and culture. The works I study work against it by articulating natural and human history in thought-provoking ways. They intervene, primarily, in language and storytelling. But if words themselves may at times compound the effects of extractivism ("meat"), they are also a site for ecological-political action. The flipside of this argument is that reading for human and nonhuman history does literature a service too: it reveals aspects of form that would otherwise go unnoticed.

Transcultural materialism infuses the realm of externality with storytelling and literary language. It presents compelling, enduring stories about people and processes which, by virtue of being outside of narrative, are an easier target for exploitation. The prefix "trans-" comes to bear in that these stories often involve different communities in conflict, but also in that the concept surpasses what we most commonly associate with culture. Indeed, it cuts across into its purported other, nature. Meanwhile, the suffix "-ion" in "transculturation" signals a dynamic process, rather than a stable condition, for "culturation" is not the same as "culture." Moreover, the root word "culture" is something of a misnomer if one associates it exclusively with some kind of collective spiritual life. "Culture" here is a concrete and, again, not just a human affair—think of how the etymology of the word relates to fermentation. These aspects will all come together more clearly through examples, including, below, the retelling of the socio-botanical history of sugar and tobacco in Fernando Ortiz (who coined the term *transculturación*). As it happens, a final distinguishing trait of transcultural materialism is that abstract definition can only go so far. Unlike the stories it deploys, as a whole it is something (to recall Wittgenstein's distinction) one can show, not tell.[3]

A useful shorthand to better grasp what this praxis is about is to consider it an *Aufhebung*, or sublation, of two distinct, and to some extent opposing, ways of thinking: historical materialism and new materialisms. One puts the human species first; the other, precisely, seeks to decenter it.[4] I regard contemporary Latin American literature as a site of articulation of these two strands. In the aggregate, the region's fiction advances the social vein that has been, traditionally, one of the strongest and most familiar features of its most prominent novels. At the same time, however, it develops an additional, complementary dimension, which one could describe as postanthropocentric. It is my contention that a corpus of recent literary works has much to teach us about such "recombined" materialism, and, reciprocally, that materialism allows us to interpret those literary works more relevantly. A central tenet of my approach is to appreciate the role of literary language in remediating the relationship of humans and objects. Such an operation has political consequences in a traditional sense, as engaged literature has had for decades, but it also extends the reach of politics to nonhumans. Critique needs fresh approaches to new materialism, and vice versa—Latin America shows the way forward.

As such, this book will be of interest to various constituencies, from my disciplinary home of Latin Americanism to comparatists and world literature scholars, from critical theorists to flat ontologists. Some schools of new materialism are, bluntly put, anti-Marxist. Among today's most influential radical thinkers, understandably, there is suspicion about schools of thought that de-emphasize the human.[5] And yet I think there are great resources in new materialism for the renewal of dialectical thinking, and many concepts of Marx himself, such as the notions of primitive accumulation and commodity fetishism, which should inform today's materialism. There will be time to get into the finer conceptual work of how such categories must adapt to today's fiction and to new materialities. For now, in broad terms, the goals of this volume are as follows: first, to show that the study of things as a means to reveal the true nature of social relations should counterbalance appraisals of objects as autonomous, nonhuman entities; and second, to explore how the nuanced and rich representations of human-nonhuman relations afforded by literature allow us to navigate that tension, providing a powerful methodological and conceptual tool to better grasp our present.

While focusing on works from the last twenty years, I also intersperse strategic mentions (Benjaminian "flashes") of historical precedents. Latin American literature has long since engaged the effects of capitalism on its peripheries, including fundamental transformations in how we relate to objects. I regard the language deployed in the region's fiction as one of the realms where different material paradigms clash. Allusions to pregnant moments of the past elucidate the present and allow a more complex, diachronic understanding of the changing role of literary language in justifying or questioning the base assumptions of human-object relations (for instance, the assumption that objects are objects and subjects are subjects, full stop, as if things did not have agency or as if humans were not also acted upon). Because of its semiperipheral condition in world literature, the corpus I study can serve as a limit case that invites a reassessment of the relationship of literature and materialism at a global level. A rising scholarly trend of the last two decades or so, which I like to call "worldliteraturism" to stress that it is indeed a trend and not a new natural state of affairs, puts forward the valuable notion that the world itself, not just nations or regions, can be a chamber of resonance for literature. However, more often than not, this is done in humanistic and idealistic terms—in short, anthropocentrically. This book advocates for reading world (and not just Latin American) literature in a less-than-humanist, materialist, and anthropodecentric way.

Among Latin Americanists—notable contributions by Mariano Siskind, Gesine Müller, Ignacio Sánchez Prado, and others notwithstanding—"world literature" is often suspect as a critical paradigm.[6] Could worldliteraturism be just another fad that distracts the field from its core mission of studying the cultural products of the region and producing quality scholarship in Spanish and Portuguese? Or worse, might it be cultural imperialism in new garbs? These are valid questions that deserve nuanced answers. The latter are best found in a posteriori, actual readings, rather than at the level of a priori discussions of principle. My work, the present volume included, develops my views on the subject; summary position-taking only conveys so much. With that caveat, let me state that I do find World Literature (I henceforth capitalize the paradigm) to be very relevant to Latin Americanism, and vice versa. The compromise of entering into worldlit conversation entails producing scholarship largely, though not exclusively, in the English language. This is to the benefit of a broader scholarly community.

Translation prevents losing monolingual readers; moreover, in literary studies, as in any other profession, and among general readers worldwide, English is increasingly common.

To boot, I am making the case for the pertinence of new materialism, a host of theories in English and French that have hitherto paid little attention to Latin America and which, it would seem, I now want to "creolize." Does this sound familiar? Similar arguments have been made about earlier "posts"—structuralist, modern, and colonial.[7] Let me reassure the skeptical reader that the present study is not a case of creolization: new materialism, despite its relative neglect of the region in formal scholarship, is not new to Latin America, which rather has a rich tradition to make explicit and to draw from. Neither is it esoteric, for all that defining a common lingo has been a priority for the movement in recent years, leading to a proliferation of terms. This I avoid as much as possible—discussions about "Anthropocene" versus "Capitalocene," say, will not be front and center.[8] Anticipating objections of a different kind, it is also worth mentioning that a focus on nonhumans does not seek to somehow cancel out the human, as in a zero-sum game. Finally, for the Great (Latin American) Book enthusiasts out there, the materialist turn does not further bury Literature with a capital L in the pit that the linguistic, textualist, and cultural turns had already dug for it—false charges to begin with, in my opinion. The triangulation of Latin Americanism, World Literature, and materialism makes sense because a rich corpus and its tangible referents sustain it.

Walter Benjamin famously wrote about "brushing history against the grain."[9] My intervention from the margins of Western culture seeks to capture the spirit of that phrase, with a twist: it finds fascinating that Benjamin, whom we traditionally read in terms of the critique of historicism, should resort to this evocative material metaphor. What brush, what grain? Is there something in those objects that leaves an imprint on his thinking? Deconstruction familiarized us with the recursivity involved in using language to think about language. Here language is material in the first order: a thing. And in the second order, it is a thing that summons other things. The instability and plasticity that new materialist thinkers celebrate in stuff is also present in language. In the opening passage of this introduction I referred to the "golden standard" of object permanence, and I have just mentioned the "spirit" of Benjamin's dictum. What's in a metaphor? Clearly, we must pay attention to language, which is something that literary critics do well, when we think about materiality. Literature, rather than being an afterthought of social science or science studies—the protagonists of historical materialism and new materialism, respectively—should be at the center of our inquiries. Another Benjaminian thinker, Hayden White, claimed something similar about Euro–North American modernist fiction and the Holocaust. In simple terms, the way Woolf, Joyce, or Dos Passos wrote, down to their word choices and plot devices, showed the historian the way to tell that ghastly story and, by extension, how to think historical discourse anew.[10] Similarly, another way to frame the present study of contemporary Latin American literature at the crux of two materialisms is as groundwork for urgent future theorization.

Lessons from Tobacco and Sugar

Allow me to present a revisionist reading of the aforementioned Fernando Ortiz's influential book *Cuban Counterpoint: Tobacco and Sugar* and the companion essay "The Human Factors of Cubanity," both from 1940, to show how Latin America developed new materialist thinking avant la lettre. Against the trend of interpreting the book *solely* in terms of commodity fetishism and cultural critique, and the essay in terms of allegory, I regard them, *additionally*, as a precursor to new materialist thought and as a literary emplotment of new materialist ideas. Bronisław Malinowski, in his prologue to the first Cuban edition, gives his seal of approval as a founding figure of modern anthropology. He offers an enthusiastic endorsement, although he hardly ever referred to Ortiz elsewhere. Consequentially, he singles out the concept of *transculturación* as the key to the book, and so the concept was minted and sanctioned. Transculturation is the notion, revolutionary at a time of rampant eugenics and racism, that there is no net loss in cultural exchange ("acculturation"), but gain. The rest is history: in the 1980s, Ángel Rama qualified the term ("transculturación narrativa") and used it as the cornerstone of his foundational study of Latin American letters.[11] In the 1990s, Mary Louise Pratt reformulated it for the cultural turn as "contact zones": "social spaces where disparate cultures meet, clash, and grapple with each other."[12] For his part, in the prologue to the new English edition, Fernando Coronil shows how

Counterpoint "counterfetishizes" its title crops, in the sense that it reveals the social relations involved in their production and circulation, countering the tendency to take them at face value.[13] This is all very well for theoretical anthropology, literary theory, cultural studies, and ideology critique. But what about tobacco and sugar?

As is well known, for Ortiz tobacco and sugar are poles that explain the development of Cuban society, for they represent two opposing forms of production and social organization. Tobacco, the native crop, traditionally revolved around artisanal labor and empowered, skillful workers; from early on, sugar demanded large plantations and disenfranchised, rote labor.[14] Point and counterpoint: one favors the growth of a middle class of independent producers; the other divides society and leads to monopoly, and so on. The resulting "tune" would be the soundtrack of Cuban history. The literature on Ortiz has reduced their rich interaction, in this treatise of over three hundred pages, to the notion of transculturation, which it supposedly illustrates. I shall put forward the rather bold claim that the many elaborations on this idea, a major staple across decades of Latin Americanist criticism, build upon what is, essentially, an oversight.[15] Every inflection point in the use of the term along the way, including Cornejo Polar's Andean adaptation or Moreiras's deconstructionist take at the turn of the twenty-first century, to name but a couple of milestones, could be subject to revision in light of this finding. Here I will only tackle the source and its more contemporary ramifications.

Now, if we accept the reductive reading, sugar and tobacco are excuses to refer to the broader, abstract problem. At best, when Ortiz goes into great detail about the specific botanical properties of plants, this amounts to digression; when he dresses them up and treats them as characters in a novel, the effect is embellishment. At worst, sugar is simply a stand-in for capitalism and tobacco for socialism, and transculturation is something of a third way. But Ortiz, who is always reluctant to reduce narrative to argument, points to a definition and yet does not quite give it: "And each of them [immigrants] torn from his native moorings, faced with the problem of disadjustment and readjustment, of deculturation and acculturation—in a word [en síntesis], of transculturation."[16] If transculturation is the synthesis of loss and gain, then what *is it not*?

Every one of the very few explicit moments in the book that might offer a definition of the term "transculturation" fails to do so. They may have performative value and literary interest, but they are not definitions in a strict sense, for they do not separate what is from what is not. Since seemingly everything, everywhere, at any moment may be called "transculturation," the term is something of an idle noun. I leave it to intellectual historians of the period to examine in detail the reasons for the successful transmission of this ambiguous term. However, it is clear that Ortiz's tooting his own horn—by reproducing in his journal Malinowski's prologue and an excerpt from the book—had something to do with it. The coinage added philosophical legitimacy to Ortiz's less abstract, more grounded intellectual efforts. The same volume of the journal features a translation from Bachelard on the psychoanalysis of fire and an article on the philosophy of Heidegger.[17] The common thread of the three pieces is an exploration of the nature of objects, from different intellectual orientations. My suspicion is that Ortiz wanted to add a patina of metaphysics to his fundamentally materialist method.

In my nominalist interpretation, *Counterpoint* exemplifies transculturation rather than explain it. Consider the most cited passage of the book: "Cultural unions, like the reproductive process between individuals, lead to offspring that partake from elements of both sources, and yet are different from them."[18] Ortiz is trying to express that transculturation is a sinuous affair. He is pointing in the direction of the totality of human-vegetable-economic history, alluded to in the "reproductive process between individuals," which evokes at one time sex, cellular reproduction, and capital accumulation. If a statement like this makes any sense at all, it is because a complex assemblage, conveyed as simple fable, stands behind it. Transculturation is less a concept one can adopt or not, agree with or take exception to, but something much broader: a methodology based on a specific worldview, one where there is a continuum between human affairs and the vegetable kingdom, both engulfed in materiality. It is as if Ortiz were saying: "To think transculturally, you must follow along the many twists and turns of my history of tobacco—take in the whole story." In importing the term into literary and cultural criticism, Rama and Pratt, writing under the aegis of the cultural turn, kept the socioeconomic narrative but discarded the veritable "life stories" of leaves and stems that Ortiz so frequently and carefully describes. Put differently, they thought, like Malinowski, that the allegorical apparatus of the book was ultimately dismissible, as if in some sense it could not *really be about* tobacco and sugar.

By contrast, that is exactly what I find most pertinent for today's critical discussion: a de-allegorization, a literalization of this fundamental study, which really is about plants *that are also* goods, for Ortiz examines them *in their becoming*. I do not just find in Ortiz a constructivist, but also a realist; not merely a precursor of cultural studies, but also of new materialism.[19] Hidden in one of the later annexes, one may find a claim that, to my mind, is the most explicit he gets about the true, indexical nature of the term *transculturación*: "The history of tobacco affords [ofrece] an example of one of the most extraordinary processes of transculturation."[20] This offering is the book itself, one that was written and should be read as if in the presence of sugarcane and tobacco plants. *Transculturación*, a narrative praxis rather than an abstract notion, posits that there is always a material basis for culture. However, it does not recur to the familiar sense of Marxist base and superstructure, a layered metaphor that leads to the separation of nature from culture. Sugar and tobacco are part of nature, as they are part of the economy, and one can follow the ways in which they seemingly go in and out of culture, that purportedly separate realm. Or one can appreciate the continuum, as Ortiz does, and use narrative to trace their becoming across disciplinary and epistemological boundaries.

Narrative has such a preeminent role in Ortiz's method that a curious plot frames the entire book. The narrator—for it is fair to call the first person that—says there ought to be a romance, written in the manner of Juan Ruiz, Archpriest of Hita (1283–1350), with sugar and tobacco as its protagonists. But finding himself unfit for the effort, he says, "All I can do is to set down, in drab prose, the amazing contrasts I have observed in the two agricultural products on which the economic history of Cuba rests."[21] This is surely an instance of false modesty, for the prose is anything but drab. It is also an affirmation of the borrowings from Ruiz, who provides the allegorical device and, perhaps more importantly, the standing of a trickster within the tradition. To be sure, Ortiz takes economic history seriously, but he wants to enliven the topic. Hence the allusions to "humor," "fables," and even, later on, "fairy tales." There would be a pedagogical objective as well, for the hypothetical counterpoint would have an "educational value"—in the original, it would serve "enseñanza popular." But does he or does he not write the alluded-to literary work? That counterpoint, which could be a *guajira*, *curro*, *rumba*, or liturgy, to mention just a few of the referents that Ortiz associates with the musical notion, is a phantom text. The narrator speculates on the beneficial effects that such a text *could have* while he is, in fact, writing it. The title-essay *is* that poem. It is a work of literature followed by documentation—annexes which, although not entirely exempt of literary interest, fall outside of the narrative unity.[22]

This explains why the first part is so thin in references to the social science literature and so rich in a doxographical collection of quotes on sugar and tobacco by a heterogeneous group of authors, including Lope de Vega, Georges Sand, and the Cuban poet Fernando Milanés—or why it goes on for pages, with obvious delight, on the whims of his characters: tobacco "heightens its inborn rank" by adopting the native woods of Cuba as its carriage, on its way to visit European aristocrats; the baby Rum is born from the marriage of Don Tobacco and Doña Sugar.[23] A reader looking for an abstract takeaway may grow impatient, but when one has followed the long history of tobacco and has accompanied the personified plant from its humble origins to its rarified consumers, a sense of irony emerges. Always in his ludic tone, Ortiz gestures toward the absurdities of transnational commerce. One gains a fuller understanding of how value is constructed over time, how it may relate to exploitation, and how it is embedded in material culture. These realizations call for narrative and poetic devices: a text within a text, a text that poses as a different text, a superposition of metaphors and allegories. The gist of the narrative operation is to estrange the very quotidian substance of sugar in order to illuminate its historical conjuncture. Instead of regarding the book as a predisciplinary, always-lacking piece of social science, one may see it as an erudite, essayistic novel. Ortiz resembles more an avant-garde writer than a disciplinary anthropologist.

Seen under this light, the companion essay has much to say. For a piece on "human factors," food is a notably central element, particularly the ingredients that different ethnic groups contributed to the national soup, *ajiaco*. Gustavo Pérez Firmat has observed that the essay makes essentially the same argument as the book on transculturation, with "a different vocabulary and style of argument."[24] That would be true if the former were indeed an essay about an abstract notion, which one could succinctly summarize or extricate from its materialist unfolding, and not the narrative experiment that it is. It is a work in which one learns to think differently about matter as one reads, and the same could be said about the *ajiaco* piece. There we read a long enumeration of the ingredients in the soup, along with the ethnic groups that contributed them. It is a long paragraph, unfit to cite in full here, framed as follows:

> For us, the image of the *ajiaco criollo* symbolizes well the formation of the Cuban people. Let's follow the metaphor. First of all, an uncovered casserole. This is Cuba, the island, the stove pot placed over the flame of the tropics . . . [enumeration of ethnic groups and ingredients] along with the fire of the tropics to warm it, the water of its skies for the broth, and the water of its seas for the sprinkling of the saltshaker. With all of that our national *ajiaco* has been made.[25]

The loving, bird's-eye view of a Caribbean island gives us an aeronautical, modernist metaphor. But years before food studies, the idea of a multiethnic nation as a cauldron of soup makes the essay just as thought-provoking as the more elaborate *Counterpoint*. And, crucially, like the occasional nod to beets and rum in that book, it hints at a "chorus"—a field of interacting forces rather than a dialectic.[26]

Note also the malleability of Ortiz's language. He says *ajiaco* symbolizes the *formation* of the Cuban people—not simply the Cuban people as a stable entity, which would mean that, say, corn stands for the indigenous people, beef for Spaniards, plantains for Africans, or spices for Asians. There a thing would take the place of a group of people, in a more straightforward symbolic function. But the soup, with all its slow brewing, stands for the *process*. Symbolization is asymmetrical and diachronic. It entails a whole that is more than the sum of its parts, a gastronomical (benignly nationalistic) affair that exceeds the more pragmatic American melting pot. And then the next line posits, rhetorically, "Sigamos la metáfora"—*Let's follow the metaphor*. One could read that as an oratorical cue, for the essay was originally a public lecture, meaning "Let us dwell on this." But when one takes into consideration what takes place in *Counterpoint*, this is more a matter of gaining elucidation through language—through the elusive but revealing qualities of literary language, that is. The passage brings to mind Maurizia Boscagli's observation that "the critique of the present through stuff demands plasticity."[27] Indeed, "plasticity," "flexibility," "malleability," or "suppleness" would aptly describe how thinkers like Ortiz open up their times—and ours—to critical scrutiny. In this case, the Cuban's "stuff" is tobacco, sugar, and language.

Ortiz's core belief seems to be that literary imagination allows us to reassess our historical *and* material situation. He founds a mode of Latin American, new materialist writing that seeks both explanation and intervention, interweaving human and nonhuman history through literary language. He shows us how objects or materiality in general can awaken history. As Coronil is keen to show, the characters in Ortiz's fable owe at least as much to Marx's Madame la Terre and Monsieur le Capital as to the Archpriest of Hita's less polemical relatives Mr. Carnival and Lady Lent.[28] Understatedly, Ortiz is integrating historical and new materialisms already. His writing transcends divides between the sciences and the social sciences, revealing phenomena that straddle botany, economics, and literature. Counterfetishism of the commodity and *longue durée* accounts of the agency of objects are both within the reach of this narrative mode, which I have called, adapting Ortiz's terminology, *transcultural materialism*. There, the nonhuman aspect of culture is revealed, without reducing it to cold facts or disingenuous description. As noted, the term has more of a deictic value than an abstract function; it signals an expansive praxis, not a distilled theory. Still, for a working definition, consider this praxis as *the noninstrumental use of stories and literary language to upset the nature-culture divide, affect our rapport with things, and reassess our place in human-nonhuman history*. In particular, I deploy it in an attempt to understand the worldwide material shift that has been taking place since roughly 1989, as represented by contemporary literature placed in conversation with relevant historical precedents.

This proposal gains traction in conversation with the work of Jane Bennett and Bruno Latour, important sources, among others, throughout this book. Bennett, who speaks of a vibrant materialism, recognizes the agency of objects: in her examples, the enticement of potato chips or the role of electricity in shaping daily life.[29] Read literally, Ortiz does something very similar in regard to objects we ultimately incorporate as smoke in the lungs or fizz in the mouth. Meanwhile, Latour notes that, when reading about a hole in the ozone layer, he finds that a newspaper's sections cannot quite "contain" the phenomenon: it is something that could equally belong under the headings "science," "society," "politics," and so on—even "fiction." The resulting "hybrid" article "mixes together chemical reactions and political reactions."[30] Mutatis mutandis, Ortiz does the same with his crossover treatise, a socio-botanical novel of sorts. Latour cites as examples of his method studies that "reconstruct" the United States "around the incandescent filament of Edison's lamp" or do something similar for French society through an examination of Pasteur's bacteria.[31] It is easy to appreciate how Ortiz carried out a similar operation in Cuba by focusing on tobacco and sugar—not just commodities but, in a more basic sense, nonhuman entities.

Today's fiction responds not only to the legacies of colonialism so vivid in Ortiz but to the unprecedented changes in our rapport with objects in the last two decades. A case in point, as I now turn to discuss, is the work of the contemporary Cuban writer Antonio José Ponte.[32]

Eros and Hunger

Flash forward from prerevolutionary to post-Soviet Cuba: in Ponte's *Las comidas profundas* (*Deep Foods*, 1997), the "Special Period" is the elephant in the room. Fidel Castro introduced the phrase "special period in time of peace" in 1990 to frame the dire years—continuing at least until 1996—after the withdrawal of the USSR's economic activities from the island. Indicative of the unique challenges this posed to the regime, a caption for photos of protests at Havana's Museum of the Revolution reads, "Groups of antisocial elements and tramps performed counterrevolutionary riots in two neighborhoods."[33] Although never explicitly mentioned, this is the backdrop of the book. It starts with the phrase "A castle in Spain . . ."—a French idiom for daydreaming.[34] True to the saying, the narrator sits at an empty table in Cuba and yearns for foods that do not come to him. His story quickly blends into that of King Charles V, expecting a royal visit: that of pineapple, "lion among fruits as he is lion among kings."[35] Struck with love for the unique, hitherto unknown fruit, Charles contemplates it, compares it to a walled city, wonders if it is a he or a she, then thinks of her as a captive queen, an offering. In his hands, readers are led to believe the pineapple is Cuba, or the colonies, or the world: a multifarious orb similar to those Peter Sloterdijk analyzes in *Spheres*, symbols of empire.[36] And, all along, also something immaterial, a dream within a dream, a mise en abyme of hunger.

Ponte went into exile a number of years ago—he defected, one could say, borrowing vocabulary from a different era. Unavoidably, reading about

Charles V, one wonders: Is this conservativeness, nostalgia for the old regime? An oblique comparison of the most powerful man in the history of Hispanic cultures and the island's aging strongman, Fidel Castro? Speculation is cut short by the startling denouement of the vignette: Charles worries that eating the pineapple will make him insane, like his mother, Juana la Loca (Joanna the Mad). Even more interestingly, he fears that "an unknown ocean would extend between them."[37] If aura is the effect that something close is at a distance, then ingesting the thing would deauratize, render banal. In this case, it would also burst the illusion of possessing distant lands never seen. Biographical fallacy permitting, here one sees the hungry writer in Havana and the *exilé* in Madrid. As this vignette suggests, reading political content in Ponte is anything but straightforward.

It's a wicked thing to write about food during a time of hunger; it is all the more wicked to do so with an eye for the historical configuration of food at a time of historical change.[38] The narrator sets himself to the task of invoking "the spirit of ancient foods."[39] The book, a collection of vignettes and ruminations with a novelistic quality, is the spiritist séance. Consider the roads not taken: not a criticism against the increasingly autarchic Castro regime for favoring scarcity over international dependency; not a condemnation of a world order—or not an obvious one, in any case—that left Cuba to its own means. Ponte chooses the more circuitous Ortizian route of imbricating material history (of Cuban foods, in this case) with history tout court. At stake is no less than the claim, which made great waves in the nineties, that history came to an end.

The idea was Francis Fukuyama's. "What we may be witnessing," he wrote in the summer of 1989, "is not just the end of the Cold War, or the passing of a particular period of postwar history, but the end of history as such: that is, the end point of mankind's ideological evolution and the universalization of Western liberal democracy as the final form of human government."[40] Writing from neoliberal Mexico, Octavio Paz reached a similar conclusion a few months later in his *Pequeña crónica de grandes días* (1990), where he also characterized said political system as the next and last step for what was once known as the Second World.[41] Paz represents a highly influential view that the Special Period had to react against; citing him illuminates Ponte's historical conjuncture. Says the Nobel laureate, unequivocally, "The revolutionary ideal has suffered fatal blows; the hardest and most devastating ones have not been from its adversaries, but from revolutionaries themselves: wherever they have conquered power, they have muzzled the people."⁴² For a sharp but revealing contrast, consider Fidel Castro's words from the speech that launched the Special Period, delivered in the Karl Marx Theater of Havana in January 1990:

> The way we see the future, we really see the Party leading indefinitely.
> Neither Carlos Marx, nor Lenin, nor Engels said on what day the party would be over—they did not say. They said that one day the State would disappear, which is something more than the party. Still, as far as one can tell, the moment in which the State comes to an end is far away. So we will have to keep on dealing with this apparatus—what is there to do? It is still undecided at the theoretical level, and, foremost, beyond theory in praxis, on what day and in what world the State will have disappeared. Then, truly, it won't be like somebody hopping onto a rocket to go to another planet—that day we will have changed this planet (APPLAUSE).
> Carlos Marx said that one day humanity will have overcome prehistory. And I think, I always did and still do, that the day that the exploitation of man by man disappears, the day that humanity as a whole is ruled by socialist principles, or beyond, by communist principles, that day prehistory would be over [habría terminado la prehistoria].⁴³

The note "applause" is part of the official, tachygraphic record from which I quote. The message is clear: the Party is not over, nor is history—here "prehistory." The caesura would be the end of the State, an apparatus that Castro appears willing to do without if only conditions were more favorable. But that project belongs to the future or to a different world. The end of history he vindicates is the ultimate resolution of contradiction by reaching the endpoint that is communism, not liberal democracy. But since that option is not viable, history must continue. In other words, the Cuban Communist Party must remain a beacon for the world. Cubans must continue *la lucha* in times of peace, diverting their efforts and energies from preparation for a possible U.S. invasion to the steadfast maintenance of the revolution in the face of economic adversity. (The more pragmatic passages of the speech mention the shortage of Soviet oil.) The speech marks the turning point that leads to Ponte's hungry narrator; its language, particularly its way of talking about history, rings very differently from the novelist's musings on Charles V, whom he successively invokes with envy, parody, and mild reverence.

Meanwhile, Ponte renders history as an erotically charged fruit. (With his usual graphic good sense, Daniel García's cover illustration for the Argentine edition captures this, with a vertically sliced pineapple that evokes, as the French painter Gustave Courbet might put it, "the origin of the world.") *Deep Foods* does not side with Castro, but neither does it align itself with Fukuyama or Paz. The book does not advocate an end of history or a continuation; it founds, in the autonomous space of literature it fiercely defends, a third temporality. A figure Ponte does side with is Lezama Lima, the great *origenista*. Ponte offers a brief commentary on Lezama's influential essay "Corona de las frutas," from 1959. It was published in *Lunes de revolución*, a short-lived literary supplement from the honeymoon period between intellectuals of all ilks and the Cuban revolution. There Lezama writes something that Ponte might find prescient: "From Charles V to Talleyrand, names of classic sturdiness or devilish demands have proclaimed the extension of their domains in the firmament of their palate."[44] At the time there were government-sanctioned recipes for making Cuban dishes out of animal parts, including skulls, that were hitherto considered industrial waste. In *Con nuestros propios esfuerzos*, published by the Cuban army in 1992, we read the following: "By taking meaty advantage of these parts of the cow, one can obtain byproducts that were earlier discarded due to lack of experience. The initiative consists in utilizing the ears of the cow, the trachea, esophagus, labia, cuts of the innards, skull and tendons in order to fabricate croquettes, homemade blood sausages, and hamburgers."[45] This is a diet suitable for a city under siege—Leningrad, say—or enduring the toll of war—Berlin. The island, an/the extension of Castro's domain, could be seen as proclaimed by those manuals of resistance through hunger.

To fully appreciate the poignancy of the Castro–Charles V comparison, consider Heberto Padilla's critique of Lezama Lima and his group, *Orígenes*, in "La poesía en su lugar," a few years before his famous, forced, public recanting divided the intelligentsia between pro- and anti-Castro factions. During his revolutionary phase Padilla describes Lezama's group as "an instance of our most pronounced bad taste . . . proof of our past ignorance, evidence of our literary colonialism, and our enslavement to old literary forms. It is not by accident that the words, the vocabulary of these poets make repeated monarchic allusion: Kingdom, crown, prince, princess, heralds."[46] As the opposition Padilla outlines here suggests, Ponte is changing the terms of the debate. His opening "monarchic allusion," combined with an empty table, is a play both on aestheticism and on social realism. In Ponte's account, Charles is essentially hungry, unsatiated. Meanwhile, Castro chose dignity for his people at the cost of scarcity; accounts of the people's choice on the matter and of their understanding of what dignity means, obviously, vary. The regime casts hunger as resistance; so does Ponte, albeit with a different, unheroic spin. Fittingly, the dense language of *Deep Foods* laments and endures its bodily effects. The book assimilates hunger to unrequited love, imagining a troubled love story of Cubans with food that transcends the ages.

But how to think *sub specie aeternitate* in the face of scarcity? This unresolved question is the driving force of Ponte's book; its dialectic is one between the will to historicize and the immediate demands of survival. Like Lezama, Ponte sets his eyes on a long historical horizon—longer, particularly, than the presence of Marxism on the island. And so his allusion to Silvestre de Balboa's *Espejo de paciencia* taps not only on its foundational, early modern evocation of Cuba as a land of fruit and riches, but also on its plotline, which is essentially the story of a kidnapping that must be endured—hence the patience, as in *pathos*. On a couple of occasions, amid heavy, neo-neo-baroque paragraphs, the narrator portrays himself as a prisoner. That is no doubt a loaded metaphor, given its context. Likewise, there is painful irony in the epithet he gives to the island, "The Place Where Tasty Foods Come From" (a pun on the phrase "de donde son los cantantes" [where singers are from]). There is further irony in the realization that fruits such as the pineapple, with its age-old evocation of *cubanidad*, were in no shortage in rural areas, but neither could they provide complete nourishment.

Arguably, the most compelling feature of Ponte's book is how he derives lessons about mankind and its relation to food from the more historically precise coordinates of the Special Period—while illuminating that moment all the same. We can then extend this line of thought to say that hunger, that original form of desire, is always embedded in literature. One can find it in texts, as one can find eros, whose imprint on culture is a major theme in psychoanalytical approaches. Here mother's milk is both about the mother and about the milk itself, the psyche and the body, life and survival. Reading hunger in literature is finding human conatus, that is, perseverance in being. There is the memory, in Ponte's simile, of having been cold.[47] Cold: the risk of losing oneself to the elements; hunger: that of losing oneself to lack. These are experiences of the human-nature continuum. Finding the traces of hunger in literature, beyond a mere heuristic device, can be part of a critical agenda that recognizes very concrete forms of precariousness and thinks alongside them. Food is of a part with language. We read about how despair (read *hunger*) multiplies metaphors: "pork chops of rice with fries, fried calamari without calamari."[48] Eating, the indispensable operation that binds human and nonhumans, is an occasion for historical, political reflection.

For his part, Latour favors the terms "nature-culture." He also prefers "collective" over "society" to account for the nonhuman elements that underpin human life; he formulates the notion of "network," a concept that cuts across multiple disciplinary divisions, for it is "simultaneously real, like nature, narrated, like discourse, and collective, like society."[49] And he talks about hybrids, as in assemblages of human and nonhuman elements, and of a Constitution with a capital C, their reified status quo.[50] Borrowing this terminology, one could say that Cuban writers like Ortiz and Ponte present networks, deal with hybrids, and undertake something of a Constitutional reform. Except their efforts, which in Ortiz's case predate Latour's by several decades, and in Ponte's run parallel to it, do not need such profusion of terminology. Latour's neo-scientistic language and the Cubans' literary experiments are different answers to a common question about how to conceive and talk about the continuum between natural and human affairs. Following the contours of their narratives could ultimately make the lingo unnecessary.

In that vein, for their theoretical value, one may revisit the seven sections of *Deep Foods*. There are many insightful discussions there of foods and of more or less known pieces about food, by a heterogeneous group of writers. We read in the second section, which deals with learning to like foods we previously disliked, that some foods "take us back to the origin." Citing Bertrand Russell's essay "On Useless Knowledge" (1935), Ponte says that an apricot *tastes better* when one knows about its long history, from its domestication in the early years of the Han dynasty in China, through its arrival in Rome in the first century CE, to the present. "Very long fibers have woven that meat that can be undone with the teeth,"[51] he reports, and by *madejas* (fibers) he means historical events. Strikingly, Russell's essay is also a defense of idleness. But how to even think of idleness in state-controlled socialism? If the system worked flawlessly, idleness would potentially be akin to dissidence, at least beyond vacation and resting periods regulated by the state. But the system does not work in that way, and idleness is not a luxury of aristocratic intellectuals like Russell but the plight of the unemployed. Ponte seems to relish precisely that condition. His Cuban present is like a time without time.

However, the third section offers a different temporal dimension, opening with an archeological excavation that, as I see it, may either take place in the present or allude to a distant future. Ponte writes about finding iron instruments, very old turtle shells, and bottles used to reinforce walls. As it happens, the province of Cienfuegos has been the site of several important archeological digs, during which turtle remains have in fact been found, as have bottles that were used as construction material.[52] Although Ponte's narrative could allude to those real-life findings, the astounding thing about his account is that, in passing, he uses the word "beer" in English: "En el calor del día se piensa en la sed de albañiles de hace siglos y la gente vuelve a empinarlas, huelen sus picos a ver qué queda de la vieja beer" (In the heat of midday people think about the thirst of bricklayers from centuries ago and lug those bottles again, smell their lips to see what's left of the old *cerveza*).[53] Is this an allusion to colonial trade, which might have brought products from a nearby English-speaking place, such as Jamaica? Or is the thirst of construction workers that of contemporary Cubans who, like in old times, make do with what is available to build houses? In the second case, the passage would be a flight forward into the future. At the risk of overinterpretation, one could even see in this *beer* the staple of a future capitulation of Cuba to the United States. The archeological dig scene is a mere two pages in length, leaving more questions posed than answered. Its unique mood, which combines stasis and discovery, further serves the cause of unsettling historical narratives.

Benjamin's thoughts on archeology come to mind. He compares the task of a critical theorist to that of digging, and (as I read him) thereby relates language to earth. Memory is "a medium for exploring the past," while earth is "the medium in which ancient cities lie buried."[54] Ponte proceeds in Benjaminian fashion, looking for certain truths (about apricots, say) hidden in language; he also leaves a reflective trace of his search as he goes. Hence his reflections on "the habit of making foods out of words."[55] One could see the book in its entirety as an impossible archeological exercise that digs the past beneath the present and at times even hints at an uncertain future.

This exercise is impossible not because of its temporal focus, or lack thereof, but because it searches for organic traces—the very kind archeologists cannot find. More than bottles, turtle skeletons, or iron tools, it is the pineapple not eaten centuries ago that Ponte seeks to unearth. In many ways, as the title suggests, his foods are "profound": they are deeply buried, forgotten during a time of hunger, yet rich in history and present value. They are a national treasure the disenfranchised narrator is somehow entitled to amass.

The third section of *Deep Foods* moves rapidly away from the archeological site, first to a reflection on Lezama Lima and then to a story about a historical meal offered by a Cuban noblewoman in Madrid. Together, these three moments compose an unusual triptych, as the more essayistic portion is in the middle of two narratives. Perhaps glossing Lezama and recounting the marquise's soiree are all part of digging—of investigating in words the profound truths of food, in fiction and nonfiction alike. And if, indeed, as the saying goes, "we are what we eat," then Ponte would be tackling ambitious questions about the Cuban, if not the human, condition. His gloss of Lezama highlights the remark "As he eats, the Cuban man incorporates the forest," only to affirm the sharp contrast between that "incorporation" and the more mainstream use of the word at the time of Lezama's writing.[56] In that period, says Lezama according to Ponte, "government propaganda" kept droning on about the verb "to incorporate," as a way of signaling the historical necessity of the dissolution of the individual: "There shouldn't be any personal goal but that of becoming a grain in the bowl where greater, superhuman forces came to eat."[57] Here dissidence becomes the desire not to be eaten alive.

This halfway point across the sections of the book raises some general questions. That Cubans incorporate the forest when they eat may mean, allegorically, that their sustenance is defiance—as it were, they join the ranks of a different army. It is an odd use of the reflexive verb "incorporarse," which usually precedes a preposition. Lezama and Ponte are purposefully playing with the object-subject divide by approximating *swallowing* and *being swallowed by*. But isn't that indistinction the point of incorporation—that is, of becoming one body? Note how the body politic, the body proper, and nature are all interconnected, thanks to the binding force of literary prose. From serving as the more or less unwitting setting for Cuba's experiment with socialism, Ponte renders the island's nature as the reason to reformulate that experiment. In so doing, *Deep Foods* comes closer to Bennett's cited notion of "vibrant materialism" than to environmentalism.

In the latter, nature and culture can be understood separately, for the "environment" is external, almost a backdrop. By contrast, Bennett maintains that "the locus of agency is always a human-nonhuman working group," while "human agency is always an assemblage of microbes, animals, plants, metals, chemicals, word-sounds, and the like."[58] The present study takes these words to heart. However, without putting too fine a point on terminology, I obviously find my coinage more precise—better to call Ponte a "transcultural materialist." Despite a general agreement between my theorization and Bennett's, differences with Bennett have to do with the meager place that colonial dynamics occupy in her thinking, hence my use of the term "neo-extractivism"—the bread and butter, pun intended, of Ponte's ruminations. This, coupled with the significant, but ultimately subordinate, role of literature in *Vibrant Matter*, provides useful distinction. Additionally, a pitfall to avoid is reproducing in criticism what happens in society at large: to apply a metropolitan theorist to a semiperipheral literature is the road most traveled. The more interesting political option is to rewrite the theory from the ground up.

Fittingly, Ponte avoids the environmentalizing effect of plain language, which is better at singling out objects than at describing the continuum that is materiality. His revision of Lezama's dictum goes beyond partisanship into a veritable politics of nature.[59] When he recognizes the agency of food, he mobilizes transculturation against state-imposed historical materialism. This is to eat so as not to be eaten, as in the cannibalistic logic of cultural critique in Virgilio Piñera, albeit extended to other organic materials. In the vignette of the Madrid dinner party, Spanish guests are treated to roots and stems, leaves and cortices. An astute guest thanks the hostess for feeding him the forests of her country. Those at the table experience, in the characteristically hypersensualized take Ponte has on Ortiz's motifs, "the same awe of those who saw for the first time how a man smoked tobacco leaves."[60] Lungs and gut take in the forest; the forest takes over the metropolis. But the forest is also a threat, and, by eating it, Cubans vanquish it. "Overeat" it, though, and there would be no Cuba left to speak of. In this fashion, Ponte's syncretic language captures a dynamic that crisscrosses the economical and the ecological, island and continent, periphery and metropolis, past and present, body and nature.

Similarly, Latour is concerned about the inability to think together the human and the nonhuman, or to articulate global and local concerns.

In the face of something like the contemporary ecological crisis, which patently cuts across all these divisions, we need to repair the fracture between "knowledge of things" and "power and human politics."[61] Wouldn't this be a fair description of Ponte's project? In his book, the long history of colonialism, the Cold War, and its aftermath all converge in Cuban foods. It is as if he were saying: "If we think deeply about food, we will arrive at significant truths." This is a recursive operation, because food does not end in food—food is of a part with language, desire, negativity, which is all the more reason to excavate these truths in literary language. Ponte goes on to note that no regime, authoritarian (*policial*) as it may be, can sever the relationship of a people with its foods, which lingers in language even when food staples are not available.[62]

Polemically, one could say that Ponte is being more radical than Castro, more materialist than the party-line historical materialists. He is "a hunger artist," to borrow the shrewdly allegorical title of a Kafka tale that—a point I will merely insinuate here—he may very well be rewriting.[63] Surely, one could describe the ideological state apparatuses of the Castro regime, different as they are from those of a capitalist state. But Althusser's explanations as to why subjects stay subject, past direct repression or coercion—that is, his analysis of internalized power structures—would fall short, in light of Ponte's work, of Cuban reality.[64] The politics of eating in the Cuba of the Special Period entail a complex dynamics of dignity and resistance. *Deeps Foods* casts it as eroticism. The ideological identification of subject with nation is about desire. In my reading of Ponte's prose, Cuba is a *matria*, a motherland, which would add a layer of meaning to a passage Adriana Kanzepolsky underlines in her afterword to the book: "All foods are an ersatz of mother's milk."[65] This departs from the more conventional reading of the acceptance of authoritarianism as fixation with the father figure. The dynamic is, in a manner of speaking, as follows: since, as censorship would have it, Ponte could not rant against the father, he takes it out on the mother. Cuba was Cuba before being socialist; islands are blessed with abundance and scarcity alike. Ponte's heterochronic narrative puts hunger in perspective, reveals its transhistorical charge of desire.

Back in the fourth section of the book, there is a musing inspired by Apollinaire: an enamored young man woos and threatens a girl by lovingly eating her shoe, which a chef has prepared. It is a gesture made "to underline his subservience to her [avasallamiento], but also talk of possession."[66]

In a peculiar, circuitous way, *Deep Foods* is Ponte's dictatorship novel, his book about prison food.

While the fifth of the seven sections of the book claims that hunger will never cease to be a part of Cuban literary language, in the way that those who have been very cold cannot shake off the feeling once they are in a temperate room, the sixth section discusses an *aliñado* or *prú*, a homemade liqueur made of fermented fruits and other staple crops that are, like rice, from the eastern part of Cuba.[67] In peasants' homes, recounts Ponte, it is customary to prepare one when a woman is pregnant: the drink ferments as the baby grows.[68] In this way, the *aliñado* will be ready for the baptism celebrations, and beyond. Because fermented drinks hold well, there are families that keep some of the beverage for years, to be had at wedding celebrations for those same children.[69] The liqueur is, quite literally, an *eau de vie*. Ponte cherishes the parallel between bottle and womb, which become "twin fermentations."[70] The image is something of an ars poetica, as his book has been a long, vitalist effervescence, a quest for satiety and celebration. And, although it goes unnamed, here there is a nod to a famous quote. The reference would not escape Cuban readers, who still congregate in the Karl Marx theaters of the island: "Force is the midwife of every old society which is pregnant with a new one."[71] Is this Ponte suggesting revolution on the revolution? Or is he casting himself as a different kind of midwife, with violence sublimated if it is present at all? This endpoint to the book's erotic charge is purposefully puzzling, and too narrow an interpretation would not do it justice. And yet it is certain that Ponte prefers a historical movement that is organic and nonteleological. This is his take at "incorporation," as in Lezama's dictum that Cubans incorporate (to) the forest as they eat—a far cry from incorporating into a Party.[72]

The other vignettes in the section contribute to this reading. The narrator ventures from the *aliñado* to Ortiz's *ajiaco* to the *Shatapatha Brahmana*, and closes with a poem by none other than Luis Marré, founder of the National Union of Writers and Artists of Cuba (UNEAC). He embraces Ortiz's use of the plate as a figuration of Cuba, adding that "moros y cristianos"—rice and beans, literally "Moors and Christians"—would extend his logic all the way to Charles, "awaiting the pineapple."[73] The fable from the Brahmanic sacred text holds that, in the afterlife, what we eat will assume human form and eat us. In the four corners of heaven, animals will slice us, trees will chop us, mute vegetables will swallow us, and water will drink us. I read this as reinforcement of the human-nature continuum and circle-of-life concepts from earlier chapters. There is also an oceanic feeling that befits the fictional reconciliation with the motherland as a land of plenty. Indeed, throughout the book Ponte makes several references to Eastern religions, the very source of the concept of "oceanic feeling" in Romain Rolland and Sigmund Freud's correspondence.[74] But here the proverbial "being one with the world," so evident in the *aliñado*-woman coupling, quickly fades into failed cosmopolitanism. Ponte quotes Marré as writing: "This loaf of bread was made with flour from the USSR. The rice came from China. The lentils were sown in old Spain. The vegetables were picked from the valley of Güines.... We drink well water. We draw it with a fourth of a horse (-power, a small engine of). The well is of blue serpentine rock and sits next to a lemon tree."[75]

The citation comes from "Nos comemos la tierra," whose title is a double entendre for "We eat dirt" and "We take the world by assault." The irony in citing this quaint prose poem lies in the fact that it was written at a time of relative abundance and integration into the world; by contrast, the Special Period was anything but. Marré harmonizes the global and the local; Ponte explores their contradictions. The one-fourth-horsepower engine, which irrupts into the poem, surrealistically, as a fraction of a horse, is in Ponte's gesturing more about scarcity than about simplicity. Worldliness, organicity, and exile all clash in this thought-provoking envoi to Ponte's chapter. Real-life implications are very real, too, if one remembers that Marré, as head of UNEAC, would have to oversee Ponte's expulsion. Indeed, after a lifetime of participation in the cultural milieu, UNEAC ostracized Ponte in 2003, which ultimately led to his leaving the island for good in 2007. (Conspicuously, Marré changes the "USSR" in the first line for "Ukraine" in later re-editions of the poem—e.g., in the selected works he published after receiving the National Literature Prize.) And so this is an overdetermined, heterodox fable, which brings together apparatchik, *ajiaco*, and Brahmanism. Its lesson of "Those who eat will be eaten" echoes concerns of historical and new materialism.

The seventh and last section of *Deep Foods* consists of the curt phrase "A table in Havana..."[76] It brings us back to the start—indeed, the origin—, to hungry dreams: a table in Havana is worth a castle in Spain. It also evokes the punch line of another notorious seven-part work, Wittgenstein's *Tractatus Logico-Philosophicus*: "Whereof one cannot speak, thereof one must be silent."[77] For the Austrian philosopher, such denouement signaled the aspiration that language could exhaust reality. For the Cuban novelist, by contrast, it posits that both language and reality are inexhaustible, try as we may to make foods out of words and eat them whole. Censorship, quite possibly, was another consideration. After all, love-hate for socialist Cuba, or for Cuba tout court, are frequent topics in the nation's diasporic literature. Without ignoring the explanatory power of exile, I have preferred instead to examine how the text actualizes the legacy of Fernando Ortiz's thought, engaging historical and new materialisms in original ways. *Deep Foods* is one of the works of contemporary Latin American literature that enriches our understanding of that intersection, and one of the texts that most explicitly realizes Fernando Ortiz's thought. Ponte illustrates, in an Ortizian vein, the interrogation of materialism that is now taking place in contemporary Latin American literature. This is precisely what the present book sets out to explore.

New Materialism Avant la Lettre

Things with a History analyzes the place of contemporary Latin American fiction within the profound material transformation of our times. After globalization, we live in an age where culture seems to become in some ways more immaterial (i.e., less bound to specific objects or places) and in other ways leaves a more irreversible material footprint (i.e., through pollution and ecological damage). This dialectic has increasingly come under the scrutiny of cultural critics and philosophers, but there are few contributions by scholars of literature in such debates. To that end, I formulate broad theoretical reflections that actualize notions such as estrangement, primitive accumulation, commodity fetishism, historical materialism, and the agency of objects. In a way, like Ponte, I seek to extend Ortiz's narrative project to a broader corpus. Inspired by *Cuban Counterpoint*, this book constructs a similarly materialist narrative that, although situated within literary theory and criticism, projects itself across the incommensurable realms of history, economy, and biology. One could see in Ortiz a forefather to a Latin Americanist political ecology of materiality—or a refreshingly jargon-free narrative praxis that pursues conceptual elucidation without sacrificing complexity.[78]

Still, if one were to borrow Latour's terminology, one could easily say that the likes of Ponte and Ortiz examine collectives and networks. As I have shown, the personification of tobacco and sugar was less a matter of poetic license than an intuition of the agency of objects; the same is clearly the case with foods. Like Latour, Ponte and Ortiz concern themselves with how the relationship between human and nonhuman entities determines a course for modernity that it is not too late to revise. The French thinker notes that when ethnographers venture outside the West, they produce unifying narratives that weave together technology, religion, botany, and so forth. This, however, is harder for them to achieve when examining the West, which is supposed to be modern and, therefore, is taken to rest on the separation of nature and culture, the human and the nonhuman. He hopes to reveal that for us too there is a "seamless fabric"; in other words, as the resounding title of his book claims, he wants to show that we have never been modern. The "amodern" project of Latour and others speaks volumes when considered side by side with the cultural products I address in the present study, particularly as they originate in what Arturo Uslar Pietri would call (transforming the phrase "Far East") "Extremo Occidente": the confines of the West.[79] In many regards, Latin America has been a site for the best and the worst experiments of Western techno-social rationality. From that position, this book examines hybrid narratives that challenge the modern separation of nature and culture.

I am interested in the ways literary works can have *an effect* similar to that of Ortiz's narrative. Fernando Coronil has wondered too about how it is that a book about commodities produces the effect that we understand the social forces that have constructed Cuban identities. He gives himself a provisional answer: "The mystery of this effect ... is perhaps resolved by realizing that Ortiz treats tobacco and sugar as highly complex metaphorical constructs that represent at once material things and human actors."[80] This explanation falls short of answering the question. Rather, I think the "mystery" has to do with Ortiz's uncommon and very early understanding of the agency of objects. The power of fascination of the book may very well rest on the fact that, ultimately, we too are objects, as are the books we write. Unlike philosophy, literature can be part and parcel to the objective world. Works like *Counterpoint* and *Deep Foods* reveal agency as something that is social, but also collective; not just human, but hybrid. Ortiz captures this most eloquently when he compares the dissemination of tobacco with that of syphilis, which is one short step away from understanding migration and human commerce as phenomena that are biological, as they are social.[81] Malinowski too, in his prologue, speaks of "the profound influence exerted by sugar on the civilization of Cuba."[82] The agency of nonhumans has been there all along, inviting us to rethink historical agency altogether—a goal that the seamless fabric of metaphor and narrative is most fit to carry out.

Indeed, because literature is so powerful at revealing the agency of nonhumans, Bennett draws many meaningful examples from poems and short stories.[83] These include Kafka's character Odradek, from "The Cares of a Family Man"—a talking spool for thread—and a striking epigraph by Henry David Thoreau: "Go not to the object; let it come to you."[84] One wishes Bennett were familiar with the work of Ortiz and Ponte when she posits, "Maybe it is worth running the risks associated with anthropomorphizing (superstition, the divinization of nature, romanticism) because it, oddly enough, works against anthropocentrism; a chord is struck between person and thing, and I am no longer above or outside a nonhuman 'environment.'"[85] From Doña Azúcar to the *aliñado*, the protagonists of the Cubans' imagination fit that description—including, of course, the "risks." It is in light of those potential pitfalls that nuanced, theoretically rich close reading gains all the more relevance.

But politics is where I part ways with Bennett, and certainly with Latour. Without turning her back on human exploitation, Bennett imagines a politics that does not deny vitality to nonhuman actants. I couldn't agree more. But out of necessity, she does this by turning her back on the human-centered methods of historical materialism: demystification, suspicion, analysis of the superstructure, and so forth. This was an important step to take in the history of materialist thought, for it greatly expands its methodological repertoire and its objects of study, and Bennett, a distinguished political theorist, does so with great success. But I think we are already in a different critical moment, when the cross-fertilization of materialisms is in order. Politics may not begin or end with human affairs, but that is no reason to neglect a tradition that, with some reformulation, can elucidate key aspects of the nature-culture continuum. As I will show, Latin American literature offers a natural bridge between these two lines of inquiry and foregrounds the viability of their articulation.

This also means that I cannot subscribe to Latour's method through and through. A minimal way of expressing my disagreement would be to say that I don't find his ideas of Actor-Network-Theory (ANT) to be fully transferable from their home in science and technology studies to the field of literary studies. For, indeed, what is literature within radical monism? One could describe how the pulp of trees becomes paper and how synthetic thread binds the cover of a book. But the moment words are printed on the page and there is a reader to interpret them, it is as if an entirely new, preeminently human realm has begun: the text is not the book. As ANT would have it, describing is transforming: because facts are not separated from values, the role of the critic is to tell the world as it is—in other words, to show how human and nonhuman actors form networks of distributed agency that define the course of events. I can envisage a reformed, invigorated practice of reception theory that engaged the circulation of books and other media in their materiality, and I am aware that cognitive approaches to literature may hold the promise of describing networks all the way from the black and white stimuli on a page to the critique of bourgeois life in *Madame Bovary*.[86] These are just different tracks: I am interested in a manner of interpretation that, although it has inspired Bennett and others, receives from their methodologies little in return.

A different, more emphatic way of drawing the line would be to affirm the pertinence of ideology critique, despite Latour's insistence that the fall of the Berlin wall and the miraculous year 1989 showed that both socialism and naturalism were utter failures. This strikes me as a hyperbolic, unnecessarily polemical position meant to scandalize his native, left-leaning Parisian intellectual milieu: the "We have never been modern" side of his argument is more amenable than the implied "We have never been socialist"—or capitalist, for that matter: Why bother discussing commodification and the exploitation of surplus labor, those entelechies, if a perspicuous narrative of networks would account for them anyway? "Ideology" is certain to inform literary works, however much it may serve as a catchall phrase for myriads of collective configurations. That does not make it a less valid category, nor does it justify dropping it from the vocabulary of critical intervention. Latour claims that socialism, which he unfairly identifies with Soviet-style communism, is predicated on the separation of nature and culture. This may be so, but it is also true that his notion of "amodernity" depends on the radical separation of moderns and premoderns. But what about Latin America, which formulated socialist ideals in different ways than the North? And what of its ways of thinking, which are not identical with those of a fully modern society but are also not premodern? These questions need to be addressed by not one but by several studies. The present one, as already mentioned, focuses on the contemporary, with some discussion of select, elucidating past moments.

The "with a history" phrase in the book's title alludes to historicism—in a nutshell, the notion that history explains the present. Historicism comes in all shapes and sizes. Some variants are inclusive (history explains the present), others exclusive (*only* history explains the present). The past may have explanatory or determining power. Compare "The United States' undistinguished track record in the sport variously known as football or soccer suggests that its national team won't do well" (a reasonable assumption for a men's World Cup bookie) with "The United States simply cannot win"—blanket determinist historicism. Historicism can be idealistic: "The values of this great nation ensure we will never fall into dictatorship," for example. The focus in that statement is on ideas. Historicism turns materialist once Marx and Engels back away from the "spirit" in Hegel, for whom history is, simply put, the unfolding of an idea. Their method bears the moniker "historical materialism" because it's a form of historicism that revolves around material conditions. In times of orthodoxy, there was but one kind of historical materialism proper, sanctioned directly from Moscow. Since then, several historical materialisms, or sometimes materialist historicisms, circulate. A bar patron claims that some people are inherently better than others. His slightly less inebriated neighbor claims that people would not be "better" than others if they hadn't had better opportunities from the get-go: the rich are the great-grandchildren of the rich. Two stools down, staring into a lukewarm beer and pondering a football match lost, I think to myself: one of these men is a material historicist. A Marxist, or someone who would subscribe to the official doctrine of midcentury international communism, he need not be.

Transcultural materialism is also a historicism. In the terms above, it is more explanatory than deterministic, although it does connect some present-day effects to their past causes (see the discussion on primitive accumulation in chapter 2). It's inclusive, precluding only recalcitrant idealism—the kind that confounds the autonomy of art with a critical pass to avoid the world entirely. One key difference with historical materialism is the scope of what counts as material: the nonhuman agents that Marx and Engels entertained were almost always, in one way or another, connected to the economy. Their approach is economicist. Nonhuman agency is expressed, primarily, through the commodity form. As the chapters of this book make clear, the connection of objects with human labor is only one aspect of their agency. Another key difference has to do with the primary domain of critique. Historical materialism was systematic and comprehensive, covering, in Marx and Engels's parlance, everything from base to superstructure. At the peak of its scientific ambitions, whether by authorial intent or Party ventriloquizing, it was a total theory of reality.

By contrast, the domain of transcultural materialism is narrower and its ambitions more modest. Its main object of study is works of literature and culture, themselves tributary to broader natural-cultural practices. A key task is explicating ideological underpinnings that go beyond (not past) class struggle into competing visions of nature, and of human labor within it. I don't regard this as an end in itself, for that would amount to instrumentalizing literature. Much as understanding art entails having at least some knowledge about the society that makes it meaningful (where does a text end and its context begin?), an appreciation of its natural-cultural presuppositions, whether explicitly or implicitly thematized, provides a fuller understanding. Immanent reading and cultural critique, in the work of late-twentieth-century thinkers from various political persuasions—Adorno, the late Derrida, and González Retamar, to name a few—were about as compatible as walking and chewing gum at the same time. The reason for this is that works of art and literature are informed by the same forces that inform society at large. Meanwhile, new materialism, and anthropodecentric thought more broadly, show that "society" is not the whole picture. Industrialization may be a function of social relations— the proletarization of the many, the capitalization of the few—but minerals, machines, farm animals, and water sources, to name merely some nonhuman actors, play their part too.

In slogan form, to Jameson's "always historicize" I add: "with things."[87] A counterpoint with the nonhuman enables new modes of analysis. Animals are not my focus, as they deserve separate studies. Neither do I venture much into disciplinary history, other than to provide a backdrop to my claims—engaging briefly, for example, with Sidney Mintz's history of sugar, John Tully's history of rubber, and so on. The closest I come to the discipline is to draw on the work of Hayden White, whose own standing within the discipline, it seems to this outsider, is that of "the great unread":

an increasingly marginal classic. (I hope to be wrong on this account.) I similarly only approximate disciplinary anthropology, enlightening conversations on tobacco with Matthew Kohrman and on earth-beings with Marisol de la Cadena notwithstanding, by way of Arjun Appadurai's disciplinarily prosperous notion of "the social life of things."[88] My *historicizing with things*, then, is foremost about Latin American and World Literary historiography. However, I do find that common structures lie at the center of a Venn diagram of partially overlapping humanities disciplines, notably literature, history, and anthropology. White addressed this with his typologies of emplotment, argumentation, and ideology. His fundamental discovery was that historians and others are affected by several of the same literary structures as anyone who tries to tell a story. Inasmuch as that is the case, and taking his often-criticized taxonomical tropology with a grain of salt, there is a common core in this book that will be of interest across disciplinary divides.[89] At the very least, *Things with a History* counters a prevailing anthropocentric thrust in literary studies. This impulse has deeper roots: we often tell stories to distinguish ourselves from nature. "We" here means the West, and criollo Latin America within it: look no further than the book of Genesis. But counterstories abound; language resists. The method and praxis of this book revolve around potentiating these other forces. This is beneficial across the board, for literature, pharmaceutically, can be a powerful agent in reinforcing the preeminence of the human *and* in interrogating it. The goal of this book will be achieved if it teaches how to preserve and think through the tension between words and things, thus understood.

This book is organized around specific material configurations.[90] In turn, the corpus that results from reading certain works together—belonging to material entanglements rather than to national concerns or aesthetic movements—will prove fruitful to the task of reimagining the contemporary. There are two sections in this book, "Part 1: Objects" and "Part 2: Assemblages." The first deals with basic elements (raw material, soil and particles, corpses) that explicate and, in some ways, constitute, from the bottom up, the more complex phenomena in the second (hyperfetishism, digital accumulation). While individual chapters may be of interest to different kinds of readers, the book is best read as a progression.

"Part 1: Objects" has three chapters. Chapter 1 focuses on so-called raw materials, such as rubber. Rubber mediates between nature and culture, the jungle and the factory. It led to the deforestation of vast stretches of the Amazonian basin, the subjugation of surviving Tupí-Guaraní indigenous peoples, a short-lived economic boom, and remarkable works of art. The chapter focuses on *Muñecas* (2008), by the Argentine writer Ariel Magnus, which tells the story of an immigrant librarian who lives alone with his silicone sex dolls. I situate the novel within its literary "rubber precedents," notably two Colombian novels, José Eustasio Rivera's classic *La vorágine* (1924; trans. *The Vortex*, 1935) and César Uribe Piedrahita's lesser-known *Toá* (1933). This constellation reflects a desire for absolute control that determines human relationships with rubber. While other works vociferously denounce the atrocities of extraction, Magnus incorporates their critique in subtler ways, ultimately leading us to rethink the role of "raw" material in historical materialism. Taking advantage of the fact that the natural rubber boom was relatively short-lived, and its cultural representation consistently comprises a smaller corpus, my goal in this chapter is to further define a model for the study of more extended commodities and their associated cultural production. Rather than approaching this period as an exceptional time, as it is often construed, I show how it is a cultural formation that participates in the broader trends of the evolution of materiality and extractivism in the region.

The second chapter goes one step further by considering works that, beyond exposing the notion of "raw" material, thematize the politics of such basic nonhumans as rocks and particles. Rather than thematization per se, which a variety of genre and media can offer, the chapter focuses on the possibilities of literary form when confronted with the ungraspable vastness of the earth or the unfathomable smallness of the subatomic. Such are the unlikely topics of the Bolivian Blanca Wiethüchter's novel *El jardín de Nora* (1998), in which the earth lays waste to a garden, and the Argentine César Aira's novella *El té de Dios* (2010), in which a subatomic particle wreaks chaos in the universe. (Neither of these would qualify as genre fiction.) I examine both works in detail, as well as in conversation with Tim Morton's notion of "hyperobjects," which would accurately describe the kind of nonhumans their plotlines depict but would willfully ignore their political dimension. My sociohistorically situated reading exploits formal resources in Wiethüchter and Aira to reveal what's at stake in their stories: unevenness on a global scale. Rocks and atoms may have no politics, but the quests for minerals for the digital age in the Andes and for the basic structure of reality in the Swiss Alps do. Throughout the chapter, I ask the question of how literature can contribute to our understanding of geological and atomic things, which transcend a human scale and life span, while at the same time remaining committed to pressing concerns.

This dialectic frames the third chapter of this book, which focuses on a limit case for the human-nonhuman divide: people's corpses. Slow to decompose and often urgent to understand, corpses are a recurrent theme in contemporary Latin American literature. And yet there is nothing Latin American about a corpse. In the case of Juárez's murdered women, for instance, their horror is something that, in a sense, as Roberto Bolaño has made clear in *2666* (2004; trans. *2666*, 2008), belongs to all concerned global citizens. Fittingly, this chapter projects the findings of the book up to this point beyond the disciplinary confines of Latin Americanism. I propose *an orientation toward the corpse* as a viable telos for the present-day revival of World Literature as critical paradigm. The argument has three parts. First, it characterizes two central tenets of the existing paradigm: a profession of dynamism for its own sake and an implicit lack of finality. Drawing on Kristeva and on Bolaño, the chapter then introduces corpse narratives that embrace the abject and reorient critical practice toward materiality. Finally, I propose a modest agenda for a different worldliteraturism, one that valorizes abject materiality over high-minded idealism. This leads to an affirmation of the value of human life without casting it as exceptional or separate from other organic and inorganic forms. The chapter concludes by exploring the implications of this proposal for literary historiography writ large.

"Part 2: Assemblages" considers the interaction of humans and nonhumans at a higher, more complex level of organization. It has two chapters. Chapter 4 interrogates the notion of commodity fetishism, as developed by Marx, from the vantage point of transcultural materialism. My revisionist reading complicates the notion that a counternarrative may reveal the social relations behind the fascination toward commodities. Instead, I characterize a mode of storytelling I call "hyperfetishist." Hyperfetishism exacerbates social tension, seeking to disturb our relationship with the object rather than to demystify it. The advantages of this mode are manifold, for it affirms the reality of fetishism and recognizes its connection to material properties instead of searching for a supposedly hidden truth. I analyze works that hyperfetishize: the Colombian José Asunción Silva's

1925 posthumous fin de siècle novel *De sobremesa* (published in translation as *After-Dinner Conversation*, 2010); his countryman Fernando Vallejo's works, which build a natural bridge between the nineteenth century and the present, notably his fictionalized biography of Silva, *Almas en pena, chapolas negras* (1995), and his more recent novel *Casablanca la bella* (2014); the Mexican Margo Glantz's mordant *Historia de una mujer que caminó por la vida con zapatos de diseñador* (2005); and, finally, her countrywoman Daniela Rossell's photographic essay *Ricas y famosas* (2002). From the softness of shoes to the glow of faux gold, from unfashionable toilets to crumbling houses, hyperfetishism makes an important contribution to the critique of emerging material paradigms.

Drawing inspiration from Benjamin's discussion of motifs in Baudelaire as a key to understanding the zeitgeist of the mid-nineteenth century, chapter 5 carries out a similar operation with regard to a constellation of Latin American creators and the early twenty-first century. I trace a red thread through sources that unmask ideologies of the digital: the cellphone as agent of alienation in the Mexican-American corrido band Los Tigres del Norte, the personal computer as broker (and breaker) of love in the work of Chilean novelist Alejandro Zambra, and dystopias of cloud computing as political fables in that of his countryman, genre author Jorge Baradit. Throughout the chapter, I revisit Bennett's reflections on the agency of objects and Jonathan Crary's coinage of the "24/7" mode of experience to show how such works deflate some of the myths associated with "digital culture." As I demonstrate, the semiperipheral condition of Latin America, a late adopter of technologies, allows the region's writers to incisively probe ideologies of the digital. This is most notably the case of an important, undertheorized strand in contemporary culture: celebratory, acritical techno-utopianism. Much in the way that digital gadgets themselves build upon simpler artifacts and labor relations, albeit under a different political sign, the chapter develops earlier claims about extractivism and commodity fetishism to further the case of art versus tech.

The book's general conclusion takes stock of the ways of representing the contemporary material turn in recent Latin American culture. These include reappropriations of raw stuff, hyperfetishism, digital ideology critique, object-centered literary historiography, and geologism. I proceed to show how, taken together, these strands challenge different aspects of a worldwide economic system, from extraction to consumption, revealing the continuities between nonhuman and human agents, including narrative. I subsume those operations under the rubric of "estranged extractivism," namely, an actualized form of estrangement that sets in creative tension humanist ideals with a renewed appreciation of our inorganic lives, always already embedded in biological and economical transaction. Bringing such externalities into narrative has an eye-opening effect. Ditto for telling "stories" and "histories" —the same term in Romance languages—of objects, and finding our own place among them. With a brief excursus into the musings on rubber boots in Norwegian author Karl Ove Knausgård, I show how the present volume's critique of neo-extractivism originates in Latin America but has World Literary implication. Beyond appreciating the affinities between bones and rocks, or blood and other life-sustaining fluids (as the work of Manuel DeLanda and other flat ontologists would do), my readings suggest a call to action, an engaged literary politics of the inorganic at a global scale.[91] I also draw inferences on how the overarching narrative of this book provides a model to invigorate traditional ideology and cultural critique with the powerful insights of new materialism.

Contemporary Latin American culture has much to offer to the mutual enrichment of critique and new materialism. Tellingly, at roughly the same time that Latour was publishing a study around the premise that "we" have never been modern, Argentine anthropologist Néstor García Canclini was publishing another around the premise that Latin Americans deploy strategies to enter and leave modernity.[92] Both works are post-1989 reactions, shake-offs of Cold War schemata. For the French thinker, dismantling modernity was an arduous task; for the Argentine, less so. Indeed, Latin America's experience with many of the techno-social underpinnings of that thing we call "modernity" offer a unique vantage point. The region has never taken it for granted or laid claim to its "we"—how could it? Interestingly, there was a fork in the road: García Canclini developed hybridity in a cultural sense, while Latour did so in a natural-cultural one. We are now at a time when critical agendas may again overlap. And yet the natural world is preeminent in a region that, by comparison, displays a less manicured, human-designed environment than Latour's North Atlantic. Contemporary Latin America produces what I have characterized as a recombined, transcultural materialism. It is a form of storytelling that elucidates critical concepts, particularly the continuity of nature and culture across human and nonhuman history. It is not subservient to any theory, metropolitan or otherwise, but a self-sustaining speculative exercise. One may cite new materialist thinking à la Latour or Bennett to footnote it—not the other way around.

Recall how we began the twentieth century trading in heavy bunches, bushels, balls, and heaps. We now exchange those very same things, but also bits, bytes, software, and intellectual property. As before, narrative can reveal the material element in culture, economically and otherwise—even botanically. The tale of two materialisms might end happily, for you can have them both, at least, in literature.

But what if it doesn't end happily? The consequences of ignoring the ties between economic and ecological systems are plain to see. As if ignoring the plights of nature and labor were not risky enough, there is also a more basic epistemological consequence: doing so paints an erroneous picture of the world. It posits two different, parallel orders—one of things and one of men—and leads to believing that solving a problem in one order has nothing to do with solving, or creating, a problem in the other. The modest but not quite negligible contribution of literary scholars has to do with a critical term mentioned above: World Literature. If we are to imagine a world that makes sense of World Literature, and vice versa, it might be beneficial to do so through the lens of transcultural materialism. "Art exists," as Viktor Shklovsky famously put it in "Art as Device," "to make the stone *stony*"; the Russian formalist's foe was habitualization and its speedy perception, which "devours work, clothes, furniture, one's wife, and the fear of war."[93] His were the early days of Soviet industrialist zeal, which he both echoes and fears: my Slavicist colleagues report that the word "device" in the title of his essay connotes machinery, such as a tractor.[94] And yet the slowing down he advocates for, which he casts as art's raison d'être, is nothing other than resisting the drudgery of Taylorism.

We are quite a way from the ¼-horsepower engine of Cuban communism, but there are family resemblances. Shklovsky was a White Russian turned Red and Marré a lifelong Party member; Ponte is a disenchanted son of a revolution. If World Literature scholars were to weave their stories together, they could show how their world was not just made of ideology but of things with a history. Shklovsky falls back on Cartesianism when he claims, a few lines below the passage cited, that "Art is a way of experiencing the artfulness of an object; the object is not important."[95] However, it is objects that brought about his estrangement [остранение], objects reconsidered and written into poems, but never quite abandoned. They are so important, in fact, that he avoids them, Scylla in a sea where the reduction of literature to algebra is Charybdis. Neither object nor symbol, literary language had to chart its way for formalism. The object *is* important, Ponte reminds us, when the object is food. But then food, and the hunger that drives us to it, model how we relate to all things. Shklovsky was a vitalist who, at least in the essay we more commonly associate with him, overlooked that sustenance is life itself.

Narrative has the power to counterfetishize commodities and historicize foods; more broadly, it can interrupt our unreflective ways of relating to objects. In the abandonment to the pleasures of literature there is a potential to repair the suture that Cartesianism has made in Western rationality. We know that we are objects ourselves; we too are matter. But the division between *res cogitans* and *res extensa*, our thinking selves and our materiality, is so entrenched that it is very difficult for us not to think in those terms. It's easier to fantasize in a literary register that tobacco and sugar are sentient beings that condition our ways of living, or that the pineapple is a traveling queen. Metaphor, metonymy, allegory, and literary figures in general supplement what deduction and inference have difficulty grappling with. Under the spell of narrative, we may reassess our social and historical conjuncture and rethink our place within the material world entirely.

PART ONE

Objects

CHAPTER ONE

Raw Stuff Disavowed

There are many terms in language that prescribe a certain relationship to nonhumans. Take the term "meat," which establishes a clear-cut separation from the living being that gave its life for it. Though the organic properties of the signified are identical, "meat" is so different from "flesh" that it would be odd, even blasphemous, for a priest to say at the altar: "Christ gave his meat to save us" (I give this example not out of religious sentiment but for emphasis). Or take the term "beef," which somehow sanitizes the fact that, well, one is eating from a calf; or "ham," a piglet; "poultry," a chick; and so on. Some are terms of untroubled consumption, others of endearment; some describe an animal mass, others a singular animal. And yet they refer to the same "thing." Or take the term "thing" to begin with! It is anthropocentrism at its best: an umbrella for everything else, a perfect device of othering. Never mind that humans are animals, and things, too: we are mammals like those we eat; we are made of carbon and water, like those things out there. The TV host–astronomer wonders that we humans are made of the same stuff as stars. Well, what else could we be made of?

This line of reasoning will be familiar to readers of new materialism and cognate critical currents. In "From Realpolitik to Dingpolitik," Bruno Latour criticizes how humans claim preeminence over "mute things"; meanwhile, Peter Singer makes an ethical argument for vegetarianism on the basis of our shared animality with livestock.[1] This chapter's contribution to those debates revolves around language, particularly the contributions of literary language in decentering the human. In the introduction, I have presented my notion of "transcultural materialism," which I continue to develop in the pages ahead and throughout this book. Two elements that I would like to flesh out at present (pun intended) are the postanthropocentric thrust of this narrative mode and the manner in which it cuts across cultural divides. This two-pronged investigation recalls a comparable pairing in the work of Fernando Ortiz: on the one hand, the idea that sugar and tobacco are actors *alongside* plantation workers; on the other, the finding that the cultural traditions of Africans and Creoles—that rub against each other, eventually configuring Cubanness—are always already *embedded in* material transformation. The German term *Geisteswissenschaften*, literally the "sciences of the spirit," is most at odds with my Ortizian approach, which foregoes the rigors of science for the insightfulness of storytelling and finds that "the spirit of the Cuban people," or any other cultural phenomena for that matter, is not ectoplasmic, like a spirit, but rather solid as clay.

I have just used a term in a foreign language to stress a specifically cultural element. The language we use to other the nonhuman does not always translate well. As Patricia Valderrama pointed out to me, Colombians would not raise an eyebrow when hearing the terms *jamón de pollo* or *jamón de cordero*: literally, "chicken ham" and "lamb ham." In the country, *jamón* is generic for sliced, processed, or cured meat; it is not specific to any one animal. This mismatch is revealing; if we read into it, we will discover an instance of how language and its gaps can reinforce or question anthropocentrism. We assert our preeminence as the earth's top predator also in words; in words, we can undo it. Meanwhile, Russian formalists considered that literary language was a different province within language—an idea that, if taken to its limits, is easily discredited by the close proximity of the everyday to the literary.[2] However, I believe we can adopt a more modest version of that view. Literary and nonliterary utterances are easy to distinguish, in fact, *in everyday life*: there can be bursts of poetry in the metro or the stadium bathroom, say, but generally poetry happens in books, readings, and similar contexts. It's all part of the same language, but it can be used literarily or not—the two modes are not always easy to distinguish, but they are distinguishable for the most part. A foreign language—which, as modern translators understand it, is horizontally and not diametrically separated from our own, like a somewhat removed city rather than a parallel universe—allows us, in the examples above, to reframe human-nonhuman interaction. Couldn't literature do the same?

In this chapter, I shall focus on a notion that is particularly adept at capturing the role of language in prescribing a certain relationship to nonhumans: "raw material"—in Spanish, *materia prima*. What is raw or primordial about a sheep, a mountain of gold, a forest of rubber trees? Primordialness, in these cases, lies in the eyes of the beholder—and in her language, novels included, unless we read them against the grain. We have understood since Ferdinand de Saussure that language signifies through differentiation. This means that the core operation of generating difference is codified in all language; arguably, it can be decodified there too. And since everyday language is straightforward and communicative, while literary language can afford a different economy, the latter seems to be the place to look for answers. With this in mind, I now focus on raw material to develop a facet of transcultural materialism. Ortiz relied on literary examples, but he did not develop the implications of his work for hermeneutics. This is, of course, a task that Ángel Rama undertook under the aegis of historical materialism.[3] As previously stated, my own take converses with that tradition but drives it in a different direction. Here, I show how transcultural materialism can be a way of reading literature. First, I will compare two narratives that, as I argue, interrogate raw material. One is from the early decades of the twentieth century, the other from those of the twenty-first. In a second moment, this comparison will allow me to further characterize the post-1989 material turn and the shifting role of fiction within it. The ultimate goal of this chapter is to make explicit the main tenets of transcultural materialism as a means for the study of contemporary literature.

The Black Flock

For a thought-provoking image of raw material, picture the massive, twenty-to-fifty-kilogram balls of natural rubber that tappers would send floating downstream in the Amazon basin to be harvested closer to major maritime ports (figure 1.1). A liberal economic historian might regard the scene as a token of ingenuity, for this process saves the redundant effort of loading the rubber onto a boat. A Marxist historian might rightly wonder about

44 ■ **Objects**

FIGURE 1.1 Workers and extracted rubber in the Amazon basin.
Arquivo historico de Manaus.

the strenuous labor involved before and after the balls are afloat. Whether one intuits here wealth-creation or exploitation, these perspectives have in common the parsing out of human and nonhuman elements: in both accounts, the life of the commodity has begun, and the organic connection to the surrounding jungle is suspended. By contrast, José Eustasio Rivera's 1924 *The Vortex* gives us the formidable metaphor of the *rebaño negro*—a "black flock," as if the rubber was ushered by an invisible human shepherd, or as if the river itself showed the way.[4] Here, in greatly condensed form, the relationship of humans, rubber, and jungle is remediated. Given the abusive, unsustainable collective of human and nonhuman elements that made the extraction possible, this is rightfully rendered as an ominous sight. The metaphor counteracts that other, more pervasive metaphor that is "raw material" in the first place.

Some of the works studied in the present volume are underappreciated local gems; others are undisputed regional classics. *The Vortex* belongs to the latter. It tells the story of how Arturo Cova, his lover Alicia, and their allies win a battle against ruthless rubber tappers who seek to enslave them, but ultimately lose the war against the jungle. The backdrop is the first rubber boom in the Amazon, periodized (by Tulio Halperín Dongui and others) between approximately 1870 and 1910.[5] The atrocities committed by rubber barons on indigenous peoples and other enslaved workers are so egregious that talking about nonhumans in this context seems, well, inhuman, even in literary criticism. But given that an ample human-centric bibliography exists and that, after all, rubber is at the heart of the matter, I would like to explore that less-traveled road. This does not suspend the political and ethical concerns that influence even the more philological, stylistic analyses. Actually, it contributes to a better understanding of such issues, for the forces of capitalism alone did not dictate the fate of the victims of the rubber boom. If Rivera wanted to write an essay about greed and the limits of the rule of law in the Amazon, he would have done so. (Indeed, some of his letters and other documents set themselves to the task.) As purposefully uneconomical as Ortiz, Rivera recreates complex assemblages that revolve around rubber: think of sliced barks of trees, whipped human backs, water currents and mood swings, guns and insects, the fevers of *beriberi*. Let us examine, then, what the novel can tell us about power relations across the human-nonhuman divide.

Glimpses of nonhuman autonomy are numerous: Cova hears the sands asking him to tread lightly and toss them into the wind, shortly before he himself fears becoming a tree; he learns that the son of Clemente Silva, his guide through the jungle, was "killed by a tree"; an "accomplice" tree tangles Silva in his lianas, aiding his persecutors; referring again to Silva, the narrator reports that "the secret voice [of things] filled his soul."[6] The jungle makes men mad; the jungle suspends moral precepts; and so forth. Eco-critical readings downplay these descriptions of Nature as ruthless and evil, favoring instead the passages where characters extol the jungle or decry the extinction of a species, as Scott DeVries observes in the case of the *balatá*.[7] Similarly, Jennifer French claims the text anticipates radical environmentalism.[8] But how can a text that vilifies the jungle so extensively be properly environmentalist? Or should we just look at the passages that suggest the opposite?

This environmentalist cherry-picking is the opposite pair of socio-critical readings that turn their backs on Nature. The Russian translation of *La vorágine*, which appeared in the Soviet Union in 1935 and may very well epitomize this trend, introduces Rivera as "a great and honest bourgeois artist" whose work offers "a view that overcame bourgeois class to appreciate the authentic social truth."[9] William Bull goes as far as to suggest that an "excessive" psychological characterization would result from Rivera not being able to grasp the objective realities of rubber tappers.[10] David Viñas, in a lucid but rather partial statement, claims that "Cova's vital immersion in peasant barbarism produces . . . the bookish emergence of Rivera in the city. The rural 'coming of age' of the protagonist ends with the publication of a book for a bourgeois readership in Bogotá."[11] Talk about not seeing the forest for the trees: those readings miss the trees to begin with. They want so much for the book to make a legible social critique that they rewrite it in their minds. Mutatis mutandis, the same can be said of some environmentalist readings, although, in addition to being partial explanations, they reproduce what they seek to challenge—that is, the separation of nature and culture.

There is no depiction of the "environment" in a novel where the jungle is a protagonist; there are networks that bind quasi subjects and quasi objects. *La vorágine* is as much about capitalism as it is about our interactions with nonhumans. Even sexual desire, which we often fancy to be an exclusive province of the human, involves the assemblage. The rich literature on *The Vortex* has rightly noted that Cova's dreams *symbolically* approximate rubber milk with semen and rubber trees with phalluses, among several other more or less veiled sexual references. In an often-overlooked passage, however, Cova is *literally* aroused by feathers:

> That afternoon, sadness possessed my spirit. Why must I always live alone? Why could I not share with someone these ermine feathers; this wing of the marine *codúa*, where the rainbow lies imprisoned; this spring-time vision of birds and colour?
>
> With humiliating pain I discovered Alicia flitting in the hazy background of my dreams; and then with crude and bitter realism I strove to blight the thoughts that harboured the intruder.[12]

The feathers in this scene would not be out of place in a story by Leopold von Sacher-Masoch, except that, given the setting, the fetish is emphatically a part of the natural world. The final allusion to ejaculation is lyrical to the point of being hermetic—that is, circuitous enough so as not to be censored for a mainstream readership of the 1920s. Yet it is unequivocal. Disturbingly, it involves rage, as the protagonist resents longing for Alicia, whom he thinks has been unfaithful. Passages like this have rightly led Monserrat Ordóñez and Sharon Magnarelli to note that the novel presents a masculinist storyline through the eyes of the protagonist, but also provides spaces for the critique of patriarchy in the silences and contradictions of his discourse.[13] Ordóñez also reminds us that feathers were commodities; indigenous gatherers picked them up in the jungle and sold them to criollos, who would export them.[14] In a sense, then, Cova is getting off to the thought of riches. Beckman elaborates on this point to show how the sexual frustrations of Cova mirror the export reveries of capital fictions.[15] I would, however, like to complement such interpretations by recentering, if you will, the feather as feather. Its materiality, which we should not ignore, reveals the hybrid cathexis of the novel.

It is useful to turn for a moment to Michael Pollan, who rethinks desire in light of the coevolution of humans and nonhumans.[16] "Coevolution" is a more accurate term than "domestication," which is one-sided. So-called domestic plants and animals get phenomenal returns from their dealings with humans: rosemary thrives on this planet, as do dogs. Nonhumans give and they receive; they domesticate us, we them—intention is beside the point. Thus a desire for sweetness informs our relationship with apples; for beauty, with tulips; and for intoxication, with marijuana. Like human bumblebees, we have favored colored tulips and other flowers; they, in turn, have an effect on our ideals of beauty, as countless metaphors attest. But of the plants Pollan analyzes, I find that none comes closer to rubber than potatoes. Potatoes codify a desire for control: the fantasy that the human species can feed any number of its individual members, any time, in any weather. This backfires, surely: think of the Great Famine of the nineteenth-century in Ireland. Or consider today's genetically enhanced potatoes, which accompany a global desire for, say, McDonald's fries to taste the same wherever we go, regardless of the unrealistic demands that makes on local agriculture.

Extrapolating, I would like to propose that a desire for *absolute* control defines our modern relationship with rubber trees, with the obvious caveat that fully developing this view would require input from a botanist-historian. Still, it is striking to see how much the literary evidence bears out this point, as *The Vortex* so vividly illustrates. The iridescent colors in Arturo Cova's ticklish feathers make a startling apparition in the title scene of the novel, in which two indigenous men, who had been enlisted to guide Cova's expedition against their will, succumb to a whirlpool—in Spanish, *vorágine*. They leave behind two spinning hats "bajo el iris que abría sus pétalos como la mariposa de la indiecita Mapiripana."[17] The understated sexual connotations become luridly clear in Earl K. James's 1935 rendering: "under the rainbow that pulsated like the butterfly of the little Indian girl Mapiripana."[18] Not coincidentally, Seymour Menton refers to a *vagina dentata*.[19] One is reminded of Rubén Darío's verse: "y los moluscos reminiscencias de mujeres."[20] Petals, feathers, butterfly wings, and labia constitute a symbolic, but also literal, material sequence in a violent form of desire that traverses the vegetable, animal, and human kingdoms.

This finding calls for a revised reading of the entire novel. As readers will recall, the drowning scene anticipates the famous ending, "¡Los devoró la selva!"—literally, "The jungle swallowed them whole."[21] Yet it also connects to Cova's variegated wet dreams, in one of which "numberless people bent over the creeping ribbon of liquid [rubber milk] and drank of it."[22] And, of course, it alludes to Mapiripana, a mythic indigenous maiden, most likely a product of Rivera's own gothic imagination and not of local traditions, who punishes a rapist priest by bearing his children, a pair composed of a bat and an owl, who suck his blood for years—that is, until he dies; then a blue butterfly illuminates the cave with its flight. Critics have struggled to make these heterogeneous and diverse elements conform to a Freudian reading. Yet instead of immoderate metaphorization, what I see here could be described as becoming, or, in Latour's terms, as nature-culture. It is the material trail of a desire for absolute control.

Note that this desire cannot be satisfied. It is akin to wanting to pull a body in a vacuum, without an opposing force. Control can only be partial; it is defined by resistance. The substance of rubber itself makes this clear, but it also promises *to become everything else*, to give *limitless satisfaction* to a will to shape. This is Arturo Cova's predicament. Alternatively, he wants control over his feelings or wants to let them loose; he desires the saint and the libertine; he is a disinterested poet and an avid entrepreneur. He has, to echo the title of an iconic rock album, a rubber soul. His will seeks to impose itself over Indians, nature, women, language, criollo male competitors and allies, and even over his own desire.

This belongs within a particularly ill-fated attempt at coevolution with rubber trees at the cost of human lives and ecological balance. Hence in the denouement, to borrow a concept of Spinoza dear to political ecologists, Cova's party loses its *conatus*, its perseverance in being. That is exactly what it means to be devoured by the jungle, an ecosystem described in another famous passage as "an enormous cemetery that rots and resuscitates."[23] The minerals in their bodies will not be lost, and yet the organisms will not endure: the biological mirror image of cultural assimilation. It is not that the object jungle prevails over human subjects, but that their collective has become untenable. Rubber is then the substratum for transculturation, as tobacco and sugar were for Ortiz, and the novel a reflection not only of an exploitative economic model but of an unsustainable experiment at coevolution. Something similar could be argued about César Uribe Piedrahita's *Toá* (1933), which takes its name from a half-Indian princess who, at the end of the novel, dies giving birth to the baby of a Covaesque protagonist.[24] The man, Antonio de Orrantia, has earlier asked her to be happy; otherwise he will leave her. Amid the pangs of death, Toá tries to smile and tells him that she is indeed happy, for fear of losing him—in the afterlife? One wonders. Perhaps this perverse scene of love surrender is one of domestic domestication. Such are the fantasies that rubber dictates. Not coincidentally, Uribe Piedrahita was also a pathologist who studied arrow poison and tropical parasites in chickens—both "obstacles" for the expansion of farming and the nation-state into the "wilderness."[25]

Beyond the natural rubber booms in the Amazon and their effects in cultural production, a trail of latex continues until this very day. Rubber is the stuff of preservatives and sex toys, but also of toys tout court, of the soles of our shoes and the raincoats that keep us dry. Along with nylon, it ushered in the plastics revolution; it was such a staple of daily life that it begot suburban Tupperware parties and the adoption of the term "plasticity" as a trait of character. Works of literature that deal with rubber allow us to interrogate our relationship with rubber and the Constitution, in the Latourian sense, that underpins it. A case in point is the underappreciated, brilliant Argentine writer Ariel Magnus's *Muñecas* (2008), to which I devote the next section of this chapter. If Ponte gave continuation to the transcultural materialism that, in my revisionist reading, Ortiz founded, Magnus does something similar for Rivera and Uribe Piedrahita. Here the past and the present illuminate each other: literature serves as the conduit for a reassessment of our place among things throughout history—not merely by representing it, as in a realist novel, but by interrogating the underexamined scaffoldings that determine our relation to nonhumans, including, above all, those implicit in language.

For the Love of Silicone

An heir to the awkward-genius tradition of César Aira, Ariel Magnus is in many ways eccentric for an Argentine writer—for one thing, he resides in Germany. This geographical fact is more or less present throughout his heterogeneous, growing oeuvre. There are two historic atrocities in the background of *Muñecas*: extermination and extractivism. The first is evident in as much as its characters are, as if part of some vulgar joke, a Jew and a "Nazi." To be more precise, they are an unnamed, immigrant librarian in Germany whose father was a socialist worker in some faraway place about which we know little, and Selin Sürginson, a library patron and daughter of a Nazi soldier who was stationed at Auschwitz. Without thinking much about it, Selin invites the librarian, whom she does not know, to her thirtieth birthday party. Almost no one goes to the party. Drunk and disappointed, she offers to drive him back home. On the way they have an unfortunate encounter with the police. Upon arriving at the librarian's place, they stop talking, as a secret is revealed about him. A certain sexual tension grows between them, and Selin ends up in his bed, offering herself up, but at the close of the narration, he does not seem inclined to reciprocate. Extractivism comes to bear regarding the librarian's secret, which is a secret not because he hides it but because it only makes itself apparent once they enter his apartment: he lives with six dolls made of inflatable silicone, which he collects, he explains, "as one would collect horses, or cars. That is, I have them in the stable or in the garage but also . . ."[26] As I see it, the long history of rubber extractivism, the dolls' historical precursor, is as present in the narration as what historian Saul Friedländer would call "the years of extermination," referring to the crimes taking place in Nazi concentration camps during World War II.[27] It is worth elucidating how Magnus situates his writing in the double erasure of these historical atrocities and their corresponding literary traditions.[28]

Rubber originates from the Amazonian tree *Hevea brasiliensis*, which the Witoto and Tupí peoples, among other ethnic groups, used for centuries before its commercial exploitation. The latter coincides with those peoples' own exploitation at the hands of Casa Arana and other colonists. As crude as it often is, Rivera's novel pales in comparison to the horrendous accounts and documentation from nonfiction sources. In the frontispiece of Walter Hardenburg's early denunciation piece *The Devil's Paradise* (1912), there are indigenous slaves in shackles; in the interior pages, there is a picture of the emaciated carcass of a woman who was reportedly condemned to die of hunger; for contrast, there later appears a picture of "free Indians" with the following caption: "Observe their robust appearance when not enslaved."[29] The understudied and insufficiently memorialized killing of thousands of natives through work exhaustion, summary execution, and outright torture was, in a strict sense, a genocide comparable in scale to the pogroms that were carried out in Eurasia. As is well known, the phenomenon that Friedländer documents was the first genocide to carry this name, the only one of its scale. Works by Rivera, Uribe Piedrahita and Euclides da Cunha accompany the first event, and those by Louis-Ferdinand Céline, Paul Celan, and many others accompany the latter one.[30] As John Tully reports in *A Social History of Rubber*, Nazi Germany synthesized rubber as part of the arms race and in response to the embargo.[31] The English had brought natural rubber to Asia, where it was cultivated on plantations and no longer in the middle of the jungle. As one can see, the trajectory of this group of substances (gutta-percha, rubber, plastic, silicone)—first natural, then artificial, and later synthetic—is rich in meaning. The twentieth century, with its neocolonialism and its wars, is inscribed in this trajectory.

The first appearance of rubber in the novel, which is 115 pages long, is on page 43, with inflated condoms that hang from the ceiling during the failed party. On page 79 Selin makes reference to the "verga de plástico" that her ex-boyfriend, Günther, had asked her to stick in him. On page 85, the dolls appear. Starting on page 87, the librarian lectures on the advances in "materia de androides," especially with the arrival of silicone. Putting to the test the work's pact of verisimilitude, which carefully borders on the absurd, he states, "The doll you see there, for example, it breathes, its heart beats, its body warms up, it menstruates every 28 days. And that's a relatively old model, I bought it a year ago. The new ones talk and carry a video camera in their eyes."[32] Noting that the plants are also plastic, Selin thinks that the librarian, "perversely ecologically-minded" is "more German than the Germans."[33] Beginning on page 113, Selin kisses the librarian, who remains undaunted. Just after, she lies down on the bed with Lais, the doll, hoping that Magnus "sticks it in me like he sticks it in Lais . . . His latex cock in my silicone hole."[34] In the end, when Selin falls asleep with the dolls, she asks if "this thing about women getting silicone implants everywhere does not take after dolls" because "nature imitates art and vice versa."[35]

These moments reveal the latex plot that runs throughout the novel. As can be seen from the page numbers that I have emphasized, the *récit* is just as or more important than the *histoire*: the novel is made up of what it tells, but the way that it tells is indispensable. Beginning on page 58, the librarian mentions that he is Jewish, and Selin talks about her father. The first fifty pages are in free indirect speech focalized on him, in a section astutely called "Her," and it goes until the end of the party. The second section, a little longer, is called "Him" and corresponds to her free indirect speech as they make their way to the librarian's apartment. This inversion of names brings to mind the expression "twin souls," yet it is also about false symmetry: the characters would almost fit into a joke or fable, but not quite. Much like César Aira, who, as Mariano García has shown, begins each of his short novels in one genre and distorts it along the way until converting it into another,[36] Magnus begins with a love story and, as I see it, skirts the boundaries of rubber novels and writings of extermination.

I interpret as ars poetica one particularly notable passage during the party when the librarian, Selin, and Ben (her landlord) resign themselves to bringing out seats to sit on, since they already suspect that no one else will arrive. In a work in which the border between animated and unanimated objects is of great importance, the librarian points out that another name for the expression "baile de las sillas" is "viaje a Jerusalén" (*Reise nach Jerusalem*).[37] Without dwelling on it, just to make conversation, Selin supposes that somewhere behind that expression there must be "a modern fable, of the sort that relegates the moral to the ethical creativity of its listeners."[38] This describes the novel as a whole. If one accepts the invitation to look for a moral, one would find that there is none (just as there is no moral in Ortiz, even though what he says about tobacco and sugar suggests a fable). The Spanish saying is, "El que va a Sevilla, pierde su silla" ("He who goes to Seville loses his seat"). Travelling to Jerusalem and back again only to be incapable of finding one's place could be related to the Crusades or to Zionism. Selin wonders if there might be something anti-Semitic in the expression, since throughout the novel she alternates between an exacerbated sensitivity to other cultures and disdain for them. One seat always corresponds to one human, singling him out: the Colombian artist Doris Salcedo represented the so-called *Holocausto del Palacio de Justicia* in Bogotá with an array of chairs in the façade of the new building that the missing judicial branch would have occupied.[39]

With a very Airean metonymic drifting, Selin goes from talking about the game to remarking that she does not understand jokes. The librarian responds by saying that he does not get thrillers:

> "I can't ever fully grasp what is one supposed to expect so impatiently."
> "First there is a corpse, and then they find the assassin," I reasoned out loud. "But to me what's dead is suspense and the scriptwriter is the killer, in the worst case with the director and the actors as accomplices."
> "By contrast, in love stories," carried on Selin, as if she were explaining my train of thought, "since the beginning you want them to kiss and you know they are going to kiss, but nonetheless you cannot step away from the TV until they do finally kiss—that's what I call suspense."[40]

This dialogue is both nonsensical party conversation and diegetic revelation. Freud showed how jokes are exudations of the unconscious. Magnus's novel is, as was his earlier work *Un chino en bicicleta* (2007), a long joke.[41] It is easy to appreciate that the political unconscious of the text, to borrow Fredric Jameson's phrase, is the memory of the Holocaust and of Nazism in a postcolonial context.[42] Add to this the memory of rubber and of other malleable substances that are as important as the chairs in the party. Like them, they index individual human bodies, but they do it to the point of molding to them. The ending is not a revelation about the profound relationship between rubber and Nazism but a realization of the possibilities of Magnus's emplotment. In the absence of a moral, what the novel does achieve is a staging of the contradictions at the heart of the memory of these events, and having them constellate—that is, if you concede that things hold a certain material and cultural memory, as plants did for Ortiz, that waits to be narrativized.

These days, silkworms are genetically modified to produce thread for industrial purposes. Latex was the original super substance: the first thing that promised to become everything else. Ambitions court hubris and tragedy, and this one was no exception. Rubber proposed a new effective border between nature and culture through the process of isolating the wet from the dry or, in a word, waterproofing. Here was a space to overcome the human, so intrinsically bound with water. As Latour points out, when attempts are made to stop hybrids between the human and nonhuman, which are in reality the norm and not the exception, such hybrids proliferate, and not necessarily with favorable consequences. Waterproofing supposes a new radical pact between objects. Racism, that organizing principle of National Socialism, is a fantasy of perfect impermeability. Its forceful institutionalization triggered a new and lamentable disruption in the order of things, which also led to the objectification of millions of human beings.

Fittingly, Selin approaches historical National Socialism in an oblique way, similar to the way Roberto Bolaño's characters do in *La literatura nazi en América* (1994), which I have analyzed in a previous study.[43] In Selin's apartment, the empty seats hardly evoke victims; however, this reading gains weight when other elements are taken into account. The phrase "imagine if there were a war and nobody came," said at the party regarding the small probability that Germany and France would participate in the war in Iraq, is iterated again at the end of the night when the librarian justifies his solitary life: "Life is a party where you're invited and when you go no one is there."[44] When a car passes by, the basement apartment is illuminated. Selin recounts, "Suddenly the room seems like a trench swept by the enemy's headlights. Are we below sea level?"[45] Notice how the latent war is represented as permeability. Before, in the party, the librarian feels in his overcoat the weight of the many gifts that he has brought for the birthday girl—like stones that drag him to the bottom of the sea.[46] That contrasts with the brutal image, impermeable and dry, of the latex penis in a silicone hole. Selin, whose Electra complex, let us remember, would have her desiring a perpetrator, here searches for total friction, violence.

Seen in a different way, she wants to be objectivized. That said, in this novel humans are no more than things. Genocide is horrific not because it reduces its victims to objecthood (there are things no one would do to *things*) but because it is the very definition of that which is horrific. It is not *tragic*, however, as Hayden White observes about the work of Saul Friedländer.[47] If ever he had it, Magnus resists the temptation to give pathos, agony, destruction, and anagnorisis to genocide, as if there existed a tragic destiny or a cosmic plan. Instead, he *displaces* that narrative onto the plot of rubber and onto the discrete drama of a bad night drinking between a shy, solitary man and a self-reproaching woman. A fable or joke would ask that a general inference be made from these characters, much in the way that the hare and tortoise teach something about patience and ethical values, or that the laughter of a Jewish joke mobilizes and dissolves (absolves?)—to say it with a German concept—*Weltschmerz* (the pain of the world). White says that Friedländer "de-narrativizes" (destorifies) extermination, as Toni Morrison did for slavery, following a modernist paradigm present in Proust, Woolf, Kafka, and Joyce.[48] Like Magnus, they prefer a presentation technique that, taking up again the vocabulary that I advanced earlier, is paratactic. Horror is incommunicable, but the unending searches to understand it are not, especially when constellation is privileged over crude data.

There are many traces of extermination literature in the novel. At the party, the librarian is a "witness to a tragedy" or, even more suggestive, "the only survivor of a personal tragedy which would keep happening in another form in Selin's memory, invisible to others and in the course of time to her as well."[49] This is not the habitual language used to speak of a trivial embarrassment, namely, that Selin's social circle left her along with her ex-boyfriend; it recalls discussion about giving testimony in Primo Levi as something both necessary and impossible.[50] It also mirrors the role of the writer facing trauma in Dominick LaCapra, for whom there would be written works about compulsive repetition and others about healing, without it being possible beforehand to distinguish between them.[51] It goes without saying that the name Selin alludes to is Louis-Ferdinand Céline, a nihilist and Nazi. The librarian refers to himself as an idiot "in the etymological sense" of the word, which is precisely the way that Hannah Arendt criticizes those who, as in the Greek root, are "for themselves": if every man focuses only on his own matters, neither political action nor a space for the commons is possible.[52] Of course, this last position fully coincides with the final monologue of the librarian, for whom the dolls appear to have been emancipated, as Rimbaud would say, from that hell that is other people.

What interest might Magnus have in collapsing a witness, a victim, an idiot, and even, potentially, a victimizer into one figure? In my view, the last line of the novel leaves space to think that when the librarian leaves the room to let Selin sleep off her drunkenness, he awaits the opportunity to possess her. Throughout the novel, he has conspicuously said on various occasions that he likes women seated (like dolls). In contrast to the first part, we do not have access to the librarian's interior speech, though by extrapolating from his previous behavior, we can imagine how excited and frightened and infuriated he must have been with the arrival of the woman in his space. However, his way of speaking as an ethical idiot who does not seek to harm anyone (just that they leave him alone), could be a façade.

Already he has lied to try to please. The novel's epigraph is from Ovid, from the episode of Pygmalion and Galatea, in which the adored sculpture turns into a woman. *Muñecas* could invert that trajectory, wherein the evening could—it remains unclear—end in consensual sex or in the rape of an unconscious woman. Recall the passage previously cited: "I wonder if this thing about women getting silicone implants everywhere does not take after the dolls. Nature imitates art, Lais. Give me your hand. First art imitates nature, then the other way around. And so on. And when you can get pregnant, it flips again. Back andforth backandforth backandforthandba [idayvueltaid]."[53]

The last line, in which the syntax breaks down, marks a rhythm like that of intercourse, which, after all, is a central motif throughout the book. Sophistication and vulgarity go hand in hand: Lais is the name of the octosyllabic medieval poems of courtly love; the truncated word "id" could be the beginning of a dream, or it might refer to the Freudian id. The fantasy about the pregnant doll does have touches of science fiction, but it could also allude to the character, Selin, who just prior has declared that she does not have any condoms because she used them all to decorate for the party. The bit about nature and art is a product of having internalized the librarian's erudite speech: the lovers become one in language, so to speak. After all, one of the few things we know about the librarian's past is that, in his mother tongue, the verb for "to go" and "to come" is the same (We also know that the route of the 36 bus reminds him of his childhood. With an autobiographical wink, Magnus pairs the Heidelberg-Handschuhsheim route, literally from "the city of the heath" to "the home of gloves," with the Palermo-Caballito route.) Having said that, in the spirit of the cultural turn for which Ortiz cleared the way, as he does now for the materialist turn, one could replace "art" with "culture." In this way, we can appreciate the final scene, with its ambiguous permeability and impermeability, as the final denarrativization of the intermingled plots of extermination and extraction. For some, the moral will be that history has ended, and that only its most distant echoes remain—or that technology will make ethical idiocy possible, or usher in the posthumanist utopia. Or the lesson might be that, facing the onslaught of androids, we must return to a state of nature.

The collapse of victimizers, victims, witnesses, and idiots could form the basis of a relativist argument and, dangerously, even one of denial. Instead, my sense is that this is both about negative critique and about confronting politically correct, thoughtless platitudes. With the important qualification that its misogynistic subplot suggests a truncated scapegoat mechanism, the novel's great merit is finding an internally coherent narrative solution for the contradictions that situate it historically. They come at a time when the memories of both extractivism and extermination lose some of their poignancy, slowly fading into the background. And yet the synthesizing of rubber and its afterlife in new materials, in which both ruthless *caucheros* and Nazi scientists played a part, provide the very fabric of the modern world. The uncanny effect of the story, which stands out among a flurry of recent works in which more or less kinky sexual fantasies play a prominent role, stems from its historical situatedness in this double erasure. We live on the brink of a sex toy revolution, says the industry.[54] We also live in the aftermath of extermination, whispers *Muñecas*, which leads me to circumscribe both epochs to a contradictory desire, self-cancelling and imperious, for absolute control.

This is why works such as *La vorágine*, *Toá*, and, decades later, *Muñecas* are fascinated with fascist and sexist ideas. The possibility of creating something that can take any form is an aspiration to omnipotence. Inventions from the fields of nanotechnology and synthetic biology, not to mention from the combination of the two, announce a very near future in which what silicone is to gutta-percha, new compounds will be to silicone. This underscores Catherine Malabou's ideas about plasticity as a figure of historical thought that reframes the relationships between the universal and the particular; hers would be an antifascist act of molding.[55] The contemporary materialist turn also enhances the status of the literary works—more *singular* than particular, and certainly *plastic*—of Latin American authors like Magnus. My related proposal is that World Literature think of itself not only in terms of space and time but also in terms of materiality.

I've allowed myself to extend the origin myth of the dolls to the domestication and exploitation of Amazonian rubber. Transactions of globalization are implicit when the librarian, granting himself the more or less precarious place of enunciation of the country where he has resided for ten years, affirms that even though the dolls began in California and are developed in Japan, "Germany is well ahead of the curve, I'll have you know."[56] It bears repeating: there would be no sex dolls, as there would be no modern syringes in hospitals nor transatlantic flights that make literary conferences possible, without the exploitation of Amazonian rubber and its synthesizing by the German military-industrial machine. The dolls in this basement are always already global. They are also and in a similar sense Latin American, of course, since they are inscribed in a tradition where librarians harken back to Borges, who wrote "El tema del traidor y del héroe" and "Deutsches Requiem," founding a thematic that Bolaño would later revisit. Magnus writes in a moment in which extraction is already a fait accompli, and the only thing left is for the dolls to be imported to Latin America as luxury goods, mutatis mutandis, as Ford's cars carried in their tires, on their way back to the Amazon, the latex of trees from that same jungle.

The novel also suggests that trauma lives in the things themselves—but neither in the way of Pierre Nora's institutionalizing figure of *lieux de mémoire* nor in the way of the boom of memoirist production in our time. If Ortiz were to write his counterpoint today, he would have to go as far as transgenic tobacco and artificial sweeteners. We can, through the transcultural materialism that *Muñecas* exemplifies, summon the things themselves: the substances, in the most basic sense, of historical content. I consider this an urgent task in the midst of a contemporary materialist turn, when our way of relating to objects is rapidly changing. It would do us well to have at our disposal other directives and figures of thought than the mere accumulation of capital. Magnus responds to the commodity counterfetishism that (as Coronil describes well) informs Ortiz's writing with a hyperfetishism that stimulates the critical imagination—or perhaps the "ethical creativity"—of the reader (see chapter 4).[57] *Muñecas* speaks to the risks and pleasures of *becoming things*, and it raises the question of a new way for humans to dwell with nonhumans.

As he contemplates the empty party, "something in the purity of the air and the overexcited stillness of the furniture" reminds the male protagonist of the library before it opens, before the books are "handled."[58] In both settings there are more seats than people. Later the apartment, where there are more dolls than people, is another sanctuary. Faced with these three impermeable spaces, curated in close proximity to one another like an artistic installation, critics must choose where to sit. But the novel is anything but hospitable: one can only sit, as Selin does, next to a thing, or hold a book and smear it with one's fingers, as one unavoidably does, in that act called "reading" that somehow evokes more spiritual and less physical phenomena. There does not appear to be any one moral or primordial scene—or is there? Infer: If it is better to have a crowded library than an empty one, and a lively party than a deserted one, would an orgy with dolls be the punch line of this long, protracted joke of a novel? In the librarian's monologue, life is either anomie or sexual perversion. To take this at face value, however, would be the same as reading the words of Sade's dying man to a priest as an authorial statement, rather than as the more puzzling literary device that they constitute. For one, what I take away from this fascinating little book is a rather consequential "as if." While Christian hermeneutics asks its readers to approach the Bible as if it were the word of God, and close reading, its secular daughter, asks them to read texts as if they were complete worlds unto themselves, my modest hermeneutical contribution, in formulating the notion of transcultural materialism, is to read *as if* in the presence of *things with a history*.

The Worst of Architects and the Best of Bees

By inoculating historical materialism with material history, works such as those studied in this chapter traverse the human-nonhuman divide to offer a postanthropocentric vision of history. They grant objects the agency and importance they are due without, in so doing, taking importance away from themes that are essentially human, political, and social, such as justice and work. Upon revisiting *Contrapunteo cubano del tabaco y del azúcar*, I made a note of how the two crops do not allow themselves to be reduced to allegories about socialism or capitalism, or to being the representatives of two cultures whose de-essentialized union Ortiz supposedly dedicated himself to celebrating. An approximation along those lines would not exhaust the literal and botanical meaning of the counterpoint. What happens to those two plants matters: from germination to their incorporation into the lungs and bloodstream of men, and from domestication as crops to their proto-industrial exploitation, each stage is associated with social orders. The effects that the plants have on the world also matter, what they give and what they receive. In this way, narrating the paratactic development of what Latour would call "nature-culture" is Ortiz's great contribution to contemporary criticism. As we have seen, Rivera prefigures some of these operations in the early twentieth century, while Magnus retraces the footsteps of these two authors in the early twenty-first century. Together, their works know how to speak simultaneously of things and humans, and permit us to understand vegetal-human history along a continuum.

Beyond rubber novels, one logical step forward would be to consider cultural products that revolve around other pivotal commodities for Latin America. These include bananas, central to García Márquez's *One Hundred Years of Solitude* (1967), whose denouement takes after the 1928 Banana Massacre in Ciénaga, one of several along the Caribbean basin to target unionizing workers. There is also Pablo Neruda's poem "The United Fruit Company" (1950), which had already rendered the banana as a symbol and agent of exploitation: "[UFC] rebaptized these countries / Banana Republics, / and over the sleeping dead, . . . encouraged envy, attracted / the dictatorship of flies: / Trujillo flies, Tacho flies."[59] The physical layout of the banana plantation itself is a matrix for material transformation: the endless rows of banana trees, shimmering under the equinoctial sun, are a model for dysfunctional human and nonhuman interaction. The story of the domestication of the Asian Cavendish banana could very well inform an understanding of its accompanying worldwide cultural products and human consequences. Something analogous could be said of cacao, a Meso-American crop predating colonization that Diego Rivera painted in heroic murals (figure 1.2) and Brazilian contemporary conceptual artist Vik Muniz featured as molten chocolate in playful portraits (figures 1.3 and 1.4). Or imagine a *longue durée*, nonhuman-centered study of the many paths that go from coca leaves to cocaine. At present, I merely insinuate these readings, inviting others to turn them into convening agendas; in my mind, they yield themselves not just for a series of articles but for a series of volumes.[60]

For its part, "raw material" has distinct stories to tell, particularly through the articulation of historical and new materialisms. Grammar sometimes gives the erroneous impression that we are in charge of nature, as if we ourselves were not also subject to it—recall the active, not passive construction of the verb "to domesticate." But literary language, which often challenges grammatical convention and explores the limits of the sayable, can contribute to reformulating our ways of thinking about these matters and potentially lead us to reconceive our place among nonhumans. Consequently, theory stands to benefit from the kind of critical exercise I have put forward in this chapter. For one, appreciating the rich language of transcultural materiality developed by the likes of Rivera and Magnus leads to

FIGURE 1.2 Diego Rivera, grisaille of cacao as Aztec currency, 1949. Palacio Nacional, Mexico City.
Author photo.

FIGURE 1.3 Vik Muniz, Sigmund Freud, from *Chocolate Pictures*, 1997.

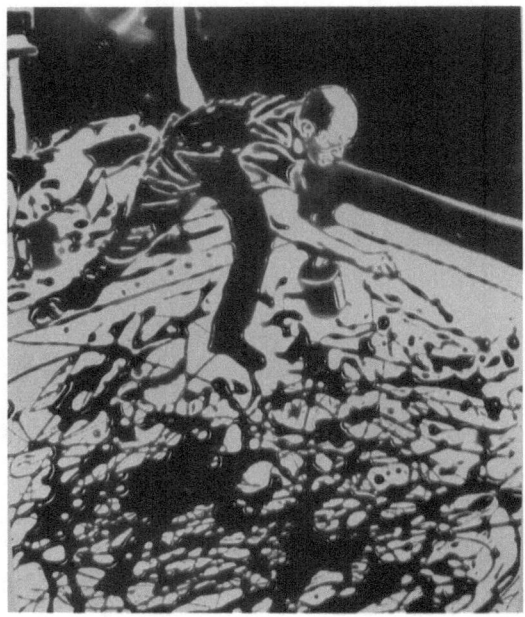

FIGURE 1.4 Vik Muniz, *Action Photo I, after Hans Namuth*, from *Chocolate Pictures*, 1997.

questioning a certain U.S.- and Eurocentrism in this emerging theoretical movement. Texts from the region articulate a new materialist theory of literature, especially as it has undergone, in a short period of time, such a radical transformation in its regimes of materiality. This would supplement the prevailing practice of citing literary works epigraphically, to elucidate critical issues, without examining what is at stake in that operation. Reciprocally, Latin Americanism stands to benefit in more ways than one. This includes stylistics, as literary figuration operates differently when regarded through the lens of nonhuman agency: an appreciation of Rivera's over-the-top language changes when one fully realizes the nonancillary role of nature in his writing. This is yet another reason to tell in cultural studies, with a nonexceptionalist Latin American emphasis, the material revolution of the century.

But before any such developments can occur, it is necessary to lay more groundwork in transcultural materialism. I now return to that task: first, by further characterizing the contributions from the above discussion of Rivera and Magnus and, second, by briefly discussing Marx's notion of raw material in order to elaborate on the theoretical import of my findings. Rivera, like Ortiz, but in a more dramatic register, throws us into the task of reassessing human rapport to things by seizing the turning points that made it into what it presently is. As a society, there are many ways in which the awareness of history leads to certain negotiations in the present. Former colonial powers face backlash from the citizens of their former colonies when they ask of them tourist visas, thereby suspending a long-standing, if often painful, bond. (This was the case when Spain, after joining the European Union, required visas for several Spanish American nations.) Affirmative action in the United States is informed by the knowledge that those descended from the formerly enslaved and disempowered do not have the same opportunities as others. The past is nowhere, someone could say, and nothing that happened centuries ago should matter in that way. I disagree, obviously, and think we ought to expand the operability of history, so to speak, to turning points in human and nonhuman history. Literature contributes plenty to the heuristics of this proposal, as it has always done for politics in an exclusively human sense.

Simply put, if historicism is the belief that history is the greatest determinant of human affairs, then this, I contend, is Magnus's framework, however idiosyncratically he may subscribe to it. Unlike Ortiz, who seeks elucidation, Magnus confounds with palpable delight. He unsettles a past that mainstream thinking takes as either solved and overcome, or enduringly problematic in "familiar" ways only (the case of extermination). At the time he writes, confounding may be as important a contribution as elucidating was in Ortiz's time. Magnus's affinities lie closer to Antonio José Ponte, whose Cuban ruminations on food I analyzed in the introduction. The Argentine's frequent allusions to Nazism and extermination, some more explicit than others, suggest in the final analysis a concern about their hollowed-out place in the daily life of disaffected, purportedly ahistorical subjects. At the same time, *Muñecas* rejects the humanist orientation of historicism. The novel, evidently, is not only about human history but also about the evolution of androids, which it describes in a gothic register, with fascination and fear. It invites us to imagine an anthropodecentric historicism, which is, in my mind, one of the essential traits of transcultural materialism. Jargon aside, the task is to think of the past through the prism of things.

How does this all square with Marxism? As is well known, Marx founds a branch of historicism that eschews the Hegelian unfoldings of the Spirit, focusing instead on economic—in this sense, material—processes. It is also a markedly anthropocentric approach. *Capital* defines "raw material" by opposition to Nature, in a passage worth citing at length:

> All those things which labour merely separates from immediate connection with their environment are objects of labour spontaneously provided by nature, such as fish caught and separated from their natural element, namely water, timber felled in virgin forests, and ores extracted from their veins. If, on the other hand, the object of labour has, so to speak, been filtered through previous labour, we call it raw material. For example, ore already extracted and ready for washing. All raw material is an object of labour [Arbeitsgegenstand], but not every object of labour is raw material; the object of labour counts as raw material only when it has already undergone some alteration by means of labour.[61]

In the examples above, while the Amazon forest itself would not qualify as raw material, the floating rubber ball would: it has already been transformed by means of (human) labor. The new materialist might retort that nature does not "spontaneously provide" in the first place: from an ecological perspective, because taking something from its environment is not without consequence; in terms of coevolution, because this taking does not happen once, or over the course of a generation, but over many. Following Michael Pollan, one could say that "the timber which we fell in the virgin forest" evolves, as do we, in this iterated operation over time. The startling thing about Marx's concept is that it seems to reify what it seeks to criticize, with a deft portmanteau: *Arbeitsgegenstand*. There is something problematic in this process that he is trying to get at, which is the accumulation of surplus value. This happens when the capitalist treats labor as just another resource, on a par with ores and fish, and then does not remunerate laborers proportionally to their contribution to a finished product, which can itself become raw material for a more complex and profitable product. In Marx's words, "Whenever products enter as means of production into new labour processes, they lose their character of being products and function only as objective factors contributing to the overall process."[62] (Think of the makers of tiny cameras for the iPhone and their labor *next to* the minerals extracted to make them.) And yet his deployment of this suspect notion of raw material, arguably, creates the problem at the outset.

The exploitation of workers is the issue that eclipses all others. This is fine, as no nineteenth-century Western thinker, not even one as visionary as Marx, should be held to the standards of the ecological thought of our day. However, it is troubling that Marx is leveraging his argument for workers on the separation of man and nature. The life of the commodity has begun, never mind that whatever the product is, it will have to be disposed of, becoming waste that may decompose in a few years or hundreds. In the vast continuum of nature-culture, the product, and its laborers, are but a snippet. And yet it would be callous to cite a *sub specie aeternitatis* perspective to neglect those exploited over a single, precious human lifespan. What Marx could have done was somehow extend the notion of exploitation to nature itself, as Rivera does, not predicate it on the basis that workers are being treated *as nature*. In a thinker who values process over product, dialectics over axiomatics, this origin story of value is rather questionable. But what are we critics to do, throw out the baby with the bathwater? This is what Latour would advocate in *We Have Never Been Modern*, as much a break with Marxism as a bolstering of ecological thinking. Transcultural materialism offers a different answer, which is preserving the dialectics while suspending the anthropocentrism.

For a case in point, consider the example Marx gives a few lines below those just quoted: "What distinguishes the worst architect from the best of bees is this, that the architect raises his structure in imagination before he erects it in reality."[63] It is startling to think that bees are Pollan's motif as well, with a very different emphasis. What worries Marx, and rightly so, is that, unlike the bee, the laborer has to *subordinate his will* to a result that only exists in his imagination. It is one that, of course, is not his own: Marx cares more about the workers who follow the architect's blueprints than about the architect who, presumably, sketches them more freely. Pollan's cheerful image of the human bumblebee implies artisanal production, not factory-grade apiaries. Coevolution with bees and certain plants has, for the most part in human history, been done at an ecologically sound scale. Today, the mass extinction of bees is all but around the corner, inextricably linked to modern agricultural production. It is not just doomsayers but people of common sense who fear for the fate of our species when we depend on bees' pollination (their "work") for our sustenance. Marx's focus on the subordination of human will is not wrong, but it is merely one part in a bigger process. That process does not start when humans take "what nature spontaneously provides," as if we were separated from nature, but when they enforce such a separation in the first place. In language, they do so with terms such as "meat," "raw material," and so on. Whether bees have a will or not is beside the question. We do, for what it's worth.

It exceeds the scope of this chapter, and of the present study, to explore that road not taken by Marx and to fully ground the notion of exploitation as it pertains to critical ecology. This will, in any case, require doing away with deceptive linguistic constructs like "raw material," trading its myth of origin for alternative narratives of material change over time—something the chapters ahead will provide. It also requires trading an abstract notion such as "labor" for actual laborers who are part of nature, or exchanging an idea such as "product" for objects that, in one way or another, result from nature and will return to it too, like discarded silicone sex dolls. Reading as if in the presence of things with a history contributes to these tasks.

CHAPTER TWO

Of Rocks and Particles

What can literature tell us about human interactions with such basic, enduring nonhumans as soil or dirt? Or elementary particles? I have already discussed how transcultural materialist narratives transcend their here and now by decades or centuries. Recall Ortiz on precolonial tobacco growing, Ponte on the foods of yore, Rivera on whispering old trees, and so on. But to write about, say, the desert is of a different order of magnitude. Here narratives, in one way or another, must hint at a time before narrative and mankind. That distant past is a site of contestation and a matrix of cultural meaning, as sources as diverse as the book of Genesis, the *Theory of the Species* or the big bang theory illustrate. Accounts of the distant past—religious, secular, scientific—are at the crux of it all. As I will show, literary accounts make distinct contributions to how we frame that past and appraise those things available to us today, such as volcanoes or sunlight, that bear witness to it.

My main goal in this chapter is to demonstrate something that may at first sound counterintuitive. In keeping with the integration of historical and new materialisms that has structured my argument so far, I will first examine the *political* dimension of something as seemingly impervious to human affairs as the desert. The desert is a void: a radical absence of polis and demos, and thus seemingly alien to politics or to political systems like democracy. But it is also a void that can be filled symbolically, with meaning, and demographically, with people. The egregious campaign to exterminate or corner indigenous populations in Patagonia (1878–1885) was precisely called the "Conquest of the Desert."[1] In North America, similar coinages include "no-man's-land" and, of course, the "Far West." The South American phrase also communicates a bloodless, all-but-peaceful settlement, when in fact it was very much the opposite. Undemocratic practices capitalized on the desert as imaginary and physical space, subordinating not just men but nature itself. Meanwhile, the Cold War revolved around harnessing the power of radioactive materials that take thousands of years more than garbage to decompose; scores of books and films address this. These "conquests" of the desert and of uranium are both instances of extractivism cutting across the human-nonhuman divide and leaving its imprint on both nature and culture.

Today, there are significant, alarming echoes of these struggles. New mining operations are taking place all over South America, displacing peoples and threatening ecosystems. Driven by digital technologies, notably the smartphone—discussed in chapter 5—there is a forceful push to extract lithium, cadmium, and other minerals from remote locations in Colombia, Bolivia, Patagonia, and elsewhere. In the colloquial terms of one first-hand account, "With these new mining techniques it is like, now you see a mountain, now you don't." Comparisons with slicing open a fruit are not uncommon. Such developments defy the age-old notion, which was already receding in antiquity but never as quickly, that nature is an obstacle to human ingenuity. (As a case in point, China has built a high-speed train over permafrost; fantasies of geo-engineering become fact.) In order to understand literature's contribution to our understanding of such unfathomable scales, I'll examine the Bolivian Blanca Wiethüchter's short novel *El jardín de Nora* (1998) in conversation with Timothy Morton's notion of hyperobjects, among other sources. The fascinating contradiction that underwrites this remarkable work is between the pressing needs of the present and the very long lithic history of the world. It is a dialectics I now turn to explicate, for it generates an alternative appraisal of the role of our species within the geological realm—and beyond it, as a novella by César Aira, *El té de Dios* (2010), thematizing the big bang and quantum particles, playfully makes clear.

Paradise Punctured

El jardín de Nora (*Nora's Garden*) is a partly autobiographical story of Austrian settlers in the *altiplano* who try to plant a European garden there, an operation that leads, literally, to the fracture of the ground beneath their feet. The novel appears to be prescient of several of tenets of the National Constitution of the Plurinational State of Bolivia, promulgated a decade later. It provides an avant la lettre thematization of new Bolivian political subjectivities—particularly of the juridical personhood of nature. One can follow this problematic throughout the narrative's ample tectonic detail. Conventional interpretations could easily dismiss this aspect as secondary by ignoring the agency of earth the novel strives to capture. However, what is at stake is an attempt to remediate the relationship of our species to "the environment"—challenging, in fact, the anthropocentrism already present in that phrase, which reduces life-sustaining systems to a mere backdrop. Wiethüchter's distinctive achievement, and her contribution to both transcultural materialism and to the present study, is to deploy a lyrically inflected narrative form that can speak *simultaneously* of natural processes and of cultural conflict. The former happens over many millennia and the latter over, at most, several centuries. And yet Wiethüchter makes their overlap, and their insurmountable tension, *thinkable*—let alone worthy of critical attention.

Article 255 of the Bolivian constitution establishes harmony with nature and the nonprivatization of biodiversity as preconditions for subscribing to international treaties, while Law 71, promulgated in 2010, goes further by granting juridical personhood to Mother Earth. We read the following in article 5 of the latter: "For effects of the protection and administration of its rights, Mother Earth is considered a collective subject of public interest."[2] The language used eschews the familiar terminology of Roman law, and leaves room to speculate whether a "collective subject" differs from a "juridical person"—namely, a legal fiction that extends the rights and obligations of "natural persons" (i.e., individual human beings) to other entities, such as corporations. The mismatch is arguably purposeful, for Bolivia has been charting for itself a path that seeks to break with Western tradition. One example is the adoption of *el reloj del sur* on the facade of Congress (figure 2.1). It runs counterclockwise, with the numbers 11 and 10 where 1 and 2 usually are, as if clocks, those visual representation of the rotation of Earth, had been modeled on the exposure to the sun in the Southern Hemisphere.

Literally a change of axis, this contrarian ethos is also present in the peculiar frame of rights accorded to nature. One cannot straightforwardly assume that "collective subjectivity" is indeed juridical personhood, despite

FIGURE 2.1 *Reloj del sur*. Plaza Murillo, La Paz, 2018.
Author photo.

the obvious nod to that legal notion. But scratch the surface of the palimpsest and Roman law is there. Similarly, the hands in the southern watch may rotate in the opposite direction, but they are still on a dial. Both are gestures of decolonization: of law and of time. Both meet real obstacles, in logic and in custom. Nature can have rights, but can it have obligations? Can an entire nation, indeed a hemisphere, unlearn how to look at a watch? To be sure, these are open questions, for the Bolivian political process, with its many supporters and not a few detractors, is still unfolding. It is too early to say whether its defiance of conventional logic will result in a different axiomatics. The ultimately arbitrary constitutive power that emerges from a phrase like "We, the people" could conceivably emerge from an assemblage of human and nonhuman: "We, the human collective embedded in nature," say. At best, we witness the rebirth of the modern state; at worst, mere sloganeering. If the convoluted history of Bolivia is any indication, these gestures might not lead to lasting institutions—one decade old is "young" for a constitution. Be that as it may, they provide a valuable thought experiment and powerful heuristic device.

Crucially, the law enshrines the rights of "Mother Nature," not nature tout court. Article 3 defines it as the "dynamic living system composed by the indivisible community of all living systems and living beings, interrelated, interdependent, and complementary, that share a common destiny."[3] One line down, with an ambiguous use of passive voice that might worry legal scholars, the article notes, as if clarifying, "Mother Earth is regarded as sacred by the worldviews of the originary indigenous *campesino* nations and peoples."[4] Three features are especially noteworthy. These are the understanding of the state as enforcer of ecological balance; the reliance on broadly defined custom and on ancestral religious beliefs as sources of legitimacy; and the emphasis on teleology: it is the common destiny of living beings and their systems of sustenance that justifies legislation. The thrust is to decolonize language. "Mother Nature" debunks "nature," which separates subjects from objects, as if trees, rivers, and sky were merely props for human affairs. Amerindian epistemologies, as Bruce Albert observes, do not take for granted the separations of human and nature, and subject and object, that sit at the cornerstone of Western, analytic thought.[5] Briefly put, there are two movements here: unsettling core principles in law and language, and then seeking to found new ones inspired by alternative traditions. Blanca Wiethüchter's writing anticipates aspects of both of these developments.

A beloved poet mostly unknown outside Bolivia, Wiethüchter produced only one novel. From its title onward, *El jardín de Nora* binds womb and earth. Etymologically, the name "Nora" is related to honor. Honorable Nora's breasts swell as holes break open the ground of her beloved garden. As I see it, the book is a *becoming* Pachamama. The plotline is simple, at first sight, and can be summarized in a few words: the earth prevails over Nora, wife of Franz, who hires an Aymara gardener to grow an Austrian garden in the highlands of Bolivia. At the onset, the gardener rushes in to share the troubling news which he thinks, we learn from indirect monologue, would "make her die from sorrow" and "bring pain to her heart."[6] "¡Señora, a ver, ven; a ver, ven!" he demands, in a phrase that denotes deference, familiarity, and genuine affliction, with the Spanish syntax of many plurilingual speakers from the *altiplano*—roughly, "See, to see, come, Madame; to see, come!"[7] Nora dallies, building suspense; it is the first of many postponements in the novella. Despite the bad feeling she's been having in her gut, she asks the man to wait while she finishes starching her husband's shirt "with infinite care," like "a loving present."[8] Franz only has three in the drawer, she muses in her own indirect monologue; the assessment heightens the tension between the inanity and seriousness of her task.

To appreciate the pregnant language the novel deploys, it is worth citing at some length from before Nora seizes the damage. There is a significant gap between what is told and the act of telling. In straightforward language, someone would merely say: "The lady makes her gardener wait while she finishes up her chores; she has a bad feeling about the man's beckoning, and she remembers her ailments." What follows says as much, and yet so much more, and not just at the level of descriptive detail:

> She took another while before getting going, waiting to feel the rumble in her chest, that murmur that was pestering her for years now ... since the day she decided to *force the soil* to produce a garden as if in Vienna. *She kept the gardener in oblivion*, self-absorbed, took the iron once again, dipped her thumb, index finger and middle finger in the cold water to mechanically spray it over non-existing clothes, until the fizzing of water on the hot surface of the iron awoke her from her daydream, but without the rumble in her chest ... *in the garden of her chest*, "who could deny the authority of a doctor, after so many exams?" she had returned home, knowing that what happened had nothing to do with nerves but with *a way of in which things express themselves, Franz, those things one does not talk about.* [My emphasis][9]

These are very long sentences, even for a Latin American tradition accustomed to baroque feats of subordination and coordination. Language here elucidates as much as it obfuscates: it gives, and it withholds. Paraphrase cannot replace it without sacrificing its qualities, particularly its remarkable concretion, which yields to manifold interpretation. Nonetheless, observe the incantation quality of the syntax; the very succinct and effective characterization; the flashbacks; the combination of dialogue and indirect monologue; and especially the thought-provoking turns of phrase I have emphasized above. To "force the earth," "retain the gardener in oblivion," hold "a garden [huerta] in the chest," or have "things express themselves" transcend poetic license: the passage seeks to sublate the oppositions between nature and culture, subject and object. Instead of enforcing these pillars of Cartesian rationality, Wiethüchter undoes them. This happens both at the level of the phenomena described and in the language upon which it is predicated. On the one hand, there is the sinister gravitation of chest and garden; on the other, a grammatical and semantic bending of the rules. That an Austrian rose garden does not belong in the *altiplano* is as much a cultural as an ecological statement. Moreover, it is a revelation that must be *experienced through the body*, and yet is always incomplete.

Numerous interpretative possibilities compound with the deft allusion to the biblical motif of paradise lost. Some references are straightforward: the cover of the book's first—and for many years only—edition features Raphael's *Adam and Eve*; at one point, Nora and Franz flip through the pages of a coffee-table book with images of Dürer's Adam and Cranach's Eve, before pausing, with a metanarrative wink, on Raphael's couple.[10] Yet subtle cues frame the relationship of Nora and the unnamed "jardinero aymara" in such a way that, at times, this bearer of bad news resembles the serpent that disrupts Eden, or rather the angel that ejects the sinner couple, or even the god (real owner) that created it all in the first place. The very denomination of *aymara* is an intromission of Franz's voice within Nora's own interior monologue; the husband, a vigorous young patriarch, is "always on the look for traces of indigenous ethnicity."[11] Conversely, in the gardener's mind, we read, "perhaps" he does not call her *señora* but *qh'ara*—white or blond—or *gringa*, or finally just *señora*.[12] The narrative voice suspends its own certainty over such matters, representing a situation where the burden of ethnic determinism happens in both directions, if asymmetrically. Nora's thrust to find paradise anew, the foundational narrative of colonization, fails to meet a tabula rasa either in the land or in the mind of the would-be colonized.

Fittingly, the storyline cultivates and then distorts allegorical expectations: we learn that the couple has children, who are at one point described as an "apple of discord"—so much for trying to map the novella onto the book of Genesis.[13] Instead of an enticing, animalized Satan, there is the premonition of a great Evil that makes Nora's breasts swell and its correlate in the ground under her feet: *huecos*, that is, voids or holes.[14] They advance relentlessly, a negative growth punctuated with alliteration and musicality: "She stared stunned at the *not being of Nothingness* that now took the place of the rosebush" (my emphasis).[15] To Wiethüchter's credit, this double negation comes across less as philosophical treatise than as anguished lament. It inspired critic Marcelo Villena Alvarado to describe the title character as an "un-Penelope," the negation of a negation.[16]

Even Evil, which Thomas Aquinas famously theorized as the absence of the good, is less important as a plot device than appears at first sight.[17] Initially, it serves to give the story its gothic, powerful thrust. But ultimately there is no one to blame for two phenomena that are mysteriously of a piece: Nora's apparent fertility (although her milk is sour) and the land's apparent infertility (although native weeds do grow). They are connected not through the familiar conventions of fantastic literature or of *lo real maravilloso* (magical realism), but through a narrative language that enacts human-nonhuman transformation: I have been calling this transcultural materialism. What underlies is a clash of temporalities: the nine months of a human pregnancy, the several-years lifespan of a garden, the slowly accruing but suddenly manifest temporality of erosion, the novel's secret protagonist. The story of the earth is not easily told in a readily comprehensible scale. As previously noted, recourse to sources like the book of Genesis is one theocentric—and, vicariously, anthropocentric—attempt to do so. Meanwhile, ecological developments are not easy to communicate, which is one of the reasons why global warming deniers abound. (They are fewer in the high Andes, where snow peaks patently recede year after year.) It is not true that nature exists as some kind of setting for man's great story. However, our narratives make that falsity verisimilar: Paul Bunyan comes to mind. Meanwhile, in a mouthful, the "human-nonhuman continuum" is real. Wiethüchter's juxtaposed temporalities confer on it a much more poetic language and an elusive narrative quality: verisimilitude.

Tim Morton has grappled with similar issues with his notion of "hyperobjects"—namely, "things that are massively distributed in time and space relative to humans."[18] Time: consider how even a millionth of a gram of radium-226 will be around for thousands of years. Space: try to "picture" the solar system. The human eye (or any other eye, for that matter) only gets to see pieces of a hyperobject, if anything at all, but its effects are unequivocal. Hyperobjects contribute to our thinking in a number of ways. They force us out of anthropocentrism, in particular out of correlationism: a form of circular reasoning that assumes that all there is to think about is what is available to human cognition in the first place. This might have, Morton asserts in passing, unaware of new Bolivian subjectivities, political consequences. "Hyperobjects have dispensed with two hundred years of careful correlationist calibration. The panic and denial and right-wing absurdity about global warming are understandable. Hyperobjects pose numerous threats to individualism, nationalism, anti-intellectualism, racism, speciesism, anthropocentrism, you name it. Possibly even capitalism itself."[19] The Bolivian legal framework, predicated on the juridical legitimacy of Pachamama, a distinctly culturally encoded hyperobject, is an example of the latter. Retroactively, Wiethüchter contributes to this task. Her textured language upends the subject-object divide that simple, declarative sentences so often and unreflectively reinforce.

As Morton asserts, hyperobjects make evident the impossibility of a metalanguage "that could account for things while remaining uncontaminated by them"; instead, intimate impressions are "footprints of hyperobjects, distorted as they always must be by the entity in which they make their mark—that is, me. I become (and so do you) a litmus test of the time of hyperobjects."[20] One such litmus test is Nora's interior monologue. That she is affected by earth is a truism; that this elemental truth comes across as verisimilar is not—hence her unhinged lyricism. Tellingly, Morton speculates that what is known as a "schizophrenic defense" in psychotic episodes could extend to our general relationship to things: we enforce a distance with things in language and in thinking at large to ward off their disquieting proximity. In literary terms, this becomes the familiar motif of the topsyturvy world: when Nora sees a doctor about the swelling of her breasts and meets his patronizing dismissal ("Es cuestión de nervios, señora"), the madwoman is in fact the sage. Moreover, *El jardín de Nora* would conform to some of the traits of what Morton describes as hyperobjective art. His quirky examples include the guitar riffs of My Bloody Valentine, which literally make the chest vibrate. In the Bolivian author, there is the representation of one such bodily reaction to/within nature, but also a humming, musical writing style that readers, in turn, internalize. Hyperobjects are "more than a little demonic," says the critic; meanwhile, evil holes spring up in the novelist's garden.[21] Less aesthetic choice than representational imperative, the gothic register of the novella serves a greater purpose of making verisimilar, and to some extent graspable, the temporality of hyperobjects.

I must tread lightly here, for the goal is not to "apply" Morton, a metropolitan theorist after all, to a literary phenomenon that belongs within an alternative genealogy, traced throughout this book, of Latin American transcultural materialism. Still, there are many instances of agreement and of complementarity. If, pressing Morton's point, one could say that the only way out of correlationism is through schizophrenia, then Wiethüchter's character would enact and embody this. We read the following: "The hole, more than a yell, seemed to her a diabolical wretched smile in the harmonious and luminous serenity of grass, green leaves and assorted flowers."[22] Once again, Wiethüchter resorts here to poetry, the medium of most of her published works, to explore the limits of her protagonist's sanity. Either we let objects speak to us, she could be saying, or we will fail to understand. Of course, talking things are the fodder that Disney peddles, for children no less. The difference is that those cartoonish characters are safely encapsulated in fantasy, while in transcultural materialism, becoming nonhuman appears as a verisimilar, disturbing possibility—death, the dissolution of a body into its constitutive elements, is just that. Nora's uncanny children are themselves, like holes in her chest, the passageway into that realization.

Wiethüchter's novel complements Morton's critical insight in two important, interconnected ways: her attention to cultural specificity and her exploration of the boundaries of the sayable. A subplot of muteness weaves into the main plot of erosion; their eventual juxtaposition leads to the story's moment of crisis and brings us back to the present of the spoiled garden. After the gardener beckons Nora to see the damage, there is a flashback to a failed rite of passage, in which the couple try to "integrate" their oldest son with the garden. Instead, the child pricks his finger on a rose stem and his blood falls on soil; it is from that moment on that the children become mute and Nora's breasts begin to swell. Clearly, this is about imbuing him with European culture: they present him with a wooden doll, a secular ornament out of place in the Andean landscape and worldview. (A garden gnome is but a very faint trace of a more enchanted relationship to nature.) But the scene is also a play on *pago a la tierra*, that is, making offerings to Pachamama or to sacred mountains—*achachilas* in Aymara and *apus* in Quecha.[23] *Pago a la tierra* is an act of reciprocity, a tit for tat: in exchange for an offering, often of coca leaves, the earth will deliver a favorable crop. But it can also chastise—in this case, with muteness and phantom pregnancy. Unmanicured, Pachamama—a hyperobject always already enmeshed in a culture, a legal system, and an ethos—rejects the cultural and ecological imprint of the garden. Wiethüchter does not so much *represent* cultural clash with gaping holes under the rose bushes, pain in Nora's chest, or a child's Babelian drift across languages when he stutters, "Kala . . . piedra . . . Stein."[24] Rather, these elements themselves are part of a clash that involves both nature and culture.

Meanwhile Morton, the posthumanist, despite engaging works of art, seems to want to get culture, that messy concept, out of the way. He does so in order to situate everyone in a shared plain of indexicality—hence his insistence on the "real" world. True, there is a planet we live on and share, whether we like it or not. It is real, out there, and beyond the hold of correlationism. But is culture any less real? "Earth" itself, as a concept, is always already culturally coded. Seeing "it," speaking about "it," is already an act of framing with decisive political, and indeed life-changing, implications. There are resources in culture and in language, her writing shows, that allow one to push the limits of correlationism. This is not just to make the unthinkable thinkable, in an ever-expanding quest for knowledge, but the opposite: to make the thinkable unthinkable—that is, to bring down a fundamentally flawed epistemological edifice. Wiethüchter knows this to be the case and makes it the core principle of her writing.

Consequently, the plotlines of secularity versus animism or Christianism versus Andean cosmology tell only part of the story: there is also the undoing of language in the face of geological might and the colonial power struggles embedded in everyday vernacular. Villena Alvarado approximates this treatment of language, with less emphasis on its political implications, when he notes that in the novel, as in the cognate long poem *Ítaca* (2000), Wiethüchter valorizes negativity: absence rather than presence, Penelope's undoing rather than her weaving—as he puts it, "the generative, motherly dimension of that absence."[25] Indeed, *El jardín de Nora* captures a different "politics of nature" through this negative poetics. Again, with Villena Alvarado, the Bolivian novelist and poet would present the "textualization of a social conflict"[26]—a conflict, one may add, that involves nature as well.

This is useful to better situate Wiethüchter's contribution. Too culturalist for a squarely posthumanist account, she is also too materialist for a humanist and not culturalist enough for a post- or decolonialist narrative, as I will show in a moment. But first, note how this speaks to the mediatory nature of transcultural materialism at large: the dwelling in narrative and literary language as a space for elucidation and contradiction, where the material and historical come to bear upon each other. The novel never presents an essentialist conflict along the lines of Aymara culture versus European culture, but neither does it leave out cues that invariably invoke such entelechies. If anything, one could talk of an Andean nature-culture that overlaps and enters into conflict with its European counterpart, in a fluid exchange that seems to suspend the principle of noncontradiction. There is both something one can objectively call "nature" and also a way in which nature is always constructed; a real thing that can, in one breath and under the spell of literary language, also be a cultural phenomenon. Aporetic as this path undoubtedly is, it is also able to narrate conflict as conflict, and not domesticate it under essentialist humanist notions like the "clash of cultures" or tautological posthumanist pleas to seize the reality of the real world.

For a humanist account of the garden, my Stanford colleague Robert Harrison's book-length essay *Gardens: An Essay into the Human Condition* is exemplary. There, as the title suggests, the critic shows how, across a vast swath of mostly Western cultures, gardens exemplify notions of mortality, order, and power.[27] His argument is eminently anthropocentric: it is fair to say that gardens, as much attention as they receive in his study, are ultimately a stage and a catalyst for cultural values and spiritual needs. Despite the obvious differences between this school of thought and my own, Harrison makes an important point that one could paraphrase as "Tell me how you garden, and I'll tell you who you are." He does so in the interest of showing some purportedly universal truths about gardens, but nonetheless he does so, dialectically, by looking at gardens across cultures. If we weigh differently the dialectic of the universal and the particular, and focus on particularity where Harrison prefers universality, we will find valuable insights for the present discussion. Moreover, in a movement that is more sympathetic to posthumanism, Harrison does confer agentic qualities to gardens, which indeed have an effect on humans and their ideas about beauty, balance, and so on. One can think of Nora when Harrison asserts, for instance, that "the garden has provided sanctuary from the frenzy and tumult of history."[28] Is this not an adequate description of what the Austrian immigrant couple was looking for? Further aligning himself with an aestheticist, humanist ideal, Harrison will go on to claim that gardens are about the cultivation of civic virtues against the destructive forces of history.

Wiethüchter has a more favorable view of history. Her novel shares the aesthetic drive, no doubt, but it goes toward history, not away from it. It is difficult to miss the dialectic of master and slave that serves as the backdrop of Nora's relationship with her Aymara gardener. Meanwhile, in *Gardens*, there are no workers with muddied clothes but rather high-minded garden designers. The point is not to criticize a thorough study, done within a certain frame of reference, but rather to use it as a point of comparison. Gardens indeed cultivate civic virtues, but they also impose them. One needs just think of settlement landscaping in early modern North and South America, where transplanting an Old World garden entailed chasing natives off their land.[29] For her part, Wiethüchter, building on the Homeric tradition and the high art of poetry that humanists *cultivate*, subjects her garden to the forces of history. Terrible or not, they are there; no gardener can fence them out. In this way, the Bolivian poet and novelist illustrates an aspect of transcultural materialism: it pays keen attention to form, as traditional humanism has done, but also to form's role within both a politics of nature and politics tout court. To understand the impact of this novel on our thinking it is relevant to appreciate its many clever formal elements—for instance, those involving changes in focalization building to a dramatic intromission by the narrative voice.[30] In this study, I engage for many a page in the laborious (humanist?) task of appreciation. But art for art's sake is only part of the equation. If the language of transcultural materialism remediates nature-culture, then its aesthetic inquiry is an exercise in political ecology.

For this to be the case, however, we must pay attention to both nature and culture. The task is easier said than done. My impression is that when one is dealing with things of a geological magnitude, it is often easy to err on the side of nature, as if human agency, every day more powerful, were all contemplation (not a bad outcome, but a wishful starting point). Anything cultural or linguistic, let alone political, is bracketed by the sheer presence of Mountain. Conversely, when scale—relative size—brings us closer to the matter at hand, then nature is suspended, and Man and his will act in the void. In this example of all-or-nothing thinking, humans are either negligible or all-important, while the truth lies somewhere in the middle. It is not easy to change ways of thinking, even when evidence to the contrary looks us in the face.

A case in point is an article by Elizabeth Monasterios, a milestone in the small but illuminating literature on Wiethüchter, which takes head-on the question of transculturation that has been a subtext of my book. In her otherwise valid critique of the notion, Monasterios pays insufficient attention to nature. There is nothing wrong with her analysis; rather, it results from the extrication of transculturation from botany that, as I discussed in the introduction, happened to this longstanding and always evolving concept once Rama and others discarded the abundant natural elements in Ortiz. She writes, "The catastrophic fulfillment of events anticipated twenty years ago by the Indian expert, who predicted the impossibility of planting roses where only *kiswaras* or *kantutas* could live, questions the success of that 'cultural plasticity' attributed to transculturation."[31] This might strike readers of *Things with a History* as counterintuitive. Recall the sequence of events: concerned about the garden, the settler couple summons a native expert—a descendant of the Uru people, per Franz's ethnographic gaze— and he tells them in so many words that a Viennese rose garden will not grow there. Monasterios takes this as a sign that there is a limit to "transculturation," but surely this only holds true if *kiswaras* and *kantutas* are symbols or allegories of Aymara culture and not, first of all, plants themselves, like sugarcane and tobacco are.

Explaining her use of the term, Monasterios describes Ortiz's transculturation as a "twofold phenomenon, both cultural and economic," when in fact, as I have been proposing, it is threefold: cultural, economic, and botanical.[32] This view informs Monasterios's reaction, as do Rama's domestication of Ortiz's constellar, interdisciplinary narrative in the late 1970s and early 1980s, alongside García Canclini's celebration of hybridity in the postmodern 1990s.[33] If transculturation means appeasement in the name of an idealized cultural blend, then clearly it does not apply here. But *ajiaco* is no light stew; if you recall my earlier discussion of Ortiz's essay: distinct elements do more than blend. And so, Monasterios goes on to note that when "los mudos" (the mutes) themselves grow a secret garden with native crops, this demonstrates that transculturation failed.[34] However, one could just as well say they got their mother's green thumb, if only more successfully. So are Nora's children a sign of the failure of transculturation or of its success? After all, babbling or not, they are acquiring the three languages: Aymara, Spanish, and German. And Wiethüchter, the second-generation immigrant author, is the mute child who broke silence and cultivates a garden of words.

In sum, while Monasterios is right in pointing out that *El jardín de Nora* challenges what circulated as transculturation in the early 2000s, her limited consideration of the role of nature in Ortiz's original formulation, and her inherited emphasis on the alleged conciliatory "products" of transculturation rather than its process, leads her to the above contradiction. Still, there is much in her findings to elaborate upon for our current critical horizon. In her words, *El jardín de Nora* is a narrative "whose inner logic has the capacity to destabilize our system of meaning."[35] I couldn't agree more with this description, reminiscent of Foucault's hysterical laughter upon reading Borges, who reportedly "shattered the familiar landscapes of [Foucault's] thought."[36] Because Monasterios writes under the aegis of postcolonialism and subalternism, such a destabilization or shattering occurs in two ways: by revealing the enduring presence of the postcolonial wound and by showing how, in cultural syncretism, there are winners and losers. In other words, we cannot idealize hybridity à la García Canclini, because it is predicated on continuing hurt and injustice. These are all valid points, as is the observation, which she shares with Villena Alvarado, that the novel lays bridges with Andean epistemologies.[37]

It appears, then, that *El jardín de Nora*, a case study for transcultural materialism, converses with, yet is not circumscribed to, humanism, posthumanism, and postcolonialism. But what about decolonialism? What circulates under this moniker is active resistance against the colonial legacy, an attempt to rid the subject of its manifold burden—down to how to read the clock, as I began this section by noting.[38] Crucially, the decolonial project has become state doctrine in Bolivia. Its conservative critics may point out that five centuries cannot be erased, which is, as with utopias more generally, no reason not to try. Other critics worry that the ruling party, MAS (Movimiento al Socialismo), concentrates power by ventriloquizing a lost past. I read this latter position between the lines of Bolivian critic's Mary Carmen Molina's appraisal of how the novel represents "continuous dissent."[39] I started out by claiming that *El jardín de Nora* anticipates some of the political and juridical developments of later years. Molina, who lives in a present where to a significant extent these are a fait accompli, poses the following rhetorical question: "How does *El jardín de Nora* distinguish itself from the affirmation of the actualization of a new, complex, disperse, and multiple subject, without affirming the subalternity of Latin America's contemporary cultural protagonists?"[40]

By way of an answer, Molina give us her notion of continuous dissent, as if there is no state under which Wiethüchter could truly become a national author. Not only is her analysis antipatrimonial, but she follows Monasterios in pointing out the mismatch of Wiethüchter with major critical currents. To this list, long already, she adds Cornejo Polar (whom Monasterios had also mentioned briefly) and *calibanismo*. Leaving aside the fascinating intricacies of these cultural theories, what matters here is her inclusion of "nuevas subjetividades," which alludes to the doctrine of President Evo Morales and the vice-president and chief ideologue Álvaro García Linera, who have held office since 2006. Theirs is a socialist, grassroots movement that, for the first time in Bolivia's republican history, congregated, successfully and enduringly, the country's multilingual indigenous majorities. In a strict sense, it coalesced a new political subject. If I read correctly between the lines of Molina's argument, Wiethüchter would share the questions posed by MAS, although not necessarily its answers. These include questions about coexistence with Mother Nature, about creole and indigenous relations, about how to appraise the country's living past, and about what new languages to forge to even formulate such questions in the first place. The novelist-poet would be at home on shaky ground, and not on the stately edifices built upon it. I agree, if not necessarily for political reasons, but because Wiethüchter, like other Latin American transcultural materialists, engages the past too thoroughly to bank the future on its repudiation.

This bears out in the novel's ending. It could be seen as an anticipation of the decolonial triumph of MAS, as a representation of the postcolonial wound, as a humanist twist on the motif of paradise lost, and as a posthuman rendering of hyperobjectivity. While each of these readings has a grain of truth, there is a supplemental element that only transcultural materialism can capture. A new teacher has been working with the mutes, and the stage is set for show and tell. Moët Chandon and beluga caviar await. The firstborn rises to the challenge: "The eldest stood up: a slight rattle, followed by a sort of hiccup that swallowed air as if to gain momentum as he closed his lips and let out a strange whistling sound like bbbbb. He breathed in and—bbbbbbaabbáa . . . And closing his lips—Mmmammá . . . Everyone applauded."[41]

It is a scene of Lacanian violence: the rupturing of silence into language, of the real into the symbolic. After all, the force of the significant has been present from the author's Germanic last name onward; autobiographically, it evokes an actual immigrant mother.[42] In this way, author, narrator, and poetic voice all take the place of the mute child who has to puncture her way into language. Lacan meets ecofeminism, for this critique of the patriarchal order has obvious ecological ramifications. Recall how Nora dwells in her symptom, still ironing shirts as the world unravels: it was an act of protest folded into one of obedience. In this final scene it appears that the mutes, those savages, are finally domesticated. But then, in one deft movement, an excited Franz urges the rest of the children to follow the lead of the stuttering firstborn. Immediately, Nora's breasts swell violently, and a grumbling, black, winged sound ("un rumor negro y alado") grows. The reader cannot quite place the sound, which may come from the mutes' throats, from Nora's chest, or indeed, from the surroundings. The protagonist is silent. But when the husband asks the kids what else they have learned to say, she senses that "the old dam is broken" (in her breasts? in the garden?) and at the same time ten "coarse and rancorous" mouths open to say:

> ¡Wwwhoooooole! [¡Bbbbuuuueeeeccccoooooo!]
> The one that opened up right there, abysmal and deep, that opened up with a wind of voices as if a throat that hurled over to the bottom, uncovering the negated fluids of a hidden garden, uncovered with a multitude of rocks like dry fruits, now precipitated over Franz and Nora, submerging them with no chance of talking into that black hole, cleared by those ten mouths unmouthed, surely designed for something else.[43]

The heart-wrenching yell of the mutes pierces with typographic emphasis the surface of a text that has been so meticulously cared for. In this powerful way, the themes that Wiethüchter has been building from the start all come together. The distant flapping of wings—a *modernista* trope—foresaw the plunge ahead. Nowhere else does her language evidence so much agentic force, generating in the reader an effect that potentiates what is being told. Squarely at odds with mere reporting, the text produces what it describes; the reader is thrust into a void, experiencing vicarious vertigo. The children speak with "viento de voces," a wind of voices. In the very tight economy of the text, alliteration makes plausible the uncanny idea that the children's yell has literally broken ground, founding anew. The hole is akin to a throat, rocks to dried fruits and, understatedly, to breasts; the swallowing earth motif is reminiscent of *novela de la tierra*, the useful if equivocal designation for works such as Rivera's *La vorágine*, discussed above, but also the Argentine Ricardo

Güiraldes's *Don Segundo Sombra* (1926) and the Venezuelan Rómulo Gallegos's *Doña Bárbara* (1929).[44] But unlike in those works, the recurrent *vagina dentata* motif is not vilified but vindicated. Nora's "garden" is genitalia within, rather than isolated from, the body and the continuum of life. A final, nonchalant allusion to the mouths' *design* suggests mammalian sucking and the absent designer: God.

The humanist has his field day: this is paradise regained. The posthumanist sees an illustration of the force of the geological, the post- and decolonialist of the imperial legacy and its overcoming. But in various ways and to different extents, all of these approaches instrumentalize language and narrative; they share a penchant for grand theory that ultimately dispenses with the literary event. They do not let the text speak. By contrast, in transcultural materialism method and narrative converge. Art makes the stone stony, as Shklovsky's previously cited phrase would have it.[45] Wiethüchter is all about making the hole holy, with every implication: making the void perceptible, rendering it sacred, giving expression to the force of the signifier through the playful lucidity of a pun.[46] Suitably, one of the phrases the mute overhear during the cure that a traditional healer practices on them is none other than *achachilas phutunku*, the protective spirit of the hole.[47] Although a roman-à-clef reading would do well in highlighting this phrase, rather than a secret message, it reveals the force of buried revelation that underwrites the entire novel.

Humor makes a noteworthy, late appearance: the hyperbole of Moët Chandon and beluga caviar in the Bolivian highlands pokes fun at the archetypal European settler couple. There is something of the serious lightheartedness of Ortiz's counterpoint also in *El jardín de Nora*. It isn't quite the comedic, if mordant, dressing up of tobacco in fancy boxes or sugar's passing as white. And yet this broken earth is laughing matter, in the way that the best of Borges can be. The pact of verisimilitude is also fracturing; the book ends much like a vignette from across the Andes, in the popular Chilean comic strip Condorito, in a "¡Plop!" (Franz would occupy the place of the perennial character who falls backward in astonishment, feet up in the air). See how the final denouement, immediately after the Bueco crisis, is purposefully absurd: "At the other side of the void, there was nothing. Phutunhuicu, said the mutes correctly when they learned to speak; Phutunhuicu, that in proper Aymara is phutunku and in proper Spanish, hole. But, well, no one understood."[48]

These are perplexing last lines for a book whose central conflict has been the overcoming of muteness. Matter-of-factly, the narrator flashes forward to a future when the children do speak and yet are not understood. That all this effort goes unheard is ironic, if not self-effacing, as the novel, unlike "the other side of the hole," is not nothing—it exists. Equal parts comedic disappointment and rage, this ending peters out into farce, disavowing the artifice the novel has been up to this last hour. Again, the text foregrounds its own theatricality, as before with the mention of champagne and caviar. This rendering of colonialism is many times removed from convention—think of Shakespeare's *The Tempest*. Having explored the limits of the sayable and of familiar allegories of paradise and hell, Wiethüchter brings readers back to the rough ground of an ongoing colonial history that plays out across the human-nonhuman continuum. It is a farce that may lead to laughter or to crying, but not to the comfort of anagnorisis. There is no final moment of recognition when true evil, as in that much different cartoon *Scooby-Doo*, is rid of its mask.

What to make of the word uttered multiple times, once incorrectly (*bueco*), once "correctly" (*phutunhuicu*), once in "proper Aymara" (*phutunku*), and once in proper Spanish (*hueco*)? I consulted with Aymara expert Roger Ricardo González Segura, from Pontificia Universidad Católica del Perú, and he observed that *phutunhuicu* is a portmanteau of *phutunku* and *hueco*. In other words, it is a mestizo term. This usage contravenes Monasterios's interpretation: that the narrator declares it "correct" amounts to a political statement in defense of hybridity. Moreover—per González Segura's account, which I corroborated using Ludovico Bertonio's authoritative dictionary—in a grammatically correct sense *phutunku* would be translated into Spanish more precisely as *hondanada*, which is a depression or low-lying land in a field, rather than as the more generic, colloquial "hueco." This is worthy of note: the incantatory utterance that seems to rupture the earth is, in a strict sense, a mistake (as was the choice in vegetation, which eroded the lowland into an abyss). This peculiar translingual word game complicates the plot of decolonization. Caliban learned the colonizer's language to curse him all the better in it; the mutes' contribution to several languages is bastardizing them. It is only fitting that, in the language of the present text, whole and hole sound alike.

Negativity is crucial to counter the effects of affirmative subalterity. Wiethüchter advocates a vision of hybridity at odds with positive formulations of identity (or of hybridity as new identity), for these are prone to commodification and political manipulation. For present purposes, hybridity is not compromising or conciliatory, but rather "savage," as Alberto Moreiras would call it in his seminal piece "Hybridity and Double-Consciousness."[49] Similarly, transcultural materialism ought to be measured more by what it problematizes than by what it solves. In this regard, it shares the familiar gesture of unmasking—arguably a philosophical revision of anagnorisis—common to many Marxist traditions. However, it does so in the negative, through literary language, binding the human and the nonhuman. Its form, then, is crucial, for it is in its deployment that this operation comes into its own. Supplementary to (post-) humanism and to (post/de-) colonialism, transcultural materialism recreates contradiction, rather than appease or hastily attempt to solve it. It does so in multiple registers, with both history and ecology in sight, exposing tensions beneath the surface.

Wiethüchter's politics of the desert playfully subvert historical materialism, making room for suspicion but not for prescription. Master-slave dialectics gives way to housewife-gardener dialectics and, at one point, to the woman's peculiar proxy rule over the household via the governess, "Frau Wunderlich" (German for whimsical or strange, possibly "Wonder Woman" by association). Wiethüchter—note the homophony once again—also transforms new materialism, whose emphasis on the autonomy of objects she takes, literalizing a metaphor, to heart. She refuses to get language and, alongside it, cultural specificity, out of the way. In this fashion, *El jardín de Nora* purports that these elements are always already part of the assemblage. Hyperobjects speak through literature too. This grounds the idea that, as short as human lifespans are in geological time, they matter. And matter they are, of course. A more transparent, less literary language would have failed at the task. There is a distinctive operation that literary form affords: aporetic exploration. Language can underscore its literariness to give voice to mute things. Literary language is a means and an end, subject and object, source and instrument of signification—if only we let it speak. A hermeneutics attuned to the performativity of language *makes reading whole*.

What to make, then, of the language of the law? Is Bolivia rendering Latour's hypothetical Constitution a reality? Personhood, as Eduardo Viveiros de Castro puts it, is a "phenomenological unity that is purely pronominal in kind applied to a real radical diversity."[50] The anthropologist-theorist writes with a certain man-jaguar from the pages of Guimarães Rosa in mind, brilliantly discussed by Gabriel Giorgi.[51] Personhood, in what arguably amounts to the most avant-gardist and polemical decision of modern American jurisprudence, has been conferred to corporations.[52] The conferral of juridical personhood to nature in the Bolivian constitution and its cognate laws may be at least in some degree aspirational (rather than functioning) components in a system of rule of law. But they are in any case important instruments of political economy: the secularization of a theological notion, Pachamama, is every bit as significant as the provisions against privatization. The water wars of 2000 loom large on the horizon. To say that water is sacred amounts to saying it cannot be privatized—neither can natural gas, which banks the Bolivian state and, by proxy, until not long ago, the Argentine and the Venezuelan states. In this way, Pachamama's legal personhood is a line of defense against foreign powers. However, government-sanctioned mining operations, with new technologies and otherwise, continue to drill *apus* and scoop salt pits relentlessly.[53] As this section has shown, regardless of any affinity to the actual regimes and parties in power, the denaturalization of our discourse on nature, which they claim as their cause and which structures Wiethüchter's fiction, extends the reach of transcultural materialism to geological time.

All Tomorrow's (Subatomic) Parties

I have made some rather large claims about recent Latin American fiction. Succinctly, I have argued that it puts forward a negative political ecology, which not only thinks together environmental and social issues but also investigates in language their blind spots, lacks, and omissions. I have also argued that it matters to the region but also to the world at large; it reveals a heightened role for literary language—for instance, by prefiguring the juridical personhood of nature; it contributes to repairing the fractures between subject and object, and language and world; it interweaves human and nonhuman history, supplementing methodologies associated with postcolonialism and other critical movements; it articulates elements from historical and new materialisms; it situates itself in a literary tradition that has critically examined extractivism since the nineteenth century; and it makes graspable geological time. But how could fiction *do* such things, or anything at all? *Books have no arms.* In the rest of this chapter I will join other critics in trying to answer this simple, challenging question, which speaks to the problem of the agency of literature itself, by focusing on César Aira's *God's Tea Party*.[54] My contribution will serve to further elucidate how transcultural materialism deploys storytelling as a form of political *and* ecological intervention.

From the vastness of earth and the very wide timeframe of geology, Aira takes us to the smallness of subatomic particles and the even wider timeframe of quantum physics. Wiethüchter wrote relatively little and has received modest critical attention; Aira, on the other hand, is a prolific and avidly discussed writer, one who is likely to be critically examined even more in the years ahead. Of the works that throughout the present study I have posited as representative of transcultural materialism, Aira's is the most idiosyncratic and, in a word, fun. It could be described as a plot-driven nonplot: a page-turner whose story, rather than build up to something meaningful, takes an absurd premise to its final, exponentially more absurd consequences. The cast of characters in this short and thought-provoking work are apes, an Ape King, God, and a particle. First published in 2010 as a slim, thirty-three-page standalone volume with a print run of two hundred by Mata-Mata, a minuscule publishing house in Guatemala, it later appeared as one of the short stories collected by the behemoth Spanish publisher Mondadori in *Relatos reunidos* (2013). Chris Andrews's capacious English translation of the latter volume was titled *The Musical Brain, and Other Stories*; it was released by New Directions in 2015. From the periphery of the global literary market to a major node of the Spanish-language publishing world to a medium-sized, discerning venue in the preeminent language of World Literature, the text's circulation has its own story to tell.[55] It is the story of a singularity—an unlikely event in contemporary culture. Meanwhile, the story that unfolds in its pages is a singularity in a different sense of the word—namely, that of physics. As I see it, its motley crew of characters provides a retelling of the foundational narrative of modern physics: the big bang.

Summary fails to do justice to the story, as the experience of reading it is all about not knowing exactly what is going on at any one moment. With that caveat, a one-sentence description could be "Apes are having a rowdy tea party to celebrate God's birthday, until a subatomic particle interlopes and truly wreaks havoc." Already the mind reels. The style is a cultivated parody of highbrow, peppered with faulty theological reasoning, which clashes in meaningful ways with the events narrated. Some episodes would not be out of place in an animated series for children.[56] There are six chapters, indicated with roman numerals, and roughly four moments. First, the narrator dwells on exploring different aspects of the comically absurd premise. Then, there is a scene in which the Ape King, sitting in for God, tries to calm down the other apes who are, well, monkeying around. He winds up raising a bigger ruckus and abusing the others. Third, the particle crashes the party—literally and figuratively—creating even more chaos, splitting space into different planes as she (*sic*) passes through. Finally, the narrator reports that God retroactively finds an explanation for the origin of the particle, which for theological reasons had to always have been part of the divine plan, but tells no one.

Readers discover each of these elements only gradually, in carefully calibrated astonishment. The opening line sets the stage by combining a sententious style, reminiscent of sacred texts, with deadpan humor. It is worth citing it in the original and in the translation. Note how Andrews prefers to channel Aira's ludic proliferation of meaning instead of trying to be faithful to his words in a literal sense. Compare the following: "According to an old and immutable tradition in the Universe, God celebrates His birthday with a magnificent and lavish Tea Party, to which only the apes are invited"; "Por una vieja e inmutable tradición del universo, Dios festeja Su cumpleaños con un suntuoso y bien provisto Té al que acuden como únicos invitados los monos."[57]

Making a nod to the ultraconservative grassroots movement known as the "Tea Party" was an opportunity not to be missed in an American translation. To the presumably mostly liberal, cultured readers of New Directions, the unexpected mention of apes at the end of the sentence would be doubly humorous—first with regard to Judeo-Christian sacred texts, parodized here through the use of capital letters to signify divinity; second with regard to the members of said political phenomenon, often portrayed as brutes. The translation charts its own path for interpretation; to the point that, as I will merely insinuate here, an American reader could read the entire short story as slapstick on the Tea Party. Aira would probably find that felicitous, though it surely never crossed his mind at the time of writing. However, I think he is more interested in apes as a way of showing the continuity of humans with nonhumans, rather than as the frontier that separates us from them. Apes, Donna Haraway writes in her eminent feminist critique of primatology and primate representation, have served humans as a means of othering.[58] Among many case studies, she discusses fearful, towering King Kong, a figure that allows mankind to extricate itself from nature and incarnates inherited gender roles, colonial impositions, and race prejudices. Mindful of this pivotal role of apes in Western culture, Aira goes on to jovially speculate that perhaps apes were not so much *invited* to the celebration as much as humans were *disinvited* from it.

In that same spirit of transforming cultural references through wordplay and subverted expectations, Andrews puns with Tea Partiers. Multilingual puns were already present in the original: the title *El té de Dios* evokes *Te Deum*, the Latin title of the early Christian hymn of praise that starts with the words "Te Deum laudamus" (We praise thee, O God). This particular *novelita*, as Aira calls his numerous and predominantly short works of fiction, takes after an altar boy's joke. So what effect could a text of this nature possibly have? It is not serious. It does not bring down American conservatives, vindicate apes, popularize quantum physics, or defy the Inquisition with anachronistic heresy. However, it is by virtue of not quite being serious that it produces many effects, whether by itself or in coordination with the rest of Aira's unique oeuvre, which is written under the aegis of what he calls "the serious smile." Some effects have to do with the subject of the book and others with the notion of literature itself; many exceed the scope of the present argument. As I now turn to show, in addition to intervening in religious and secular stories of origin, *El té de Dios* provides a model of how fiction *acts*.

What god do readers imagine? Aira is aware that divinity has many forms and is always culturally embedded—this is already a question for World Literature. The book, for it is fair to call it that in its original form, features in its Guatemalan edition an uncredited illustration that, to the uneducated Western eye, may at first glance look like Indian decor. When mainstream Western readers finish the book, they might choose to ignore the cover as an additional whim on the part of the author or editor. Or they might be puzzled and intrigued by the fact that, while so many things in the text seem to allude to a Judeo-Christian god, there on the cover is what appears to be a Hindu deity (figure 2.2).

FIGURE 2.2 Cover of César Aira's *El té de Dios*. Guatemala City: Mata-Mata, 2010. Princeps edition.

As it turns out, the cover depicts Hanuman, the Monkey God, a popular character from the Ramayana who is Rama's aid against the devil Ramana. A statuette of the epic hero stands approvingly in the background while he plays a *chipliya*.⁵⁹ Hanuman is often portrayed in classical and modern Hindu iconography, and would be immediately recognizable to millions of people, but not to most of Aira's readers. They would see here an image of the book's tea party, say, of the Ape King calling other apes to order. It is a two-way mirror, which produces a different image when looked at from different vantage points—in this case, that of cultural expertise. Yet the image is also an enticement to speculation. Interestingly, at a time when World Literature writers often strive for immediate cross-cultural intelligibility, Aira prefers to harness mediation in order to multiply possible interpretations rather than find a one-size-fits-all account.⁶⁰ (Andrews gets this.)

The Ape King only tangentially resembles a Hindu deity, as when he dreams about having a thousand hands to slap every guest at the same time.[61] He is mostly a caricature of a fear-instilling Old Testament God, mixed perhaps with a heightened version of King Kong. God cannot make himself present at the party, readers learn through amusing aphorism, for that would entail his absence elsewhere. And so the appointed "Acting-God" Ape King, inebriated with power, relishes in exerting sovereign violence against the bodies of the other apes.

At this point, intertextual references juxtapose. Think of a different tea party gone awry, the one convened by Lewis Carroll's memorable Mad Hatter in *Alice's Adventures in Wonderland*.[62] At first, Carroll promises such a civilized gathering that even animals can partake, only to later use them to liberate the child from a regimented life. For his part, Aira gives us the Ape King, who is an exacerbated version of that dialectics of order and chaos. Suspense and disbelief peak and reach relief through cartoonish, hyperbolic violence:

> [The Ape King] sprays lemon juice in [the] eyes [of the weaker apes], dips their fingertips into the boiling tea, plugs their ears with candy and their noses with marmalade, pushes silver spoons into their anuses. . . . In the breaks, he downs gallons of tea, to fuel his causeless fury. There must be something in that tea.[63]

Aggression quickly escalates, in a manner best captured with children's literature and pop culture references. In a polysyndeton, we go from the benign buffoonery of a Mad Hatter dipping his pocket watch in tea, to the sadism of, say, Tom and Jerry: lemon-sprayed eyes and burned fingertips. Then we move to the perversity of the latter's crasser avatars, *The Simpsons*' Itchy and Scratchy: candies are plugged into ear canals, marmalade into nostrils. The next step in this genre-bending passage is entirely off-color, the hysterical climax of a penetration sequence that would not be out of place in a racy stand-up comedy routine: silver spoons into anuses. An ellipsis follows, giving readers a chance to burst into laughter. To top things off, the narrator states matter-of-factly that "in the breaks" the Ape King gulps down tea, as if abusing others were his day job, yet this tea fuels his "causeless fury"—theological mumbo jumbo again. The icing on the cake, pun intended, is the phrase "There must be something in that tea."

It is none other than God's tea. Surely, Aristotle never foresaw this objection to his argument: that perhaps what moves the unmoved mover is a natural stimulant.

Meanwhile, lemon juice, ready to burst from turgid cells at a moment's notice, with no reliable connection to how vigorously the fruit is squeezed, is just the right material-semiotic reminder of the limits of domestication—in this case, of animals, nourishment, and appetite. The agency of a halved fruit can disrupt a codified ritual, turning the world on its head. (This suggests a reason for stretch wraps, which also capture seeds—civility in a membrane.) Aira is enlisting nonhumans in his tale, conferring them unusual forms of agency. The "original" (i.e., Western) "God's birthday" is Christmas, an event that also convenes nonhumans, whether the star of Bethlehem or the donkey and ox who warm the baby with their breaths. For his part, Carroll punctuates his own mad tea party with this unsolved riddle: "Why is a raven like a writing desk?" The flat ontologist would reply: *Why not?* Aira, by going from apes to a subatomic particle, is equally invested in such continuities across the organic and the inorganic. The particle "glided through a meteorite of nickel and iron as a bird crosses the blue sky on a spring morning.... With the same oblivious fluidity, she passed through an atom. Or a sheet of paper, a flower, a boat, a dog, a brain, a hair."[64] This is taking the disruptive potential of the tea scene to a different level altogether. The new materialist in Aira appreciates, and fools around with, the connections between ravens, desks, apes, and atoms.

The historical materialist in Aira, however, involves a different, political dimension. It might strike one as surprising that quantum physics even have this aspect to it, had Wiethüchter not made the case for geology. What monkeys and tea have in common is that they both come from the Indian subcontinent, as Hanuman does. Britain's tea parties were affirmations of imperial might. (Arguably, this made the original eighteenth-century coinage of the "Boston Tea Party," in that other former British colony, all the more rhetorically effective.) In the twentieth century, laboratory research demanded the extraction of apes from India to Europe and North America. The more or less successful imposition of religious beliefs, textbook postcolonialism and plain common sense tells us, happened in the opposite direction. To an extent, Hinduism and the coexistence of apes and humans made Indians reluctant exporters of laboratory subjects. Moreover, the presence of monkeys themselves, Haraway notes, questioned the epistemological basis of the colonial enterprise: "Hardly always harmonious, the historical interaction of monkeys with people in India, in practical affairs of everyday life, makes cultural nonsense of the notion of primates as revealing the secret and primitive nature of 'man.'"[65] Contemporary India is no ecological utopia. Regardless, ape-man coexistence, which might lump together locals and animals in the colonial mind, further reinforcing hierarchy, suggests, in fact, a more horizontal relation among humans, be they colonizers or colonized, and apes. The Ape King could stand for "man" as much as for God, thereby questioning that triumphalist narrative in all its heteronormative, racist, speciesist, colonial glory.

It is telling of Aira's guerrilla-style (gorilla-style?) publication strategy that the Chilean first edition, a fourteen-page affair which appeared from Sazón publishing house (as miniscule as its Guatemalan counterpart) in 2011, features a drawing of what appears to be a Muslim man wearing a taqiya and a *thawb* serving a single cup of tea that sits off-center on a tray. Readers may wonder, Why the tray, if it's only one serving? Recalling that the Prophet cannot be represented stops reflection in its tracks: this is a one-man God's tea party. With the cover of this edition, which works too well in conversation with its Guatemalan iteration for there not to be some form of authorial intent, Aira is again short-circuiting World Literature.[66] God only knows what hurdles Andrew's counterparts, translators to Hindi and Arabic, will have to overcome.

The point is not to turn Aira into a theologist, a postcolonial critic, or a proponent of animal studies or object-oriented ontology. Rather, it is important to appreciate how his work manages to destabilize at the same time different stories of origin. This is the case of creationism, obviously—the kind of doctrine that, as it happens, many actual Tea Partiers adhere to. But it is also the case of Darwinism, social or otherwise, deftly intertwined here with behaviorism: "The invitations, addressed 'To Evolution,' are automatically transmitted to the ape's instincts, like the sound of a doorbell."[67] In a different passage, evolution is layered with the civilizing mission, as the narrator wonders whether manners themselves will evolve to such a degree that, in a distant future, "we would arrive at a divine, unprecedented spectacle: a gathering of apes sitting quietly around a table, lifting their teacups in one hand, their little fingers pointing at the surrounding void . . . , perfectly demure and genteel."[68] This is reminiscent of evolution-themed comic strips in which, from left to right, amoeba become fish become reptiles and so on, until they become man and then, say, a golfer or a white-collar worker. Despite its concretion and expressive economy, the text draws from many narratives and visual and cultural referents to produce its powerful, intricate effect of double take.

The particle is the most powerful agent of all. It takes after a modern, secular, scientific origin story that has fueled public imagination in recent years: the quest to find the Higgs boson, nicknamed "the God particle," conducted at CERN, the multibillion-euro facilities along the Franco-Swiss border. Bruno Latour, in one of the few articles in which he makes explicit his views on literature, to which I shall return, rightfully remarks that "as usual, whenever the hard questions of constructivism are tackled, God appears—no matter how ironic his appearance may be."[69] This is true both of the Higgs boson's nickname and of Aira's quantum physics–themed story. The Argentine's particle bears no Higgs moniker, but the allusion is obvious, and its implications are worthy of note. Aira does not engage in great detail with what goes on in laboratories, but rather works with its ripple effect among a general public. Fascination with the big bang has an analogous role to those concurrent, circulating narratives of evolution, civilization, and creation, thematized above. The intromission of the particle into the party could be read allegorically, given that for many the existence of the Higgs boson calls into question religious belief and various aspects of anthropocentrism. More interestingly for present purposes, it illustrates the agency of literature.

For one, there is the generative power of spoken language itself, down to its most basic material component: sound. Homophony, as Diego Vecchio has perceptively demonstrated, is the starting point of many of Aira's improvisatory acts of storytelling.[70] Reflecting on how likely it is for a *partícula* to show up uninvited, the narrator muses that maybe they are attracted to social gatherings, for it is not for nothing that the word for *fiesta* in English is "party."[71] *Bosón de Higgs* approximates "baboon." Puns occur naturally within a language and across languages; this is what Derrida might call the "freeplay of signifiers." Aira does not choose just any word, however, but one that denotes a building block of matter. Deliberately or not, it is a notion that would interest the deconstructionist and the constructivist, one that sits at the crossroads of the linguistic and material turns.[72] He does not simply make a note of the pun, but runs with it as far as it will take him, past any non sequiturs along the way. Above, Wiethüchter did something similar across German, Latin, Aymara, and Spanish—here the languages are English, Latin, French (briefly, as seen below), and Spanish, plus the languages evoked by the different cover art.

If infiltrating was an aesthetic ideal of subversive literature in the past, interloping is what this is all about. The particle "was there and not there . . . she was the prototypical interloper."[73] This statement amounts to an ars poetica, for Aira clearly understands his writing as having in some sense that effect, but it also corresponds to his vision of the transformative power of art at large. In a different metaphor he uses elsewhere, the goal would be to short-circuit—again, Borgesian shattering laughter. The particle's interruption of the ape tale plays out along gender lines. King Kongs are unlike the majority of male apes, who are in fact more social and less dominant than females, thus unsuitable as mirror images of mighty man. As Haraway notes, many Western primatologists and writers saw in apes what they wanted to see. In Aira, that narrative reached its hypermasculine climax in a thousand-hand orgy of anal rape. To counterbalance this (but drawing on the same logic of a caricature of patriarchy), a few lines down the next chapter introduces a fragile, feminine, and cautiously eroticized subatomic particle: "Her tiny little body [su cuerpecito huidizo], on which not even the finest brush could have inscribed a single letter."[74] This wandering less-than-Aleph packs a punch.

The particle is a "she" just as Time, in Lewis Carroll, is a "he." "If you knew Time as well as I do," ripostes an indignant Hatter to Alice, "you wouldn't talk about wasting *IT*. It's **HIM**."[75] These are idle pronouns and capitalizations, to be sure. And still they generate meaning, signaling agency at a very basic level, this time of script, rather than sound. "March Hare" and "Ape King" turn words into characters and personify animals with the most minimal of gestures. Meanwhile, the climactic event of the story, the particle's grand entrance, deploys the power of language to feed the spatial imagination:

> Coquettishly, the particle identified as a geometric point, which meant that her manifestation in reality was linear, because over time a point will always trace a line. And since a line is the intersection of an infinity of planes inclined at different angles, when this line entered God's Tea Party, something like a windmill of superfine screens appeared, screens tilted at various, changing angles, over which the apes went slipping and sliding. . . . Since there were

so many planes, it was very rare for two apes to be on the same one, which didn't stop them fighting—on the contrary.⁷⁶

What makes the particle flirtatious, or "coquettish," as Andrews puts it, is that she identifies herself as a geometric point—a masculine *punto*. A template for this story could be a cowgirl who walks into a bar brawl, making things worse. The geometrical basis is midschool Euclidean axiomatics, which the passage seems to recite in quick succession, translating each axiom into action, the a priori into a posteriori. First the point, then the line, then the multiple planes that make up space: each of these utterances titillates readers' minds, banking on the suspense that sound and script had helped to build. Delight comes, and the release of psychic energy. The particle is not making the world whole again, as Lukács wished for the novel as genre, but beautifully shattering it into a million pieces. Or is it? It is hard to miss the other template: the big bang, origin of origins.

What is most fascinating of all is that, later on, the denouement approximates words themselves to the particle: "At bottom, it was a question of language. There weren't any things in reality, only words, words that cut the world into pieces, which people end up taking for things."⁷⁷ Non sequitur is an art that Aira cultivates all too well. The particle may slice God's tea party, but it ties the work together. The title *El té de Dios*, in some cases the label of a book cover, singles out this work from the continuum of improvisation and recombining motifs that constitutes Aira's oeuvre. If there are no things in reality but only words that cut the world into pieces, then what world would there be for words to cut in the first place? A chicken-or-the-egg dilemma, this is the nominalist versus realist debate folded into one circular, hilarious sentence. It is also reminiscent of Jacques Rancière's well-known notion of the partition of the sensible, rendered both literally and literarily.⁷⁸ "The windmill of superfine screens," as Andrews puts it, is a radical illustration of how words cause an effect.⁷⁹ An alternative one would be showing how the phrase "just an ape," used in derogatory fashion, can justify rather ignominious experiments.

Upon closer examination, the way Aira frames the dilemma of words versus things provides a key to the parable and to the model of literary agency it espouses. For laypeople, the search for the Higgs boson resembles what for realists, Tim Morton included, is the quest to find the bedrock of indexicality. Some fifty years after its existence was hypothesized, the boson was finally "found" in 2012, prompting other scientific questions and (contrary to some forecasts) no landslide, worldwide crisis of faith. The drive to an origin story remained intact. In Aira, the narrator tells us that God finds an origin of the particle that, by "logical necessity," always must have been, but he does not tell it. (The English translation calls this discovery "her birth certificate": Obama's birth certificate for the "birthers" in the Tea Party?)[80] The final solution is not in a thing, out there, anterior to language and culture, the original point of reference. Neither is it in an originary word, unavoidably embedded in some culture, whence everything results. "In the beginning was the Word," says the Gospel, "and the Word was with God, and the Word was God" (John 1:1). Aira's *partycle* disrupts these isomorphisms with an unassimilable remainder: "And the particle was not a detail in a story; she didn't contribute any information or advance the plot: she was an accident and nothing more."[81] Early deconstruction thought that this ultimate undecidability affects signification at large—a position that Latour and many others have, more or less validly, rallied against.

Yet the ultimate certainty would be God's Word, the nano-brushstroke on the particle. The very end of this mutating novella, *novelita*, or short story is, as might be expected, an overdetermined deus ex machina. God, who has never spoken (he is there and not there) would have to utter the particle's birth certificate into existence. It is not an obvious task for him, we learn, as he has every language to choose from, "living, dead, and potential," and is thus afflicted by *l'embarras du choix*.[82] One can read here the Spanish false friend *embarazo*, pregnancy, for he is, after all, giving birth. He is also breaching his way into language, like a Wiethüchter-Lacanian infant ("[God] had no choice but to take part in the linguistic game") and piling a Sapir-Whorfian reference onto the many allusions already implicit in this comedy ("Each of them carved the world up differently").[83] The turning point, though, is the Higgs boson, which is, as the journal *Nature* explains, "a key part of a mechanism that gives all particles their masses."[84] True to fact, Aira situates the particle at a crossroads, "from which the paths of mass and energy depart."[85] Reportedly, it takes God less time to solve the riddle than for the narrator to explain it, and then it is already solved, and always has been. The deus ex machina in this Borgesian garden of forking paths keeps the secret to Himself.

Other than upsetting origin stories across religion, politics, and physics, Aira is providing, via metonymic displacement, an inquiry not into the convertibility of energy into the matter, as CERN scientists did, but of matter into language. He represents a hyperobject, in Morton's nomenclature, that is both a powerful cultural trope and a subject of scientific inquiry. What the fantasy about the "God particle" shows is that even the quest for the building blocks of the universe cannot let go entirely of language, literature, and culture. It does not provide a culturalist reading of science or a scientific reading of culture, but multiplies contradictions to an effect. It teaches one to see words as mediators between matters of fact and matters of concern. And fiction slides along. Like the particle, "To her the Void and the All were one; She roamed them both, in free fall, idle and unattached."[86] *El té de Dios* is but one of Aira's *novelitas*; to date, he has published over a hundred. Each one is its own agent, capable of making the mind trip.

The Other Literary Agents

Democritus, the founding figure of materialism in its atomist variant, was known in antiquity as "the laughing philosopher," so much did he value cheerfulness for philosophy. In Greek, "atoms" are literally "uncuttables," which seems a fitting etymology for Aira's antics. But imagine a less cheerful materialist who came along to ask, Where, exactly, is the indivisible unit of action of literature, the final cut? Show me the atom, so to speak, where literature *does*: the moment in which *El jardín de Nora* resituates the reader vis-à-vis nature, the instant when *El té de Dios* subverts tales of origin, the mechanism by which *Las comidas profundas* transforms our rapport with food, and so on. Many possibilities could open up here, including reception theory, phenomenology, neurological approaches to literature, or sociologies of literature. But allow me to turn briefly to a recurrent interlocutor throughout the present study, Latourian thought, to extrapolate and formulate theoretical takeaways for this chapter. Again, I do so with a caveat, because the experience of reading works like the above is not easily replaced by abstraction.

Aira coincides with Latour in many respects; in some important ways, some more obvious than others, they differ. The French thinker does science studies, including formal, theoretically-rich ethnologies of laboratory practices; the closest Aira comes to that is, arguably, *God's Tea Party*. To my knowledge, Latour's sole sustained engagement with literature is his article on the American novelist Richard Powers. Still, as Rita Felski eloquently puts it in an influential 2015 article, the "pact of mutual noninterference is reaching its end."[87] In my mind, Latour has been scapegoating critique for too long; Felski does something similar with suspicion.[88] I find this unnecessary now that Latour has situated himself (having contributed to establishing the field of science studies itself) at a third position that is neither "pure science" nor "humanities." My own contribution to these debates, the notion of transcultural materialism as a sublation of historical and new materialisms, is keen on not throwing away the baby with the bathwater. Felski's own rather apologetic defense of literary studies does not go far enough: critique, suspicion, and interpretation are all alive and well. Perhaps they enjoy better health in Latin Americanism than in other subdisciplines. Be that as it may, materialist literary exegesis that combines attention to form and to social content, as outlined in this chapter and elsewhere throughout this book, illustrates this.

What Felski, paraphrasing Latour, gets quite right is her understanding of "actor" as "any and all phenomena whose existence makes a difference."[89] A "Latour litany" (the term is Ian Bogost's) conveys the radically equal footing on which this puts all nonhuman and human actors.[90] Felski's example is "strawberries, stinkbugs, quarks, corgis, tornadoes, Tin-Tin, and captain Haddock."[91] Recall Aira, above, having the particle go across a sheet of paper, a flower, a boat, a dog, a brain, and a hair; similarly, we read that the particle could have emanated from anywhere, including "a flare from the surface of Alpha Centauri or a pan used to fry a dove's egg in China [la sartén en la que un chino freía un huevo de paloma], in a child's tear or the curvature of space, in hydrogen, blotting paper, a desire for revenge, a cube root, Lord Cavendish, a hair, or the unicorn."[92] At different levels, one could talk about the agency of each of these elements, of their assembly, or of their place within a work of literature. Aira's second list seems to obfuscate rather than to elucidate, throwing in the mythological creature at the end chiefly for comedic purposes. Nonetheless, *God's Tea Party* would subscribe to a distributed, nonhierarchical view of agency. A single book, with all its powers to capture our attention—from its cover through its typography to its storyline, metaphors and puns—is an actor too.

The less-than-jovial materialist might object that, clearly, there is a categorical mistake at work here. It would require some kind of subatomic Bovarism, or indeed magical thinking, to believe that Wiethüchter's collapsing soil or Aira's erratic particle could do something *in the world*. Reading about an earthquake and experiencing one at the same time would be a fantastic coincidence; only a radioactive book, should such a thing exist, could literally project a particle that could slide through our bodies. But where, if not in the world, do these things cause an effect? One may hypothesize that neurological studies of literature include MRIs of the moment when something changes in the brain's circuitry at the exact moment that a reader *understands* something. That would be one way of showing how the soil and particle on the pages *do* something. This, however, is not necessarily the best way of answering a question that Latour borrows from Alfred North Whitehead: "Can we write *about* an event, that is, *extend* its eventfulness?"[93] This is where interpretation inevitably and rightfully comes into the picture. Referring to this same problem, I quipped above that "books don't have arms." They do, as it turns out: readers are their arms. The road for a renewed take on reception theory and sociologies of literature lies open, but this should not subtract from close reading and interpretation, for what do readers "receive" in the first place, or what do reader communities revolve around? Interpretation is the sine qua non of extending the eventfulness of literature.

By necessity, suspicion comes along. Without it, *El jardín de Nora* would be but a convoluted tale about a suffering housewife and her tortured children, *El té de Dios* the random result of improvisation in storytelling. To make recourse to metaphor: if no one connects the dots, there is no drawing in the first place. But what makes a work of art interesting is often not found in the work alone but in societal concerns, such as the quest for minerals in the Andes or for the basic structure of reality in the Swiss Alps. The eventfulness of literature, down to the very circulation of books, depends on more than what immanent reading, narrowly construed, can offer. It also depends on the place of authors within World Literature, which is, to a significant degree, a function of history and politics. Foregoing suspicion would lead to overlooking this, as the Latin American cases studied throughout the present volume demonstrate. Represented hyperobjects, such as a subatomic particle or Pachamama, can do plenty—that is, once interpretation elucidates their place within works of literature as well as within other, more complex assemblages.

At stake is what the anthropologist Elizabeth Povinelli lucidly identifies as the new frontier of contemporary politics: the opposition of life versus nonlife, which underlies Foucaultian biopower—"geontopower," in her coinage. Organic and inorganic chemistry exist in a continuum: "we" are made of the same carbon as, well, carbon.[94] Although scientists themselves do not know where to draw the line, the state always seem to know. Who has the right over what (inanimate, unliving) rocks or particles is a watershed question in many arenas, from mining to nuclear disarmament. Rationalization of such legality, more or less valid, hinges upon humanist, Cartesian ideals, a policing of the separation of subject and object at all costs. "Animist beliefs" should pose no contest, for *bios* and *zoe*—the axis of Foucault's distinction— are not *geos*. (However, corpses, the subject of the next chapter, are revered without qualm, as if they were still animated.) Povinelli reports how, in Australia, indigenous people are invited to participate in government only as an animist voice, which is already a step toward domination: "The demand on Indigenous people to couch their analytics of existence in the form of a cultural belief and obligation to totemic sites . . . is a crucial longstanding tactic wherein settler late liberalism attempts to absorb Indigenous analytics in geontopower."[95] I leave it to more qualified politologists to ground my suspicion that strikingly similar dynamics may operate under a socialist, indigenous regime in the Andes that is, nonetheless, keen on mining.

Whatever the case may be, there are conclusions to be drawn about how we study and teach literature, Latin American literature in particular. My disciplinary formation allows me only second-hand familiarity with the many non-Western languages and traditions that populate the continent. Many of them have a keen relationship with the lithic entities addressed in this chapter or conceive of the constitutive elements of reality in ways sharply different from the vulgar, mechanicist atomicism typically taught in primary school. (Few things strike me as more animistic and superstitious than pointing at an atom or solar system modeled by colored Styrofoam spheres and telling a six-year-old that *that* is reality.) Wiethüchter and Aira, and my reading of their work, explore alternative epistemologies and ontologies mostly from within Western coordinates, if also pointing at their limits. However, one way to redraw the field of Latin Americanism, and to reform its scholarly training, would be to carry out more substantive comparison. This would not happen so much among "different cultures" but among differentiated, though contiguous, experiences of nature-culture. Understanding this requires building bridges between anthropology and literary studies—clearly, it's high time to stop talking past each other.

Yet this conversation too must be historicized. Not long ago, in the pivotal year 1968, the famous New York intellectual Lionel Trilling claimed condescendingly from his lectern at Columbia that Latin American literature had "an anthropological interest."[96] (*One Hundred Years of Solitude* had been published a year earlier.) Latin America reproduces internally this ethnocentric anthropologization of the alleged Other: its globally celebrated Spanish- and Portuguese-language novels and poetry, squarely situated within an art form and its genres, are its Western bits, while the region's cultural production in other languages, including rich, underexamined oral traditions, are objects of anthropological interest. Remedies are not easy to come by. Looking for commonalities in the world rather than primarily in cultural production, as transcultural materialism does in the wake of Ortiz's sugar and tobacco, is a step forward. Peruvian anthropologist Marisol de la Cadena's account of the inauguration of President Alejandro Toledo in Machu Picchu as "an occasion when earth-beings and the state shared the same public stage" might offer a model to follow.[97] (She shows how the same event, and the same "mountain," registers differently among the audiences congregated.) For his part, Jeffrey Cohen shows how medieval Christian writers, notably in the Arthurian cycle, are fascinated by the erotic properties of stones or think of love in lithic ways.[98] The medieval urtext to Fernando Ortiz's *Contrapunteo*, the Archpriest of Hita's *The Book of Good Love* (1343), also bears this evidence out.[99] Indeed, comparison across literatures, and beyond "literature," should keep us busy in the years ahead.

For now, as the present chapter suggests, it is important to note that animism can be both a literary and a legal category. It stands to reason that reading literature differently may lead to reformulating the law or, at least, to interrogating its bedrock of "common sense." We confer life through acts of reading or legislating; we also take it away.

CHAPTER THREE

Corpse Narratives as Literary History

As we have seen, the stakes of transcultural materialism reach beyond the disciplinary confines of Latin Americanism into World Literature. For a remarkably successful critical trend, the revival of the latter over the last three decades has made few explicit pronouncements about its future. Although no one knows for sure where present-day tendencies are headed, they often feature visions of what is to come. The startling thing about the critical discourse surrounding World Literature is how effectively generative it has been despite—or perhaps because of—its very modest projections. What currently defines the telos of World Literature is its own dynamism, rather than a specific goal, even one broadly defined. At best, this amounts to a celebration of the converging creative energies of scholars; at worst, one sees a bias toward action for its own sake, scholarly busyness. I will approach the problem of projection through a related phenomenon: abjection. To that end, I shall draw from a constellation of theoretical referents and from several literary examples, with a nonexclusive emphasis on contemporary Latin American fiction. My goal in this chapter, building on the work done so far, is to propose an *orientation toward the corpse* as a viable telos for world—and, of course, Latin American—literature.

In the sections to follow, I will first speculate about the implicit telos of the worldlit movement to situate my ideas. Second, I analyze corpse narratives, in Roberto Bolaño and other sources, that embrace the abject and point critical practice toward materiality. Finally, I will draw conclusions from the chapter's various discussions. Purposefully cacophonous, I occasionally adopt the suffix "-ism" (as in "worldliteraturism") to keep in mind that we are dealing with one approach among others, as opposed to a metatheory. Similarly, as I mentioned in the introduction, I stress the caps in World Literature to refer to the more institutionalized, mainstream avatar of the phenomenon, as represented by the Journal of and the Institute for World Literature (full disclosure: I count myself a collaborator of the institute). I find it useful to estrange all cognate terms surrounding *Weltliteratur*, lest we adopt them acritically. Thus, I will occasionally continue to use the more colloquial term "worldlit," following increasingly common usage in the field, based on the template of the hitherto widely used "complit." The crux of my Latin America–centered argument is to contribute to World Literature with affinity for the emerging paradigm, while also questioning some of its developments and offering a more defined sense of finality for the movement consistent with transcultural materialism.

Purposeless Purposiveness Turns Ugly

Some may have no quibble with conceiving of worldlit criticism as purely autotelic. Increased exchange among critics who were previously not in conversation is a good thing. The reasons why such conversation should revolve around World Literature, and not any other encompassing category, are less apparent. But that could be secondary if the conversation, in itself, is worthwhile. In such a nominalist approach, "World Literature" could be replaced by any other catchphrase that spurs the conversation. *Différance* served similar purposes back in its heyday. And yet the critical trend we came to know as deconstruction, to continue with the example, had very concrete ideas about what it sought to achieve—namely, debunking binarisms.[1] Meanwhile, there is a symptomatic void of goals, let alone theory, in such otherwise enlightening reference works as Theo D'haen's *The Routledge Concise History of World Literature* (2012).[2] That volume does a formidable job at telling the "story" of World Literature, from the influential aphorization of the term by Goethe, through Curtius and Auerbach, leading to Moretti, Casanova, and contemporary debates. Non-European, pedagogical, and translation topics are also explored. However, this capacious account of the past and present of World Literature lacks a section devoted to imagining the future of the paradigm, as well as a general conclusion. (Each chapter ends with bullet-point conclusions intended as takeaways for the student.) I see in this conspicuous absence an affirmation of the intrinsic good of worldliteraturism.

Mads Rosendahl Thomsen makes this more evident in *Mapping World Literature* (2008), where he notes: "The important aspect of the future of world literature is the way in which it is being used to make institutional changes in a situation where fields of research are being redefined, and curricula are being determined to some degree by the idea of what will be relevant to the future."[3] Note the circularity in this reasoning, best described as self-referential reformism: World Literature deserves to be taught because it is worth studying. There is not much room left for literature outside of institutions, or for the referential in literature, that is, how it connects to the world at large, to be front and center. Later work by Rosendahl Thomsen is more nuanced, and I shall return to it later on. But this early formulation illustrates the point: either these are tautological, read ideological, pronouncements, or, as I prefer to think, the markings of a leap of faith.

In the first case, we face what Žižek would call a sublime object of ideology, that is, those "signifiers without signified" that constitute political communities who identify "with the very gesture of identification."[4] There is some traction to that assessment, to be developed elsewhere. But ultimately, World Literature comes across as a rather benign sublime object of ideology, if it registers as such at all. The worst possible ideological fallout that can be imagined is very far removed from the calamitous scenarios that might ensue in society at large from manipulating discursive elements like, say, "security." Additionally, as David Damrosch notes, "cross-cultural literary relations" predate modern nations and literary institutions by many centuries, as exchanges along the Silk Road or the Indian Ocean illustrate.[5] Such factual observations would dispel the fear that, in the final analysis, "there is no there there": circulation is something we can point to and call World Literature. This leaves open the question of whether a critic's task is to provide accounts of the circulation of textual and oral traditions, past and present. However, as focusing on circulation produces, well, more circulation, the self-fulfilling prophecy is then complete. In other words, autotelic axiology and virtuoso exhibitions of connoisseurship replace discussions about finality.

The leap-of-faith option is not unproblematic. Projection without content, moored in self-affirmation and institutional expansion, excludes by fiat. Regardless of a remarkably (and salutary) inclusive ethos, the risk is to exclude through inclusion, mutatis mutandis, like the Catholic Church does. This is an ironic turn, given Goethe's Lutheran background and polytheistic sympathies, but the "invisible church" of World Literature tutors he hoped for in the 1830s sits more squarely with the Church of Rome.[6] Catholicism is a host of contradictions, notes Carl Schmitt, for "there appears to be no antithesis it does not embrace. It has long and proudly claimed to have united within itself all forms of state and government. . . . But this *complexio oppositorum* also holds sway over everything theological."[7] World Literature is open to all literatures, sidestepping the thornier question of opening itself to incompatible visions of what literature is. One could argue that such differences can be hammered out along the way, but first we need to "sit at the table." The counterargument would be: Why that table in the first place? Canonization, a secularized theological notion like the state structures that Schmitt had in mind, is increasingly about *complexio oppositorum*. This, of course, gives certain privileged institutions an outsized role in orchestrating the whole affair, with pontifical nudges in lieu of party lines. Convening power becomes power tout court. (It might also be the reason why the paradigm feels most at home in partially overlapping readers, genealogies, and surveys than in major monographs with a sustained line of scrutiny.) I am not keen on restating here familiar arguments that have been made against World Literature. Rather, I seek to underline the recursive structure that leads to the absorption of opposing views within the paradigm.

The most notorious example is Emily Apter's thoughtful and suitably entitled *Against World Literature* (2013), a case for recovering what is lost in translation.[8] It is an exercise both in refutation and in loyal opposition. As Gloria Fisk aptly puts it, "While Apter pretends to fire against world literature like an enemy, she leans against it like a plank on a wall to join a critical conversation."[9] The contagious enthusiasm of World Literature transcends stark methodological differences: Apter stresses "traditional" theorization in her works, while others emphasize erudition or sociological analysis. These approaches would normally be incompatible, if not outright antagonical, were it not for the very wide institutional umbrella above them. Faith in dynamism for its own sake can also be seen in Amir Eshel's work, which advocates for futurity (openness) without utopia (prescription, per his account), and in Damrosch's claim that that "true history [of world literature] lies in the future rather than in the past."[10] What future?, one may ask. Answers are less forthcoming. The gist of the project is creating the frames, not filling them, or in a different metaphor, establishing a minimal set of rules of a game for others to play.

This same spirit is to be found in the founding charter of the *Journal of World Literature*. The aspirations of bringing together scholars, creating a forum, and fostering "wider and deeper" discussions feature prominently in the journal's masthead.[11] As befits an ecumenical publication, there is little in the way of the prescriptive or the axiological other than, respectively, going beyond the national and favoring a cosmopolitan approach. There is plenty about the how (collaboration, networks) and precious little about the what. Unless by the latter we understand: everything. Now, this all-encompassing agenda is prone to suffering from an expansive version of what Gerald Graff described in 1986 as "taking cover in coverage."[12] A more capacious account of the facts of literature on a global scale would allow scholars to leave uninspected, to put it in terms Graff borrows from Norman Foerster, "the theory upon which their practice rests."[13] In this context, "everything" is a logical impossibility. Absent an Aleph, the Borgesian imaginary object that shows all points in the universe and all points of view at the same time, things happen in succession.[14] The elusive quid of World Literature would be a variedly infinite task that, nonetheless, we must promptly undertake.

The basis for this paradoxical, hypergenerative endeavor is already present in Goethe's most-cited dictum on the matter: "The epoch of World-literature is at hand, and everyone must strive to hasten its approach."[15] Compare this statement to "Godot is coming; quick, we must tidy up the house now!" "At hand"—or "upon us," as it is also translated—is *an der Zeit*; "hasten" is *beschleunigen*. They are both, unequivocally, about speed. This oft-quoted phrase remains elusive. If the epoch is already here, then why hasten it? "*Everyone* must hasten its approach" acts like a critical-mass resort to self-validation: indeed, if nearly everyone does, the epoch would have, in a sense, arrived. But if that threshold is not met, dynamism suffers. Hospitality entails risks, including the possibility that guests do not show up—or, in this case, join in the active expectation of the new era. The weak spot of convening power is that it is required, in fact, to convene.

Its strength is that no one wants to be left without an invitation. Everyone *must*. Goethe's dictum instills enthusiasm (*begeistert*), inaugurating a theme that runs all the way through *JWL*. This coincides with what Pheng Cheah, in a kindred intervention, has rightly called "spiritualism": the tendency to think that literary exchange configures a higher, spiritual order.[16] Autotelism flies high.

We cannot expect Johann Peter Eckermann's recollections of his conversations with Goethe, or the romantic poet's scattered mentions of the term, to become an oracle for contemporary scholarship. Piecing together what Goethe meant or figuring out what we want to do with it make for fascinating pursuits. So should debating the baggage of his aestheticist classicism, a retreat from the politics of his day that Adorno regarded as compromise and Benjamin as capitulation.[17] (A few lines down, in fact, Goethe invokes the Greeks as ahistorical representation of the beauty of mankind—no need to hurry there.)[18] For present purposes, suffice it to note, with a different German thinker, that when dealing with Weltliteratur we appear to be dealing with a thing of beauty. "*Beauty*," says Kant, "is an object's form of *purposiveness* insofar as it is perceived in the object *without the presentation of a purpose*."[19] *Zweckmäßigkeit ohne Zweck* is an apt description for the enthusiasm that is World Literature. A sunset or a poem does not need to exist in the way that a hammer does. Like the hammer, they appear to serve a purpose, but not one in particular. The same can be said about World Literature. As with beauty at large, we will do well in taking it with a grain of salt.

Take the following case in point: genealogies of World Literature such as D'haen's downplay the role that postmodernism, postcolonialism, and the linguistic turn play in the 1990s emergence of the paradigm. (Instead, they prefer longer historical-critical timeframes and focus on seemingly converging themes across cultural traditions.) Others are better suited to weigh in on the *posts*. As pertains to the linguistic turn, before there is "world and literature," we must problematize "world and language."

World Literature can be infinite in one sense and completely flat in another, limitless in coverage but absolutely limited in referentiality, if it does not take this problem into consideration. Thinkers ranging from Laozi in sixth-century-BCE China, through medieval European scholasticism, leading to Wittgenstein and Kristeva in the twentieth century have all, in multiple ways, explored how the relationship between world and language is not one to be taken for granted. Literature takes part in such inquiries, "from *Faust* to Hollywood films, and from the Babylonian court of Šulgi in the twenty-first century BCE to the global Babel of our own twenty-first century today," as Damrosch has put it.[20] How can these works "connect" to the world? One short answer is that they cannot, but that is no reason not to try. Another is that they always already do. These answers are not incompatible, so long as we do not try to solve the referentiality problem by falling into dualism, imagining there is a world "out there" that literature across the epochs manages to render somehow, like a series of maps or miniature paintings.

I am briefly reminded of the Cuban Alejo Carpentier's famous 1949 prologue to *The Kingdom of This World*, where he formulates the highly influential notion of *lo real maravilloso americano* (roughly "magical realism"). There a narrator enumerates his travels through China, Islam (*sic*), and the USSR, before returning to Latin America to better understand the region's marvelousness and specificity.[21] No list, no matter how long, will ever re-present the world. And none leaves it unchanged, either: lists affect readers, broadening their horizons, establishing new connections, transforming others. The same is true of lists of authors, recipients of minimally renewed, already differentiated attention. Lists communicate the power of language despite its limited referentiality. They share an important additional trait, aptly identified by Umberto Eco in the context of discussing one of his later works: "We like lists because we don't want to die."[22] I suspect that fear of death is a driving force behind the rebirth of World Literature, a paradigm riddled with ars-longa-vita-brevis anxiety or, in words Damrosch borrows from the metaphysical poet Andrew Marvell, the predicament of not having "world enough and time."[23] If life is too short to read an expanded canon of books from various cultures, then at least we can approach them more or less superficially.

But what if, instead of retreating at the sight of death, we face it? "Death" we never really see, for it is already an abstract, spiritualist notion. The more radically materialist move is to turn toward the corpse, which the rest of this chapter sets out to do. "A wound with blood and pus, or the sickly, acrid smell of sweat, of decay, does not *signify death*," says Kristeva. "Without makeup or masks, refuse and corpses *show me* what I permanently thrust aside in order to live."[24] I am reintroducing a notion to which preworldlit students were no strangers: the abject, that which is cast off. Lacanian psychoanalysis holds it as a basis for subjectivity, which defines itself in opposition to what it rejects.[25] "To every ego its object, to every superego its abject," notes Kristeva a few lines above.[26] Spiritualist, aspirational World Literature, by merging the represented and the real, inflicts upon itself the violence of thoroughly disowning its own refuse. In an image, the superegoic, deathless ideal critic contemplates monuments of culture, forgetful of the rotting flesh that marble, in a sense, outlives. All along, the corpse teaches how to navigate the tension between literature and world.

Anus Mundi

I am taking my cues from the Chilean writer Roberto Bolaño (1953–2003), a strong gravitational force in World Literature and the entryway into global relevance for a broader canon of Latin American writers, contemporary and otherwise. Passionate, traveling women and men of letters are his favorite characters; their passion is equal parts *eros* and *thanatos*, be it death wish or killer instinct. In Bolaño, literature is always a matter of life or death until, paradoxically, the futility of it all sweeps in, and readers are struck by how little literature can contribute to repairing the world's woes. Therein lies the constitutive aporia in Bolaño's writing: he sees literature as a historically situated, politically charged vital impulse, flanked by death, both fruitless and indispensable. Drawing, yet also departing, from my earlier work, the following sections present an original, encompassing theory about the Chilean's oeuvre from the vantage point of the corpse.

Consider the following parable, a secondary plotline in *Nocturno de Chile* (2000; trans. *By Night in Chile*, 2003), a novella about a dying priest who is also a prominent literary critic. A Viennese court shoemaker, out of equal parts patriotic zeal and the desire to increase his social status, spends all his modest fortune in building a cemetery and sculpture park for the heroes of the Austro-Hungarian empire. He finds a suitable plot of land for that purpose and calls it "Heldenberg" (Heroes Hill). The joke is on the shoemaker, it seems: he has himself buried there before the outbreak of World War I, with no way of knowing that there would be no more heroes of the Austro-Hungarian empire, nor any empire at all. When

Soviet tanks roll in—note the ellipsis—they find his vault-like crypt atop the desolated hill, and inside, his corpse, with "eye sockets empty . . . and his jaw hanging open, as if he were still laughing after having glimpsed immortality."[27] Alas, the joke is on us, readers who embark on similarly futile enterprises, equally unaware of historical contingency, and will perish all the same. *Cadáver*, Spanish for corpse, originates in the Latin verb for "to fall." This corpse perched upon a hill emphasizes the collapse of high and low, the unavoidable abjection in projection, the decomposing carnality of imagined futures. Reinforcing this idea, the novella's main storyline features the recurrent motif of a body tortured by the Pinochet regime that haunts the priest's last-hour recollections. The suppressed memory of that corpse surfaces in the denouement, as in a book-length fictionalization of habeas corpus.

Other than setting the stage for those somber revelations, the shoemaker parable lambasts the petty search for greatness and subservience to fickle politics that, allegedly, underwrite literary history. Bolaño's fiction has very unflattering things to say about critics and idolizes unprofessional readers. (He exaggerates.) The Chilean allows for, even cultivates, a naively vitalist, almost anti-intellectual reading of his work. In that vein, Bolaño's answer to the "ars longa, vita brevis" conundrum would be to live more and to read less. But of course, that moment is part of a more complex operation: some of his most memorable characters are such passionate readers that they read in the shower.[28] On a different level, Bolaño is summoning the powers of horror, as Kristeva calls them, to infuse global literary history with a renewed attention to materiality. The literary and cultural transactions across locales that populate the pages of his books, both the hefty and the thin ones, are all about bodies, not just ideas, traveling. In fact, one can regard the entirety of Bolaño's writing as permutations, often extreme, of three elements: sex, literature, and travel.[29] For a brief illustration, consider a deranged poet who roams the American Southwest in *La literatura nazi en América* (1996, trans. *Nazi Literature in the Americas*, 2008). He imagines a centenarian Ernst Jünger and a nonagenarian Leni Riefenstahl, practically corpses, furiously making love: "bones and dead tissue bumping and grinding."[30] It's a harrowing image, to say the least, somehow aggravated by the figures' fascist proclivities—reminders, like the fine boots the shoemaker made, of the heteronomy of literature. The point here is that World Literature cannot be about pure souls.

Bolaño furthers this idea both subtly and forcefully. He swiftly became the darling of World Literature spiritualists even when, upon closer inspection, his work is a source for the critique of this very tendency. As Sarah Pollack has demonstrated, Bolaño's initial success was due to a much-hyped Latin American rebelliousness, allegedly present in *Los detectives salvajes* (1998, trans. *The Savage Detectives*, 2007)—consider it an extension of the realm of the spirit to the playful South.[31] The serious materialist thrust can easily go unnoticed amid the often-playful tone and the plot-twisting enthusiasm. I regard this as something of a Trojan-horse move: once admitted into the citadel of literary history, Bolaño changes the rules of engagement from within. Rather than merely an author whose work may belong to a canon, or to several, Bolaño is an event that both exposes and unsettles canon formation itself. The necessity of World Literature in this day and age stems from the interdependence witnessed foremost not in novels or epics but in finance, migration, and communication, fields that more readily acknowledge imperialism, cultural or otherwise, than the generally more hopeful, utopian enterprise of studying literature beyond narrow national frames. Bolaño contributes to the debate by problematizing the historicity and referentiality of World Literature, its realpolitik and its troubled rapport with geopolitics.

Immanuel Wallerstein's world-system theory provides the conceptual backbone to many modern approximations to World Literature.[32] The Bolaño phenomenon evidences the great extent to which such approximations downplay an important facet of Wallerstein's oeuvre, namely, the fundamental role the thinker attributes to 1968 in his later work. In a piece he published in the *annus mirabilis* 1989, too close to the fall of the Berlin wall and its spectacularization by Fukuyama acolytes to have been adequately assimilated, he puts forward theses such as the following: "1968 was a revolution in and of the world-system" and "Counter-culture was part of revolutionary euphoria, but was not politically central to 1968."[33] This late Wallerstein is, quite simply, antisystemic. He also seems to subscribe to a school of thinking about 1968 as more than mere youth revolt, but rather a profoundly transformative event with implications the world over. In a related fashion, Salvador Allende, the brutally overthrown Chilean president and Bolaño's inspiration, gave a speech in Guadalajara in 1972 in which he posited that "to be young and not a revolutionary is a contradiction, even a biological contradiction."[34] Stopping short of politicizing life itself, here the socialist posits youth as a form of antisystemic resistance.

A few years apart from *soixante-huitards*, Bolaño writes time and again about the violent fate of Latin Americans who were close to twenty years of age at the time that Allende died, to paraphrase the short story "El Ojo Silva" (trans. "Mauricio 'The Eye' Silva").[35] Bolaño does politics where he knows best, in fiction. He is not one to ignore the unsavory aftermaths of the sixties, nor one to throw away the baby with the bathwater. His writing does not so seek to represent a narrowly defined political position but to activate the social politicity of literature. Bolaño exacerbates tension and contradiction in the realpolitik of World Literature—in *2666*, as I will show below, by cultivating the aura of an apocryphal lost German classic to shed light on the women assassinated in the Sonoran Desert. The book is not reducible to a human rights plea, however, no matter how urgent the massive feminicide it denounces. Rather, it exposes the frailty of both human life and literature, seeking to make art at their limits.

If the goal is to revitalize an antisystemic, global youth politics à la 1968, the means are rekindling historical avant-gardes. In particular, the Chilean deploys a critical stance similar in many ways to Georges Bataille's base materialism. A potent set of images that stimulate a certain kind of thinking rather than a rigorous philosophical doctrine, base materialism confounds high and low, sophisticated and crass, head and ass. In one deft movement of recurrence, it sets free the agency of language to derail meaning even while it deploys it to produce meaning. Ramifications of these ideas are more familiar to contemporary readers through the work of Jacques Derrida or Philippe Sollers. As it happens, the latter is a character, alongside the rest of the *Tel Quel* group, in Bolaño's short story "Labyrinth." (There Bolaño imagines an interloping Central American outside the frame of an iconic photo of the group; the story itself is an act of self-inclusion within, and disruption of, cultural capital.) But the key thinker behind Bolaño's writing is the earlier figure, Bataille.

The Frenchman, in turn, channels Francisco de Quevedo, the Spanish seventeenth-century classic. Bataille may well have drawn inspiration from the underexamined, mordant *Gracias y desgracias del ojo del culo*, approximately *Fortunes and Misfortunes of the Asshole* (circa 1628). (This is just the kind of work Bataille had access to as custodian of the *enfer* of censored books in the National Library in Paris). Quevedo compares the centrality of the anus with that of the sun; he calls attention to the fact that every one of us readers is endowed with an anus. "More necessary is the lonely eye of the ass than those in the face," says the Spanish bard, "for one may live without eyes in the latter, but without an eye in the former neither defecate nor live."[36] Crassly humorous, but insightful. Globalization has renewed the search for universal truths, to little avail—here is one. This basic common denominator conjures both pleasure and pain, not to mention compassion and community, across classes, races, even species. Bolaño, as we shall see, takes note.

For his part, Bataille transforms this ethos into broad theorizations of the bodily. His thought experiments with human sacrifice include having everyone in his headless collective, *Acéphale*, pledge to be a sacrificial victim, provided someone else in the group would be the victimary—a role nobody undertook, in the end. This provocation intervenes in the power dynamics within avant-garde movements and turns the individual body of every participant into a touchstone for speculative thought. In this vein, Bataille's uncategorizable prose poem–essays of 1931 and 1933—respectively, "The Solar Anus" and "Base Materialism and Gnosticism"—provide a defense of baseness and a purposefully failed attempt to think the cosmos through the body. In the first text, Bataille imagines "organic coitus of the earth with the sun" or the terrestrial globe "covered with volcanoes, which serve as its anus."[37] Idiosyncratically, cryptically, he fancies the earth jerking off with an eruptive force that accumulates in the underclass: "As in the case of violent love, [erotic revolutionary and volcanic deflagrations] take place beyond the constraints of fecundity."[38]

In the ultimate expenditure of energy, Bataille's narrator wants his throat slashed as he violates a girl he calls the Night. The text's peculiar envoi is an eclipse of sorts: "The *solar annulus* is the intact anus of her body at eighteen years to which nothing sufficiently blinding can be compared except the sun, even though the *anus* is *night*."[39] Clearly, there is no easy methodological takeaway here. However, note how the final image interrupts the thrust toward totalization, from body parts and workers to earth and cosmos. Bataille builds on the force of the word "revolution," but the absolute indexical necessity of the individual body forecloses transcendence. The delirious sacrificial storyline explores its own logical constraints. In the words of Benjamin Noys, Bataille "argues that any attempt to reach the heights is doomed to an inevitable fall back into the dirt."[40] One thing that Bolaño will achieve by recuperating the motif of the solar anus is similarly countering the idealist totalizations of World Literature practitioners who, in their abstractions, forget individual bodies or do not otherwise bound their thinking, inextricably, to the body.

There are two ways in which Bataille leaves his mark on Bolaño: through implicit solar economy and explicit, if often subtle, allusion to anuses. For Bataille, the sun is an image of perfect expenditure: it burns away, and gives, without retribution. Expenditure is a trait of life, an exuberant drive that cannot be contained. Bolaño's final years of illness and copious writing paid tribute to this idea. In his aptly titled lecture "Literature + Illness = Illness," he claims literature itself puts up a useless, valiant fight.[41] Here Bolaño purports that traveling made him ill and equates traveling with living. Since his travels, and those of his characters, configure the global picture one gets from reading Bolaño, it is safe to conclude that worlding in his oeuvre is expenditure, too. He wrote from the affect of a dying sun; the writing reflects this. Earlier narrative work is measured, consistent with genre conventions. His novellas read like novellas. Later work such as the novel 2666, by contrast, reads as expenditure of the novel genre itself. There is also the often-cited anecdote, whether authorial legend or fact, that Bolaño, formerly a young poet, set out to write fiction upon learning of his illness. Reportedly, he did so in order to sustain his family, having solar and home economy bear upon each other.

I dare posit that the entirety of Bolaño's oeuvre is written under the sign of the anus. Its discernment of global transactions, and its concomitant appeal to the all-encompassing project of World Literature, stems from no other place—hence the recurrent motif. There is the autobiographical character in *The Savage Detectives*, a naive aspiring poet, "Belano" (beautiful anus). Or the aforementioned "El Ojo Silva," a Spanish pun for "the whistling [read farting] eye." *By Night in Chile* has but two paragraphs, the first straddled across a hundred odd pages, the second a single line: "And then the storm of shit begins."[42] Early article collections on Bolaño by Karim Benmiloud and Raphaël Estève, and by Patricia Espinosa, took up the motif of melancholic black suns (*astres noirs*) in Bolaño. Their bodily dimension as anuses is no less important, for it speaks to the base condition of all agents in World Literature, potentially victims or victimaries. Bolaño's less-than-heteronormative take on Bataille's motif presents free association under different, equally transgressive garb. Having witnessed the twentieth century, it is arguably less jovial about violence. Still, it cultivates its aesthetic in order to open new paths at the expressive limits of language.

These limits include the untimely, literal death of the author, from liver failure, at age fifty—clearly, a limit we are making headways into overcoming. But for every path Bolaño's work continues to open, there is only one it seeks to shutter close: a World Literature of pure souls.

One may briefly recall the character Auxilio Lacouture's bathroom-stall account of the breach in university autonomy that accompanied the Tlatelolco massacre (*Amuleto* 1999; trans. *Amulet*, 2006;). The delirious character, a clairvoyant, self-proclaimed Uruguayan mother of Mexican literature, portrays the bathroom as the last stronghold of autonomy in the university.[43] The language of her internal monologue constantly compares the breach with rape. Bolaño's oblique take on the much-depicted Tlatelolco events foregrounds the problem of artistic autonomy in Mexican and Latin American literature; his oeuvre extends the gesture to World Literature at large. Bolaño names his characters in ways that expand, rather than narrow, meaning. For one, "Auxilio Lacouture" is a bilingual pun for "I repair the stitch"—and yet an anus is open by definition. The notion of aporia, with its etymology of pores and pathlessness, is doubly pertinent. Autonomy must be and cannot be; complete autonomy would entail irrelevance and removal from the world; complete heteronomy leaves no room for the imagination. Neither ivory tower nor weapon of class warfare, the bathroom stall embodies the precariousness of literature. The anus, in its openness and fragility, is indispensable. Ditto for novels. Lacouture evokes the textile and the textual, as well as the suture between subject and language introduced by Lacanian psychoanalysis. The moment one is inclined to map a center-periphery World Literary system onto Bolaño's poetics, with an anus for the sun, is the moment when that very enterprise is disavowed. There is no single anus, but multitudes.

Kristeva establishes a connection between anuses and corpses in the chapter "Semiotics of Biblical Abomination," from *The Powers of Horror*, notably in a section entitled "Waste-Body, Corpse-Body." There we read, "Contrary to what enters the mouth and nourishes, what goes out of the body, out of its pores and openings, points to the infinitude of the body proper and gives rise to abjection."[44] The difference between refuse and the corpse is one of degree. The idiom "shitting oneself from fear," identical in Spanish, speaks the truth: the odd use of the reflexive there ("oneself") is about the objectness of the body itself, already intuited in our rapport with corpses and refuse. "We are what we eat" is a platitude more easily adopted than its logical consequence (what we excrete). Throughout Bolaño's oeuvre, there is an underlying emplotment of abjection that plays out in multiple registers, some tragicomical, others downright ghastly. What's most striking about this macro-storyline is not just what it thematizes but the use of language it deploys. Considering this aspect in some detail will shed light on the referentiality or "literature and world" conundrum.

Take Bolaño's short story "El retorno," from *Putas asesinas* (2001), translated by Chris Andrews as "The Return" in an eponymous 2010 collection. (The hilarious B-movie connotations of the original book title, "Murderous Whores," fall flat in English.) Like *Memórias Póstumas de Brás Cubas*, by the Brazilian master Machado de Assis, it is a first-person account of a deceased person. It is also a story of necrophilia, and a love story at that: the ghost of an unnamed party animal, knocked down by a heart attack on the dance floor, witnesses his body being smuggled from the morgue to a Parisian mansion. There, Jean-Claude Villeneuve, a celebrated fashion designer, has sex with his corpse. The ghost confronts him; apologies are made and accepted. As the story comes to a close, the morgue smugglers come to pick up the corpse. The ghost-narrator chooses to stay in the mansion, while the lonely necrophiliac confides in him or talks to himself, endlessly. The tale is reminiscent of Derrida's "La loi du genre" in its simultaneous unsettling of genre and gender—genre because it effectively blurs the boundaries between a fantastic ghost story (like Machado's) and a realist, very straightforward story; and gender because it maps a coming-out confession, a pervert's lot in Western psychiatry pre-DSM-IV, onto a sort of coming-in perversion: a straight man turns gay, a necrophiliac turns domestic partner. As Villeneuve strokes the dead man's genitals, the ghost thinks of Cécile Lamballe, "the woman of his dreams," who left him dead at the disco.[45]

In the Lacanian tradition, corpses and bodily excretions *always* mediate between world and language—and, therefore, literature. This is the case here, on a metalevel. Readers are not confronted with the real (unless they should choose to have a reading séance at an actual morgue) but read about it. Still, the story conveys to some degree the limit case for language that corpses are. Signification is at a loss. The protagonist ruminates: "My body or my ex-body (I don't know how to put it)"; he utters the impossible phrase "my corpse"; he talks about the remains in the first person, with dark humor ("I didn't have the stomach to watch them open me up") only to totter back into the third.⁴⁶ This is verisimilar because "he" is only just getting used to being dead, just as it is plausible, within the economy of the short story, that the protagonist should forgive and oddly befriend Villeneuve, because "his" body is not *his* anymore, and ultimately, a ghost is neither a "he" nor a "she." The conceit confronts us with the arbitrariness of the signifier, not just pronouns and possessives but the word "corpse" itself. As Natalie Depraz reports in *The Dictionary of Untranslatables*, the German triad *Leib/Körper/Fleisch* can only be rendered as *carne/cuerpo* in Spanish or as the rather awkward lived-body/body/flesh in English.⁴⁷ Saying "Please fetch a chicken corpse from the refrigerator" is both elucidating, as conscientious eaters know well, and ominous. It is funny too, in a nervous-laughter sort of way: again, we are what we eat.

While the story builds upon the strong connotations of a word like "corpse," it also relies on smart, silly puns. Read "el retorno" as *el re-torno*, a rewriting of the famous potter's wheel (*torno*) scene in the 1980s Hollywood drama *Ghost*, a film the protagonist mentions in passing.⁴⁸ Or read "Cécile Lamballe" as *ceci l'emballe*, "this wraps or covers it," which becomes all the more meaningful in light of Villeneuve's profession as "wrapper of bodies," as one might call a fashion designer. *Emballer* is also used colloquially for seducing, exciting, or making someone get onto a police car, all usages that multiply the possible readings of the story, whether Bolaño intended them or not. Further clues can be found when the narrator recounts how Villeneuve contemplates (his) corpse and presumably wonders about the hopes and desires that "had once agitated the contents of that plastic body bag."⁴⁹ Also in a thought-provoking passage from the morgue, before the mansion, is the following: "In life I was afraid of being a toy (or less than a toy) for Cécile, and now that I was dead, that fate, once the cause of my insomnia and pervasive insecurity, seemed sweet, and not without a certain grace [elegancia] and substance: the solidity of the real."⁵⁰

In the metaphorical sense of "being a toy for someone," the passage provides characterization of the timid narrator-protagonist, who remembers his lover as a femme fatale. She may even have been literally fatal, for all he knows, adding yet another layer, in more ways than one, to her enveloping last name. But the parenthesis is puzzling: something *less* than the animistic attachment of children to objects is hard to imagine. One reading is that Cécile, the imagined child in the metaphor, plays with him whenever she wants. Another points at a more elementary rapport between a living human and an inanimate object. Not coincidentally, the protagonist yearns for human touch, a common trope in ghost stories, foretelling the sexual acts to follow. I see here Bolaño using all the literary resources at his disposal to try to convey something that lies beyond words, a very primordial chiasm between language and world. Note the overall telos of this story, relevant for World Literature at large: toward the unassailable, uttermost, basic actuality of matter.

Abjection-Projection

The cult of youth and vitality in Bolaño has its heights in the exuberant literary movement at the onset of *The Savage Detectives*, which I have analyzed in detail elsewhere, and its abysses in the brutally murdered women in *2666*—lives, futures literally wasted.[51] It's a slow, violent arc from *real visceralismo*, as the movement is called, to scattered viscera; from "savagery" to savagery. A gargantuan, unfinished novel, *2666* is a grimly cosmopolitan affair, over a thousand pages in length, that transcends the lighthearted countercultural appeal of the not-quite-as-extensive, but still-very-sizable, six-hundred-odd-page earlier work. The two books share an antisystemic, political take on the World Literary transactions they depict—a scale model for a different Weltliteratur. Crucially, they focus on bodies desired, desiring: alive, dead, and everything in between.

Their open-ended main storylines revolve around a similar quest to find an imaginary author (dead or alive?): first Cesárea Tinajero, then Benno von Archimboldi, avatars of what Lacan would call *objet petit a*, a punctum for desire, impossible to satisfy. Both are worlding novels that sweep readers away to places as distant as Bersheeba, Cologne, Kostekino, and Managua, to name a few. African and especially Asian locales are less represented, because Bolaño's worldview is Latin America–centric and also, presumably, for verisimilitude, given how less common literary exchange between the regions has been until very recently. (A great number of events in his fiction take place in Western Europe, but this is also the case for Latin American literature at large: see Cortázar's *Hopscotch*.) Bolaño captures one form of the drive toward World Literature, which, first and foremost, he himself participates in—the quest for genius—and does something of a "bait and switch." In the earlier novel, the Mexican mother of all avant-garde poetry is finally found, but dies; in the posthumous novel, the German master of twentieth-century literature ultimately peters out. Bolaño did not have "world enough and time" to see himself become a missing author too.

There are five sections to 2666, each the length of a conventional novel, each entitled "The Part About" something in particular: "the Critics," "Amalfitano," "Fate," "the Crimes," and "Archimboldi." The first focuses on European literary scholars and provides the overall plot for the novel, the search to find Archimboldi, rumored to be in northern Mexico. The second leaves behind the scholars and focuses instead on the Chilean exile–philosophy professor who hosted them in Mexico, Óscar Amalfitano, and on his half-Spanish daughter, Rosa, who has a brush with death. The third focuses on the African American box journalist who ends up driving Rosa north, to the United States and safety from cartel-related sexual violence. The fourth leaves aside the increasingly distant transitive connections to Archimboldi, from his search party, to their acquaintances, to their acquaintances' acquaintances. It focuses, instead, on thinly fictionalized forensic reports of assassinated, mangled women, based on horrific real-life crimes committed along the border, who *could have been* Rosa. However, there are also enough hints that allow for a paranoid, demonic interpretation ("666"), according to which Archimboldi would somehow be behind all of the crimes. The fifth section dispels that impression, recounting the fictionalized biography of a writer who lived in the wake of World War II and bore many names. At the end, we are left with Archimboldi traveling to Mexico as an old, reclusive, famous writer, searching for his nephew, Klaus Haas, a brutally violent man introduced in the third section, who is nonetheless imprisoned on unsubstantiated charges.

This six-degrees-of-separation novel ultimately shows that, in an interconnected world, there is someone who knows someone and so on who knows a victim or a Nazi or a narco perpetrator. Then it asks the question of what is left of compassion or outrage across this long chain of missed connections, providing the probing ground for an ethics of globalization, a politics of World Literature, and vice versa. A growing scholarship on the novel has explored these issues.[52] Presently, I would like to underline that, if the long-winded premise of this irresolute novel has been able to move a generation of readers, it's because the common denominator is the body.

Consider, from "The Part About the Critics," the story of the Pakistani cab driver whom a Frenchman and a Spaniard, in the presence of an Englishwoman, beat "until he was unconscious and bleeding from every orifice in the head, except the eyes."[53] At this point in the novel, violence erupts to release narrative tension and let off steam from the characters' frustrations, notably the unrequited love of Liz Norton, the Englishwoman. The triggers are a rapid succession of translation-related misunderstandings: the passengers laugh at the driver's missing a Borgesian reference of London as labyrinth, which he takes as an insult to his taxi-driving skills, insulting them in turn after mistaking the trio's flirtations for proxenetism, or outright regarding them as such. To the credit of the novel's robust suspension of disbelief, readers find it not preposterous but terrifying when the aggressors, cosmopolitan scholars of literature, kick him once for Salman Rushdie, twice for Valérie Solanas, and so on. This open-ended parable thematizes the liberal West's tormented relations with Muslims—while kicking him, they ask the man to shove Islam up his ass—and gives expression to the political unconscious of World Literature. The setting, a long, protracted joke along the lines of "A Frenchman and a Spaniard enter a taxi," provides a Freudian return of the repressed in cosmopolitanism.

Competing for the love of Norton, whose last name not for nothing evokes the prominent anthology, condenses and displaces the quest for canonization that is the main theme in the first of five sections, "The Part About the Critics." Such a contest presents a rather grim view of the realpolitik of World Literature, which foretells the even darker, apocalyptic mood of the later "Part About the Crimes." Given the paratactical unfolding that is characteristic of Bolaño's prose, it is telling that the cabbie scene, a Borgesian Aleph rendered violent potlatch, sits roughly halfway between the petty politics of a literary congress and a more brutal beating of a different taxi driver in Mexico. Compare these two instances of violent exclusion, one implicit and institutionally sanctioned, the other explicit and symptomatic of utter institutional breakdown:

> On a last-minute whim, the organizers—the same people who'd left out contemporary Spanish and Polish and Swedish literature for lack of time or money—earmarked most of the funds to provide luxurious accommodations for the stars of English literature, and with the money left over they brought in three French novelists.[54]

At the entrance to the hotel, the two doormen were beating the taxi driver, who was on the ground. It wasn't a sustained attack. They might kick him four or six times, then stop and give him the chance to talk or go, but the taxi driver, doubled over, would open his mouth and swear at them, then another round of blows would follow.[55]

Beyond insinuating that conference organizers are white-glove hoodlums, Bolaño is sickening his readers into realizing the full weight of literary and political inequality. Against the grain of the predominantly celebratory discourse of World Literature revival, Bolaño cultivates a timely malaise. After the assault on the Pakistani man, Norton stops frequenting her devotees for a while, because she has to "think this over."[56] She could have denounced them, admitted some degree of complicity, or finally fallen in love with them, à la wisdom for Nietzsche, who infamously wrote that "[wisdom] is a woman and never loves anyone but a warrior."[57] Eventually, Norton, the Medusa-gazed anthology in this open-ended allegory, will wisely choose Morini, a decent suitor in a wheelchair (not a warrior), but not before travelling with the other two to Mexico, a place where numb doormen beat cab drivers to favor a certain taxi company over another. There she has a crisis in front of two mirrors, looking at herself, a woman like those women disappeared there.[58] It dawns on readers, on the one hand, that Western women's long-fought-for right to self-determination—even basic personal safety—is relatively rare on the world stage. On the other hand, one realizes that such inequalities are part of a broader and more complex state of affairs. As recent news demonstrates, lives lost to terrorist attacks on European soil are exponentially more telegenic than forty-three missing Ayotzinapa students or countless Syrian military "casualties." *2666* compels World Literature not to forget structural inequalities.

As a case in point, the cosmopolitan European academics in "The Part About the Critics" casually compare their lecturing at small university in northern Mexico to a massacre, and themselves to butchers, gutters, and disembowelers.[59] Fittingly, a few pages earlier, they are treated to barbecue:

> On the patio where the barbecue was being held they gazed at several smoke pits [múltiples agujeros humeantes]. The professors of the University of Santa Teresa displayed a rare talent for feats of country living . . . they dug up the barbecue, and a smell of meat and hot earth spread over the patio in

a thin curtain of smoke that enveloped them all like the fog that drifts before a murder, and vanished mysteriously as the women carried the plates to the table, leaving clothing and skin [las vestimentas y las pieles] impregnated with its aroma.[60]

The rapport between lecturing and murder is not causal, but neither is it casual. Their proximity in the plot is about allowing the stench of death to permeate all the seemingly impervious realms of culture. Two aspects bring this point home: the hyperaesthesia of women's "clothing and skin" impregnated with the smell of meat, and the poignant ambiguity of "piel" referring both to animal hide and to human skin. Speaking of home, it is there that European critics can return, waving their privileged passports the moment something starts to smell bad. Other legally sanctioned traveling bodies, in the broad spectrum of precariousness that is 2666, don't have it so easy. When Rosa and Fate—What's in a name?—are crossing the border into the United States at the end of the third part, a policeman sizes them up. They are an attractive woman and a black man. When the policeman learns from their travel documents that they are not Mexicans but Spanish and U.S. passport holders, "a shadow of frustration crossed [his] face."[61] The subtext here, a lesson in intersectionality, is that they cannot be messed with as much as they could be if they were Mexicans. They flee to safety, we are led to believe, while their travel companion, Mexico City journalist Guadalupe Roncal, goes on to interview Haas in prison. In a feverish dream of that prison, Fate thinks about the killings and hears "shouts, as if a bachelor party were being held in one of the prison chambers. . . . Distant laughter. Mooing."[62] Sounds and smells render northern Mexico a prison, the prison a slaughterhouse.

And then the novel plunges into the scattered atrocities of "The Part About the Crimes." The experience of reading this section of the novel is a multifarious succession of moral outrage, guilt by omission, morbid fascination, disgust, and anaesthesia. There is dread and ennui, as the book's epigraph (from Baudelaire's "Le Voyage") suggests: "An oasis of horror in a desert of boredom." An often unbearable, relatively plotless mass of corpse narratives dominates the section, as police, journalists, and bereaved family members try to make sense of mauled corpses. This is an exercise in purposely excessive, redundant storytelling that engages the book as an object. In the pre-internet, bygone era of analog communication, you could get a sense of how big a city was by holding its telephone directory in your hand. In something of a gothic reversal, you gain an awareness of the magnitude of femicide by starting to flip pages on the unbearable, still-fictional account provided by Bolaño. "Respite" is offered by disquieting stories from Haas's imprisonment and his time behind bars. The reader totters between assuming the roles of forensic detective and criminal defense lawyer. However, besides trying to discern means and motives, there is also, at a purely diegetic level, a question about how the events at hand connect to what came before, if at all—what even holds the novel together. Could Haas be the same diabolically tall German author? Only much later will we know this to be a red herring.

As it happens, there is a solar anus moment in the fourth section ("Crimes") that binds the seemingly disconnected fifth section ("Archimboldi") with the loose narrative thread that continues through the first three. A prison-hardened Haas gives exemplary punishment to El Anillo (ring or small anus) by introducing a knife blade, as a Brit might put it, up his arse:

> Haas took the shiv away from El Guajolote and told El Anillo to get down on all fours. If you don't move, cocksucker, nothing will happen. If you move or you're scared, you'll end up with two holes to shit from . . . Discipline, motherfucker, all I ask for is a little discipline and respect, said Haas as he stepped into the line of stalls. Then he kneeled behind El Anillo, whispered to him to spread his legs, and pushed in the shiv slowly all the way to the handle.[63]

While the forensic clues in desert corpses already speak to atrocity, this is the most graphic and violent moment up to this point in the novel: a sick scene of potty training. There is no returning to the merry gallops of Arturo Belano—a beautiful anus, a beautiful soul—after this. Things will arguably get worse, but this is the first occasion in which the pact of verisimilitude established earlier, with those gallantly perverse academic love stories, gives way to something so grim. Other than the damage inflicted upon the fellow inmate, it is the display of mastery and subordination that takes readers aback. This is all the more meaningful because, throughout Bolaño's oeuvre until this point, the anus has stood for something ostensibly more playful. The apocalyptic last novel is willing to expend even this. The solar economy of Bolaño's writing is expletive, hypergenerative: the name Haas ("hate" by homophony) remits to an earlier character, in *By*

Night in Chile, whose last name (Etah in English, Oido in Spanish) is an anagram for *hate*. Bolaño is cannibalizing his own motifs, driving them to exhaustion via compulsive *ars combinatoria*. In this decisive moment, fear touches the anus.

Worlding in Bolaño's writing is linked to anal fixation. In the monograph *Cosmopolitan Desires* (2014), Mariano Siskind has convincingly demonstrated that an urge to belong in global modernity has been a determinant factor in twentieth-century Latin American literature. Such cosmopolitan desire is also present in Bolaño, with two important qualifications: Bolaño complicates desire itself, notably through perversion, and speaks to the cosmopolitical rather than to the cosmopolitan. The Chilean, multinational author never allows his readers to forget that, on the world stage, some bodies matter more than others. Some make headlines, their lives celebrated; others die in anonymity. As Rosa Amalfitano puts it, commenting on the effectiveness of narco-assassins: "We're alive because we haven't seen anything and we don't know anything."[64] Bolaño reminds readers of their privilege and its precariousness, both conditions of possibility for the social practice of literature at a global level. Adorno asked the poignant question of whether there could be poetry after Auschwitz. Mutatis mutandis, the question here is: Can we talk about the travels of literature when the mobility of actual bodies is so regimented?

Bolaño's sexualization and abjectification of global literary transactions gives pause. Imagine a perfectly thorough sociology of worldwide literary cultures. A transnational team of scholars achieves a complete description of the social dynamics at festivals, publishing houses, bookstores, libraries, and so on—even their own collaboration. Could such a project account for the why of literature? The closest that Bolaño's oeuvre comes to answering that eternal question is by framing it in terms of desire and bodily engagement. It's the reason why his literati characters recurrently encounter various forms of eroticism, including perversions ranging from the kinky to the mass murderous. The defining testament is the drive to live and to survive, in literature as elsewhere. The unit of meaning is always an individual lifespan, contingent upon a body. Against the trend toward the autonomization, institutionalization, and professionalization of World Literature that underwrites literary encyclopedias, Bolaño constantly reminds us that fiction, and art more generally, is a fragile, heteronomous affair, embedded in lay forms of life.

If, pace Eco, above, we make lists out of fear of death, then what to make of a list of forensic reports, the urtext of "The Part About the Crimes"? As a list, it would provide comfort to readers, who contemplate from a safe distance, many times removed, much like museum goers experience the sublime painting of a harrowing storm at sea. But the contents of that list are horrendous, resulting in veritable commotion. The fictional peeling of layers of separation from horror builds the novel's suspense. This movement brings readers closer to the aweful corpse—in the etymological sense of "awe" as that which inspires reverential fear—and reveals the insurmountable distance from it, in a different metaphor, like a dolly zoom. I leave it to biographers to speculate on the import of Bolaño's writing about botched bodies (corpses) while his own was fatally failing him. There is, however, an obvious commitment to the cause. Bolaño dedicates what little life he may have left to writing the Juárez femicide into literary history. He does not know he is going to die so soon—an organ transplant was coming—and cannot anticipate the importance of his work—he is one of many talented contemporary Latin American authors writing on the subject. But he is willing to wager the entire solar economy of his oeuvre in telling that one story that is many stories. We read the following:

> According to the medical examiners, the cause of death was strangulation, with a fracture of the hyoid bone. Despite the body's state of decomposition, signs of battery with a blunt object were still evident about the head, hands, and legs. The victim had probably also been raped. As indicated by the fauna found on the body, the date of death was approximately the first or second week of February. There was nothing to identify the victim, although her particulars matched those of Guadalupe Guzmán Prieto, eleven years old, disappeared the evening of February 8, in Colonia San Bartolomé.[65]

A discarded corpse is a thing without history. But corpses, as forensic specialists and archeologists know well, tell stories. Bolaño, building upon such arts, tries to give the corpse *una historia*, in the double sense of "history" and "story." Someone else may have done things differently. Bolaño knew that the corpse of the character in the passage, Guadalupe Guzmán Prieto, corresponds in real life to Brenda Mejía Flores.[66] One could imagine, say, a documentary biopic that tried to piece the girl's life together, reach out to any acquaintances, give a face to a bigger tragedy, appeal for viewers to relate. Instead of questioning the subject-object divide or the irrepresentability of such horror, that hypothetical work would adopt the representation conventions of its day, turn the object into a subject inasmuch as possible, and hope for the best. Well, this is not the practice of *2666*, and someone could legitimately criticize it for this. The novel does try to singularize every victim on its pages in its own way. It dryly registers the impossibility of going any further, as in the case of unnamed corpses, but also, for the most part, chooses not to focalize on the bereaved families of named victims. Bolaño wants to get at the systemic, historical dimension of these deaths, while still doing his literature. Rather than shift registers or media (into activist filmmaking, in the counterfactual scenario), he incorporates the problem of representability at the metalevel and explores what happens to his anal craft of fiction when exposed to these events.

Meanwhile, World Literature deals with phenomena on a global scale, and of transnational historical significance, all the time. Whether tackling the expansion of the novel form across the continents or the transcultural resonances of epic, scholarly work is increasingly at home among networks and complex interconnections. At the same time, six women are assassinated in Mexico every day, which is already a staggering statistic, but the phenomenon is much larger worldwide: according to the UN, Mexico ranks sixteenth in the world in femicides.[67] Why shouldn't literary scholars, then, engage with something as significant, prevalent, rhizomatic, and urgent? One blasé answer would be that we are not activists, journalists, criminologists, or forensic experts. Neither is Bolaño, as we have seen, but he assimilates all four discourses to a significant extent, both in the research behind the novel and in the writing itself. Without ceasing to be a work of literary art, however narrowly we wish to construe one, *2666* stretches the limits of the novel form so as to rub against those other domains. The forensic hermeneutics in the passage above is a case in point: in a mise en abyme, coroners "read" cadaveric fauna for clues while readers do the same.

The embeddedness of "The Part About the Crimes" within *2666*, and within Bolaño's writing at large, provides an illustration of what it might mean to bank the future of World Literature on a search for justice, always the more pressing concern than global literary historiography. Bolaño is no social realist, and neither is the agenda for World Literature I advocate. More important than thematizing atrocious deeds, there is the question of what to do, not just in terms of advocacy: What needs to happen to form?

This is something critics can adapt and adopt for their own practice and methods, again, whether they are activist scholars or not. In my mind, a significant part of what distinguishes wordlit approaches is a certain transcendental condition: namely, that we write with a renewed awareness of the world, as if in the presence of more and less distant peers who have deeper knowledge of other traditions and languages. This chapter has been making the case to invigorate that awareness with the bodily: alive, suffering, dead. Writing literary history and engaging with the world should not be an either/or proposition, but neither are these poles easily bridged.

Bolaño's model is encapsulated in an image: a book Óscar Amalfitano hangs out to dry on a clothesline in the second section of the novel, at the mercy of the sandy winds of the Sonoran Desert—and of the smell of barbecue, one supposes. "It's a Duchamp idea," he explains, "leaving a geometry book hanging exposed to the elements to see if it learns something about real life."[68] The book is a work of poetry he acquired while in Europe, Rafael Dieste's *Testamento geométrico*, that he would have forgotten all about had there been a mugging, a car accident, or a "suicide in the subway" on his way home when he acquired it. In that case, he ruminates, "I would remember whatever had made me forget the *Testamento geométrico*."[69] Hanging the book is clearly a futile act, much like literature and the arts, coldly considered. Doing so either calms Amalfitano's nerves—he fears for his daughter—or evidences that he is unravelling. With this fictional ready-made, Bolaño situates creation at the crossroads of desperation and solace, escapism and commitment. A few lines down, Amalfitano fancies his "ideas or feelings or ramblings" (read *literature*), not unproblematically, as vicarious experience: they turn "the pain of others into memories of one's own."[70] Bolaño also impossibly approximates his pages to the stench of death. He does so with ample qualification, obviously, because something as banal as one's minor car accident can wipe the memory of reading about another's atrocity. This is a different formulation of the referentiality problem in World Literature, and again, no reason not to try to make words count.

Understatedly, as to avoid impossible comparison, 2666 traces an arc from genocide to femicide. Explicit mentions of the Shoah are scarce, but the novel evokes it through the Nazi barbarism that surrounds Hans Reiter, Archimboldi's given name. Bolaño may have drawn inspiration from Adorno and Horkheimer's *Dialectic of Enlightenment*, and certainly from their impulse to call into question the entirety of Western civilization in light of the horrors of their day. After a careful close reading of perpetrator rationale in Sade, they note: "The [purported] explanation for the hatred of woman as the weaker in mental and physical power, who bears the mark of domination on her brow, is the same as for the hatred of the Jews."[71] There is no room to do justice here to their very nuanced argument, but it is worth remembering that they regard anti-Semitism as an unfolding of the contradictions of Enlightenment thought, which they in turn seek to truly enlighten. If the comparison between Bolaño and Adorno and Horkheimer holds, then future readings of the novel will do well in looking for insights about the broad cultural dynamics that pave the way to femicide (of brown, impoverished, global factory workers in particular). As far as the present argument is concerned, the takeaway is that Bolaño's thrust to approximate the symbolic and the real, however impossible a task to complete, drives him all the way from Hollywoodesque necrophilia into facing a major social issue. It is a phenomenon whose comprehension, let alone resolution, still exceeds us. Bolaño writes the shortest, most modest global Latin American novel necessary to approximate the scale and world historical significance of its horror.

The feminicides in Juárez are an extreme case for the moral imagination, which struggles to understand suffering *at the same time* in its singularity and multiplicity, with one pole in the dialectic not eclipsing the other. In that regard alone it is akin to the Shoah, a singular horror that, nonetheless, unavoidably informs discussion of mass exterminations of a different scale.[72] In "The Part About Archimboldi," a verbose man who rents a typewriter to the writer—who has used for the first time his nom de plume during the transaction—muses over a cup of tea: "Jesus is the masterpiece. The thieves are minor works. Why are they there? Not to frame [realzar] the crucifixion, as some innocent souls believe, but to hide it."[73] The geometrical, symmetrical disposition of three crucified bodies asks us to take in from a distance, as an artistic composition, something that, up close, is ripped flesh and necrotized limbs. Christianism tries to repair the gap between individual and collective suffering, singularity and Church. Bolaño, via a base materialist negative theology, gives readers, instead, an open wound.

Form follows suit. So open-ended is "The Part About Archimboldi" that in the end it doesn't really matter who the lost author is.

Approaching its thousandth page, the novel disavows its own conceit. The section reads as that which comes after the end of the world: a long, barren epilogue. And yet it is rich in more ways than I can address here. It's worth noting that the solar economy is out of whack. There is a story within a story within a story, a third-level mise an abyme, of a peaceful indigenous tribe that turns violent when a Frenchman abruptly shakes one native's hand, presumably a grave offense. The native yells "dayiyi," which translates (note the double quotation marks) as " 'man who rapes me in the ass,' or 'cannibal who fucks me in the ass and then eats my body,' though it could also mean 'man who touches me (or rapes me) and stares me in the eyes (to eat my soul).' "[74] A made-up word, a third-hand parable, a parody of colonization, colonoscopy, and cultural difference: the combinatory possibilities of the anal motif have come to this. If the novel and the oeuvre were a body—a *corpus*—this body would already be decomposing.

And yet neither the novel nor Archimboldi is quite a body. While there were more bodies than names among the corpses of Juárez, the mysterious writer has more names than body. Né Hans Reiter, he "becomes" Benno von Archimboldi, is at one point thought to be identical to Klaus Haas, and even appears briefly in *The Savage Detectives* as J. M. G. Arcimboldi. The *von* particle confers nobility; the last name sounds Italian, though it is actually French Huguenot (38); the upbringing is German: this man seems to summon all the powers of European high culture combined. His notoriety largely exceeds his individual body; the corpses of "The Part About the Crimes" remain, despite the novel's efforts, an anonymous mass. The flesh to notability ratio speaks to a fundamental injustice that lives on in language. Cultural milestones are built, among other things, upon deficits of attention: some individual bodies are conferred inordinate amounts of attention, others hardly any.

There are two, complementary nonhuman allusions that reveal the kind of body that Archimboldi is, illustrate the peculiar proliferating structure that *2666* is, and, more broadly, emblematize the telos of Bolaño's unfinished oeuvre. One is the insistent and rather bewildering identification of Archimboldi with seaweed—*alga* in Spanish. Algae drift across national borders, multiply sexually and asexually, are essential to life. They aren't companion species and cannot be easily anthropomorphized in the imagination. Archimboldi's taking to the water creature befits his cold, saturnine, distant personality, his rootless cosmopolitanism. If previously he appeared as more than human, he now fancies himself as less or other than. After the horrors in the fourth section, and the horrors of World War II obliquely narrated in the fifth, *2666* renounces humanity. The Chinese character for algae, I learned serendipitously, is 藻, which is also the character for literary talent. This is the final ars poetica: Bolaño, who has been shown to write under the aegis of the constellation and the rhizome, turns in the last moment to the spore. Its "flesh"—the green, gooey stuff, inanimate and nurturing—is everywhere and nowhere: democratic, viscous, promiscuous, making sunlight breathable via photosynthesis. Autotrophs like algae, plants, and many bacteria produce their own sustenance from the environment. In other words, they have no need for an anus. The mind reels from imagining where Bolaño could have taken this premise. My suspicion is that, as in the present volume, the author saw the need to imbricate natural and human history.

And then there is the matter of Archimboldi's chosen name and its connection to the sixteenth-century Italian mannerist Giuseppe Arcimboldo, famous for making human likenesses out of nonhuman elements: the sometimes charming, sometimes disquieting trompe l'oeil faces made of flowers (spring), fruit (summer), and so on. Talented sci-fi ghostwriter Boris Ansky, a major inspiration for Archimboldi, sees in the painter "happiness personified" and "the end of semblances [apariencias]." Other than a celebration of the joyful vitality in Bolaño's multifariously composite writing, "end" here means both goal and interruption. "Apariencia" is more ambiguous: presence, fakery, apparition—as in a ghost. The word is also used for a theater curtain behind the theater curtain, revealed during a play for an effect of surprise. True to form, Ansky veers into an ekphrasis of the painting alternatively known as *The Cook* or *The Roast*. Happiness aside, he considers it a "horror painting":

> A reversible canvas that, hung one way, looked like a big metal platter of roast meats, including a suckling pig and a rabbit, with a pair of hands, probably a woman's or an adolescent's, trying to cover the meat so it won't get cold, and, hung the other way, showed the bust of a soldier, in helmet and armor, with a bold, satisfied smile missing some teeth, the terrible smile of an old mercenary who looks at you. . . . Everything in everything, writes Ansky. As if Arcimboldo had learned a single lesson, but one of vital importance.[75]

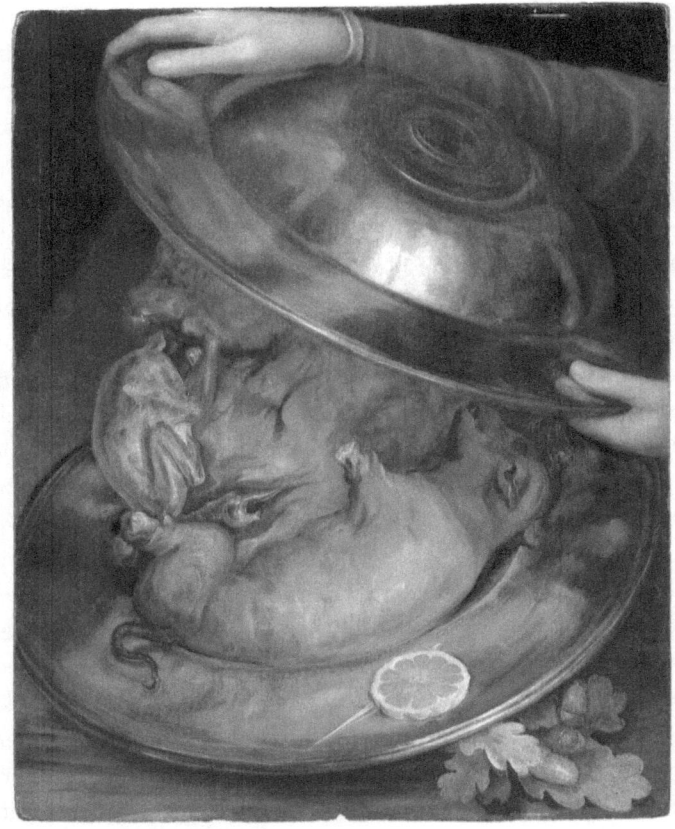

FIGURE 3.1 Giuseppe Arcimboldo, *The Cook*, 1570. Oil on panel, 53 × 41 cm. Nationalmuseum, Stockholm.

The above is an illustration of the painting's mirroring effect (figure 3.1) Bolaño is a maximalist. He works by overdetermination, accumulation, iteration. See here (smell) the Mexican barbecue; a ghost made of flesh—a corpse—popping up behind the theater curtain; Hans *Reiter*—writer, horseback rider—an impossible approximation of representation and referent; a topsy-turvy world; the intromission of war at home, of the military among civilians; surrealism—and *real visceralismo*—avant la lettre; a rumination on singularity and collectivity; the eerie proximity of "a woman or an adolescent's" living hand and the suckling pig's dead head;

Benjamin's dictum that "every document of civilization is a document of barbarism."[76] Archimboldi, the great, sought-after author, is purportedly an Event at a time when Authors are not really events anymore, when chasing them with blind humanist zeal or belletristic devotion is particularly inane, both in itself and in light of more pressing, terrible events. This is a contradiction Bolaño, and the present argument, must gingerly embrace. The only way not to overly spiritualize art and culture is to regard them as monuments of flesh.

The most famous sentence in the novel is as follows: "No one pays attention to these killings [in Juárez], but the secret of the world is hidden in them."[77] It would be a fool's errand to give a narrow interpretation to this ars poetica. Chris Andrews, Osvaldo Zavala, and others have pointed to the enormous economic forces unleashed along the border as the novel's real culprits;[78] Sergio González Ramírez, who wrote the original account (2002) of the dead that Bolaño overlays his fictional narrative upon, had already done so for the crimes themselves.[79] Be this as it may, one thing that is certain about this "secret" is its double etymology of things unsaid and of things *secreted*. *2666* confronts literary culture with its refuse. Meanwhile, Gloria Fisk remarks that World Literature "has worked historically to map the lines of inheritance—cultural and otherwise—that separate high from low, smart from dumb, timeless from temporary, haves from have-nots."[80] Bolaño's global Latin American novel, and the whole and hole of his oeuvre, work in the opposite direction.

There's More to Death Than This

Bolaño is not alone, among post-1989 writers, in confronting extreme forms of the abject. The Chilean is a distinguished figure among an accomplished group of contemporaries that haven't received the international recognition that earlier generations did in the wake of the 1959 Cuban revolution, yet continue to formulate some of the most daring aesthetic proposals in contemporary fiction. They come from all major subregions, each a nodal point for Latin American literature deserving of robust institutional attention: the Southern Cone, Brazil, the Andean region, the Greater Caribbean, Mexico and Central America, plus their connections to U.S. Latino and

Peninsular literatures. I am thinking of authors like the Colombian Evelio Rosero, the Argentine José Pablo Feinmann, the Chilean Diamela Eltit, the Guatemalans Rodrigo Rey Rosa and Eduardo Halfon.

For a brief overview, consider Rosero's *Los ejércitos* (2006; trans. *The Armies*, 2008), a jarringly musical portrayal of paramilitary violence in the Colombian backlands, which purposefully involves corpse abuse in ways unfit to describe here. The novel extends readers' capacity to take in the horror of history while remaining empathetic.[81] Or take Feinmann's light-hearted short story "Dieguito," where an idiot child by that name sews back together the corpse of global football icon Diego Armando Maradona. When his father asks him what he is up to, he explains: "Dieguito Armando Maradona."[82] It is a hysterically funny punchline if one is familiar with the uses and abuses of the Spanish gerund, as in *armando*: to assemble. Thought-provokingly, the abject figure may be synecdoche for Argentina. For her part, Eltit, an immensely influential figure whose translations into English unfortunately lag behind, has pegged her writing to the suffering real in numerous ways, resulting in dense, experimental works like *Impuesto a la carne* (2010). The title is already informative, wordplay for "a tax on meat" and "an imposition on the flesh."[83] Rey Rosa's *El material humano* (2009) fictionalizes Guatemala's criminology archives to produce a textured collage of past and present violence, while Halfon's short story "Han vuelto las aves" (2015), which I will revisit in the conclusions of this book, subtly hints at the corpse of an assassinated community leader, via negativa, by dwelling on the overgrown coffee plants left behind in the family plot.[84]

Even works that deal with the living body describe it in forensic detail, in several registers, from the sophisticated exercise in fictionalized autobiography in the Mexican Guadalupe Nettel's *The Body Where I Was Born* (2011) and in her countrywoman Valeria Luiselli's *The Story of My Teeth* (2014) to the scandalously masculinist "dirty realism" of the Cuban Pedro Juan Gutiérrez, of *Tropical Animal* (2000) repute.[85] It is not unfair to say that the lead characters in each of these books is defined, respectively, by one body part: an eye, teeth, the penis. For dying, as opposed to dead bodies, look no further than the epoch-defining novel of the 1990s, Mario Bellatin's *Beauty Salon*, which deals with a decommissioned salon turned into a *moridero*: a place where marginalized subjects go to die from an unnamed sexually-transmitted illness.

Meanwhile, honorary Latin American writer Patti Smith, a well-known punk rocker and memoirist, dedicated her hundred-verse, stanzaless poem "Hecatomb" to Roberto Bolaño. (She has also championed the Argentine César Aira on numerous occasions.) A few relevant lines include the following: "A poet's coat is skin"; "A poem of perpetual death / Trumping the Greeks / In the precinct of the muse."[86] Smith is clearly ruminating on the corpses of Juárez's women, fictionalized in Bolaño's Santa Teresa ("a city shaped like a dress"), and on the author's reputation, which caught like wildfire after his death ("we the worthless / unsolicited revelators / cash in our chips"). Lest anyone think that an orientation toward the corpse is all about macabre realism, Colombian draughtsman José Antonio Suárez, in a beautifully illustrated 2013 booklet by Medellín's Ediciones SML, re-edited in 2015 by Bogotá's La Casa del Doctor and Cologne's Walther König, renders the sacrifice of one hundred oxen in the poem as brightly colored, deceivingly naive iterations of pierced cattle. Both Suárez and Smith take something from the playbook of Roberto Bolaño: the slow building up of a sensibility toward human "flesh" by way of "meat." Through his sister, Suárez quite understandably declined to grant reproduction rights for the auratic drawings in this very singular art book: picture a white cow midair against a textured gray backdrop—dark sky or rising mud?

If the return of World Literature has arguably been dominated by the visionary, idealist tenet of Don Quixote, the present chapter has emphasized down-to-earth, materialist Sancho Panza. "Panza" means "belly" and stands for irreducible corporeality. Even the most materialist of thinkers shy away from fully considering literature in this embodied way. We read, as part of the brief reflection on *Weltliteratur* in the *Communist Manifesto*, that as international commerce expands, the "spiritual products" of individual nations become "common property": *Gemeingut*.[87] Corpse narratives put the gut back into *Gemeingut*, pun intended. Translation, a sine qua non of World Literature Marx and Engels neglect, entails more than the accumulation of capital and meaning. There is also the potential for their dispersion and disruption—hence my projecting Gregory L. Ulmer's notion of the "puncept" across languages.[88] Transnational literary relevance cannot be entirely scripted, cultural hegemonies notwithstanding. World Literature as dynamic principle gains with the realization that ideas are, in one way or the other, bound to actual bodies. This does not entail reducing literature to goods, as the humanist may fear, or neglecting the commercial aspects of circulation and copyright, so prominent in the Frankfurt or Guadalajara book fairs. It is rather a call to setting ideas in conversation with the corporeal, including the surfaces, membranes, and contact zones where transaction takes place.

The narrativization of corpses provides a bridge between the agency of language and the agency of (other) matter. The words "corpse" and "meat" have an almost totemic quality: they prescribe a differentiated behavior between human and nonhuman animals and their remains. Denaturalizing the use of such terms can have powerful effects. It would be callous to refer to a loved one's corpse as "corpse"—let alone "meat"! There one would rely on an impossible possessive, saying "her" and "his" *body*, although bodies must be alive to merit the name, and ownership too requires life. The abject and its misnomers bring us closer to humanity in a nonhumanist sense: rather than exceptionality from the rest of nature, they underscore the continuity. It is safe to generalize that World Literature, an influential trend among several, has been overly humanist. Meanwhile, other contemporary trends are markedly postanthropocentric, be they animal studies, new materialism, posthumanism, and so on. It is time to have these trends bear upon each other.

For one, Rosendahl Thomsen's *The New Human in Literature* (2014) has done so persuasively regarding the thematization of posthuman topics—prosthetics, living longer lives, and so on. Through readings of Woolf, Achebe, Céline, DeLillo, and others, the study makes an eloquent case for how literature can contribute to thinking critically about biomedical innovation, and conversely, how modern science can inform hermeneutic practices.[89] However, the more fundamental question of the relationship between world and language, and therefore literature, holds. The same is true of Vilashini Cooppan's timely proposal for a nonlinear history of World Literature, understood as nonhierarchical description of the phenomenon as networked flow. My proposal supplements, rather than contradicts, the latter approach, albeit with a different approach to death, which she addresses via Friedrich Kittler.[90] Where she notes that all books are books of the dead, I would—and the difference, as we have seen, is not negligible—emphasize that they are books of the corpse.

Cheah has warned us against the "teleology of the concept," a trait of Hegelian Eurocentrism. As he puts it, "As spirit, the concept develops itself by externalizing itself in the sphere of objective existence that is other to it."[91]

A spiritualist telos for World Literature would see its job accomplished when the world becomes legible to itself at the level of abstraction, as if the word "corpse" could produce the same impact that contemplating one such *human thing* does. Leaving the institutional project of World Literature with no clear sense of direction, as purposeless enthusiasm, opens the door for the prevailing ideologies of the present to determine the whole enterprise. The productive dispersion of attention, blindly exclusionary ecumenism, over-professionalization, and trickle-down economies of cultural prestige rank high on the list of teloi this would impose. Instead, we could take a closer look at the soil under our feet. My interest in corpse narratives falls within transcultural materialism and its efforts to blur the line between nature and culture. World Literature has yet to assimilate how much of the world is *not* human; the abject, in its liminality, is a useful starting point. Only then can we return to the corpse's Other: the youthful living body, protean like algae or bound like our own, whose preservation and plenitude inform our practice as necessary condition and indispensable, if ultimately unfulfillable, goal.

Deconstruction and poststructuralism saw each word as a potential pun, its disseminating energy waiting to be liberated. Building on corpse narratives, a subtext to this chapter has been a similar attempt in regard to "World Literature." All permutations are welcome: world and literature, world or literature, war literature, worm literature—iteratur. Such errancies will bring us closer to the real than reifying the notion would. Contemporary Latin American literature, a fascinating field of study that increasingly welcomes global readers through better, timelier translations, bears this out. Let the literatures of the world theorize, as they are theorized upon. Just temper Goethe's haste and its teleology of progress with a dialectical, paradoxical image, one that Bolaño brings to the table on several occasions, namely, "los grandes cementerios a la velocidad de la luz" (the great cemeteries at light speed).[92]

PART TWO

Assemblages

CHAPTER FOUR

Politics and Praxis of Hyperfetishism

Philosophers and political theorists often confine literature to serve as illustration to their ideas. That literature qua literature could think through specific issues seems counterintuitive, because interpretation is indispensable for such thinking to emerge. At the same time, the new materialist turn of the last few decades, which decenters the human as object of study, has no qualm with appreciating the agentic properties of, say, a hammer. And yet the object has to be banged with to *do* something. Mutatis mutandis, books, by way of their sheer semantic density, and by nudging readers in various ways, *do*. Note I do not say texts, or works, or authorial intentions, but point at the material substratum of a series of practices.

Examples of nudging include reminding us of the presence of an author or work we have familiarity with, but have not quite read—*Don Quixote*, *The Complete Works of Shakespeare*— or serving as cumbersome affective binds to our earlier selves—via adolescent readings of Herman Hesse, Andrés Caicedo, or Arthur Rimbaud. Books prefigure interpretation like a hammer prefigures banging. There are many things one may do with one or the other, but some behaviors are more commonly scripted than others, and the habit of using books or hammers to, say, swat flies, has not really taken on.[1] Nor has regarding *Madame Bovary* as illustration of Maya astronomy or the *Popol Vuh* as a critique of social mores in nineteenth-century France. Someone might object that in this last claim I have shifted from the physical properties of books to their spiritual qualities, their cultural belonging, or the "reception" (What's in a metaphor?) of the stories they "contain" (ditto). Alas, I am a monist, and find that such elements are contiguous, not parallel. Another likely objection is that I seem to leave e-books out of the party, and indeed I do: e-books are no more books than smartphones are telephones, friending someone on Facebook is making a friend, or Amazon is a bookstore. Thinking otherwise is falling prey to ideology. Short of a perspicuous description of the agentic entanglements of a given book, a task I hereby entrust to abler hands, this chapter exposes the conceptual purchase of a selected corpus of books—and, yes, their stories—in affecting our basic rapport with other things.

I understand this domain as always already mediated by the social, but not reducible to it. From part 1, you may already recognize the Scylla and Charybdis that flank my navigation as historical and new materialism. The former, in the Marxist tradition, seeks to denounce the social relations that magically endowed things, such as luxury items or privately owned land, hide from view. The latter, in the more recent Latourian vein, suspends social systemic analysis, or carries it out only in piece-meal fashion. It focuses on the agency of things while eclipsing the question of social relations, particularly of labor. One seeks to debunk an order of things by demonstrating its arbitrariness; the other assumes it as its starting point and intervenes within it through thought-provoking accounts of the techno-social. As discussed in chapter 2, Rita Felski pits one against the other, favoring the latter; I do not so much reconcile them as offer a third position, consonant with transcultural materialism. I am reminded once again of how Borges shattered Foucault's mental schemes, and seek, in the present chapter, to bring about a similar effect in relation to objects whose exchange value eclipses their use value—in a word, commodities.

My focus is one instance of transcultural materialist intervention, namely, the practice of hyperfetishism. I call "hyperfetishism" an exacerbation of commodity fetishism that disrupts unreflective ways of relating to objects without reducing them to abstractions. Where cultural critics traditionally unmask, hyperfetishists play along so thoroughly with the masquerade that the artifice is revealed and transformed by way of excess. As we shall see, this allows them to chart something of a middle path between social critique and descriptive analysis. The elucidation that ensues contributes to one of the present volume's central goals, that of examining the ways in which contemporary Latin American literature allows us to better grasp the notion of human-nonhuman history. Whereas part 1 of this book dealt with basic things—food staples, rubber, earth, atoms, corpses—part 2 addresses more complex assemblages—hyperfetishes in the present chapter and digitalia in the following. Complexity here is less about physics than about economics: small, constitutive elements are already plenty complex (the atom whirls with fermions and bosons), and some highly prized commodities are strikingly simple (a purse, say). The primary difference I want to emphasize in this chapter is not one of scale but one of escalation in added value. On the other hand, chapter 5 will look at instances where the market does reward mastery over physical complexity, as in chip manufacturing and quantum computing—nothing is outside the purview of literature.

Three sections follow. First, I further define the concept of hyperfetishism by opposition to Marx's original coinage. Then I discuss works that successfully carry out this operation: the Colombian José Asunción Silva's 1925 posthumous fin de siècle novel *De sobremesa* (*After-Dinner Conversation*); his countryman Fernando Vallejo's works, which build a natural bridge between the nineteenth century and the present, notably his 1995 fictionalized biography of Silva, *Almas en pena, chapolas negras*, and his more recent novel *Casablanca la bella* (2014). Third, I elaborate on the broader methodological implications with a consideration of the Mexican Margo Glantz's mordant *Historia de una mujer que caminó por la vida con zapatos de diseñador* (2005) and her countrywoman Daniela Rossell's photographic essay *Ricas y famosas* (1999–2002).

The Case for Exacerbation

I find primitive accumulation and commodity fetishism particularly useful categories for contemporary criticism. The former has provided a subtext to the chapters above, as it informs my analyses of tobacco, sugar, food, soil, subatomic particles, and the body (corpse) in literature. Rather than apply Marx, I have engaged in the critique of value, complementing it with findings from new materialism and Latin American culture. As I now turn to commodity fetishism, I am mindful that, as with primitive accumulation, some adaptation and recontextualization are in order. Accumulation and fetishism will overlap in my discussion of digital technology, as they do in such gadgets themselves—but that is the subject of the next chapter. For now, although they do occasionally intersect, the focus is the fetish.

Marx defines commodity fetishism as when "the relationships between the producers, within which the social characteristics of their labours are manifested, take on the form of a social relation between the products of labour."[2] It's a things-are-not-as-they-appear kind of argument. We are under the illusion that transactions revolve around objects, and not the other way around. We forget or fail to appreciate the social relations that are indispensable for something to emerge as a coveted good. Belonging to the often-cited first section of *Capital* (1867), volume 1, commodity fetishism has received ample attention.[3] In terms of exposition, even pedagogy, it comes before primitive accumulation, discussed only until the eighth section of the volume. (Conceptually and historically, primitive accumulation comes first, which is the reason why I have engaged with primitive accumulation earlier.) The persuasive power of Marx's conceptualization of commodity fetishism rests, I contend, on two things: a simple fact—typical consumers do ignore most things about production—and a thought-provoking reconceptualization of what constitutes fantasy and what constitutes reality. Fantasy is, of course, a literary category. Given the important role it plays in this crucial step of Marxist dialectics, closer examination is necessary.

Picture the most coveted commodity: the car of one's dreams, the rarest of perfumes, the latest iPhone. For Marx, it seems, the surprising attachment to such things is the fantasy—a dream one can wake up from. The *reality* is the complex interplay of supply chains, factories, marketing, and especially the labor and social relations that bring about commodities. Capitalism is predicated upon *fantasies*: you do not really need that car, perfume, or gizmo; social relations that appear reified could always be otherwise. That said, fake needs (luxury) become about as pressing as real ones (shelter, food); social structures are most arduous to transform. If only we could debunk those myths, Marx thinks, in the same way that we have cleared "the misty realm of religion."[4] Religion has turned out more resilient than Marx (or Nietzsche) anticipated: the mist lingers at noon. Leaving aside the question of whether the parallelism between religion and capitalism is entirely adequate, I think Marx is significantly wrong about fantasy and moderately wrong about commodities. The most thorough exposition of the social relations involved in the design, assembly, and commercialization of the car of one's dreams will hardly sway the infatuated buyer. The commodity is both real and fantastic—a point Marx would concede—but in a different fashion as he claims it to be.

The first of these objections is already present in Benjamin's "Capitalism as Religion" (1921). There he couches capitalism as a "purely cultic religion" that "creates guilt [Schuld], not atonement."[5] One difference with Marx is the insistence on the "permanence" and self-sustaining structure of this religion. Guilt or debt here are harder to shake or "wake up" from. The fantasy is not the kind that dispels easily. Marx was certainly aware of this, otherwise he would not have taken the trouble of writing so extensively against it—approximating organized religion and economic system is a partly rhetorical move. However, the opposition of reality and fantasy is compromised, long before Althusser would complicate things with the notion of ideological state apparatuses. By the looks of the looming 2020s, the cult is not only strong, but the lines between reality and fantasy are as blurred as ever. My position in this debate has to do with the truism that a rhetorical move is never just rhetorical: it causes an effect. Marx's treatment of fantasy in these influential, indeed foundational pages has the regrettable consequence of siding fantasy with capitalism and untruth, versus reality—or realism?—socialism, and truth. This forecloses a promising path: looking for truth in fantasy. Not just as representation or thematization of utopian alternatives (the past most taken) but, as I will illustrate in the next section, as something that may outright affect commodity fetishism—counter cultish practices with different chants, to borrow Benjamin's metaphor.

The second objection has to do with another questionable separation in *Capital*. Marx strives to be both materialist and analytic: sometimes the latter gets in the way of the former. And so he separates things that belong together, unwittingly becoming an idealist. Read the following under that light: "The existence of the things quâ commodities, and the value relations between the products of labour which stamps them as commodities, have absolutely no connection with their physical properties and with the material relations arising therefrom."[6] My quibble is with the "absolutely no connection" part, which hinges upon a strategic and unmaterialist use of the particle "quâ." Marx is free to define his terms anyway he wants, and he can distinguish a commodity from a thing even while he is pointing at the same object. But this is a slippery slope to dualism and spiritualism. From a certain perspective, a Louis Vuitton bag is a thing like a fishnet is a thing; from another, a commodity like an emerald ring is a commodity. Some objects are endowed with the soul of value—*and this is in no way material.*

In the interest of questioning the relatively arbitrary connection between thing and value, Marx is being arbitrary himself. "So far no chemist has ever discovered exchange value either in a pearl or a diamond" he notes triumphantly, to claim that nothing intrinsic makes these things tradeable. (Here Marx is rebutting the classic economic theories of British economist-philosophers Walter Bailey and David Ricardo.) But is this so? For pearls, yes, but diamonds are notoriously scarce and cut through nearly everything. They may not exist *for* humans, but they are very useful to them and consequently prescribe human behavior—as quasi subjects with agentic properties, a new materialist might say. The existence of things qua commodities will happen, as will any existence, in connection with physical properties and material relations, even if value is not reducible to immediate interactions with an object or to its constitutive elements.

To recapitulate, fantasy and the imagination don't quite work the way Marx envisages it; commodities are never just commodities, not even at a "purely conceptual" or physical level. There is much to gain from parsing out the material entanglements of objects and their roles in the creation of value. But affecting them is the point, as per the eleventh thesis on Feuerbach, from 1845: "Philosophers have hitherto only *interpreted* the world in various ways; the point is to *change* it."[7] A performative contradiction that has been pointed out several times is that Marx remains a philosopher when he utters this. However, arguably the theses do change the world, as they affect ways of thinking. Regardless, one can hold Marx to his own standard, as set forth in the earlier piece, of breaking with old, contemplative materialism (*anscheuende Materialismus*), which I think lurks behind this radical separation of commodity and thing. Adopting, adapting the notion of commodity fetishism for still newer materialisms calls for the revision of the role of fantasy, simply put, from foe to ally. "We fail to see in these articles the material receptacles of homogeneous human labor," notes Marx, concerned that we measure commodities by the fascination they produce and not by the actual work involved in them.[8] Fantasy can expose, not just mask, that process. An added benefit is not reducing object agency, in anthropocentric fashion, to human labor—as important as it is.

Paradoxically, Marx himself anticipates this move. For a work that denounces the fascination with commodities as fantasy, *Capital* draws quite liberally from it. To demonstrate how articles are mere receptacles, Marx treats them as anything but. Note his rhetorical use of personification:

> If commodities could speak, they would say this: our use-value may interest men, but it does not belong to us as objects. What does belong to us as objects, however, is our value. Our own intercourse [Verkehr] as commodities proves it. We relate to each other merely as exchange-values.[9]

This fascinating thought experiment is predicated on the separation of object and commodity—two facets of the same thing. Taking the experiment further: wouldn't the object have a hard time speaking "just as" commodity? A uniformed employee can speak as a private person when in plain clothes. But it is less apparent what an object must shed to speak exclusively as one of its facets. Here it wears the mantle of exchange value; there it doesn't. The point is that neither use nor value are intrinsic to the thing—both stem from its interaction with humans. Value is what defines a commodity, and value is brought about by social relations. This is all well and good, but what is the status of fantasy, then? There would be an unsound fantasy of seeing the extrinsic properties of an article as intrinsic, but there would also be a corrective, sound fantasy of extrication—as if value somehow could, after all, alter the chemical properties of a thing. And so the opposition wouldn't be between reality and fantasy but between fantasies that measure up to the reality of the social constructedness of value. Marx is having it both ways at this point in the book, denouncing fantasy *and* enlisting its services (he also cites *Much Ado About Nothing* and *Robinson Crusoe*.)[10] *Capital* will ultimately continue in the vein of social realism, turning away from such flights of fancy and toward scientificism, preferring equations over metaphors. However, one takeaway for present purposes, consonant with what has been established throughout this study, is the effective role of storytelling in reformulating our relationship to things, valuable and otherwise.

Another takeaway has to do with the broader task of articulating historical and new materialisms. The entire argument of *Capital* hinges upon the distinction of use and exchange value established thanks to the notion of commodity fetishism. Revisiting that notion could have significant consequences for the whole edifice. I don't think there's anything particularly wrong about it, and am not intent in bringing the edifice down, but I would suggest two actualizations. One is to make room for less inert things. This is something of an urgent task. Marx takes issue with money, the great equalizer, for being the all-powerful stand-in for all things. But he does proceed to analyze the political economy of money, leaving aside, as capitalism does, the specifics of things. (If they are cherished, like a family heirloom is, this is but an expression of exchange value—someone might be willing to pay a lot of money for a certain chair, and not any other, because a late parent used to sit on it.) In chapter 2, on "exchange," Marx closes the window of opportunity that personification, or outright animism, had opened at the end of chapter 1, on the commodity. He starts by dismissing the fantasy of speaking commodities:

> Commodities cannot themselves go to market and perform exchanges in their own right. We must, therefore, have recourse to their *guardians*, who are the *possessors* of commodities. Commodities are things, and therefore *lack the power to resist* man. If they are *unwilling*, he can use force; in other words, he can take possession of them. In order that these objects may enter into relation with each other as commodities, their guardians must place themselves in relation to one another *as persons whose will resides in those objects*, and must behave in such a way that each does not appropriate the commodity of the other, and alienate his own, except through an act to which both parties *consent*.[11]

Am I the only one to read here a form of eroticism? We are, after all, referring to intercourse [Verkehr]. I have emphasized word choices that speak to a triangular desire; in René Girard's parlance, we desire what we think the other desires.[12] But the other here is seemingly inert: humans wanting what the object wants. "Docility" is both reading too much (an unnecessary catexis) and too little (a misrecognition of agentiality) into things. Marx abandons the more upbeat animist fantasy via an understatedly sadist one. From receptacles of labor to receptacles of will, things must be reined in, punished. Surely, Marx wants to question the instrumentalization of things by capitalism, but he participates in that process all the same. These days, commodities quite literally do make exchanges of their own account, given the rise of algorithmic trading and artificial intelligence in the stock exchange.[13] But long before that development, which no nineteenth-century thinker could have anticipated, there is the underlying arbitrariness of *possessing things*. Marx will famously debunk private property, but not that basic fantasy. The one-way street of possession, with a clear subject and a clear object, was already questioned by the Latin proverb *Qui capit, capitur*: "The one who owns is owned." Marx was surely aware. In this book, I have referred to coevolution and pointed out how domestication is a two-way street. An interesting kindred path to explore, in a revisionist reading of *Capital*, would be to go beyond object masochism.

The other actualization of Marx, which I shall delve into in what follows, is to consider commodity fetishism as one fantasy among several possible fantasies that "negotiate," for lack of a better term, our relationship to things. If the fraught opposition of real-social and fantastic-object relations gives way, an alternative emerges: commodity hyperfetishism. Marx anticipates it, as noted, but quickly disavows it. Instead of waking up from the fetish, the gist of this operation is to dwell on it, that is, to follow the fetish to its final consequences. Note that, although I have alluded to sensuousness, I am not thinking of fetishism à la Freud or Sacher-Masoch. There is plenty of eroticism, already, in coveting a luxury good—in wanting what the thing wants. After faltering somewhat, *Capital* opts for deflating the fascination with things endowed with magic properties that obscure the fact of labor. However, that fact would emerge all the more clearly through the exacerbation of that desire, without overly instrumentalizing things or reducing them to exchange value.

Commodities Speak!

Although *modernismo*—the art-for-art's-sake fin de siècle movement that cemented Spanish American cultural autonomy—is often associated with the great Nicaraguan poet-diplomat Rubén Darío (1867–1916), the phenomenon left a deep impression in Colombia.[14] A case in point is the early verses of one José Eustasio Rivera, before his turning to *La vorágine*, or the musings of that novel's autobiographical protagonist, Arturo Cova. But the figure that most keenly represents the movement's ethos and pathos in the country is the poet and novelist José Asunción Silva (1865–1896). Silva left behind a blazing trail of writing despite dying, at age thirty-one, of a self-inflicted gunshot to the heart.[15] Like his more illustrious contemporary, Karl Marx, Silva toys with the idea of letting things speak. His poem "La voz de las cosas," published posthumously in 1908, illustrates key aspects of commodity hyperfetishism. (As noted in chapter 1, Rivera's secondary character, Clemente Silva—What's in a name?—borrows the phrase.) Under the title "The Voice of Things," Silva presents two eight-verse, rhythmic, rhyming stanzas *about the impossibility* of capturing the voice of things in verse. The refrain insists on the conditional: "if my stanzas could lock you in"; "if verse could imprison you."[16] Variations of the refrain appear, symmetrically, at the onset and demise of each individual stanza, as if containing the inventory of things in the six remaining "internal" verses. In the first stanza, this inventory includes Silvana—things readers associate with the melancholy writer—like a withering flower, a ray of moonlight, or a warm May breeze. The second raises the ante, attempting to capture more aethereal things, like feverish dreams, ghosts, or a kiss—a fleshy event rendered spiritual by proximity.

It is a testament to the lopsidedness of cultural flows that my version below is, to my knowledge, the very first English translation in print of this remarkable work—and a very hesitant one at that:

> If I locked you into my stanzas
> brittle smiling things
> pale lily shedding your leaves,
> moonray over a tapestry
> of moist flowers, and green leaves
> blooming to May's warm breath;
> If I locked you into my stanzas,
> Pale smiling things!
>
> If verse could hold you prisoner,
> gray ghosts, when drifting,
> fickle contours of the Universe,
> baffling dreams, beings gone,
> an osculation sad, soft and perverse
> to the soul amid the shadows
> If verse could hold you prisoner
> gray drifting ghosts![17]

From its title onward, the poem calls into question the difference between a thing and a person. I made a number of translation decisions to convey this and to foreground the contributions of "The Voice of Things" for the notion of commodity hyperfetishism. Obviously, my rhyme is less consistent. An unforeseen alliteration, gray ghosts, emerged in the process, a modest compensation for lost musicality. I replaced an iterating relative clause in Spanish (*que sonreís, que te deshojas*, etc.), which can refer to a thing or a person, with the present progressive. I did so to preserve some of the cadence without rendering the original repetitive, but also because such clauses are arguably less common in English-language poetry. Moreover, relative clauses in English unambiguously refer to a thing (that-plus-verb) *or* a person (who-plus-verb). I preserved "osculation" to match Silva's equivalent choice, already a cultism in the nineteenth century. "Kiss" (beso) was always an option, then and now, but it is important, for the poem's gradual unveiling, that the consummation of love remain somewhat elusive. Who-kisses-what and what-kisses-whom remain open questions, as the painful memory of a blissful spring haunts the second stanza. This befits the blurring of the subject-object, living-dead divides in the poem.

Who speaks? The poetic voice can be attributed to a mournful lover, to a thing, to the month of May, to the universe, to a ghost. It's tempting to point in the latter direction, as the death of Silva's sister, Elvira, is a leitmotif in his late poetry, notably in "Nocturno III"—a staple of Spanish-language poetry anthologies. But grief here engulfs all things transient, which is all things. The tangible is ghostly, and vice versa. A universe as brittle as a withering flower is *almost* saved by *less than* a kiss. Words remain contained in the poem, despite aspirations to the contrary. The author himself, as the contemporary Colombian poet Juan Manuel Roca suggests in a perceptive essay, *becomes* the voice of things.[18] In a sense, all that is left of Silva, and of his beloved sister, is a perverse (incestuous?) grave in the Central Cemetery of Bogotá (figure 4.1). Anticipating the poet's death, however, the poem speaks as if from the great beyond. A failed reliquary, it rekindles a profound sense of doubt about the limits and contours of the subject—and, pace Roca, of the object: "a dubitation in the face of the simplest things."[19] Cartesian rationalism is built upon "methodical" doubt, but all too swiftly overcomes it, parsing out the cogito from the res extensa. Silva's pure, profane love for a ghost, regardless of biographical speculation about incest proper, does celebrate an unnatural marriage of soul and object, voice and deed.

154 ◾ **Assemblages**

FIGURE 4.1 Tombstone of José Asunción Silva and Elvira Silva, Central Cemetery, Bogotá.
Courtesy of Cristian Felipe Soler, 2018.

Commodity hyperfetishism, like the poem, upsets our relation to things. It is not exactly a rational strategy, but neither is our attachment to luxury goods and coveted items. Marx thought he could reason his way out of fascination; the likes of Silva plunge ever deeper into it. Any elucidation the latter may provide requires reading between the lines. A crucial feature is the role of form: what we learn cannot be parsed out from literary structure or artistic convention. It wouldn't be "all the same" had Silva chosen to compose, instead, an essay in phenomenology or a still-life painting. (Affinities exist.) Part of what makes the poem compelling is the rich tension between the what and the how, between the substance of substance and its transformation into poetic language. Someone might object that commodities, the kind one trades, are not mentioned in the poem: only things tout court. While this is the case, "tapestry" in the fourth verse leads to a puzzling enjambment that, for the following verse at least, reads both literally as an indoors space with an ornate tapestry or figuratively as an outdoors space with a blooming field. A third possibility emerges, quasi-surrealistically, of a blooming carpet. If I don't discard the latter interpretation, and read commodities into a poem about the voice of things, it's because Silva's work is known to frequent animism.

A case in point is the famous opening to Silva's sui generis novel, *After-Dinner Conversation* (*De sobremesa*, 1925).[20] He rewrote the considerable work, having lost the manuscript to shipwreck in 1895, a year before taking his life. (There are various reasons, as we'll continue to see, for Silva to cherish lost things.) I cite Kelly Washbourne's professional translation:

> Secluded by the shade of gauze and lace, the warm light of the lamp fell in a circle over the crimson velvet of the tablecloth, and as it lit up the three china cups, which were golden in the bottom from the traces of thick coffee, and a cut-crystal bottle full of transparent liqueur shining with gold particles, it left the rest of the large and silent chamber awash in a gloomy purple semidarkness, the effect of the cast of the carpet, the tapestries, and the wall hangings.[21]

Three similar paragraphs follow, with light bouncing off and diffusing from candlesticks, engravings, a piano, crossed swords over a shield, and so on. Cigarette smoke introduces cigarettes, cigarettes introduce hands, and only by the fifth paragraph do the hands introduce silhouettes and short descriptions of characters. "Some after-dinner conversation *this* is!" notes one such character, Juan Rovira, in the sixth paragraph, as if breaking a spell. "We've been as silent as three corpses for half an hour."[22] The conversation has been going on, one could say, among things—it's an animated party, so to speak. As unconventional as this opening gambit is, it does achieve a straightforward, conventional characterization of the protagonist, José Fernández, a rich Colombian parvenu who will recount his European travels in the mise en abyme that follows. (His dandyish sejour in the Old World is all about acquisition, refinement, and exoticized love.) Again, form is indispensable.

Had Karl Marx confronted this lengthy description, he might have noted that china cups are made by, well, Chinese craftsmen, cut-crystal by Bohemian, and so forth. Transnational networks of commerce and patronage make possible this flight of fancy. It's all invisible to the bourgeois, whereas commodities are front and center. The coffee they sip—after a lavish meal furnished by servants, one may safely presume—titillates the taste buds and contributes aroma to the general ambiance. The highland campesinos that produce it (to this day) and the social structure that sustains such production are invisible. In fact, the closest Marx comes to confronting this passage is through Ericka Beckman's notion of "import catalogue," which she aptly deploys in an encompassing reading of *modernista* fascination with commodities.[23] In short, in rather orthodox Marxist fashion, and building explicitly on the notion of commodity fetishism, Beckman claims that such cultural production is the superstructural output of an economic structure built around the complementary forces of raw material exportation (coffee) and luxury good importation (pianos). I agree with this important study insofar as this is an apt application of Marx. My problem with this reading is that a whole lot of words become unnecessary, which is why I think we should reformulate for literary studies, as previously with primitive accumulation, the notion of commodity fetishism itself.[24] Reading Silva's excesses against the grain facilitates this task.

The most lucid, if strikingly heterodox take on the issue can be found in a fascinating contemporary Colombian novelist and memoirist, Fernando Vallejo, a critically acclaimed and widely read author whose work I have previously analyzed.[25] Vallejo is most famous for *Our Lady of the Assassins* (*La Virgen de los sicarios*, 1994), a gay romantic crime novel set in Pablo Escobar's Medellín.[26] This is ironical, for that work is the furthest Vallejo ventures away from his usual register of semiautobiographical fictionalization. While it is implausible that the actual Vallejo dated underage hitmen—the premise of that celebrated novel—it is certainly the case that he immersed himself in all things José Asunción Silva for *Almas en pena, chapolas negras*.[27] Part biographical essay on Silva, part memoir on the act of conducting literary research, the book, over five hundred pages long, is anything but economical. Vallejo identifies with his object of study to the point of Bovarism. In a knowledgeable but colloquial, often irate style, he discusses well-known and obscure sources. Vallejo blames Silva's death on prudish Colombia. Along the way, an Annales-style portrait of late nineteenth-century Bogotá emerges and is brought to bear upon the present.

The document Vallejo considers that sheds the most light on commodity hyperfetishism is Silva's accounting notebook. Debts, incurred and owed, become social relations under Vallejo's imaginative recreation. The notable poet Ricardo Silva, José Asunción's father, owned a fine-goods store.[28]

When Silva took over, mismanagement and a drastically changed economic climate led to ruin. To acquire the luxury goods he wrote about, Silva sold them. He wasn't breaking even, but he defaulted and brought his creditors down with him. At best, Silva was a naive, lousy entrepreneur—at worst, a crook. Vallejo can only redeem his hero, justified in his pursuit of beauty. But despite himself, Vallejo gives ample evidence of social relations becoming products, becoming financial gains, as in the process of abstraction of labor that bolsters modern capitalism. As it turns out, Silva, the original Colombian bourgeois bohemian, was a failed industrialist. (A foreclosed tile factory was to save him from the store debacle). At the same time, Vallejo turns finance into social relations, transforming accounting into storytelling, and binding the whole affair to precious *modernista* objects.

Like Marx, Vallejo has to deal with the fact of credit—capitalist parlance for "capital." Marx progresses in some ways like Hegel before him. The master made his way through dialectical argument from simple perception to complex Spirit. The reformist gave the dialectic a different political sign, arguing from simple commodity fetishism to complex capitalist system. Credit—and debt, its Janus face—is a crucial turning point. The buyer, notes Marx in chapter 3 of *Capital*,

> buys it before he pays for it. The seller sells an existing commodity, the buyer buys as the mere representative of money, or rather as the representative of future money. The seller becomes a creditor, the buyer becomes a debtor. Since the metamorphosis of commodities, or the development of their form of value, has undergone a change here, money receives a new function as well. It becomes the means of payment.[29]

Note how many times the word and notion of "becoming" appears in this short passage. I read here the remnants of Hegelian eschatology and teleology, but also something wholly animistic. The magical properties of coveted things are connected to the magical properties of those rectangular pieces of paper we call money. This Marx must demystify. Vallejo, rather, remystifies. Extrapolating from Silva's accounting notebook, he flatly brings theology back into the picture: "For Silva, God didn't exist, Credit did. God is Credit."[30]

Vallejo goes on to elaborate how, for the Silvas, owing was "a philosophy," according to which, in order to truly exist, a person must owe. Some of this is a play on the book's pre-text, namely, the accounting notebook. After all, it is Vallejo who needs names to show up there in order to tell his story. But the deeper truth is that debt is never just about arithmetic but has always had religious and moral overtones. As David Graeber notes, since the Middle Ages, moral relations have been conceived as debts.[31] For the Silvas, according to Vallejo, being in the red was laudable, almost ascetic, rather than reproachable: "Silva didn't have anything but empty hands that squandered in luxury what came in from loans."[32] Perhaps the Silvas thought themselves beyond good and evil. Whatever the case may be, owing to the fine-goods stores of the metropolis was indeed a way of life, a shortcut to the riches of metropolitan capitalism from the periphery. Brecht's famous dictum "What is robbing a bank compared to the founding of a bank?" applies, with qualification.[33] The Silvas traded in luxury, not in their individual manpower. Still, from a moral standpoint, they are both in the wrong and in the right. They lied and cheated in a system of debt and credit that was already corrupt.

The quip on the Silva God also has to do with the ebbs and flows of convertibility from money to gold, which conservative president Miguel Antonio Caro had restricted, to the chagrin of importers. (A Catholic zealot and also a poet, Caro re-Christianized the country via the 1886 clericalist constitution; everything about him, down to his classicist aesthetics and religious beliefs, reeked contrary to Silva's *modernismo*.)[34] Certainly, Parisian luxury providers would not take pesos. Importers gave away the country's gold in exchange for goods, but then limited access to bullion aggravated what was already a vicious circle of debt. Caro rejected modernity; for Silva, to be modern was to owe. Anyone studying nineteenth-century Colombia will encounter thought-provoking alternatives to the Weberian tale of capitalist expansion—some more failed than others. What interests me about Vallejo's contemporary rendering of Silva is the revelation of the utter nonsense of the whole enterprise. As the saying goes—I am no expert—finance is not about working for money but about having money work for you. Commodity hyperfetishism takes a step further back, before commodities are abstracted (transformed) into money and arithmetic. Simple economic self-preservation dictates that no object is so sacred, or even cherished, to go bankrupt over. Conspicuously oblivious to labor, and counter to financial common sense and its cognate morality, it points at the underlying absurdity of it all.

How far Vallejo takes this idea is something to behold. In a later installment of his multivolume fictionalized memoir, *Casablanca la bella*, the biographer turns his attention to restoring a derelict house in Medellín. Vallejo left the city decades ago to settle in Mexico, but frequently returns to it in the imagination.³⁵ His alter-ego narrator, Fernando, is to instill an ersatz dwelling with the grandeur of his long-lost family home, Santa Anita. Endless decisions about construction materials, layout, and décor are necessary, which provides many an occasion for unbridled fetishism. Finding a toilet to the exacting specifications of the character's nostalgia, which extends to even such mundane things, becomes a major undertaking. The narrator fetishizes the heavyset, inefficient contraptions of yore. As the protagonist walks down the aisles of big-box stores looking for the prized object, to no avail, readers cannot help but wonder about his mental state. (He soliloquizes to the house rats, to boot.) When he finally succumbs to the evidence that such toilets are not on the market, and for good reason, it seems Fernando is coming to his senses. Or is he? Citing at length reveals hyperbole and irony:

> [Water-saving sanitaries] truly are the best, given: the space they take (hardly any); the water they save (a lot); the float (infallible: a valve). . . . Regard such a lovely "bowl" or "water surface area." Toilet secured to the ground with PVC, lightweight but firm. Two flush buttons: eight liters for solids and six liters for liquids. I am most pleased with them. Using them is such a delight. So glad I bought them!³⁶

Note the ellipsis: Vallejo actually sings the praises of the toilet for longer than shown in the extract above. Blending promotional catalog with technical dictionary, the style is pompous to the point of comedy, leading to the broken, overenthusiastic syntax of a product review. Part of the effect has to do with the collapse of high and low, that is, with the treating of a profane object as if it were sacred, of a simple artifact as if it had a prodigiously complex mechanism. But there is also is a potent, paradoxical subtext of personification. Just as Silva constructs his characters by portraying their object world, and vice versa, Vallejo is revealing the soul—and bowels!—of his hero with this charade. For an instant, the dysfunctional, impractical misanthrope becomes functional, pragmatic consumer. Social relations and means of production seem to harmonize in the big-box store:

customers inadvertently work the warehouse in search of their wares, and so does Fernando, uncharacteristically. He might as well start loving his fellow man. But here we reach aporia, for the ode to the toilet is still a delirious rant.[37]

True to form, the novel ends in the sweeping nihilism Vallejo is known for. Casablanca, like Santa Anita before it, and, synecdochically, like the entire country of Colombia, collapses. The apparent therapeutic breakthrough at the big-box store—an apparent sublation of the character's nostalgia, objectified as water-saving toilet—unravels. Fernando is no more attuned to the modern world, nor is he more hopeful about the fate of his country of birth. As Juanita Aristizábal notes in a perceptive essay, this amounts to a negative critique of the rotten foundations still at work in a nation that, at the time of Vallejo's writing, was experiencing a real-estate boom.[38] Vallejo gives voice to the extreme, underacknowledged classism, racism, and misogyny that have marred the country since its nineteenth-century inception. I think he also voices a profound disarrangement with things— the kind of burning love for objects that led Silva, the national poet, to his ruin. (Mutatis mutandis, the gaudy splendor of Pablo Escobar's estates also come to mind.) The symptom here might be Colombian, but the illness belongs to global capitalism.

Commodity fetishism does not dwell on the object, nor think with it, but hastens to the accumulation of value it may be involved with. Hyperfetishism does not do so, producing instead a more oblique elucidation of an affective structure that is also economical. The toilet in Vallejo illustrates some aspects of what Sherry Turkle would call an "evocative object," that is, "a companion of life experience." As she puts it, "We think with the objects we love; we love the objects we think with."[39] Vallejo contributes to this line of reasoning by pointing out that such a love can itself be suspect. "It is necessary to name things to call them into existence," Fernando is told, "but you name them so that they cease to exist."[40] This is a fitting description of *Casablanca*'s ars poetica as unmemory palace, reminiscent of the wavering "voice of things" in Silva. But it also points to the depth of experience that literature brings to the task of thinking with and about objects, both present and missing. Not to belabor the point, but when Marx discusses *Robinson Crusoe*, it is only as illustration of what he thinks he already knows about our fascination with commodities. Hyperfetishism, as we have seen so far, complicates the picture.

Conspicuous Consumption Revisited

The most thoughtful interventions I know on the subject of the love of things come from Mexico. Margo Glantz, for one, writes about designer shoes with gusto. As a scholar and an essayist, Glantz is noted for her work on a major feminist avant la lettre, the colonial writer Sor Juana Inés de la Cruz (1651–1695). Fittingly, as a creative writer of fiction, memoir, and poetry, Glantz rethinks the body and the experience of the female intellectual in modern Mexico.

The witty title of the work at hand, literally *Story of a Woman Who Walked Through Life in Designer Shoes*, does not translate well. Recall how the Spanish word for "story" is the same as the word for "history": one version gives the intimate, the other the monumental.[41] The book is both. Then there is the matter of *The Devil Wears Prada*, Lauren Weisberger's best seller from two years prior, which exemplifies, critics of the genre note, "chick lit."[42] Deliberate quote or not, Glantz does revisit themes like the purported banality of feminine literature or the infantilization of women via an identification with, and overattachment to, "pretty things." Throughout her oeuvre, she writes more broadly about women's issues. (An example is a clever retelling of a doctor visit and breast cancer scare that criticizes, in one deft movement, the medicalization of the female body and *machismo* in Octavio Paz's poetry.[43]) The title of the book at hand is ironic only to an extent, however, for Glantz very much owns her fetish. Beyond providing the occasional soundbite at literary festivals and author interviews—to audiences' delight—Glantz's public love of shoes is serious stuff. The path she *doesn't* take to get recognition is to go on the defensive, as if arguing for women's literature were more important than writing it. Instead of opposing misogyny, Glantz subverts it. Instead of de-objectifying women, she subjectifies things: a more effective strategy, as the element of surprise would have it, for a similar goal.

Under the playful heading "Andante con variaciones,"—*andante* signaling both slow tempo and the act of walking—the book opens with a first-person, autobiographical rumination on the etymology of *zapato*. We learn the word is of Turkish origin and dates back to the Renaissance. The collective noun *calzado* takes after a participle for those who wear shoes (calzados), as opposed to members of mendicant monastic orders (descalzos). In Glantz's retelling of the cultural history of shoes, *calzado* is liminal: noun and adjective, sacred and profane, religious and secular, high and low, local and universal, luxury and necessity, personal and impersonal, even human and nonhuman—feet themselves are "the original shoe." Heidegger famously discussed van Gogh's painting of shoes, focalizing an entire philosophy of art around them. (He problematically identifies the worn-out work shoes as those of a peasant woman, seemingly content with the natural order of things.)[44] Glantz attempts a similar undertaking, except these are no pauper's shoes—this devil wears Ferragamo. Her alter ego, Nora García, ruminates:

> I am most interested by the life of Ferragamo, I was thinking to myself this afternoon. It's, at least, a curious thought coming from someone who has deformed feet and is at the beach in a bathing suit, barefoot; from someone who, moreover, flaunts a bunion she cannot dissimulate when barefoot. And I wonder, how can I be interested by the life of a fat man who spent his life hunched over someone's feet, taking measurements, studying their anatomy and structure, and then carving wood lasts; on someone who on top of it all was a fascist?[45]

Talk about things with a history: in this deceivingly lighthearted passage, Glantz bridges personal and world events, providing an embodied reflection about the surface and depth of our attachment to things. Ferragamo, the global luxury brand, is commodity fetishism abstracted, perfected: a "cultural icon," in Douglas Holt's parlance. (For years, Holt held the L'Oreal Chair in Marketing at Oxford—such honorary professorships exist.) The links between cherished brands and fascism are sometimes plain to see, as in Volkswagen's stylized acronym-cum-swastika logo; other times they are buried in corporate history, as in Siemens's slave-labor-driven Nazi years. That those names were not irrevocably sullied by their connotation gives much to think about. Modestly, Glantz wonders about her own fascination, which endures even after scratching past the timeless patina of the brand (Ferragamo®) to reveal the last name (Ferragamo) and the Italian fascist artisan (a fat man hunched over clients' feet) who went by it.

The bunion breaks the spell. Even the finest shoe is pedestrian, pun intended; the most iconic brand, mundane. Timeless luxury is historically situated, nasty understories and all. Idols, the protagonist included, have feet of clay. The passage establishes a parallelism between her and the shoemaker, inviting the question of whether the craft of literature is somehow akin to clothing the feet of the rich and powerful in exchange for cultural standing. Glantz's writing wavers, andante style, between self-deprecation and self-appreciation. Think of a love-hate gaze in front of a mirror, choosing the right shoes to wear to a job interview. The opening movement of *Story of a Woman* tells the agony of becoming. The protagonist refers to herself in the third person, then assumes the first person. Her thinking of Ferragamo is "curious" because she is a lowly commoner with deformed feet, first, and then because the man is a lowly craftsman beneath her dignity—and a fascist, no less. Throughout, things become words become things: shoes become a name become a corporation—and backward again. Meanwhile, the self-aware, insecure dresser irrevocably becomes a writer:

> Resolute, she returns to Ferragamo, tries the shoes again; the saleswoman tells her, you've been here before, Nora nods, pleads to be shown the shoes again, contemplates them, caresses them, wears them, verifies that the bunion doesn't stand out too much, makes up her mind . . . she will use them solely when she sits down to write, as she does now, with her shoes on, her Ferragamo shoes she has purchased at an exclusive boutique in Bond Street, London.[46]

A statement of cosmopolitanism and petit bourgeois sensibility, the polysyndetic incantation brings hyperfetishism to its musical climax. Many threads are woven together in the passage, too long to cite in its entirety: stasis and movement, the connection of brand names with both honor and infamy, the purposefully embraced contradiction of taking up the monk's cloak—asceticism—and wrapping herself in luxury—indulgence. Nora García is neither too poor to afford such fancy shoes nor rich enough to do so without second thought. She sits in a maelstrom of contradictions she can only attempt to resolve by writing, metafictionally, the book itself. Additionally, as Erin Graff notes, the text combines Jewish and Christian referents, including the medieval trope of the deformed, devil-like Jewish foot or the Glantzs' own shoemaker background as Eastern European immigrants to Mexico.[47] (The author's more sustained reflection on her Jewish ancestry appears in her 1981 *Las genealogías*, translated in 1991 as *The Family Tree*.[48]) Clearly, García is not modeled on the traditional politically committed intellectual. Whatever insights she has to offer about the trappings of capitalism, she offers understatedly.

Now, while she does share the above trait, Margo Glantz is obviously not Nora García. To some extent, the author is vicariously building an author myth for herself by tapping into the mana of the brand to build her own. But these days, authors do this unironically: their literary agents, whose awareness of the product they put on the shelves supplements literary appreciation (however narrowly defined) with market savviness, encourage them to build brands for themselves. Nora takes pains to explore this theme dialectically. The musical subtext (andante), as in Ortiz (counterpoint), mobilizes form to interrogate extractivism in language. As far as "variations" go, the work that ensues after this opening andante section could be described as a short-story cycle or composite novel—it's also a rewrite of the collection that appeared in Argentina under the title *Zona de derrumbe*, after a different section.[49] Shifting the order of the sections, focalizing one as the title story over another, and adding or subtracting passages are not radical changes. This is consonant with a vision in which shoes are simple and complex, writing is heroic and mundane, inner life is rich and iterative. Extractivism, like brand fascination, is part of daily life.

If commodity fetishism were an illness for a Freudian talking cure to overcome, hyperfetishism would be better fit for a Lacanian exercise of dwelling in the symptom. García, artisan and one-woman corporation, illustrates this. She is also wearing history and vanquishing fascism (outsmarting it, at least), one step at a time—while sitting at her desk. However, there is no turning back the clock to that original scene of craftsmanship. At the time of writing, Ferragamo is already a global luxury brand. Ferragamo himself lived as a jetsetter for half of his life, having clothed the feet of Marilyn Monroe and Eva Perón. Risk here is mainly aesthetic: that of producing prose that is also a commodity. Crucially, hyperfetishism reveals the blurry borders of commodities. It does not take for granted the difference between use and exchange value. Likewise, it shows how commodities permeate language and private life. Thorstein Veblen famously observed that "conspicuous consumption of valuable goods is a means of reputability to the gentleman of leisure."[50] Glantz exacerbates this logic to thought-provoking contradiction: García is an industrious, pedestrian gentlewoman of leisure. She debases herself *and* acquires social status, exhibiting both *less than* consumption—sitting down, shoes won't wear or tear—but also *more than* consumption—buyer infatuation overgrows into author myth. Note the family resemblance with Silva and Vallejo above and, in chapter 3, with Bolaño's Viennese court shoemaker.

By way of the present chapter's conclusions, it's worth considering a final, emblematic case of Mexican hyperfetishism. Roughly contemporary with Glantz, photographer Daniela Rossell gained worldwide notoriety with a series of provocative portraits of young Mexican women—and, less frequently, their mothers and servants—in opulent settings. Silva's imagined interiors are sparse in comparison. The series grew from a small-scale exhibition to a national mediatic phenomenon, thanks to a scandal about the women photographed: daughters and granddaughters of prominent politicians of the Partido Revolucionario Institucional (PRI, Institutional Revolutionary Party). These days, Rossell's emblematic early work is exhibited, alongside superstars like Cindy Sherman and Rineke Dijkstra, at key venues of the art world, big and small, such as New York's Museum of Modern Art and Berlin's Olbricht Foundation. Many aspects of these eye-catching photographs have been discussed, notably by Princeton's Rubén Gallo, who comments on their scathing implicit critique of Mexican plutocracy and on the missed opportunity of making such critique more pointed and explicit. (He accuses Rossell of "bad faith" by omitting the names of the heiresses depicted.)[51] Artist intentions aside—the photographer herself was a gilded youth, the subjects her personal acquaintances—I find that commodity hyperfetishism provides a better framework to appreciate them. Conversely, Rossell sheds light on this phenomenon.

Take the case of Rossell's untitled picture, reminiscent of a harem, ostensibly a revision of an orientalist motif (figure 4.2). Is this a feminist take on an art history motif, à la Martha Rosler's famous "Hothouse (Harem)" collage of 1972? Rossell's picture and composition is indeed visually aware of Rosler, who cut out pictures of naked women from *Playboy* and composed them anachronistically, so as to confront the masculinist gaze in high art and popular culture, seventeenth-century monumental painting and twentieth-century mass magazines. (An illustration would be too explicit and bedeviled by copyright issues to include here.) As there is hardly any space between the mostly reclining bodies in Rosler, the *horror vacui* that characterizes the motif was taken to its limit: the aestheticizing of the subordination of women rendered into a canvas of flesh. This is part of what made her negative feminist critique so effective, for it visually demonstrates that all

FIGURE 4.2 Daniela Rossell, *Untitled (Ricas y Famosas)*, 2002. C-print, 30 × 40 in. Edition of 5 (1134).

the paraphernalia of men's magazines—at the time they included articles by reputed literary authors—are but frills and justification, like the rich tapestries of a harem. And yet Rossell sharply differs from Rosler, for all that their names are anagrammatic, because the relationship between ornament and subject is suspect, the extensive feminist critical apparatus is lacking, and, more simply, because the women she depicts are legitimately posing in good fun.

This is, of course, disquieting. Such ambiguities uncharacteristically prompt Gallo, a nuanced reader, to request explicit engagement from Rossell. Is she, at the end of the day, criticizing PRI or celebrating its uncontested seventy-year reign? Objectivizing or subjectivizing women? Oblivious to Mexican poverty or summoning it via negativa? The bonsai palms and blackamoor candelabra—eunuchs?—turn the women into powerful giants; the continuity of foreground staging and backdrop painting reduces them to lively decoration. The puma hide sits ambiguously among hunters or prey. One relatively alert woman looks away—toward the arriving prince (whom the tray bearer also faces?)—but lounging seems to be an end in itself. Color overload takes over, and yet the wooden floor visible in the bottom-right corner reveals the artifice. Do we witness an enthusiastic celebration or a comical repudiation of "bad taste"? Impossibly eclectic geometric patterns hint toward postmodernism: a conceptual trompe l'oeuil. And yet the piece conspires against its own compositional perfection, for instance, with the lone plastic water bottle in the bottom left. What brings the work together, in my mind, is an exacerbation of the fetish that prompts critical thinking, providing questions rather than answers. It's a visual-arts manifestation of the phenomenon the present chapter addresses.

Similarly, another captivating photograph, also untitled, features an unnaturally blond woman draped in revolutionary red, or rather an electric hue thereof, sitting on a coffee table, as if a coffee table book herself (figure 4.3). The backdrop, red as well, features a large-scale portrait of Emiliano Zapata, the indigenous peasant revolutionary, presiding over the chimney like a patron saint or yet another hunting trophy. (The latter is a

FIGURE 4.3 Daniela Rossell, *Untitled (Ricas y Famosas)*, 1999. C-print, 30 × 40 in. Edition of 5 (DR.1388).

recurrent motif throughout *Ricas y famosas* and, presumably, the homes of the better off—notice, in this photograph, the little bear standing on a rock.) As a library scene, this is, on one level, an allegorization of the production of knowledge. Facing away from the camera, a maid dusts redundant encyclopedias, some of which most likely sit there on account of their stately leather spines, which dress the room and contribute to solving the predicament of too much space to fill. At the right, a clock from Porfirio Díaz's day keeps time. Zapata and the *fresa*—slang for "preppy," but also literally a strawberry, which she resembles—lock eyes with the viewer; the maid doesn't have the chance. Other than the forceful condemnation of a plutocracy that speaks in the name of the people (Gallo has reservations), I see in this photograph an enormous empathy and pathos, as if every human and nonhuman element were held prisoner to every other. The voice of things is overheard. Subjectification of the object and objectification of the subject, the commodity here combines what Bill Brown calls "misuse value" with a stark sense of materialized, if perverse, historicity.[52]

The above merely scratches at the surface of Rossell's complex work—but then again, surface is all there is. The photographer complicates *Capital*'s teleology from use to exchange value to financial abstraction in a striking number of ways that, nonetheless, are more performative than speculative. Her compositions, despite being meticulously staged, reimagine social situations rather than analyze them. Objects are parts and parcel of this operation. In a different work in the series, another svelte heiress, wrapped in gold lamé, lounges on a plush leather coach, personifying ennui while staring at the camera (figure 4.4). Standing beside her, slumping, a plump maid in uniform also stares on, albeit uncomfortably. The two equally young women evoke a master-slave dialectic, but they are hardly the *punctum* of the grand photograph. Taken from an impossible angle, as if by an angel, the photograph gives away much of the field of vision to a foregrounded crystal lamp. There must be another source of light so as to cast such dramatic shadows. Regardless, the lamp achieves a chiaroscuro effect against the opposing dark corner, a synecdochal maid's quarters.

In Guy Debord's definition, "the spectacle is capital to such a degree of accumulation that it becomes an image."[53] This is the case here quite literally, with a twist: Rossell's manicured images depict things and, in turn, become objects themselves with exchange value in the art market. *Détournement*, Debord's favored technique, is akin to rearranging a dream, rather than to

FIGURE 4.4 Daniela Rossell, Untitled *(Ricas y Famosas)*, 1999. C-print, 30 × 40 in. Edition of 5 (1076).

waking up from it. (His examples include renaming Beethoven's Third Symphony (*Eroica*), originally dedicated to Napoleon, as the "Lenin Symphony.")[54] Rossell, activating misuse value, achieves a sort of détournement with things, her own work included. The rippling effect goes in many directions, affecting many constituencies. European and U.S. art buyers may recognize the gaudiness in their own curated interiors. Underprivileged Mexicans peek into the rarified environments of an overclass estranged from the people, or perhaps recognize them as familiar—as those they themselves would inhabit could they afford them. (Gallo cringes.) This multifariousness may very well be what gives her work an iconic status in contemporary Latin American art. Be that as it may, an important takeaway for present purposes is that, in hyperfetishism, conspicuous consumption complicates, rather than affirms, social status. The accoutrements that bolster privilege can also reveal its weaker underpinnings. Social mobility, and lack thereof, are also a function of human nonhuman relations.

To be clear, I am not suggesting that any of the authors or visual artists considered in this chapter are "progressive" in some fashion. They may well be the opposite. But despite themselves, they present a different way of revealing the seams of the commodity. Heideggerian attempts to recover the thingness that exceeds the object, à la Brown, pay scant attention to economical dimensions; Marxist takes ignore thingness, if not objects themselves, to focus on the bottom line. Hyperfetishists build up noninstrumental, expressive language as counterforce to both mystification and economicism. That Latin American cultural products develop that third possibility has less to do with the region's ingenuity or aesthetic prowess, however much these traits may be in evidence, than with its unique positionality at both the receiving and giving ends of modern extractivism.

CHAPTER FIVE

Digitalia from the Margins

In 1849, thousands of experienced Chilean miners left the port of Valparaíso to join the California Gold Rush. They carried with them tools and skills essential to the extraction of gold, a formidable mineral essential to the accumulation of wealth and, as it would later turn out, to digital technology. From 1971 to its abrupt end in 1973, Salvador Allende's government appointed a transnational team of scientists to develop a national computer system that would manage the country's socialist, centrally planned economy; the unfinished project was known as Cybersyn in English and *Synco* in Spanish. It featured an orange, 1970s-futurism control room for president and ministers to make decisions based on real-time data from nationalized factories across industrial sectors. At the dawn of the twenty-first century, as data mining and mining proper drive each other in a feedback loop, Chilean writers, like their counterparts from elsewhere, reflect on the importance of the digital in our changing relationship to objects. Putting together these three moments invites a defamiliarization of the digital technologies that so decisively inform our daily lives. Contingent, they result from historical processes and express a certain world order. They could be *different*.

One cannot overstate the impact of the so-called digital revolution, and yet it is easy to dismiss its long history and its ideological underpinnings. A smartphone sitting on a table at a restaurant in Santiago has a long story to tell, from the minerals and manpower extracted around the world to assemble it, to the startling fact that so much computing power—indeed, more than would have managed a socialist utopia in the seventies—is conferred upon any one individual, the customer. There are no brands of Chilean computers, as there are none for cars or airplanes. A long history of extractivism and uneven development, of failed alternative modernities, is built into the smartphone. Yesterday, Latin America provided essential rubber for Ford's cars and then bought the finished product at a disproportionate cost; today, it provides essential coltan, gold and other minerals, and then does the same as before. Digital surplus value is disproportionately accumulated in northern centers of capital. Meanwhile, scholars in science and technology studies have long debated such pregnant questions as that of whether artifacts have a politics; how technologies reflect societal values and, in turn, may condition them; and how transnational technological transformation affects the world.[1] But how to awaken sleeping objects? In other words, how to reveal the historicity of the digital? As I argue in this chapter, contemporary Latin American literature, when read within the broader material turn that this book traces, offers an answer to this question.

Smartphones and other highly portable technology provide a useful illustration of the material turn that has been occurring in recent years. Thanks to them, many in the developed and developing worlds will readily recognize that, in their lifetime, their relationship to objects has significantly changed. However, such gadgets can also eclipse the broader shift they belong to; it is easy to take the part for the whole. To the contrary, this chapter builds on the insights about raw material and luxury goods developed in chapters 1 and 2, respectively. A bedazzled smartphone, that bundle of minerals and consumer desires, mobilizes everything we have learned about extractivism and commodity fetishism—also about the potential role of literary language in, fittingly, "throwing a wrench" into their workings. As I now turn to show, the semiperipheral condition of Latin America, a late adopter of technologies, allows the region's writers to incisively probe ideologies of the digital. In particular, as my transcultural materialist reading will demonstrate, they estrange the notion of *personal* computer, confront the nasty underside of cloud computing, and ultimately upend and denaturalize a phenomenon that the cultural critics Richard Barbrook and Andy Cameron called in 1995 the "Californian Ideology"—the self-serving techno-utopianism of a new digital ruling class.

Cellular Dreams on a Porous Border

Carlos Slim has been described as the Warren Buffett of Mexico. Having surpassed in wealth the American investor by "a few" billion dollars, one might as well say the opposite: Buffett is the United States' Slim. The largest stakeholder in the *New York Times* and, reportedly, its savior from bankruptcy, Slim is at the time of writing the second wealthiest man alive, second only to Bill Gates. Yale Law School professor Amy Chua noted in 2004 that the mogul made $5000 every two minutes, which was more than the average Mexican earned in a year.[2] Like Gates, whose fortune of $79.2 billion tops the *Forbes* list of wealthiest people, Slim amassed his $77.1 billion from the digital turn[3]—not computers, in this case, but telecommunications, especially cell phones. (The irony of Slim bankrolling print media with profits from digital media has not escaped cultural critics.) The turning point in his accumulation of capital coincides with neoliberal policies in Latin America. In fact, it is the deregulation of Mexican telecommunications in the 1990s that gave Slim the opportunity to amass his fortune. President Salinas privatized Telmex, the state telephone company, in a move that later caused a corruption scandal, leading him to exile and loss of reputation. Meanwhile, Slim saved face and profited at a historically unprecedented rate.

When does a phone stop being a phone? Clearly, today's "smartphones" are not telephones: rather, they are portable computers, one of whose functions is to make and receive calls. We do not call a Swiss army knife a "smartknife," and do not confuse it with a knife proper. This semantic slippage is partly due to the nature of technological change: Benjamin was fascinated with how the first electric light bulbs were shaped like gas flames or how iron was shaped to resemble wood.[4] However, "smartphone" is marketeering language; the term itself is part of an apparatus that compels users to "upgrade," creating needs and desires that previously did not exist. The cell phone was—it is about time to refer to it in the past tense—something in between. Its name came from the network technology that made communication independent of copper lines, the rudiments of that technology since Alexander Graham Bell. Not that it was independent of infrastructure, mind you. Slim's cunning, as his detractors have observed, was to have the Mexican state pay for the new infrastructure he needed to replace the old one, and then reap the benefits of establishing a new technological standard. Clearly, there is more than one way to think of the "smarts" in the smartphone. But can literature and other cultural production, as Ortiz, Rivera, Magnus, and others have shown us in previous chapters of the present volume, allow us to estrange a language that obscures the historicity of the material turn?

One of the first works to critically engage cell phones, unwittingly binding the worlds of Slim and of Gates, is the *corrido* "El celular." Corridos have a long history, which goes back to colonial Mexico and originates in medieval Spanish *romances*. Like modern troubadours, its first practitioners in the Americas used its stanzas, typically composed of four rhyming, octosyllabic verses, to carry news from one village to the next. Myths are born in corridos; they recount the exploits of famous men and women, including *caudillos* and *soldaderas* of the Mexican Revolution. The piece at hand is a hit song from the 1992 album *Con sentimiento y sabor (Tan bonita)*, by the popular *norteño* band Los Tigres del Norte. The band's members grew up in Sinaloa and live in San Jose, at opposite sides of a digital divide and an increasingly militarized border that are, nonetheless, home to a diversely bilingual and binational people. Sinaloa is a Mexican state famous for corridos and, in the last decade, unfortunately, also for narcotrafficking. (Los Tigres went on to pioneer the subgenre of *narcocorridos*, which memorialize the war on drugs from below.) San Jose is a Californian city that, with Palo Alto, where the author of the present study resides, is a focal point in the string of suburbs that have come to be known as "Silicon Valley." As a *New Yorker* article put it, "Los Tigres sing in Spanish—mainly about things that happen to poor people in Mexico, or to Mexicans in America."[5]

"El celular" is a case in point. To the straightforward bouncy waltz of modern, rock-infused corrido, its eight stanzas portray a man who goes from honeymoon with his cell phone to disappointment. At first, he flaunts it. "Call me at any time and anywhere," he says, "'cause I've already got my cell phone."[6] By the second stanza he is qualifying the invitation, asking his interlocutor not to call home at night, but rather (as he specifies in the third) when there are many people around to see him pick up the phone. He looks like a "man of influence," he says.[7] Listeners presumably warm up to this likable goof, who masquerades as a rich man, in the manner of popular comedic characters Tin-Tan, Cantinflas, and Chespirito, who have made Mexicans and Latin Americans at large laugh out loud for decades.

The song indulges in this goofiness for several stanzas: our hero compares his poise to that of an ancient Roman and a top executive. He claims the gadget gives him "personality," and confides that he carries it even when it does not have a battery, merely to "flash around." Interestingly, the verb he uses is "apantallar," literally "to screen"—one is reminded that, per Freud, projection is indeed a key aspect of constructing a personality and building memories. The imperial figures of the Roman and the executive are projections, we learn in the climactic sixth stanza, from a disgruntled employee, possibly a day worker:

> The boss gave it to me at work
> because an executive I am so
> the truth is I'm straight up fucked
> he controls me wherever I go.[8]

The genre does not care much for nuance, nor does it aspire to sophistication. Still, the song's moment of truth could not be more poignant. Tragicomically, we discover what we knew all along: that the cellular-wielding chap is no Carlos Slim. Rather, the gadget feeds delusions of grandeur while increasing "productivity," if not outright exploitation. Some twenty-five years later, this unlikely document of technological shift captures a zeitgeist. Call it cultural critique for the undocumented masses: this is a song about alienation, the invasion of private life, and a changing rapport with means of production. It is little wonder it should be a hit—all corridos sound the same, but some, in a fitting metaphor, *click*. Playful variations on the throbbing bass rhythm in the seventh stanza dramatize the anticlimactic, overly farcical moment when the song almost slips away into crass comedy. When the boss has an emergency, "he drags me out of the bathroom, doesn't let me ... think [pensar]." *Pensar* unequivocally rhymes with *cagar*, to shit, the omitted term here. The bass falters only for a moment, but then the note drops on the verb *to think*, and the song continues to its denouement. In the interim, the coupling of thinking and shitting vindicates the reflective agency of what Marx would call *Lumpenproletariat*. More generally, it gives a twist to the topsy-turvy-world motif that underwrites the song. The rich and poor do not quite trade places—but don't they equally, in the end, obey bowel movements more pressing than any work demand or phone call?

Having gone from new-gadget bliss to abjection, the song closes with a conventionally picaresque (and *machista*) envoi. It turns out the plebeian hero has a second boss. He can't fool around with girls anymore, or go party with his buddies: "My wife almost caught me / she keeps tabs on me with my cell phone."[9] Years before the NSA surveillance scandal, the age-old plot of jealousy and treachery comes across as naive. The third boss is the cell phone, of course, but there is an entire apparatus of overlords that gravitate around it; a shifting social pyramid, governed by company take-overs and transnational financial operations at an unfathomable scale, still has the same localized workers at their base. In the song, disruption economy enters into family politics, possibly for the better. In compensation, a masculinist fantasy asserts itself. The digital turn is transforming society in many ways, some salutary and others less so. It is a mixed bag: access to information empowers women and men everywhere; concentrations of capital are one evident cause of concern. At the prospect of further disempowerment, cultural products take refuge in machismo. There are multiple examples. In the late aughts and onward, they range from the unfortunate to the unmemorable. There is an over-the-top urban Mexican song that plays on the double entendre of a "byte" being about data and about teeth, egregiously insinuating that the scroll button in certain Windows mice resembles a clitoris ("Byte, byte, byte / Yo quiero un byte, byte, byte / Déjame jugar con la bolita de tu mouse"). Or witness the Puerto Rican reggaeton superstar Daddy Yankee—What's in a name?—in a suit and a crisp white shirt, a muscular businessman with oversize graduation rings, praising the bling of smartphones. In Colombia, *prepago* went from being the term used for off-contract cell phones to the euphemism for escorts.[10]

Are these moments vulgar displays of power or desperate cries of disempowerment? It is too soon to tell, but these poles are part of a dialectic. We live in an age of social experimentation via the digital. In one narrative, connectivity and instant gratification become the norm rather than the exception. In another, the upper hand belongs to a false sense of proximity and to insatiable desire. In this changing environment, cultural products may adopt various stances, from the celebratory to the critical to mere social commentary. Among the latter, Andrés López's epochal stand-up act, *Pelota de letras*, stands out. It depicts a digital generational gap with vignettes such as a grandfather who has an uncanny ability to fold newspaper pages flat but cannot pronounce the Anglicism "DVD" (el sirirí) or use a mouse (he looks at the device, not the screen).[11] If we connect the dots, we will appreciate the popular culture of an entire continent exploring the frictions of the digital turn and the specific ways in which it has been conducted: through neoliberal policy, capital accumulation, and hegemony of the English language. Over 95 percent of the World Wide Web is in that language, and yet its supremacy rests on the privatization of Latin American telecommunications—by homebred industrialists, no less. In isolation, the cultural products I have discussed up to this point make a modest contribution to the historicization and critique of the digital turn; together, they make a stronger case. However, it is in works of fiction, embedded within broader cultural formations, where I find the most complex and thoughtful reflection.[12] I now turn to consider them in more detail, going from cell phones and peripherals to what has been the main event of the domestic digital ecosystem: the personal computer.

Happiness Is a Warm Computer

The oeuvre of Alejandro Zambra (born in 1975) is composed of several short novels, available in English translations, including *Bonsái* (2006), *Formas de volver a casa* (2011), and the experimental work *Facsímil* (2014).[13] He has also authored several collections: two of poetry, one of essays, and a book of short stories. His recurrent theme is seemingly naive love stories that comment more or less obliquely on Chilean history. Against the trend of revisiting the 1970s that one can find in many Southern Cone writers and film directors from both sides of the Andes, Zambra speaks from democracy, although looking back at childhood years marked by dictatorship. Fittingly, Patricio "Pato" Fernández, writing for the culture section of the Spanish newspaper *El País*, referred to his work as "the great light [leve] novel."[14] *Levedad* or lightness, in this context, does not imply lack of ambition. Zambra's love stories are not so much political allegories as they are metonymies: he does not write about dictatorship; he writes about love. We slip from domesticity to History with a capital *H* with ease and without heroism.

One can see in the title of Zambra's short story collection, *Mis documentos* (2014), a reflection on the relationship of technology and writing, a gesture toward obsolescence, and a white-glove attack on Alberto Fuguet.[15] The title alludes to the discontinued name that Microsoft's operating system, Windows, gave to its user file-folder from 1995 to 2005: My Documents. Ostensibly, the company chose this name for pedagogical as well as for brand-name-recognition purposes. It also evokes Fuguet's idealization of Apple's Macintosh computers as one of the traits of newness in his often-cited 1996 coinage "McOndo"—a riff on García Márquez's fictional town, joined with condos, the computer brand, and the hamburger chain.[16] Fuguet is Mac, while Zambra is PC. Except Zambra knows that these terms might not mean much in fifteen years, let alone in cultural history writ large. On the one hand, there is opportunistic avant-garde posturing; on the other, a critical reflection on obsolescence. The book's savvy poetics of everyday life submits the present to the gaze of the future. Put in terms of a different Chilean writer, Roberto Bolaño, Zambra knows that "My Documents" will have but a fleeting normalcy from the vantage point of the distant year of 2666.

Files are "mine" as they are yours and everybody's; the possessive pronoun seeks precisely to establish a connection between the so-called personal computer and the mass of users. In a parodic mode, Zambra's title cultivates a similar effect, as the stories in the book are for the most part exercises in *petite histoire*. They include love stories that, for lack of a better word, one could indeed call superficial, in that any reader could feel identified with them. Microsoft eventually abandoned the possessive pronoun because it was no longer necessary: users did not have to be seduced or convinced to spend numerous hours a day in front of the screens. Moreover, the company Apple, with its minimalistic hyperproductivity and branding, established the doctrine that, in matters of design, what does not serve a purpose is in excess. Meanwhile, it relegated the other files in the computer, the ones that determine the relationship between the physical machine and the user, to a digital backstage from where they would never return. There files guard trade secrets, increase company revenue, and give users—for the most part unconcerned by the profit they generate—a sense of ease and lightness.

The most remarkable text in the collection is "Recuerdos de un computador personal," a re-elaboration of a short story that appeared in the Mexican journal *Letras libres* in 2008 under the title "Historia de un computador."[17] Set mostly in Santiago, it is essentially the parable of a couple,

Max and Claudia, who fall in and out of love, as told from the vantage point of their mutual relationship with their home computer. Summary does not do justice to a text that hinges upon its *récit*, and whose carefully chosen words suggest many rich subtexts. And yet, for present purposes, suffice it to say that Max and Claudia's relationship grows in parallel to the embedding of the computer in their lives; that it reaches its plenitude as the computer reveals the full extent of its functionality; and that they both become obsolete at the same time. Other than the arrival and decay of the computer, the main diegetic elements are Claudia's snooping into Max's files, which leads to her discovery of his philandering, merely suggested in the first version and rendered explicit in the second; and the late revelation that Max has a child, Sebastián, in Temuco. The story ends there, as Max gives away the computer to his neglected son:

> Once by himself, Sebastián set the computer up and ascertained what he already suspected: that it was considerably inferior, from all points of view, to the one he already had. They had a good laugh with his mother's man, after lunch. Then they both made room in the basement to store away the computer, still there since many years ago, waiting, as they say, for better times.[18]

Zambra's vignette of everyday life in the early 2000s comes to us complete with the thermal sensation of the CPU, which gives warmth to the protagonist, and mention of by-now-archaic games such as *Minesweeper* and *Solitaire*. Like Baudelaire to Benjamin, Zambra speaks to us from what is already a distant time.[19] But while contemporary capitalism thrives in producing an ever-shorter lifespan of products, leaving behind literally mountains of waste, Zambra dwells on the object. In step with new materialism, he tells the becoming of an assemblage of human and nonhuman elements. For elucidation, consider that when the National Rifle Association defends gun ownership on grounds that "weapons do not kill; people do," they obscure the fact that it is precisely *people with weapons* who kill. The "locus of agency," to revisit Bennett's term, lies in the assemblage.[20] Similarly, in Zambra's story, it is not people who love, but *people with computers* who do.

As I see it, the unity of action of the story, Achilles's rage, is the computer's agency. At the onset, Max buys the machine in installments, "as if on impulse and not through rational decision-making."[21] Once the machine

180 ◾ Assemblages

becomes a staple of his household, he writes "short lines *he called* free verses."[22] The insinuation is that the "medium" conditions Max's, and possibly Zambra's, writing. At the pivotal moment when the couple connects the computer to the internet, they both become "addicted" to email, and in Max's case, to pornography; we first learn that he has a son because Claudia asks that a user profile be created for him; when an unfortunate repair wipes the hard drive, this is compared to an amputation. In these examples of computer agency, connectivity spawns verbosity and sexual consumerism; software architecture elicits diegesis and characterization; hardware becomes an extension of human body. It is to Zambra's credit as a storyteller that there is hardly any animism in a story that, closely read, shows what computers *do*.

Provocatively, the computer comes to occupy its place in the assemblage of objects that is the household by affecting its composition and circadian rhythms, not unlike Claudia. She settles in by bringing a towel and a mirror, and by being the first, of the few women who have visited the apartment, who stays to sleep and have breakfast. Meanwhile, the machine makes room for itself by displacing the ashtrays and coffee cups on the table, like the new stimulant it is. Its hum is a "slight roar" (leve rugido), that becomes part of "a familiar soundscape" (un sonido hogareño) along with the "muffled buzz" (ronquera) of the refrigerator and the noises that come from the street.[23] When the couple—or trio—move to a bigger apartment, it gets its own room: "They allocated it a single bedroom."[24] The computer registers multifariously as Max's first companion, pet, or other son. Claudia, then, either usurps the machine's place or "adopts" it, as one would a child or a purring cat. For all the overdeterminacy of this human-nonhuman collective, it is clear that the computer has the power of turning the household on its head: from the sleepless nights it enables to the peculiar desk it gets in the bigger apartment, a salvaged door atop easels.

The computer in the story congregates involuntary memory and conditions voluntary memory. Claudia spends days organizing pictures from the couple's vacations, giving them clever titles and storing them in several folders, "as if from different trips."[25] Note that her assimilation of experiences, prefigured by the clunky engineers of yore, is now the province of "user experience designers" in Silicon Valley. See Apple's iPhoto, which organizes images around what it calls "Events"—a usage that must make Alain Badiou cringe. Contrast this with the above-cited bygone era when

"My Documents," with the possessive, was necessary to instruct users on what to do with computational power. As happens with other features of ideology, the very idea of a "personal computer" is by now second nature, although there is no fundamental reason to allot a society's computational resources along the lines of consumerist individualism. Although it is an imperfect analogy, one could think of the difference between developing infrastructure with cars or with trains in mind as the principal means of transportation. Computation has hitherto developed in a way more akin to cars, but it could still take a different form; it could become a public good rather than private property.

In *You Are Not a Gadget* (2010), Jaron Lanier appears skeptical of such paradigm shifts. Drawing examples form several digital platforms, which are embedded into all hitherto software even when technically superior options are available, he speaks of a "lock-in" effect in new technologies.[26] Engineers build on shaky ground, but more importantly, although this is not a term that the politically moderate Lanier would use, on what one could call an *ideologically-conditioned* medium. Software turns into thoughts turns into facts. Lanier does use the term "digital reification" to refer, for instance, to how a young musician's creativity and musical formation is unavoidably filtered by MIDI, the Musical Instrument Digital Interface that, in simple terms, allows instruments and computers to connect.[27] More germane to Zambra's story, the computer scientist and cultural critic also tells us that "files" were not there from the beginning, as early programmers considered other options, like a single, all-encompassing file. The file is now quintessential "locked-in idea." It might be easier to get rid of the concept of photons: "Our conception of files may be more persistent than our ideas about nature."[28] Moreover, Lanier tells us a few sentences later that a file reifies "the notion that human expression comes in severable chunks that can be organized as leaves on an abstract tree."[29] With this in mind, "Historia de un computador" becomes an artistic document of the (perhaps futile) resistance to lock-in. Claudia's attempt to organize memories into files and folders mirrors Zambra's act of writing. The love story's fundamental narrative tension is between unbound feeling and what Lanier might call a "severable chunk."

There is an added component, which is the position of the story on the global stage. Lanier's cultural critique is the work of an insider who can exert an actual influence on the debates that inform the next generation of software and, as a consequence, the shape of some portion of our lives. Zambra's assessment does not stand a chance, and not because he is a fiction writer, but because he is Chilean. This brings to the fore the broader problem of belatedness and dependency, which have been central concerns of Latin Americanist criticism for as long as the field has existed. But what of this so-called digital revolution, which seems to arrive in all corners of the world roughly at the same time? The frontier of innovation, from which entrepreneurs profit, seems always closer but yet remains unattainable. We seem to live in a time of trickle-down economics in fast motion. No matter how fast the flow, the structure remains fundamentally uneven.

Added value and native technology (imagine once more a Chilean *brand* of computers) seems as unlikely today as in the heyday of dependency theory. The same extractive economic model that informed the rubber boom and Rivera's *La Vorágine*, analyzed in chapter 1, looms on the horizon. What "Historia de un computador" makes us painfully aware of is that what is being extracted from users is the quality of their lives. This neo-Luddite line of thinking, to be sure, has been articulated in northern locales, notably by Nicholas Carr in *The Shallows* (2011), a psychology-divulgation manifesto on how new technologies deprive us of deep thoughts.[30] But by formulating his critique from Chile, Zambra offers a glimpse into what the situation is like for the rest of the world, namely, for those who cannot afford the latest or the second-latest model, but only the one that is already several steps closer to the dumpster. Paradoxically, Zambra tells us of a time when computers did last, particularly in the peripheries of digital capitalism. His nostalgia for Windows deserves a place in world literature, as it allows us to reflect on a fundamentally asymmetrical relationship between locales that is part of everyday technologies.

The political unconscious of the text is work's takeover of the household, reinvigorated over the last decade at a global level. "It is a common characteristic of all capitalist production," quotes Benjamin from Marx, "that the worker does not make use of the working conditions. The working conditions make use of the worker; but it takes machinery to give this reversal a technologically concrete form."[31] There is a quantitative difference between Marx's or Benjamin's time and our own, for machines have proliferated, but also a qualitative one, because alienation does not just affect the factory worker but spreads across the social spectrum and is intrinsic to our technology. It also colonizes spaces of private life that were once left relatively unaffected, such as sleep, which Jonathan Crary defines as "an uncompromising interruption of the theft of time from us by capitalism."[32] Sleep is an obstacle to 24/7 productivity. With the constant stimulation of the soft light it casts upon us, and with its alluring organization of electrons into zeros and ones—subatomic particles like Aira's in chapter 2—the personal computer leads the charge against it.

It is a sleepless Claudia who discovers Max's secret, in the dead of night, trying out passwords while her partner sleeps. She goes through *charles, baudelaire, tindersticks, los prisioneros, laetitia casta, mónica belluci* [sic], and *marihuana*. This evocative series includes some of the referents discussed above, which speaks to the flattening effect of postmodern cultural consumption, contributes to character development, and may be in part a bona fide statement of the author's influences. Ironically, *claudia* is the password that gives her access to the relationship's undoing. Her own name is the purloined letter; the computer that earlier solidified the couple's love is the conduit for its dissolution. A night-shift worker of sorts, Claudia is unwittingly contributing to the obsolescence of her love relationship (although Max was seemingly well ahead of her in that regard). Given the imbrication of love and technology present throughout the story, this turning point signals the submission of love itself into the waning moments of a production cycle.

As Chellis Glendinning observes in her "Notes Toward a Neo-Luddite Manifesto," all technology is political.[33] True to form, the machine in "Historia de un computador" is both about story and about history. On the one hand, there is the common narrative of a transnational middle class and its gadgets; on the other, there is the specifically Chilean problematic of patriarchy, masculinity, and the generational gap. As Ana Peluffo pointed out to me, the gap that interests Zambra is, foremost, the one that exists between his generation and those that follow, not so much the one between his generation and the ones that were more directly touched by the coup itself. This forward-looking gaze, however, does not entail negating the past, but rethinking it in light of its unanticipated ramifications, including synchronization with techno-centric capitalism.[34] Between "Historia de un computador" and its lower-key, more psychological and individualistic rewrite as "Recuerdos de un computador personal" comes a somewhat disappointing, but ultimately accurate assessment of the normalization of a technology that at one point could have had a critical edge.

The text is so keenly aware of the ideological, historical contingencies of computation that its second version carries one step forward the deauratization of love initiated in the first. Initially there is a series of evocative scenes that goes from the couple's love-making in front of the computer, "un polvo largo y lento" (a long, slow fuck) with the screensaver reflecting on Claudia's back—call it *ménage à trois avec ordinateur*—to a private ritual in which, after learning Max's secret, Claudia strips herself naked and wipes the computer screen with her underwear and her tears.[35] Numbed by years of pornography, the narrator in the second version describes Max as obsessed with anal sex and "facials," and recounts their breakup scene as involving rough sex, possibly rape, and a kick in the nuts.[36] In the unpublished fragment "Baudelaire," of 1921–22, Benjamin imagines that time is a photographer that portrays the essence of things, and that Baudelaire, although he does not know how to reveal the plaques, can interpret them "with infinite mental efforts."[37] The daguerreotypes of Claudia's reflection on the computer or her silhouette portrait against its backlight, followed by her abuse in the rewrite, tell the story of an objectified woman who appears distant in her proximity becoming one whose proximity is unbearable and who, in an alienated, digitally conditioned macho logic, must be destroyed.

Zambra's love stories bring to mind Zygmunt Bauman's proposal of "liquid love" as a rising phenomenon in contemporary relationships. Per the sociologist, this is an extension of consumerism into the private realm. Not too loose and not too serious either, but rigorously "casual," it replaces commitment to one person with a laborious courting of a network of potential partners, each node activated when the time comes. Liquid love is a lot of work, but "worth it," as it redefines the feeling in terms of a return on investment. Bauman speculates that today sex is the epitome of a self-sufficient, "pure relationship."[38] I would venture to say that a significant part of Zambra's oeuvre to date revolves around such moments of coagulation, so to speak, of liquid love. This is certainly the case of the relationship in the short story and in others throughout the collection. We zero in on a couple, see them fall apart, and move on to others. These are not just failed love stories, but variations on a mode of production, as seen through private life.

Readers of *Bonsái* will recall a memorable conversation between Julia and Emilio, the novel's main couple. It is worth citing both in the original and in Carolina De Robertis's courageous, if awkward, translation: "Éste es un problema de los chilenos jóvenes, somos demasiado jóvenes para hacer el amor, y en Chile si no haces el amor sólo puedes culear o culiar, pero a mí no me agradaría culiar o culear contigo, preferiría que folláramos, como en España."[39] (This is a problem for Chilean youth, we're too young to make love, and in Chile if you don't make love you can only fuck, but it would be disagreeable to fuck you, I'd prefer it if we shagged, si *follaramos* [sic], as they do in Spain.)[40] For all its wit, the passage expresses Zambra's maladjustment with his time and provenance. As Agamben puts it, "The contemporary is he who firmly holds his gaze on his own time so as to perceive not its light, but rather its darkness."[41] Zambra's estrangement of a verb so basic should give us pause.[42] His character yearns for an earlier cultural construction of love in Chile, and for just the right kind of raunchiness—one that, as it happens, can only be found on the other side of the Atlantic. Is this, perhaps because Spanish society is more egalitarian than Chilean, which means that popular language is not jarring to intellectual types? Be that as it may, note how Zambra is playing the part of Agamben's contemporary with his many experiments in love, including its more digital variants. He does not, however, renounce yearning. In liquid love proper, if we adopt Bauman's vague but inspiring category, love becomes an automatic response, a nonsubject.[43] That Zambra, precisely, *writes about love* signals his discomfort with this form of productivity.

A devil's advocate might say that the scope of Zambra's critique of the contemporary is limited because it stems from Santiago and not from a major metropolis. And yet, as Naomi Klein has reminded us, neoliberalism, a mode of production that capitalizes on shock, was born in Chile.[44] What attracted Benjamin to Haussmannized Paris was a sense of historical pregnancy: the city was a beacon for things to come and offered a connection to a disavowed past. Something similar could be said of Santiago, with its own experience of shock and with its physical layout. These are prescient of the turn that other Latin American capitals are undergoing and, if we follow Klein, are phenomena of world-historical importance. Peppered with shopping malls and hypermarkets and crisscrossed by highways, Santiago maintains many a Hispanic square and not a few direct architectonic quotes from the French belle époque—see its old market, with its iron and glass ceiling, or its art museum, a scale copy of the Grand Palais. Zambra might be the contemporary narrator to capture this space and its historical conjuncture. Indoor love stories and resignified everyday objects are merely two aspects of that broader topic.

As a subject in history, Zambra proceeds from that major experience of shock that was the coup of 1973. But he is born a couple of years later and spends his adolescence, after 1989, under the democracy of the watchful Senador Vitalicio—Pinochet, the self-appointed senator for life. His adult years coincide with the death of that figure and with the gradual and still unfinished awakening of Chilean society. Meanwhile, his country and cultural milieu went from trauma to melancholy, followed by denial and mourning, in a process that Idelber Avelar, Nelly Richard, and Alberto Moreiras have aptly analyzed.[45] Nostalgia becomes an aesthetic possibility just now, and Zambra comes to its encounter. It is a mode full of risks. It is easily coopted, serving as a backdoor for reactionary domesticity. But it also has great political potential; it mobilizes. Zambra's writing *affects* with subtle estrangements—of objects and love, as this chapter shows, but not only they. Its proposal of interrupting nostalgia with digital obsolescence allows us to regard time as time and not as monument or consumer good.

To recapitulate, the importance of Zambra's tale rests on its untimely contemporaneity and on its portrayal of a new form of alienation, that of technological heteronomy and sentimental entropy. It is not a blanket diagnosis: the future can be found in Temuco, even the promise of a different domesticity, where the remnants of the past are also stored. Zambra does not commit to an anticapitalist or neo-Luddite critique, but he does explore those positions, which are global in nature, from the vantage point of Chilean society. Some readers will miss a more forceful recourse to indignation or straightforward position-taking on the pressing contemporary question of the effects of new technologies on literature. Zambra merely sets the stage for such a reflection. The story shows that, surrounded by technological gadgets of foreseeable obsolescence, we live among ruins.

Accumulation of the Invisible

What is the endpoint to the arc that goes from flip- to smartphones, and from mainframes to personal computers? This is a question that angel investors, I imagine, must pose to themselves every day. At the time of writing, the buzz in Silicon Valley and in publications such as *Wired* magazine is that cloud computing and the "Internet of Things" are the telos of modern gadgetry—by the time of revising proofs, bioengineering seems to be on the rise. These are all about the seamless integration of computation with everyday objects. It is a transformation that, if ever achieved, would require many more studies like the present one, focusing solely on its cultural aspects. Already, entrepreneurs profit vigorously from the aspects of this ideal that have been implemented. A casual, even affectionate utterance, "the cloud" is a branded, sanitized term for server-based computing. This is a particularly fruitful case study to understand ideologies of the digital and the role that artists and writers can have in unmasking them. There is no "cloud"; there is farm upon farm of computer servers, growing exponentially around the world, producing enormous amounts of heat and requiring equally vast amounts of energy to cool them down. For all that we may pause in awe at the term, as if it dictated our very destiny; "technology" itself does not exist in any strong sense. As Heidegger puts it in his well-known "The Question Concerning Technology," "The essence of technology is by no means anything technological."[46] Parting ways with that text's individualist, aestheticist, and humanist elements, one could say that technology is a state of affairs composed primordially of social relations, copyright law, and reified assemblages of humans and nonhumans. That individualist consumerism should define computation is not written in stone—only in sand-based microchips.

As previously discussed, Marx devoted an entire section of volume 1 of *Capital* to what he called "primitive accumulation." True to the book's intended purpose of critiquing political economy in the double sense of analyzing and interrogating it, he examines a foundational myth of modern economics. "Previous accumulation," as Adam Smith dubbed it, is the idea that there was a concentration of capital prior to capitalism that resulted from men's natural talents. In this fabled origin story, the lazy started off on the wrong foot and the diligent flourished. Private property does not stem from violent acts of land-seizing but from merit and chance alone. Marx compares primitive accumulation to original sin: the idea that falling from paradise at the dawn of time accounts for all hitherto misfortune. In reality, however, "so-called primitive accumulation, therefore, is nothing else than the historical process of divorcing the producer from the means of production. It appears as 'primitive' because it forms the prehistory of capital, and of the mode of production corresponding to capital."[47] Could we not entertain the possibility that we now live at a time of digital primitive accumulation? As yesterday's lords fenced off public land and farmed it, today's digital moguls privatize data and, well, also farm it. The abysmal differentials in wealth that already ensue feature entrepreneurship as their original virtue.

A valuable counterargument would be that cloud computing has allowed the entry of scores of smaller players into the internet economy. This is true. There are so-called public clouds and private clouds. The former, such as Amazon's EC2, are available for hire and provide computational services at a scale that was previously impossible. I consulted a technical report from the electrical engineering and computer sciences department at the University of California, Berkeley on the subject; it notes that it costs the same to use a thousand servers for one hour as one server for a thousand hours. But the aspiring entrepreneur—the next Candy Crush Saga billionaire, say—does not have to *own* a server or a thousand, but merely rent them. So, going back to Marx, wouldn't the cloud bring the producer *closer* to the means of production, instead of divorcing her from them? In order to elucidate this, it is worth citing the report at length:

> Cloud Computing is likely to have the same impact on software that foundries have had on the hardware industry. At one time, leading hardware companies required a captive semiconductor fabrication facility, and companies had to be large enough to afford to build and operate it economically.... Only a handful of major "merchant" companies with very high chip volumes, such as Intel and Samsung, can still justify owning and operating their own fabrication lines. This motivated the rise of semiconductor foundries that build chips for others.... Similarly, the advantages of the economy of scale and statistical multiplexing may ultimately lead to a handful of Cloud Computing providers who can amortize the cost of their large datacenters over the products of many "datacenter-less" companies.[48]

Does everyone profit? Yes. This is not a separation of the haves and the have-nots, as Marx's more dialectical model would have it. This is stratification. There are those who profit exponentially from owning the very few state-of-the art fabrication lines or data center infrastructures. For the rest, it's trickle-down economics. And so, in a sense, digital primitive accumulation does separate the producer from the means of production. Add to this that, on the internet, general users are producers too: every click generates profit, and we are nowhere near to profiting from it. Still we retweet; we "like." If the allure and entrapments of bourgeois culture configured the ideological scaffolding for early modern workers to give away their labor power, it is the hype of entrepreneur culture that does the same for our age. And so Steve Jobs and now Tim Cook, with playful seriousness, launch each new Apple product as a revelation or a papal decree.

Personal computers, we now come to realize, were merely a stage: the miniaturization of mainframe computers may have alienated many, turning hobbyists into night-shift workers. But at least computational power and user information were *there*. The cloud brings a new twist to the history of domestic computation. Now computers are primarily portals into privately-owned server farms that process and store elsewhere. The architecture of the cloud reifies social imbalance, at a local and global level.

The question invariably arises: What is to be done? At a techno-social level, answers will likely take years to coalesce, involving multiple actors across different fields of knowledge and spheres of influence. As far as literary and cultural studies go, the present chapter has already pointed to one provisional answer—namely, critique. I have thus far read between the lines a number of works in order to articulate their critique of technology. For what it's worth, I can say that my own experience with these works has been one of gaining consciousness; listening in to Los Tigres or reading Zambra has had something of an awakening effect. Consequently, potentiating and accompanying such works strike me as sensible critical tasks—connecting the dots they often present scattered. Ideologies of the digital are so pervasive and, in a word, *successful*, that the suspicion we reserve for so many other phenomena easily falls mute to a shared enthusiasm. Artworks, short stories and corridos included, allow us to realize that there is room for malaise and more in this brave new digital world. I have not so much interpreted these works as *used* them—not in an unfair or reductionist way, I should hope. But in any case, my goal has not so much been reading *them* as having them read *us*. The belle-lettrist dream of the work as a world unto itself is fine for appreciation, but doing something with it requires following its threads back to the bigger tapestry of modern life.

This does not solve the problem of what to do with the cloud in art or criticism. Representing it is something that cloud ideologues already do; the "cloud" itself is a clever catachresis for the tons upon tons of whirring equipment it evaporates into thin air. I find that another Chilean author,

Jorge Baradit, offers a prescient critique of the cloud, written at a time when computer-server farms had not yet taken over. Clearly, a mere interpretation that sought to understand the author's intentions or appreciate his contributions to a literary genre would fail to see this. However, before I *use* Baradit to present the final part of this chapter's argument, allow me to engage in a brief excursus, for it is in the plastic arts that we can find some of the earliest and finest insights on the matter of undoing clouds.

Consider the work of John Gerrard, an Irish artist born in 1974. He gained international notoriety for his installation *Solar Reserve (Tonopah, Nevada)* at the Lincoln Center in New York in 2014. Its depiction of an industrial facility devoted to harnessing the energy of the sun was something to be seen. With support from the Public Arts Fund, the artist set a massive LED wall, several stories high, on the esplanade (figure 5.1). It harmonized with the surrounding buildings by usurping the architectural function of the central fountain, which it hid from frontal view. At a distance, this new centerpiece to the theater and opera complex appeared to be a screen of epic proportions, projecting a video. Upon closer examination, the screen

FIGURE 5.1 John Gerrard, *Solar Reserve (Tonopah, Nevada)*, 2014. Lincoln Center, New York.

was recognized as more of a cube, the video turned out to be a computer simulation, and its scale was seen to be rather modest for the ungraspable enormity of the power plant. A tower, surrounded by ten thousand mirrors that reflect sunlight, may look like the stem of a flower to an unsuspecting passerby; come closer, and the pedestrian turned art spectator would find herself immersed in the simulation, which offered bird's-eye views impossible to the human eye and choreographic rotations of the sun-seeking mirrors (figure 5.2).

There are many possible readings for a piece like this. There is celebration of human ingenuity, reverential fear of technology, collapse of desert and metropolis, coordination of city rhythms to astronomic-industrial homeostasis, erasure of the borders between the virtual and the real. Crucially for present purposes, there is a commentary on accumulation. Gerrard invites us to ponder what it means to store ("reserve") solar energy. Who benefits from such a sensational, if still-evolving, technology? Framing it as public art cuts to the chase: the sun belongs to all and to no one; solar reserve is of the commons. Contrast this to a different piece that Gerrard exhibited at

FIGURE 5.2 John Gerrard, *Solar Reserve (Tonopah, Nevada)*, 2014. Lincoln Center, New York.

FIGURE 5.3 John Gerrard, *Farm (Pryor Creek, Oklahoma)*, 2015. Thomas Dane Gallery, London.

the Thomas Dane Gallery in London, next to a room-size rendering of his Nevada-inspired masterpiece. In *Farm (Pryor Creek, Oklahoma)* (2015), photographs are stitched together to create an effect of animation or cinematic movement, producing an effect at once familiar and uncanny (figure 5.3). The pictures show, in this arresting way, cooling towers, pumps, and blank walls from a Google data center, or server farm, in Oklahoma. Spectators may feel like giants prying about when, upon further reflection, the company is the prying giant. While the solar power plant was about public accumulation, this one is strikingly private, try as Google may to cast itself as a shared resource: call it a "mock commons."

As it happens, Gerrard approached the company about documenting its facilities for artistic purposes. Google declined, which led the artist to rent a helicopter, fly around the facility, and shoot pictures. Reportedly, when he consulted with state police about whether the company had any right to stop him, they said: "All we can say is, the air is free." And so a unique "farm" came to be, one that, as the artist remarks, "eats us as we eat it." Make no mistake: with its simulations and deftly computerized imagery, this is high-tech art about the highest tech around. It is, as a *Guardian* review accurately puts it, an attempt to "out-Google Google." The company that snatches personal information by the exabyte and trades in such catchy euphemisms as "street view" or "big data" may have met its artistic match. "It's better to ask forgiveness than permission" deserves a spot as the company's motto, next to "Don't be evil." First take pictures of thousands of people on the street, then blur out their faces at the company's sole discretion. First sweep in and "data mine" all there is to know about people, then deal with potential liability. And so on. For once, Gerrard turns the tables.

But what is it that we see when we see the piece? A farm, obviously, and a pigsty at that—except, unsettlingly, the unsuspecting users of the internet start to appear, ever so slightly, porcine. We also see a bank, a fortress, a technological wonder; an ugly façade that is pretty in its ugliness, like the Georges Pompidou Center inspired by mid-twentieth-century factories. Clearly, these artworks go against the grain of digital ideology. At the very least we, the pigs in this unflattering comparison, might think twice before trotting happily to the butchers.

Something similar could be said about the photographic study of technology that Kim Steele did for the *New York Times*. It was published in 2013 with a selection from forty years of capturing the might and austerity of technology. Like Gerrard, Steele also seeks a technological détournement, for her camera of choice through all these years has been a now-discontinued Hasselblad 503—a stubborn mechanical eye facing machines old and new. We see the Hoover Dam and are reminded of Heidegger once again, with his observation of how a dam on the Rhine turned the river from nature into "standing-reserve," that is, into an instrument. We see a new proton-beam facility in San Diego for cancer treatment and are reminded that technology saves lives. We see a Global Hawk drone and shudder at its sleekness and destructive power; we also appreciate its place among the technologies that define U.S. industrial supremacy. Finally, we peek into Facebook's server farm in Prineville, Oregon (figure 5.4). It ties it all together: irrigating, healing, killing . . . and then playing *Farmville* on the social network or scrolling down through mostly mindless chatter. Now remember—there are those who profit at an unprecedented rate from all this inanity. They *accumulate*.

FIGURE 5.4 Kim Steele, *Facebook's Server Farm*, Prineville, Oregon, 2013.

This is where the position of contemporary Latin American writers becomes most interesting. One step removed from the centers of the art world that Gerrard and Steele participate in, they are nonetheless as significantly impacted by the cloud as everyone else. The situation is reminiscent of earlier stages in capitalism when, for instance, the United Fruit Company brought to Latin America the worst of extractivism without the benefit of the vast cultural market that existed in the company's country of origin. In other words, it brought the stick of exploitation without the carrot of freedom of speech (and the institutions that make it possible). By the time writers and other artists formulated their critiques, it was in a sense already too late. This needs not happen again with digital primitive accumulation. We can take what the likes of Gerrard and Steele teach us and bring it to bear upon our hermeneutic practices as literary scholars. In turn, given the many communicating vessels between Latin Americanist scholars and writers, one may expect this will have an impact on creative projects now in the making.

In this spirit, Jorge Baradit's science fiction novel *Synco* becomes quite elucidating.[49] Its artistic merit has attracted little critical enthusiasm; its contributions to the novel as form, sci-fi or otherwise, are meager. And yet many things happen in *Synco*, almost despite itself, which are worthy of note. Baradit imagines an alternate universe where Pinochet stops the coup in Chile in 1973 and Allende brings the eponymous cybernetic project to completion. The novel features many amusing counterfactuals, such as a Poet Pablo Neruda Airport, a Cyberbolivarianist movement, and transistors the size of buildings (for microcomputing had not been invented). Other counterfactuals are more alarming, such as the assassination of now-president Bachelet as a young woman or the refashioning of notorious torturer and CIA operator Michael Townley as a mostly bored and horny IBM employee. The novel's politics are, in a word, confused. Its plot peters into an esoteric conspiracy, as the purported socialist utopia reveals itself as left-wing totalitarianism, then outright fascism. Tidbits of *mapuche* religion and iconography punctuate the delirious political system much as orientalist myths and imagery informed Nazi hermeticism. For all its gimmicks, the novel's premise remains unparalleled: what if Cybersyn had succeeded? For present purposes, What if something such as the cloud had coalesced under state socialism, not neoliberalism? What if locales like Santiago de Chile were the capitals, and not the backlands, of technological modernity?

Stafford Beer, the real-life British developer behind Synco, believed that information is a national resource—not in the way that the snooping NSA might understand the phrase, but in the sense of its service to a common cause. His Chilean collaborator Fernando Flores becomes a character in Baradit's novel. The character explains the goals of their project as "a harmonic dance of consumption patterns and popular needs" and a "system that self-regulates mathematically, not politically."[50] The actual Synco, which computer historian Edén Medina and others have recently examined in great detail, did in fact aspire to homeostasis and self-regulation, although it was neither so naive nor cunning to proclaim itself as apolitical, and it did not aspire to be the harbinger of the end of history. Crucially, it revolved around worker participation, which Baradit fictionalizes as totalitarian control (perhaps because, as Beer complained, the project bureaucratized over time). A 2014 *New Yorker* article made the case for revisiting Beer and Flores's progressive system for contemporary technological pursuits; it called it "a dispatch from the future," prescient of such developments as Nest thermostats and the "Internet of Things," except one driven by citizen needs and not corporate profit.[51]

Baradit offers memorable images. It is one thing to know that the Internet, like so many other technologies, is an offshoot of the Cold War, as is space exploration. Indeed, the idea of a networked communication system that, unlike phone lines, did not depend on central hubs, was originally a cautionary measure against the potential nuclear destruction of conventional infrastructure, buttressed in vulnerable major cities.[52] But it is another thing to visualize a military parade that revolves around a microcomputer, as such spectacles centered, at the peak of Soviet power, on nuclear warheads. Past a squad of the fearful, AK-47-wielding super-goons of the regime, and following the red flag of the totalitarian regime-cum-mainframe, enter the microcomputer:

> Behind them a squadron of flaming Fiat 600 carried the personal microcomputer developed by Institute Miguel Enríquez for Synco's field operators, a marvel of miniaturization that had caused amazement at the last world technological fair in Paris. The last Fiat 600 towed a small lorry with the "Atacama X-12" model, a modern, fully wireless computer that weighed a mere 80 kilos.[53]

The public demonstration that ensues consists of the computer's technician wirelessly beaming an image of himself past the podium of the Compañero Presidente. The reader chuckles, as intended: Why make such a fuss about the transmission of images, given today's Skype or FaceTime? A "mere" eighty kilograms, as in a hundred and sixty pounds? For some, the parade will restitute an element of amazement to that now commonplace sight; for others, it will merely add to the disparate collection of novelties that the novel has become by that point. Regardless, what is fascinating is the protagonism given to the "macro" microcomputer, dramatically set against a Fiat parade of Italian fascist connotation, in all its massive glory. After giving us circuitry the size of entire neighborhoods, the progress is patent; after exposing us to the lugubrious workings of Synco, this new concentrated system promises to be evil condensed. This is overly dramatic, but effective: the microcomputer is indeed the endpoint of an arms race, and Baradit disabuses us from thinking otherwise. Computational power is power too. Hence, the messiah-like character of Capitán Proxy "protects the fatherland from its own history," and, provocatively, an offline country is a dead country: "La señal muerta es el síntoma de un país en coma."[54]

But what would it mean for that country to live? For a fleeting moment, before succumbing to the apocalyptic imperative of genre fiction, the novel imagines the technology of a different, more just social order. Baradit imagines socialist computing, if all too hastily he has it degrade into totalitarianism. And yet, before its monstrous collapse of Stalinism and Nazism, *Synco* fancies Santiago as a world capital for the Third Way. The novel wants Allende alive, then kills him again. It is even more ambivalent about Pinochet. However, through its unabashed staging of contradiction against the monologue of present-day technologism, *Synco* allows us to estrange and renegotiate our digital present and its accompanying world order.[55]

Today, California is undergoing another gold rush of sorts, luring away the world's most talented programmers and calling forth mining operations of all kinds. Not only is the utopian vision that sustains it in many respects at odds with Allende's, it is also understated to the point of being invisible (like the cloud), if ever present (like the cloud again). As I have shown, cultural products can counter the corporate-driven fantasy of behind-the-curtain, benign technocracy. I am no neo-Luddite, nor do I ignore the many beneficial aspects of recent technological developments. What I have sought to challenge, however, is the ideological self-deceit at work when users create profit in the name of gratuity or express themselves "freely" in highly restrictive protocols.

In data, what makes lives special is also what makes them generic. Digital primitive accumulation is about affective extraction; servers quite literally bank on the quality of our lives. The works analyzed here bring us back to Barbrook and Cameron and their unmasking of technologist optimism as ideology. Having lived in the heart of Silicon Valley since 2008, and drawing from anecdotal evidence, I take some of its underlying assumptions to be the following: we shall innovate our way out of social contradiction; technological expansion is inevitable; if technology is involved in x, x is always better; software and gadgetry are the endpoint of all technology; technology is out in the world, not inside the subject; it is best to think a bit, but not too much, about the ecological and human implications of overseas production; entrepreneurs create riches out of thin air. I take issue with these, and I think that contemporary Latin American cultural production does, too. We may "like" this—or not.

Conclusions

Extractivism Estranged

Transcultural materialism is a remediation of human and natural history. It's both found object and method. "Transcultural," per my revision and extension of Ortiz's argument, signals a materialist approach that is always already natural-cultural. I have associated it with ways of reading that expose underlying assumptions about human-nonhuman coexistence and reveal literature's potential, qua literature, to provide insight into political ecology. As the chapters of this book have demonstrated, there is an undercurrent in contemporary Latin American fiction and in selected historical precedents that deploys it. As the present general conclusions seek to establish, one can further it into a mode of intervention. Its telos is to carry out a critique of extractivism, in language, onto the world.

Works written in this vein do not merely represent human and natural history, in the manner of an ecologically capacious realist novel—think Tolstoy with climate change—but interrogate its underexamined scaffoldings in language: say, the subject/object divide implicit in calling something "nature," "animal," or "thing," as if we weren't ourselves all of the above, however not reducible to any one of them. Words like these easily turn distinction into separation; for the ecologically minded, they are also relatively easy to spot as potential pitfalls, or markers, of "speciesism"—the assertion of the preeminence of our species over everything else. But there is more to language than nouns. Verbs often render nature passive and man active ("hunt," "mine"); narratives, more broadly, separate human from natural history as if they weren't always already intertwined. It takes careful work with language (interpretation, close reading) to even aspire to undo what centuries of anthropocentrism and Cartesianism have done. Given its complexity and richness, literary fiction is a good place to start.

It's important to keep in mind that, while the transcultural materialist works studied in this volume blur the line between nature and culture, defamiliarize objectifying language, interrogate the power dynamics that affect human-nonhuman interaction, and so forth, most literature actually contributes to, rather than critiques, the status quo. The good news is that novels waver, explore counterfactuals, allow one to think in the recesses. Part I of this book analyzed works that revolve around basic objects. A case in point, examined in chapter 1, "Raw Stuff Disavowed," is José Eustasio Rivera's *The Vortex*. Ultimately, that rubber-boom novel expresses deep frustration over the inability to effectively extend human dominion— if only with less brutality to the enslaved—over the Amazon basin. Nature is a femme fatale that, at the end of the day, prevails. Recall its telegrammatic punchline: "The jungle devoured them!"[1] The net effect is like a call to arms, which indeed the Colombian state and other actors have heeded, to desertify, cultivate, and colonize wilderness in practice while admiring it in theory. And yet the novel, despite its prevailing narrative, features rich counternarratives and a thought-provoking use of language to delve into. Materialist interpretation unleashes their potential.

Language is the key. I have focused on how novels—and, to a lesser extent, other genre and media—conceptualize the role of humans among nonhumans and vice versa. Some do so explicitly, as in the case of Blanca Wiethüchter's *El jardín de Nora*, discussed in chapter 2, "Of Rocks and Particles," which narrates the planting of an Austrian garden in the Bolivian highlands. But thematization and emplotment only go so far. Ditto for authorial intent. The main agent of this book is textuality, from the integrity of the novel form to the timely use of an interjection. Storytelling and authors have a role, of course, but it is the power of words themselves I have paid the most attention to. Novelists and poets just happen to be very keen at putting them to work.

Implications for World Literature as critical paradigm, as discussed in detail in chapter 3, "Corpse Narratives as Literary History," include an orientation toward the corpse—that is, a reappraisal of the role of the abject in literary history. With discussions of Roberto Bolaño and others, I have explored how the abject communicates humans and their nonhuman counterparts, surroundings, kin. We are beings that ingest, excrete, and die, even when fiction and the arts often cast us as disembodied, angelic, immortal. Recovering that suppurating, radically earthly dimension serves us well when thinking about phenomena, literature included, on a planetary scale. It leads to a different realization of the ethical, political, and ecological relevance of working with words. In one way or another, to greater or lesser degrees, literature participates in and responds to, rather than just reflects, processes as vast as climate change or industrialization. One instantiation of this idea would be to blur the line between textual and book history. (Literature is *also* dead trees.) The study of the book object is not exactly a new trend, but neither is it as central to literary studies as it should be if, indeed, we are materialists. Actor-network theories of literature can be fascinating provided one does not assume, with naive positivism, that suspicion has no role, or that everything that literature does is inherently benign.

Clearly, I don't think critique is, per Bruno Latour's dictum, "running out of steam."[2] I do find that World Literature is losing momentum, however, and will continue to do so unless we ground it in a manner consistent with the findings of this book. "Material World Literature" is too unfortunate a coinage to put forward, however aptly it would emphasize engagement with the planetary in all its nonhuman glory, as in Ursula Heise's eco-critical model, or with the ethico-political dimension of literature, as in Pheng Cheah's deconstructionist model.[3] Mine has been a kindred intervention with a foothold in Latin Americanism. (As I have previously argued, I find it less productive to model Latin American literature after World literature than to attempt to do the opposite.) The other foothold is in critical theory, a natural traveling companion to a literary tradition that often reflects on issues pertaining to power.

Speaking of critical theory, there are implications worth considering in this domain as well. With speculative exegeses of rubber novels, I have suggested that the category of "raw material" is for Marx something of a leap of faith, or an outright faulty premise. As theoretically informed as the present monograph has strived to be, it is not a work of theory as such. Others have made similar claims in a different fashion: Jason Moore's *Capitalism in the Web of Life: Ecology and the Accumulation of Capital* (2015) comes to mind.⁴ Moore shows how modernization created a separation of nature and humans to better exploit both; in so doing, he ushers in a revision of Marx's own modern, unavoidably eschewed premises. With regard to Marxist literary criticism—a tall edifice that ultimately stands on shaky ground—recognizing that nature never is "raw" gives another reason to revise findings and approaches. Ecological thought that reinforces the separation of nature and culture may be a contradiction in terms, and yet it is not uncommon in society at large and in eco-critical literary criticism in particular. Historians like Moore, versed as they are in natural and social history, cannot, for reasons of disciplinary specificity, concern themselves with language to the extent that literary critics can. Transcultural materialism, as a method for the study of literature, reveals the traces of successive material paradigms in language, and intervenes therein to change them. Put differently, this approach complements emerging, natural-cultural approaches to critical theory.

Conversely, Latin American novels of extractivism make the case for the politicization of new materialism. An exacerbated variant of what happens in other places of the world, Latin America has been subject and object of extractivism, plundered and plunderer. Its colonial exploitation predates that of the African continent and continues through the present through various forms of neocolonialism; its criollo elites benefit from modern mining operations that destroy the environment and affect the livelihood of the poor, much like their European or American counterparts do. Novels and cognate cultural products benefit from a rich tradition of experimentation and aesthetic risk. They offer, not surprisingly, a privileged site to reflect about the language of extractivism, which is part and parcel with the phenomenon itself. Part 2 of this book addressed it more comprehensively. Chapter 4, "Politics and Praxis of Hyperfetishism," considered the flipside of extraction, which is conspicuous consumption. The works I analyzed there, by authors such as Margo Glantz and Fernando Vallejo, take the prevalent and acritical celebration of luxury goods—"magical, clean" objects somehow removed from "prosaic, dirty" production—and turn it on its head. They don't necessarily do so programmatically, for works and authors alike may very well participate in the glee of consumerism. However, their engagement with, on the one hand, the cycle of production and consumption and, on the other, the effects of this cycle on literary form, make for thought-provoking fiction.

Note that extractivism is not new, nor does it belong to the realm of fiction alone. It does have a very specific Latin American configuration. A classical source to understand this is *el Libertador* Simón Bolívar's "Letter from Jamaica" (1815). At the time of writing, the visionary, authoritarian leader credited with quite literally spearheading the end of Spanish colonial rule in the Americas is looking for allies in England. He criticizes Spanish rule for reducing locals to being either "serfs" or "consumers" when it comes to commerce: "O, you wish to know what our future held?," he asks his addressee, Henry Cullen. He then dramatizes an answer: "Simply the cultivation of the fields of indigo, grain, coffee, sugar cane, cacao, and cotton; cattle raising on the broad plains; hunting wild game in the jungles; digging in the earth to mine its gold—but even these limitations could never satisfy the greed of Spain."[5] In Marxist terms, Bolívar is bemoaning the colonial status quo, whereby raw stuff and consumption are within the reach of *americanos*, but added value is not. At the same time, he is defending the extractivist model and reducing nature to mere economic resource, advocating for changes in management rather than for structural reform. (In the letter, indigenous cultures are cast as something from a heroic past.) Bolívar's ideas were, of course, plenty radical as they were—it's astounding, to begin with, that he no longer sees himself as a Spanish subject. What is interesting here is his symptomatic identification of extractivism as a staple of Latin America at the time the region was only recently coming into its own.

Brought to bear upon the present, Bolívar's prescient lament—which can and has been read both from the left and from the right—reads either like a poignant critique or a call to creolize neo-extractivism. In chapter 5, "Digitalia from the Margins," I mentioned how, with the exception of a handful of plutocrats, Mexican mogul Carlos Slim among them, few Latin Americans truly reap the benefits of added value in today's technologically driven economy. Those who do arguably do so thanks to the exploitation of the region's nature and people. Leaders of the receding Pink Tide—Bolivia's Evo Morales, Ecuador's Rafael Correa, Brazil's Dilma Roussef, Argentina's Cristina Kirchner—all gingerly embraced modern mining, despite its toll on the ecology and social equality of their lands. As the region swings to the right, this is unlikely to change.[6] The shift from extractivism to neo-extractivism is qualitative, for new technology is literally built from differentials of added value and reinforces them in turn. This is part of a virtuous circle for those who profit and a vicious one for those, nonhumans included, who are profited upon. We have replaced "the cultivation of the fields of indigo" for the mining of coltan, but the underlying logic continues. So does the thrust of literary language, equally present in Bolívar's eye-opening enumeration and in Zambra's invocation of love and computers, to offer whatever counterweight it can.

This can happen in unforeseen ways. Explicitly, this book has close-read works of literature that showcase how historical materialism enriches new materialist approaches. Implicitly, some of its findings contribute to the opposite: infusing critical theory methods with the findings of new materialism. Take Bruno Bosteels's *The Actuality of Communism* (2011), a thoughtful study that achieves many important things.[7] It uncouples Marxism from communism, as there are more communisms than those informed directly or indirectly by Karl Marx, and avoids the unsalutary—indeed, complementary—extremes of ignoring altogether the bloodshed that has occurred in the name of and against communism, on the one hand, and dismissing communism entirely because of it, on the other. More broadly, Bosteels demonstrates, as the title of his book suggests, the actuality—*Wirklichkeit*, also "effectiveness" and, paradoxically, "potency"—of communism. However, there are aspects of this actuality that the author's conceptual framework cannot account for. In the context of a discussion of the dialectical inversion of actuality and possibility, a theme he derives from Žižek, Bosteels notes, "The point is *somehow* to perceive communism not as a utopian not-yet for which reality will always fail to offer an adequate match, but as something that is always already here, in every moment of refusal of private appropriation and in every act of collective reappropriation."[8] At the very least, anthropodecentric thought contributes to this "somehow" by revealing the force of the signifier "communism": an actant in its own right, a word-deed. Just voice it aloud at the next faculty meeting for corroboration. The effects far exceed the utterer's intentions, the word itself being a nonhuman agent that—in a modified, less than semantic take on speech-act theory—quite simply stirs the humans in the room.

My methodology has revisited and repurposed particular concepts in Marx it finds especially compelling, such as primitive accumulation or commodity fetishism, rather than attempt to address Marxism or communism as a whole. I would be surprised if, in the eyes of the reader, this colors the book as Marxist, let alone communist—a matter about which

I have little control. I do envisage a horizon where, rather than have critical thinking engulf and override new materialism, or vice versa, these poles continue to build upon each other, contrapuntally. This is consonant with two other themes Bosteels develops, namely, the ontological turn in speculative leftism and its neo-Spinozist instantiation.

The former refers to a renewed interest—see Chantal Mouffe, Ernesto Laclau, Alain Badiou, and others—in the ontology of the political, as opposed to the straightforward practice of politics.[9] The inquiry into what constitutes the political has its own politics, to be sure, but it happens at a metalevel; nothing prevents subtle philosophers from also engaging with straightforward partisan issues. Still, in a caricature, the question of speculative leftism is "What is an event?" rather than "Where do we stand on the issue of subsidized transportation in our city?" Here too, recent approaches lend a hand. For a quick illustration, consider electrons as part of the political. An interdisciplinary approach grounded in science and technology studies (STS) has much to contribute to the study of actual power—"power grid" and "electric power" being more than naturalized metaphors—but also to political theory writ large, speculative leftism included. For materialists of any persuasion practicing in our technological era, thinking about ideology solely in abstract terms is, at best, shortsighted; at worst, it is misleading. Thinking about ideology in this day and age, as explored in chapter 5, benefits from considering what Sheila Jasanoff calls "sociotechnical imaginaries."[10] Understanding totality, as Lukács might put it, calls for a different kind of awareness. For a more or less banal example: posting radical claims on Facebook about housing costs in the San Francisco Bay Area (The rich must pay!), on aggregate, raises rent prices by funneling money into the pockets of a notorious real estate hoarder: Facebook. Because we live and signify in a corporate-designed world, a priori exercises in political ontology simply have to turn a posteriori.

Neo-Spinozism provides a common platform across critical paradigms. Bosteels laments that, in speculative leftism, the Heideggerian-Lacanian framework often overrides neo-Spinozist or Deleuzian ontologies of substance. Bosteels is thinking primarily of Antonio Negri and Michael Hardt, who put forward a famous argument about the multitude: "the living alternative that grows within empire," a composition of the "diverse figures of social production," similar to the internet in being a distributed network.[11] To their credit, they formulate an original political ontology, distinct from more familiar categories like "the masses," "the people," or "the working class." As Bosteels notes, however, critics find Negri and Hardt's notions too ghostly (Where does the multitude begin or end?) or not ghostly enough (What's the multitude's conceptual purchase?). The way forward in this impasse is anthropodecentric Spinozism. When Hardt and Negri evoke Saint Paul's "power of the flesh," we should at the same time think of its cognate, "meat": a single substance that humans and animals share (see chapter 1). A different political ontology emerges then. Speculative leftism could take stock of the various ways in which new materialism has advanced Spinozist thinking. Take Rosi Braidotti's "zoe-centered egalitarianism": "a materialist, secular, grounded and unsentimental response to the opportunistic trans-species commodification of Life that is the logic of advanced capitalism."[12] As she goes on to note, her work draws from Deleuze and Guattari's neo-Spinozism "reworked" with feminist and postcolonial theories.

New materialism also invites reconsiderations of the historical materialist archive.[13] In the context of a lengthy rebuttal of Trotsky and Bukharin, Lenin writes in 1921:

> A tumbler is assuredly both a glass cylinder and a drinking vessel. But there are more than these two properties, qualities or facets to it; there are an infinite number of them, an infinite number of "mediacies" and inter-relation-ships with the rest of the world. A tumbler is a heavy object which can be used as a missile; it can serve as a paper-weight, a receptacle for a captive butterfly, or a valuable object with an artistic engraving or design, and this has nothing at all to do with whether or not it can be used for drinking, is made of glass, is cylindrical or not quite, and so on and so forth.[14]

The literary value of this enumeration is, in a manner of speaking, crystal clear. We can almost see the revolutionary leader feeling the object in his hand, noticing its heft, pondering what to do next. The passage conjures the mundane and the exceptional, action and philosophy—the missile and the paperweight—beauty and violence—the captive butterfly, twice over. On one level, the point is that dialectical thinking has to consider *all* possibilities, and not the modest dichotomy that narrow-minded, scholastic Bukharin had used as an example in an earlier dispute: glass cylinder and drinking vessel. But then there is the implicit political ontology, which becomes graspable only in hindsight, where the very locus of revolutionary action lies in a multimodal human-nonhuman assemblage. The literary qualities of the passage, it bears noting, contribute to this realization. In closing his discussion of the tumbler, Lenin notes that "a full 'definition' of an object must include the whole of human experience, both as a criterion of truth and a practical indicator of its connection with human wants" and reminds his readers, citing Plekhanov, that "truth is always concrete, never abstract."[15] The mind reels.

For readers who may feel that the above paragraphs carry a few "isms" too many, or who wonder if Leninism or Spinozism have much to do with literature, let alone Latin American literature, I'll grant that, to some extent, we can dispense with the abstruse theoretical discussion. Not because, again, "critique has run out of steam," "suspicion is overrated," "theory is passé," or, heavens, because texts are to be data mined rather than read. Such ideologemes feed the niche specialization-irrelevance vicious circle in the humanities, itself reflective of broader trends in cognitive capitalism.[16] It is, rather, a matter of charitable interpretation and economy: works of literature already think for themselves. (This heuristic point of departure broadens, rather than narrows, the space for theoretically informed interpretation.) The present volume has shown how literature both represents and *enacts* materialist thinking. It provides more than mere illustration to the task of renewing the materialist scaffolding of contemporary speculative leftism.

To appreciate how this might be the case, recall the distinction between actors and actants: works of literature are the latter.[17] An actor is often a conscious, willing human; an actant needs neither of these attributes. "Actant" encompasses humans and nonhumans, individuals and collectives. My sense is that an indispensable aspect of the agency of literature, thus construed, is precisely its literariness. Theme, embeddedness within communities, symbolic value, social function, and so on matter plenty, but the event that is literature is not reducible to any of these features. On the contrary, it is the assemblage of these interactions, as they crystallize around books and other stuff, that matters: the sum total of the forces it unleashes, the matrix of possibilities, the breaking down of language—and its building up, once again.

Supply-Chain Critique versus Global Extractivism

Retrospectively, the arc of the present volume can be seen as a disassembling of the proverbial personal computer. Under the aegis of a recombined (historical and new) materialism I have called "transcultural," the book has progressed from raw material (chapter 1) to digital artifacts (chapter 5), with stopovers at crucial turning points. The latter include basic, enduring entities such as soil and atoms (chapter 2); corpses, essential to understanding the porous border between human and nonhuman (chapter 3); and hyperfetishes, a distinctive, recent phenomenon that anticipates infatuation with digital gadgets (chapter 4). At this point, it is worth taking this multilayered critique of commodity fetishism one step further by tackling, in literature, the various compounding forms of extractivism involved in recent technology. *Contemporary* literature, as previously noted, allows us to appreciate the present in its opacity, rather than in its deceiving transparency.

To that end, in this section I would like to formulate the rudiments of a corpus that works against the accumulation of surplus value in supply chains. Increasingly sophisticated—read *exploitative*—contemporary supply chains crisscross several continents with exacting precision. While upper management has a perspicuous view of supply chains, views from the ground are partial at best. Indeed, something that allows capitalists to extract hyperbolic margins from unsuspecting producers and consumers is their exploitees' lack of awareness of the scripted paths from raw material to purchased product, where the chain ends, and of its continuation, often unwieldy, from use to waste. This is in part a problem of storytelling. Products (commodity fetishes) are storied in all their banal glory, from enthusiastic reviews, through publicity, to infinite variations of consumer reverie. Their production, and the social relations that make it possible, are another "great untold." I hold no illusion that piecing together stories about traveling goods and their afterlives will spark worldwide revolution. But I do find it salutary, in today's largely postpolitical World Literature criticism, to engage with stuff—literally.

For a working definition of a supply chain, consider a pencil: its supply chain encompasses all logistics from sourcing wood and graphite, through assembly, to the sale that brings it to an end customer.[18] Ecologically responsible manufacturers would factor into their calculations what happens to the object afterward, notably decomposition—or lack thereof, as in the case of plastic. Before globalization—a technosocial process of integration that gained speed around 1989, the spur for the critical revival of World Literature—most of those steps happened locally. (Yes, there was trade along the Silk Road centuries ago, but at a radically different order of magnitude.) Extractivism has intensified accordingly. It is an economic model in which some nations specialize in producing raw goods while others specialize in manufacturing products.[19] Purportedly, this leads to increased overall efficiency, but it in fact solidifies an uneven scheme in which profit differentials can never be leveled out. Extractivism and supply chains compound to maintain global inequality despite net growth. Meanwhile, World Literature preaches a baseline equality among the literatures of the world. It is easy to read in this contrast bad faith, self-deception, compensation, utopianism, complicity, or a combination thereof.

In fact, World Literature has never been alien to such matters. Consider *The Manifesto of the Communist Party*, Marx and Engel's seminal work of 1848, which provides one of the first notes on record of the term *Weltliteratur*. Famously, the authors describe how "new wants" require satisfaction from distant lands, leading to economic interdependence.[20] "And as in material, so also in intellectual production," they go on to claim, adding that "national one-sidedness and narrow-mindedness become more and more impossible, and from the numerous national and local literatures, there arises a world literature."[21] Approaching the passage dialectically requires appreciating its internal contradictions, implied sublations, and overall teleology. I read it both as celebration of an unintended favorable consequence of the consolidation of the bourgeoisie at a global level *and* as budding critique of its emerging, integrated culture. It should give us pause that the manifesto should end on the still-unheeded call for proletarians of the world to unite. The international bourgeoisie was already several steps ahead of that. One side of the argument is the invocation of a proletarian World Literature, of which the manifesto itself would serve as an illustration; the other a condemnation of World Literature altogether. The heights and abysses of later socialist realism can be seen under the light of this contradiction, be they state-sanctioned (Maxim Gorky), antistate (George Orwell), or stateless (Roberto Arlt).[22]

As others are better suited to dwell on Marxian exegesis or social-realist literary historiography, I will turn to a different way of building on the parallelism of goods and literature. It is not exactly descriptive, in the way that Bourdieuan sociologies of literature, themselves beholden to the isomorphism of *Weltmarkt* and *Weltliteratur*, are. Rather, salvaging for a different era the fundamentals of socialist realism and adopting them as methodological imperatives, I seek to use cultural production to expose social reality and thereby participate, however modestly, in its transformation. I take my cues from the chapters above. Recall the following: it is ironic, to say the least, that the seemingly abstract, speculative action of pondering literature and biopolitics should take place on a very concrete laptop computer. The latter is always already a reification of transnational social relations and biopolitical entanglements, including coltan from Congo and lithium from Bolivia. Its nether parts report: "Designed by Apple in California. Assembled in China." As much a product of human ingenuity as the novel is, the computer speaks to the global condition in an entirely different key. We could ignore it as an externality to "spiritual" production (an epic misunderstanding best captured in the German agglutination *Geisteswissenschaften cited above*), ruminate humanistically on its role in how we think (à la Friedrich Kittler), or engage it on its own terms. As I see it, literature can either turn a blind eye to its conditions of production or, on the other hand, call them into question.

When teaching Zambra's "Historia de un computador" (chapter 5), time and again I ask my students, teasingly: "What is your favorite brand of Chilean computers?" "None" is the right answer, as there is comparatively little in the way of high-surplus-value technological products from Latin America. And yet Zambra's story, already tinted with nostalgia for a time when daily computation was limited to the living room, has been taken up by avid readers in its successful translations into several languages. This is but a pyrrhic victory in commercial terms, for Latin American literary fiction—with the arguable exception of the Boom writers, Roberto Bolaño and, possibly, Yuri Herrera and Valeria Luiselli—is rarely a high-surplus-value affair. And yet it is meaningful that this literary critique of technology should go against the grain of hegemony. If one realizes, moreover, that personal computers are but a chapter in the long history of computation, and that they are ideologically conditioned—computation need not be "personal"; i.e., individualist—then it becomes apparent that Zambra, from Santiago, is driving technological commodity fetishism to its exhaustion. The point is well taken that literature can estrange our relationship to computers. In this case, it does so by inscribing them into narratives more complex than planned obsolescence, parodied in the short story.

I have followed this trail in the work of a more famous countryman of Zambra's: Roberto Bolaño, author of *2666*, the 2004 classic (chapter 3). At this point it's worth recalling that Klaus Haas, a person of interest in the investigations of the Juárez femicides and the nephew of Archimboldi—the lost German luminary whose search provides the lengthy novel its unity of action—sodomizes his prison mates with cool detachment (and a cold knife blade). Well before such horrors, while Haas is still a free man, we learn something rather meaningful: he owns a computer store.

The construction of this character is too important in the novel for this to be an idle detail. At this point in the novel, the wants of the forlorn, well-established European academics of the first part align themselves with the broader wants of the market and, inconclusively, with the wants of one or several killers. They all travel to distant lands to satisfy them. Detective Epifanio Galindo cross-examines women who work for Haas— read, through homophony with the German noun, *Hate*. The detective is flirtatious, belittling, and oddly caring. He investigates the murder of their coworker Estrella Ruiz Sandoval and wants to know if she was an habitué of nightclubs. The intimation and misogynistic overtone is that somehow she had it coming. A coworker categorically denies the accusation: "Estrella wanted to know things about computers, she wanted to learn, she wanted to get ahead, said the girl. Computers, computers, I don't believe a word you're saying, cupcake, said Epifanio. I'm not your fucking cupcake, said the girl."[23]

The woman's self-assured, defiant stance is met with the patronizing, derogatory "tortita" (translated here as "cupcake"), Mexican slang for "fatty," "vagina," or "lesbian" (nuances the translation misses). Women in the computer store are defying gender roles. Estrella herself used to work in a *maquiladora*: by working for Haas, she has moved up in the world. In Epifanio's eyes, Madonna-whore Manicheism becomes butch-victim. Hence the disdain for his interviewee. Meanwhile, when Haas is thrown in prison, justly or not, he introduces himself to the hardened *narcos* there as "a computer expert who started his own business."[24] Bolaño has a knack for making the most mundane phrase seem eerie, and this is one such occasion. The self-defined computer expert, to put the matter in the prison slang, will make bitches of them all. Computation then provides the link between several compounding factors: the aspirations for social mobility that drive women from the Mexican countryside to a lawless, chauvinist, desert town; a geography ripe for both impunity and deregulation; a global desire for gadgets of all ilk that reshaped northern Mexico in the wake of NAFTA. Scores of brown women sit in a maelstrom of power differentials.

2666 sits somewhere between the all-knowing, evil computer in Stanley Kubrick's *2001: A Space Odyssey* and the fascist propaganda screens in George Orwell's *1984*. Much can be said about its slow, paratactical unfolding from European universities and high culture to the depths of border-town femicide. I am characterizing this movement, tendentiously, as taking us, knowledge workers par excellence, from the spiritual achievements that software like Microsoft Word make possible to hardware and the social conditions of its production. In this account, high and low not just collapse in an evocative figure like Bataille's solar anus, but in the more prosaic and quite physical body of modern gadgets. The latest "personal" computer or equivalent novelty is the embodiment, and corporate resolution, of social contradiction. Mining, foundry, fabrication, stocking, distribution, design, engineering—these are worldwide class dynamics and levels of education brought together in seeming harmony, provided there is a narrative. And indeed there is one, thanks to techno-utopianism: the story that this benefits the whole. Transcultural materialism complicates that story.

For its part, *Maquilápolis*, Vicky Funari and Sergio de la Torre's eye-opening 2006 documentary, shows a different facet of the same workers Bolaño writes about.[25] In the haunting opening sequence, we see their disciplined bodies casting shadows on the desert as they replicate the movements they would do in the factory. Uniformed women wave their hands in the air rhythmically, as if carefully operating machinery, miming their daily routine. The visual quotation of the famous sequence in Charlie Chaplin's *Modern Times* (1936) is apt. In the silent cinema classic, the conveyor belt is a central element; here it is absent, for the cogs and wheels of these women's employment extend themselves along an invisible, transnational assembly-line. Long sequences portray the daily lives of specific workers (Carmen Durán, Lourdes Luján) and their plight for labor and ecological justice.[26] Shots of blue uniforms hanging from a thread—against the backdrop of distant factories or highway overpasses—conjure domesticity and work, private life and globalization. In a close-up, women utter the names of their employer companies. Their bodies rotate, as if standing on an off-frame lazy Susan, resembling exhibited products. Later, they showcase the finished products of their labor (TV parts, pantyhose) in their hands. Here supply-chain critique, in the vein of transcultural materialism, interweaves social relations with means of production, domains that orthodox Marxism held separate. *Stories of things* and *stories of people* bear upon each other.

What drives goods around the world is added value. More than the sum of its parts, a computer derives profit from every link in the supply chain. The company makes a killing at each transaction, from the mining of mercury and gold in Africa and South America; through the aluminum foundries for the computer's frame and motherboard assembly in China; to its rote software coding in India and its design in Cupertino; to its glorified commercialization in all of these locales. Think once more of rubber trees coming back to the Amazon, many times more expensive, as truck tires. To get a sense of the magnitude of modern extractivism, multiply this by each of the numerous components in a tech gadget—then bundle and copyright them. Each additional level of accumulation makes the human labor involved in the process more abstract and harder to grasp. Glendinning's previously cited dictum resounds, "All technology is political."[27] Any computer reflects social relations of production at a global level.

Addressing this requires us to venture beyond the boundaries of Latin Americanist literary criticism, narrowly construed, far beyond auteur-activist documentaries like *Maquinápolis*, across media, genres, and locales. Consider, for the sake of simplicity, the two other crucial moments in computer supply chain literature: mineral extraction and artifact disposal. Regarding the former, prolific genre writer Alberto Vásquez-Figueroa, something of a Spanish Simenon, gives us the 2008 novel *Coltán*. It is a hard-boiled rewrite of Christie's *Ten Little Indians* (1939) with the board of Dall & Houston, an ersatz Haliburton, as the dying Indians. The premise is smart: Aarohum Al Rashid, a mysterious figure evocative of Islamist insurgents, starts murdering them one by one for not paying a Robin Hoodesque ransom: the rebuilding of Iraqi infrastructure. Coltan comes into play because Dall & Houston has sought to rein back its trade.[28] This leads to plot twists and a chase across the continents that results, unsurprisingly, in the revelation that Al Rashid was a board member all along.

What interests me in this cultural product is how it both denounces and symbolically exploits the coltan trade. Take a character, the Belgian swindler Marcel Valerie. We see through his eyes Congolese child coltan miners for the first time, covered in dust and always at risk of being buried alive in mine shafts, like an "army of ghosts."[29] Valerie learns from his Kazakh guide that their day shift is worth twenty cents (in euros); he's amazed, but not appalled. Seizing a business opportunity, he purchases the mine from the Kazakh for a bargain of thirty million euros. With a heavy hand, here Vásquez-Figueroa communicates the mind-bending scalability of modern profit. Yet he is also complicit in what he denounces, for he builds a European bestseller upon sensationalist myths about coltan. As Michael Nest shows in an eponymous 2011 study, it is false that 80 percent of the world reserves are under control of mass rapists in Congo, a legend that once prompted a well-meaning Democratic U.S. senator to say that "without knowing it, tens of millions of people in the United States may be putting money in the pockets of some of the worst human rights violators in the world simply by using a cellphone or a laptop computer."[30] Alas, if only systemic responsibility were so simple. *Coltán*, the novel, serves as cautionary tale against a certain kind of simplification.

Ironically, simplicity in form can convey ideological complexity. Colombian conceptual artist Antonio Caro presents a powerful, straightforward work of art that comments on mineral extraction: *Minería* (2012). In this work, it looks as if the Colombian flag—a stripe of blue sandwiched between two parts of yellow above and one of red below—had forgone its yellow stripe in favor of the word "MINERIA." Achieving the not-insignificant task of seeing his country's flag as *objet trouvé*, Caro nods to the representation of riches by the flag's yellow—that is, gold. The viewer is reminded that gold does not happen spontaneously but through laborious, indeed toxic, extraction. The blue of oceans and the red of founders' blood look orphaned when the yellow of gold retreats into the sans-serif, bulky all caps of the title word, forcefully presiding over the piece. The artwork puts in stark relief that national identity hinges on surrendering natural resources to foreign powers: then for mercantilist, now for digital accumulation. This revisits familiar motifs in Caro's lifelong, playful rumination on names, symbols, and catchphrases, which include the late seventies pop-art gesture of writing the name "Colombia" in unmistakable "Coca-Cola" font. It solidifies the impression, cultivated throughout his oeuvre, that the country is for sale. Caro extracts and transfers the gold from the nation's symbolic reserves onto the fraught terrain of contemporary debates on nature and culture.

Carolina Caycedo, born in 1978, pursues similar goals with her *Be Damned* series, notably the piece *YUMA, or the Land of Friends* (2014) (figure 6.1). Commissioned for the Berlin Biennale, it documents, in a grand, Jacques Louis David–like format, the construction of a river dam in El Quimbo, Colombia. It is a dizzying experience to stand in front of the work, as if carelessly soaring above the terrain, while also being reminded of one's smallness vis-à-vis the towering, flat image. High-definition depiction, paradoxically, gains the qualities of abstraction. A different kind of found object, the piece originates in a satellite photograph from the exact coordinates of the construction site, seemingly a click away, yet shrouded in lush tropical nature—if not for long. Yuma is the Muisca name for the

FIGURE 6.1 Carolina Caycedo, *YUMA, or the Land of Friends*, 2014. Digital prints on acrylic glass, satellite images, 580 × 473 cm., 100 × 100 cm. Exhibited at the eighth Berlin Biennale for Contemporary Art, Museen Dahlem.

river. Caycedo would agree with Heidegger on how a dam instrumentalizes nature, with the added component of turning entire displaced, meagerly compensated indigenous and mestizo populations into similarly instrumentalized "nature." This is the contemporary, Latin American instantiation of the biopolitics of neoliberalism that Michel Foucault discussed in his late opus *The Birth of Biopolitics*.[31] It bears noting that all this scarring of the earth happens in the name of the electricity that fuels our gadgets.

Vásquez-Figueroa's coltan, Caro's gold, and Caycedo's hydropower stand to gain when set in conversation with each other. The Spaniard might sensationalize more than elucidate, uproot problems in the name of localization, and contribute very meagerly to the genre of the novel, his chosen art form. But he also reveals, by contrast, a certain nationalistic myopia in his Colombian conceptual-artist interlocutors. How many nations' flags could, in how many languages, replace their colors with the word "mining"? How many "natural resource" exploitation sites could be photographed and exhibited in German galleries? *Coltán*, for better or for worse, reaches out to those other *other* locales. Similarly, what I am attempting to do here is deploy the resources of World Literature to fill the vacuum of storytelling in supply chains that, in turn, make the paradigm possible in the first place. Consider, heuristically, that Zambra's tale about computation does not begin or end where its plot does. It belongs to a single cultural assemblage with the *maquila* prehistory and e-wasteyard future of its title gadget; it informs the articles that frequent-flying intellectuals produce.

Consider computer waste. A quasi-foundational work is the 2008 Pixar animation blockbuster *Wall-E*. The title character is a postapocalyptic, rubbish-sorting robot that, after many adventures, becomes instrumental to the rebirth of planet earth. As much as I regard the film as a masterpiece of the genre, if the medium is the message, and the medium is mass entertainment, then the message here is just further commodification. I am moved by the robot's romantic loneliness and his built-up encounter with a feminine, more advanced robot, EVE, endowed with fertility in a barren world. But the extreme embellishment of actual e-wasteyards is hyperbolic,[32] particularly when coupled with highly mediated aesthetic practices, dependent on powerful computing, such as corporate computer animation and 3D rendering.[33]

There are different, more productive responses, such as the South Korean poet Kim Hyesoon's aptly titled 2011 collection *All the Garbage of the World,*

Unite! Kim finds gods among the refuse and expresses their divinity with jarring effect, building up to garbled words on the page: "Do you know all the dearest gods that are hanging onto our limbs? / On the seat you left, a wet towel, a wad of gum, a crushed tomato. . . . Yournostrilssingledropofapricklynosehairearth god!"[34] One could also think of the Zambian Ellen Banda-Aaku's witty children's short story "E is for E-Waste" (2013) and the instructive San Francisco activist video "The Story of Electronics" (2011).[35]

On disposal, however, the most thoughtful works I know are Brazilian. A case in point is Jorge Furtado's 1989 avant-garde documentary *Ilha das Flores*.[36] Throughout the thirteen-minute short, a Guy Debord–inspired voiceover, the sound of which is reminiscent of a science documentary, describes the logic of consumerism. Meanwhile, the film follows a tomato from the plot of a Nisei farmer, to a petty-bourgeois family kitchen in Porto Alegre, to the eponymous wasteland in the outskirts of the city. Crude, iterative images of money changing hands splice the already-staccato sequences, themselves introduced by rudimentary computer graphics. At one point, piles of corpses from Nazi factories of death are shoveled into graves. To a jarring electric-guitar riff, the tomato ends up in a pile of organic waste that feeds the homeless denizens of the garbage dump—though not before a dumpster farmer's pigs get the first pick.

Clearly, Furtado does not film for the faint of heart. However, his work retains a playful lyricism, lost in Eduardo Coutinho's later, grittier portrait on a similar subject, *Boca do lixo* (1993), and beautified in Vik Muniz's paintings with trash and their accompanying documentary, *Waste Land* (2010).[37] Be that as it may, the important links established here are, on the one hand, between freedom and the control of life—Foucault's dyad—and, on the other, between supply chains and exploitation. The script's envoi interrupts the by-then established repetition of brain and opposable thumbs as human traits. It introduces freedom as a third, unexpected trait, precisely in the moment when the subject depicted would be, at least in the eyes of the well-to-do, most thoroughly dehumanized. The final lines are a tautology by the modernist poet Cecília Meireles: "Free is the state of one who has freedom. Freedom is a word nourished by human aspirations, that no one can explain, and no one can understand."[38] Rather than a late-romantic invocation of the ineffable or merely an ironic *épater les bourgeois*, the operation at hand is rigorously dialectic. Shopper "freedom" and obscene differentials in value extraction are of a piece.

In this sense, a computer is very much like a tomato. Electronic wasteyards in rural China and Bangladesh are smoldering no-man's-lands where day laborers "cook" motherboards to scavenge mineral.[39] Nurturing effective forms of solidarity for our present biopolitical conjuncture must cut across facile oppositions: local-global, digital-analog, producer-consumer, human-nonhuman, organic-inorganic. Mobilizing cultural production to illuminate different moments in exploitative global supply chains, as I have strived to do here in short form, may contribute to this task. The next logical task remains to extend these insights from cultural products that relate mimetically to actual production and consumption to those that allude to them only indirectly. The wheels of commerce will be there still, covered by a very thin veil. As of late, their movement subsumes more and more of human activity, literature being no exception. Arguably, sharply differentiated accumulation of surplus value will continue to occur whether we describe it or not, challenge it or not. But so will a cognate literary corpus continue to exist, brought about by its own internal logic. Examining it will, at the very least, raise important questions about the autonomy of literature.

Alternatives include addressing a corpus of World Literature as handed down to us by critical consensus or by the culture industry. The latter offers fine representatives of literary genres, the former a snapshot of today's society and values; they overlap, partially. But neither necessarily speaks to, recalling Jasanoff's term, "sociotechnical imaginaries."[40] These vary widely among locales and have significant impact. The harmonizing agenda of World Literature may fail to appreciate those aspects. They do not always emerge in a single work but, as I have shown, in a host of works that revolve around a singular object. Heuristically, again, the object in focus has been a computer, including some of its parts and some aspects of its afterlife. It bears repeating that I write from a place known by the moniker "Silicon Valley," named after the eponymous semiconductor. Most service workers here speak Spanish at home, are more likely to come across a movie like *Wall-E* than any work of highbrow Latin American fiction, and could not afford engineering or literary criticism careers. In more ways than I intuit, my book reflects this.

Now, for all that a computer may reflect global social relations of production in its hardware and software, a skeptic might say that the act of writing "with" one is free from that backstory. I would disagree, obviously, at various levels, ranging from my understanding of what writing *is* (here I do side with Kittler), to, more importantly, my commitment to recognizing and engaging with the materiality of cultural production. The goods and literature debate has been framed in terms of parallelism, to various degrees of proximity. I regard it, rather, as a matter of imbrication. To my mind, the question is not whether they are imbricated, but how. Computation is an interesting starting point because it is becoming the sine qua non of literary culture, as it is of cinematic culture: a purportedly disembodied process that is in fact very tangible; a seemingly gratuitous affair with vast economic consequences. The most brilliant algorithm has little effect without supply chains and all they entail. Should one ignore this epoch-defining phenomenon? (For its part, "applying" the tools of digital humanities raises the question of who the agent is and who, alas, is the tool.) Projecting the stories of objects into their real-world material entanglements cultivates a different ethos—one of thinking with literature wherever it may take us. It has been the path charted here, and it is but one of several ways of thinking with, not past, the imbrication.

Paradoxically, reconnecting material and intellectual production may serve well those who seek to "liberate" the former from the latter, as bourgeois piety dictates. "Art for art's sake" is not achieved by fiat. Of course, it may also rekindle a political streak that the Marxist tradition of World Literature has lost to the more tepid Goethean vein. In either case, it is a sensible measure, lest the debate on the global autonomization of literature happen in a denial of historicity. There is similarly much work to do, self-consciously, to not replicate extractivism by plucking from the cultures of the world to build upon them conceptually, thereby adding value, and then shipping them back to their places of provenance as theory. If the present study has, unavoidably, skirted this position, it has done so as a necessary moment in throwing the proverbial wrench into ever-expanding forms of accumulation.

Things with a History

Where to go from here? A succinct comparison of noteworthy contemporary authors, as captured in the contrast between their respective material invocations, leads the way. Take the Norwegian Karl Ove Knausgård (b. 1968), whose six-novel autobiographical work *My Struggle* (2009–11) is something of a twenty-first-century World Literature classic. He went on to pen the very remarkable *Autumn* (2015), a collection of short texts with the stated goal of explaining the world to the author-narrator's unborn daughter, one "thing" at a time (Knausgård is no stranger to hubris). The heterogeneous collection that ensues—dawn, telephones, Flaubert, vomit—is thought-provokingly idiosyncratic. Individual pieces double as prose poems or the entries of a personal encyclopedia. Under the heading "Rubber Boots," we read about a pair that belonged to the author's late father. Walking in them gives the narrator "great pleasure," for as "the foot sinks down into the mud without anything penetrating its protective cover, the mud oozes up around the boot but the foot remains dry—and sovereign somehow."[41] This feeling of sovereignty amounts to a triumph over death. The subject wills itself away from mourning his father or commemorating him reverentially via his personal objects. At the same time, the narrator celebrates the impermeable capacities of rubber, a turning point in the separation of nature and culture, ahistorically.

Contrast this with the short story "Han vuelto las aves," by the Guatemalan author Eduardo Halfon (b. 1971), in which mourning means stepping deeply into history, natural and otherwise. Halfon writes genre-defying, recombining, episodic narratives. Across several volumes—notably *El boxeador polaco* (2008), *Monasterio* (2014), *Signor Hoffman* (2015), and *Duelo* (2017)—such episodes compose a loosely autobiographical *Künstlerroman*. Recurrent themes include the imminence of intimacy between the author-protagonist and traveling, mysterious women; echoes of violence in rural Central America; and the memories of his grandfather, who survived Auschwitz. The story at hand, masterfully suspenseful, is set in the coffee-growing region of Huehuetango, near the Mexican border. In medias res, the author-protagonist arrives at the Martínez's house, with a purpose readers are not privy to, but which entails learning from the residents, as if taking notes for some report. (Per the book's copyright page, the piece was originally commissioned by the Inter-American Development Bank.) Residents gradually open up to *señor Halfon*, leading to the revelation that their son has been assassinated, readers gather, in the long struggle to establish fair and sustainable farming practices. The denouement is worth citing at length, as Mr. Martínez penetrates into his son's unattended shrub of a coffee plant:

> Don Juan turned his back to us and seemed to step into the enormous, lone coffee plant. As though hiding among its green leaves, searching for something among its green leaves. As though wishing the old plant would protect him. His back still to us, he was plucking beans off the old plant, slowly, tenderly, his campesino hands letting the red fruit fall soundlessly onto the dry ground. He bent a little and picked the lower beans. He stretched to the upper branches, pulled them toward him, and his expert hands stripped them clean. The ground around his feet was turning red. His straw hat crackled in the branches. He now looked more hunched, smaller. He kept on plucking beans and dropping them onto the ground. He kept entering the foliage of the old plant, the greenery of the leaves and branches, until the whole of him disappeared entirely.[42]

It's an overdetermined image, to be sure. "Don Juan" here is an enamored, heartbroken *picaflor*, a hummingbird, serving as accessory to life at a site where life itself commemorates death—a de facto botanical memorial. (This comes within an oeuvre in which Shoah memorials are not uncommon, effectively leveraging recognition of the Guatemalan *genocide* on the original historical phenomenon that led to the juridical notion of extermination of a *genus*.) We learn, in this sentimental education of a short story, that *deshijar*, that is, plucking beans in order for plants to yield fewer and better-quality beans, is a verb. The irony is unsettling, as is to "witness" a private act of mourning in full color: red and green. Breakthrough in healing or dwelling in the symptom, we don't know. Anagnoresis is only partial, because the process of getting here matters more than the revelation itself. The story is not about the assassination of a coffee cooperative *campesino*, but about everything that surrounds it, down to the fraught origins of "fair trade." The true realization is that family history, the history of Guatemala, and world and natural history are all organically connected.

Simone de Beauvoir was moved by a deliberately long take in Claude Lanzmann's *Shoah* (1985) of the grass that continues to grow, to this day, on the train tracks of extermination.[43] "The basic quality of the transience of the earthly," wrote Adorno in his 1932 essay "The Idea of Natural-History," "signifies nothing but just such a relationship between nature and history:

all being or everything existing is to be grasped as the interweaving of historical and natural being."[44] Halfon illustrates what Beauvoir and Adorno meant[45]—not at the abstract level, for there is nothing abstract about it, but as tangible, embodied experience. Again, the contrast with Knausgård is enlightening. For the Norwegian, the milky rubber tree remains in the margins of history. Less than a relic, it is a disavowed pre-text for the late father's (synthetic?) rubber boots, themselves an instrument for the separation of nature and culture, human and nonhuman history. For the Guatemalan, the bushy coffee plant *is history*. More than a relic—a living being—it bears the fruit of the lost son's botched effort, situated at the crossroads of Guatemalan history, natural and otherwise. Whereas extractivism plays a role in both bereavements, one engages it critically and the other doesn't. The uptake, and an important conclusion for the present volume, is the following: *whereas cultural production carries with it the traces of material-social transformation, it often also covers these traces.* This dialectic of exposure and erasure justifies the expanded hermeneutical practice I have called "transcultural materialism."

I have read for disclosure and for concealment of such matters as abusive, epoch-defining "social pacts" with things; coinages and other linguistic practices that reinforce fixed hierarchies among humans and nonhumans, first, and among humans and nations, consequently; and separation of humans from nature, coupled with narratives in which humans can just take and take without ever giving back. Narrative and language alone do not and cannot determine such facets of extractivism, but they can certainly make them worse or better. Recall, from the introduction, the role that Hayden White gives to accounts that destorify or denarrativize the Holocaust. Unified narratives give the impression that one can grasp that event. Disassembling such narratives, and letting constellations and fragments speak for themselves—incidentally, as Halfon does—communicates anew the scale and poignancy, the sheer incomprehensibility, of the Shoah. When it comes to communicating the "slow violence" of extractivism, to adapt Rob Nixon's term, storifying may actually contribute to a better understanding of human-nonhuman relations. As the above take on supply-chain critique suggests, extractivism profits from scatteredness in storytelling. Piecing together bouts of narrative has a salutary effect. Sometimes individual works of literature achieve this; other times it's the critic's task to, at a metalevel, facilitate this effect. This can be done by reassessing a single work—for example, by interrogating how its verisimilitude may hinge upon a certain understanding of the nonhuman—or by setting several works into conversation—on the issue of primitive accumulation, say. As previously noted, in Romance languages, Spanish and Portuguese among them, there is a single word for "history" and "story": *historia*. Hence things *with a history*.

In order to intervene in a material-social status quo, one measure is to lay in the open traces of nonhuman domination. This involves a combination of the textual and the contextual, the negative and the positive. Methodologically, the implication is for literary studies to cultivate, at the same time, strategies that may seem antithetical: close reading and sociohistorical (even botanical) interpretation, ideology critique and description. Luckily, there is a rich Latin American tradition—showcased in this book under the aegis of revised *transculturación*—that makes this possible. The region's literature has two distinctive features that contribute to this endeavor, bolstering its relevance for literary studies writ large: a thematic investment with making art at the frontier of Western capitalist expansion and a formal investment with language. Some of the most accomplished products of Latin American literary culture marry formal sophistication with political relevance. Early examples include Darío's short story-cum-manifesto "The Bourgeois King" (1888);[46] examples from the 1960s zenith include Castellanos's counterfactual historical novel *The Book of Lamentations* (1962) and Cortázar's experimental novel *Hopscotch* (1963).[47] While this is more readily appreciated regarding politics in a conventional sense (as a humancentric, partisan affair), it holds true for political ecology as well.

Several reading practices emerge. One is to identify and interrogate moments of articulation in which immanent material properties are emplotted or codified through language. The chapters above offer ample illustration. In terms of rhetorical analysis, this often means stopping short of allegory and metaphor. Sometimes, a cigar is just a cigar. Similarly, for all that abstraction is essential to thought, it can be easily overused. Novels about the rubber boom, say, may be about commodification, but ascribing to them that abstract operation alone leads to overlooking many a description, setting, and plot twist: to not reading, in short, and also to ignoring plants, rocks, corpses, and things that may have more centrality to *historias* than we credit them with. Another emerging reading practice is more heuristic in nature, involving proposing alternatives narratives of imbrication between the human and nonhuman. This entails filling gaps and heeding the questions about nature and culture that literary works, more or less explicitly, engage with. The path to a more radical, creative interdisciplinarity—mineralogy and narratology?—lays open.

The critique of extractivism may start in literary works and continue in criticism. By force of custom, unsustainable human-nonhuman assemblages are invisible to the eye. Estranging them makes them visible. A *mot juste* here or there goes a long way, as does, more broadly, casting doubt onto what appears to be settled. As a case in point, as previously noted, coinages such as "meat" or "raw material" give the appearance, at the very surface of everyday language, that eating animals or extracting minerals has always been the default state of affairs. The very signifier justifies; it gives the standing of a fait accompli to what is, at a tangible level, much more contentious. What to make, then, of entire narratives and discourses built upon the edifice of such equivocations? It may take decades to think our way out of the Cartesian split that informs our unsustainable relation to (within) nature. Rewriting history as natural history, while still doing justice to very human concerns such as labor, would take years for disciplinary historians to achieve, should they choose to do so. And yet time is pressing, as global warming reminds us. Transcultural materialism, by summoning the powers of literature to estrange extractivism, may elicit new ways of thinking about old problems.

A dialectical praxis based on close reading and metalinguistic awareness, the approach I have espoused has an impact on a number of domains. Latin Americanism is an obvious first. Fernando Ortiz's use of the term *transculturación*, and its various permutations throughout decades of criticism, is central to the field. The notion has stood for a foundational socioeconomical force in Cuba (Ortiz), a literary integration of disparate elements (Rama), cultural hybridity in the region at large (García Canclini), a specifically Andean dialogue between Quechua and Spanish traditions (Cornejo Polar), a problematic acculturation mechanism (Moreiras), and a racially fraught Caribbeanist cultural narrative (Arroyo), among many others. Trying to pin down this rich, variegating drift is something of a lost cause. This book's modest but far-reaching proposal with regard to Latin Americanism could be construed as a call to revise—to *materialize*—this entire genealogy in light of the misapprehension of the more "natural" (botanical, agricultural) aspects in Ortiz's coinage. The nonhuman is present all along, at every turning point: the invitation is for scholars with granular knowledge of the subfields to explore the implications of this finding. For instance, one task would be to explicate the role that dry highland savannas of Perú and Bolivia (*la puna*) may have in Cornejo Polar's thinking; another would be to revise Rama's discussion of mountains as "natural fortresses" in Arguedas and Mariátegui; and so on.[48]

Everything established so far is expandable in and transferrable to several provinces of literary and cultural studies. The starting point is simple and the ramifications manifold. I began by making the case for establishing a counterpoint between new materialisms, with their emphasis on nonhuman agency, and historical materialism, with its emphasis on human labor conditions and their historical unfolding. Approaching cultural products in this dialectic fashion does not necessarily lead to a unified analysis, nor is it meant to. Instead, it exposes an important dimension of the tensions and contradictions that literature, like art more generally, plays a part in. The contributions of this approach to present-day criticism include presenting an alternative to the false dichotomy of positivist description versus suspicion that underlies sociologies of literature (Casanova, Moretti) and actor-network theorizations (Felski), while supplementing the cultural-critique impulse prevalent within the field of Latin Americanism (Beasley-Murray, Beverley, Bosteels—to cover the letter *b* alone). Close reading and (materialist) interpretation get their dues. Suspicion recovers its place as an important methodological principle—and retains suspicion of power, that is, of the mediation of words in shaping human interaction with the world.

But where does transcultural materialism end? In other words, how broad is the corpus of this study, and to what kinds of objects might its findings apply? As naive as it would be to try to script the reception of a book, it's worth noting that, though expansive, transcultural materialism is meant to have certain bounds. The same is true for Fernando Ortiz's *transculturación*, even while, as we have seen, that notion continues to shift contexts and speak to different questions. Many things can be described with the dynamic, diachronic, "slow friction" Ortizian model. At times, it seems that *any* cultural process—and, per my revision, any natural-cultural process—could be framed in those terms. But when the semantic field of a concept is too vast, the concept becomes useless. Fortunately, many elements do not sit well with *transculturación*, which allows it to remain meaningful.

The term may overcome contradictions and hold opposites within itself, but it does have an outside: it persistently antagonizes essentialism, racism, and ill-founded feelings of cultural superiority. This applies to the notion both as found object and as method, aspects that Ortiz tends to blur together in the development of his views. In the former sense, not everything that has happened in Cuba can be described as *transculturación*. In the latter, *transculturación* could not apply to just anything. For an extreme example, consider that, although Nazism drew inspiration from Germanic mythology, American racial laws, and Hindu iconography (swastikas), it would be foolish to describe it as the result of transculturation.[49]

Similarly, although transcultural materialism could be brought to bear on more issues than I can anticipate—the aspiration of any book—there are limits as to how this might unfold. As I have theorized it, the two central elements here are language and extractivism. The first is the domain that I have focused on, for obvious reasons of disciplinary affordance and bias. Surely, there are social-sciences aspects that could be developed, not least in disciplinary history, whose mainstream instantiation in academic departments has drifted away from the self-awareness about language thoughtfully put forward by the likes of Hayden White, Dominick LaCapra, or the siblings Benedict and Perry Anderson. As an outsider to the discipline—despite the phrase "with a History" in this book's title—my one plea, coming from the neighboring field of literary studies, is for any historian inclined to take up these ideas to make a significant investment in language—not for stylistic preference or for reasons of methodological affinity, but because my study shows that extractivism continues in language, and so in language it must be, at least partially, dispelled. An analogous entreaty could be made vis-à-vis the more strictly ecological ramifications of this natural-cultural study: minimally, practitioners would do well in considering the role of metaphor in their thinking. The internal connection between extractive language and economic exploitation raises the second limit: acritical takes on material transformation may provide many valuable descriptive leads, but they fall short of the sort of recombined materialism the present volume has grounded. Human labor should not be left out of the picture as we pay attention to nonhuman elements. For a quick literary illustration, recall how the yellow butterflies so celebrated in García Márquez's *One Hundred Years of Solitude*, in a famous signifying chain, bear the color of bananas and allude to massacred plantation workers.

The above suggests that depoliticizing, purportedly "materialist" approaches to literary studies are less relevant than those that in some way continue to engage the enormous power differentials the world is fraught with, and which are in some ways alleviated, in others compounded, by digital technology and the coming revolutions of genomics and material science. Literature is concerned with the world, and the world is an unfair place that develops unevenly. Reading literature and ignoring unfairness is not reading at all. If the time for ideology critique is over, then surely we must live in the best of worlds. Alas, this is not the case, not least because a sharp subject/object distinction has led humans, some more than others, to fancy themselves owners of the world. Extraction of the labor of fellow humans and of "natural resources" preys on a suspended sense of debt and of reciprocity: namely, the fantasy that forces of production, human or not, will just surrender their resources without exhaustion—or rebellion. Ecological damage and most, if not all, variants of capitalism feed of each other in a vicious circle, as proponents of notions such as the "Capitalocene" know full well and as, increasingly, common sense tell us. So the idea that literature and literary studies had a more pressing political role in the smoky-London-sky days of Dickens forgets that much of the world is exposed to the poison of industrial growth, but also that plenty of political-ecological worries besiege even the most greenified of cosmopolitan cities.

At this point, I may already be preaching to the chorus. But I hope to have persuaded readers interested in the nonhuman to take such considerations into account, and to have convinced readers interested in the literary to understand form, as Adorno would have it, as "sedimented content"—with the provision that "sediment" is not a neutral metaphor.[50] The thing mediates between cultures like sugar cane mediated between the masters and the enslaved. We use the word "sweet" to describe things pleasant and endearing because, over time, the titillated palates of consumers had more of a say than the tired arms of producers.[51] History, with a capital *H*, rests upon a truce between words and things that narrative and literary language can help bring back into question.

A final vignette drives these points home. In the late aughts, a British Petroleum employee won an internal contest to name a well off the coast of Louisiana "Macondo," after García Márquez's accursed fictional town.[52] The largest oil spill in U.S. history took place there in 2010. If the media mostly referred to this event as the "Deepwater Horizon" oil spill (pointing, oddly enough, to the malfunctioning drilling rig and not the site itself), it's because the connotations of depth and distance served the purpose of assuaging reactions to the catastrophe better than the name of the fictional site of the real-life Banana massacre of 1928, ushered in, in turn, by United Fruit Company extractivism. "Macondo," the magical-realist signifier, probably felt "magical"—read *justifying*—at the time the risky underwater exploration project was named. The employee, presumably a Latin culture enthusiast, must have been gratified; the company must have found the name good publicity. But the signifier, with its apocalyptic overtones, became "realist," and was therefore disavowed, after the debacle. (In *One Hundred Years of Solitude*, Macondo is wiped out by the wind.) It bears noting this took place in a mass of water called the "Gulf of Mexico" that, despite its name, belongs mostly to the United States. Words, too, are things with a history.

One can try to shield novels from the world, as it were, by either actively claiming this has nothing to do with the transnational literary phenomenon that is García Márquez, or by passively ignoring such a major ecological catastrophe—and the extractivist push that, again, scripted it—as mere happenstance. Alternatively, one can let words do the talking, historicizing nature-culture as needed. Marxist criticism holds literature to be entangled in ideology: it does not just *represent* it—ideology determines its form. Why wouldn't this also be the case for political ecology? The most basic tenet of our time's prevailing material paradigm, namely, that man is above everything else, is constantly mobilized and rekindled in language, literary or not. The frequent spiritualist objection that literature can only represent reality, as if it somehow existed in a parallel universe, becomes something of a moot point. Being a monist and reading books are not at odds, because stories don't exist in a Platonic realm of perfect archetypal ideas. Stories exist and have consequences, some more tangible than others. It is not that the moniker "Macondo" caused the debacle, as superstition might have it. But ex post facto, it resignifies it, giving it historical depth and narrative poignancy. The force of the signifier is of a piece with the event itself, which is literary (it affects the afterlife of the novel), ecological (think maritime birds covered in iridescent, black muck), and economical (millions of dollars "lost"). It is easier to brush oil from feathers than to parse out the literature from everything else here.

Allow me to extrapolate: to define what a literary object or event is, as if looking for the indivisible atoms of literature, is not necessarily a task worth undertaking. "There is a fallacy of 'agency' to match every fallacy of 'application,'" notes Neil Larsen. "A poem or a novel no more *acts* than a dream or a fantasy does—that is to say, they act only insofar as no *conscious* social action is possible *except* as mediated by such mimetic objects."[53] The Macondo oil spill, thus named and thought alongside the novel, is a nightmare that moves to action—and also to reaction: a "media storm" to be contained. While surrealists literalized metaphor, as in Dali's "ruby lips" precious stone brooch, this is a spillover of metaphor into the literal, and of literature into reality. But "Macondo" is also a cypher for a different, better pact between humans and nature, as Raymond L. Williams has demonstrated in a perceptive eco-critical reading of García Márquez's novel.[54]

More broadly, one important feature of Latin American literature is to serve as repository for alternative political ecologies. Transcultural materialism articulates the positive of eco-criticism with the negative of ideology critique not by choice, but by necessity. History and nature are always already interwoven, often to the benefit of extractivism. Consequences, like climate change and ecological displacement, are very real. Literature, without ceasing to be literature, can contribute to the urgent task of intervention. One could even ask again the question: Where does literature end and the world begin?

Notes

Introduction: A Tale of Two Materialisms

1. See Héctor Hoyos, *Beyond Bolaño: The Global Latin American Novel* (New York: Columbia University Press, 2015).
2. A related work that considers forms of cultural resistance to extractive capitalism is Macarena Gómez-Barris, *The Extractive Zone: Social Ecologies and Decolonial Perspectives* (Durham, N.C.: Duke University Press, 2017). Unflinchingly, Gómez understands extractivism as theft, particularly against indigenous and Afro-descendent territories (xviii). With a "decolonial femme methodology" and an emphasis on activist art practices, the book aligns indigenous sovereignty with ecological preservation in the Yasuní region of Ecuador, the Bío Bío region of Chile, and the Cauca Valley in Colombia, among others.
3. See Ludwig Wittgenstein, *Tractatus Logico-Philosophicus*, trans. Charles Kay Ogden (Mineola, N.Y.: Dover, 1999), esp. 2.171–2.172 and 4.1212. For discussions of the distinction see Marie McGinn, "Saying and Showing and the Continuity of Wittgenstein's Thought," *Harvard Review of Philosophy* 9 (2001): 24–36; and Adrian W. Moore, "On Saying and Showing," *Philosophy* 62 (1987): 473–97.
4. Similarly, Jennifer French thinks that ecological and radical thought should be reconciled, especially in the Latin American context. She also offers a convincing explanation as to why this synthesis has not yet taken hold: "What could be more ecological than dialectics, or more dialectical than ecology? The similarity of these two critical models is both obvious and all too often overlooked, perhaps because Marxism's decline and environmentalism's rise have been largely contemporaneous among progressive intellectuals in the United States and Latin America." Jennifer L. French, *Nature, Neo-Colonialism, and the Spanish American Regional Writers* (Hanover, N.H.: Dartmouth College Press, 2005), 157.

5. In the words of one prominent critic: "The New Materialism emerged in part to replace a currently unfashionable historical materialism. Yet whole currents of it would seem to have no particular concern, as historical materialism does, with the destiny of men and women in an exploitative world." Terry Eagleton, *Materialism* (New Haven, Conn.: Yale University Press, 2016), 17.
6. The defensive stance against worldlit comes across most vividly in Ignacio Sánchez Prado's early edited collection, *América Latina en la "literatura mundial"* (Pittsburgh, Pa.: University of Pittsburgh Press, 2006). Note the scare quotes in the title. Sánchez Prado's more recent *Strategic Occidentalism: On Mexican Fiction, the Neoliberal Book Market, and the Question of World Literature* (Evanston, Ill.: Northwestern University Press, 2018) presents a Bourdieu-inspired account of Mexican literary exceptionalism vis-à-vis global trends. Mariano Siskind's unsurpassed *Cosmopolitan Desires: Global Modernity and World Literature in Latin America* (Evanston, Ill.: Northwestern University Press, 2014) is a de rigueur referent, while Gesine Müller's co-edited collections provide states of the art—notably, the volume co-edited with Jorge Locane and Benjamin Loy, *Re-Mapping World Literature: Writing, Book Markets and Epistemologies between Latin America and the Global South* (Berlin: De Gruyter, 2018). Another useful source is the special issue "Rethinking World Literature in Latin American and Spanish Contexts," ed. Annalisa Mirizio and Marta Puxan-Oliva, *Journal of World Literature* 2, no. 1 (2017): 1–9.
7. See, for instance, John Beverley, Michael Aronna, and José Oviedo, eds., *The Postmodernism Debate in Latin America* (Durham, N.C.: Duke University Press, 1995).
8. Donna Haraway draws important terminological distinctions in "Anthropocene, Capitalocene, Plantationocene, Chthulucene: Making Kin," *Environmental Humanities* 6, no. 1 (2015): 159–65. In a 2017 blog post, Steve Mentz, a scholar of oceanic literature and eco-criticism, tallies close to twenty neologisms for the new era: see "The Neologismcene," *Arcade: Literature, the Humanities and the World* (blog), https://arcade.stanford.edu/blogs/neologismcene.
9. Walter Benjamin, "Theses on the Philosophy of History," in *Illuminations*, ed. and introd. Hannah Arendt, trans. Harry Zohn (New York: Schocken, 1969), 257.
10. White ruminated on this idea throughout his scholarship, from his classic work *The Historical Imagination in Nineteenth-Century Europe* (Baltimore, Md.: Johns Hopkins University Press, 1973) to a late text that, via a reading of Saul Friedländer, develops the connection of metahistory and the Holocaust: White, "Historical Truth, Estrangement, and Disbelief," in *Probing the Ethics of Holocaust Culture*, ed. Claudio Fogu, Wulf Kansteiner, and Todd Presner (Cambridge, Mass.: Harvard University Press, 2016), 53–71.
11. See Ángel Rama, *Transculturación narrativa en América Latina* (Buenos Aires: Andariego, 1984); Bronislaw Malinowski, introduction to *Contrapunteo cubano del tabaco y azúcar: Advertencia de sus contrastes agrarios, económicos, históricos y sociales, su etnografía y su transculturación*, by Fernando Ortiz, 2nd ed. (Havana: Universidad Central de las Villas, 1963), xi–xix. For a multidisciplinary approach to the legacy of Fernando Ortiz, see Mauricio A. Font and Alfonso W. Quiroz,

eds., *Cuban Counterpoints: The Legacy of Fernando Ortiz* (Lanham, Md.: Lexington, 2005). In the latter work, especially worthy of note is Jean Stubbs' extrapolation of counterpoint to today's transnational *habano* commerce. See "Tobacco in the *Contrapunteo*: Ortiz and the Havana Cigar," in *Cuban Counterpoints: The Legacy of Fernando Ortiz*, ed. Mauricio A. Font and Alfonso W. Quiroz (Lanham, Md.: Lexington, 2005), 105–23.

12. Mary Louise Pratt, *Imperial Eyes: Travel Writing and Transculturation* (New York: Routledge, 1992), 7.
13. Fernando Coronil, introduction to *Cuban Counterpoint: Tobacco and Sugar*, by Fernando Ortiz, trans. Harriet de Onis (Durham, N.C.: Duke University Press, 1995), ix–lvi.
14. Ortiz worries that a certain enlightened worker is falling prey to the stultifying effects of radio. He refers to the fascinating practice of public reading in *tabacaleras*, which allowed workers to instruct themselves as they rolled cigars. Ortiz admires such "factory graduates"—the term is José Martí's—for "the tobacco worker is a nonconformist who thinks and insists upon a new design for living [renuevo del modo de vivir]." Fernando Ortiz, *Contrapunteo cubano del tabaco y el azúcar: Advertencia de sus contrastes agrarios, económicos, históricos y sociales, su etnografía y su transculturación*, 2nd ed. (Havana: Universidad Central de las Villas, 1963), 92. Radio was part of a broader mechanization that led to the collapse of that mode of production and worker culture. For a contemporary play that depicts this shift in factories of Cuban émigrés in Florida, see Nilo Cruz's Pulitzer Prize–winning *Anna in the Tropics* (New York: Theatre Communications Group, 2003).
15. For an overview of the discussion on *transculturación* from 1940 onward, see Jossiana Arroyo-Martínez, "Transculturation, Syncretism, and Hybridity," in *Critical Terms in Caribbean and Latin American Thought: Historical and Institutional Trajectories*, ed. Yolanda Martínez-San Miguel and Ben Sifuentes Jáuregui (New York: Palgrave, 2016), 133–45.
16. Fernando Ortiz, *Cuban Counterpoint: Tobacco and Sugar*, trans. Harriet de Onis (Durham, N.C.: Duke University Press, 1995), 98.
17. See *Revista Bimestre Cubana* 45, no. 1 (1940). Ortiz was a liberal democrat who favored compromise throughout his life, including staying in Cuba after the 1959 revolution. It is reasonable to suppose that the progressive gesturing in *Counterpoint* harmonized with the ideals of the Castro regime. At the same time, its lightheartedness and subtlety did not quite make him a threat to Batista and his proxy rulers. For a fascinating account of the debates on the monoculture of sugar that frame the original publication in 1940, see Enrico Mario Santí, "Towards a Reading of Fernando Ortiz's *Cuban Counterpoint*," *Review: Literature and Arts of the Americas* 37, no. 1 (2004): 11–13.
18. This is a modified version of Coronil's translation in his introduction to *Cuban Counterpoint*, xxvi. "En todo abrazo de culturas sucede lo que en la cópula genética de los individuos: la criatura siempre tiene algo de ambos progenitores, pero también siempre es distinta de cada uno de los dos." Ortiz, *Contrapunteo cubano*, 103.

19. For a recent discussion of the relations between realism and new materialism, see the book-length conversation between Manuel DeLanda and Graham Harman. The latter is of the opinion that "all *coherent* materialisms must be forms of realism": "If human history ha[s] been so deeply affected by the material culture of weapons and battles, of vaccines and quarantines, of matter and energy flows in industry and trade, then a belief in a mind-independent world follow[s] logically." Manuel DeLanda and Graham Harman, *The Rise of Realism* (Cambridge: Polity, 2017), 3.
20. Ortiz, *Contrapunteo cubano*, 183.
21. Ortiz, 3.
22. There is a notable gap between the roughly one-hundred-page title essay and the remaining two hundred pages of "annexes" (whose length varies by edition). Judging from the way the twelve annexes are cited throughout the essay, my sense is they should be read as elaborations on specific points, almost extended endnotes. On this point I disagree with Coronil, who thinks there is a "counterpoint" between the first essay and the remaining sections, as well as with Santí, who finds them "complementary."
23. Ortiz, *Cuban Counterpoint*, 43–46.
24. Gustavo Pérez Firmat, *The Cuban Condition: Translation and Identity in Modern Cuban Literature* (Cambridge: Cambridge University Press, 1989), 24.
25. "La imagen del ajiaco criollo nos simboliza bien la formación del pueblo cubano. Sigamos la metáfora. Ante todo una cazuela abierta. Esta es Cuba, la isla, la olla puesta al fuego de los trópicos . . . junto con el fogaje del trópico para calentarlo, el agua de sus cielos para el caldo y el agua de sus mares para las salpicaduras del salero. Con todo ello se ha hecho nuestro nacional ajiaco." Fernando Ortiz, "Los factores humanos de la cubanidad," in *Fernando Ortiz*, ed. Julio Le Riverend (Havana: Unión de Escritores y Artistas, 1973), 155–56. Unless otherwise indicated, henceforth all translations from sources in languages other than English will be my own.
26. Absent from the English translation, the section on beets provides one of the book's most interesting and contradictory moments. Beets in the tropics represent the worst of imperialism for Ortiz—although he does not use the term. Ortiz advocates for a certain rational economic order of "true universal exchange" (verdadero librecambio universal) where all the sugar of the world of the tropics is produced in the tropics (*Contrapunteo cubano*, 462). Contrast that free market stance with one of his most openly socialist statements, in the following page: "Hoy día, con azúcar de caña o con azúcar de remolacha, el problema va siendo igual. Una misma estructura económica, mecanizada, monetizada y deshumanizada, determina fenómenos análogos para las dos, en las llanuras frías como en las sabanas tropicales. En los campos remolacheros como en los azucareros es una misma la angustia. Las tierras que producen los azúcares no son de quienes las labran y los provechos se van lejos" (*Contrapunteo cubano*, 463). It belongs to a different study to elucidate the idiosyncratic blend of free enterprise and agrarian reform in these underexamined pages.

27. See Maurizia Boscagli, *Stuff Theory: Everyday Objects, Radical Materialism* (New York: Bloomsbury, 2014), 14. Boscagli pursues a kindred goal to that of this book while focusing on a Euro-American corpus.
28. Coronil, introduction to *Cuban Counterpoint*, xxviii.
29. See Jane Bennett, *Vibrant Matter: A Political Ecology of Things* (Durham, N.C.: Duke University Press, 2010), esp. chap. 2 ("The Agency of Assemblages") and chap. 3 ("Edible Matter").
30. Bruno Latour, *We Have Never Been Modern*, trans. Catherine Porter (Cambridge, Mass.: Harvard University Press, 1993), 1.
31. Latour, 4.
32. On Ponte's oeuvre up to the mid-aughts, see the special issue on the author in the journal *La Habana elegante* 31 (2005). Carlos Alonso offers another comprehensive view in "La escritura fetichizadora de Antonio José Ponte," *Revista de Estudios Hispánicos* 43, no. 1 (2009): 93–108.
33. Katherine Gordy, "Dollarization, Consumer Capitalism and Popular Response," in *Cuba Today: Continuity and Change since the 'Período Especial'*, ed. Mauricio A. Font, Scott Larsen, and Danielle Xuereb (New York: Bildner Center for Western Hemisphere Studies, 2004), 23.
34. "Un castillo en España . . ." Antonio José Ponte, *Las comidas profundas* (Rosario, Argentina: Beatriz Viterbo Editora, 2010), 9. Mark Schafer translated an excerpt of Ponte's work under the title "Meaning to Eat," *BOMB Magazine* 78 (January 1, 2002), http://bombmagazine.org/article/2448/meaning-to-eat.
35. "La piña es el león de las frutas y Carlos el león entre los monarcas." Ponte, *Las comidas profundas*, 12.
36. Peter Sloterdijk, *Spheres*, trans. Wieland Hoband (Los Angeles: Semiotext(e), 2011–16).
37. "Se extendería entre ellos el océano que desconoce." Ponte, *Las comidas profundas*, 14.
38. The definitive study of gastro-criticism in Cuban literature is Rita De Maeseneer's *Devorando a lo cubano: Una aproximación gastrocrítica a textos relacionados con el siglo XIX y el Período Especial* (Madrid: Iberoamericana, 2012). There she situates Ponte in the long history of the island's writings about food, and also vis-à-vis contemporaries like Zoe Valdés and Daína Chaviano. See, especially, 240–63. For a study that examines the theme of lack across Ponte's essayistic oeuvre as a recasting of *origenismo*, see Isabel Alvarez-Borland, "El silencio del hambre: Figuras de la carencia en Antonio José Ponte," *Hispania: A Journal Devoted to the Teaching of Spanish and Portuguese* 90, no. 3 (2007): 443–52.
39. "El espíritu de las viejas comidas." Ponte, *Las comidas profundas*, 16.
40. Francis Fukuyama, "The End of History?," *The National Interest* 16 (1989): 4.
41. Octavio Paz, *Pequeña crónica de grandes días* (Mexico City: Fondo de Cultura Económica, 1990), 25.
42. "La idea revolucionaria ha sufrido golpes mortales; lo más duros y devastadores no han sido los de sus adversarios sino los de los revolucionarios mismos: allí donde han conquistado el poder han amordazado a los pueblos." Paz, *Pequeña crónica*, 98.

43. "[T]al como vemos el futuro, vemos en la realidad al Partido dirigiendo indefinidamente.

    > Ni Carlos Marx, ni Lenin, ni Engels dijeron qué día se acababa el partido, no lo dijeron; dijeron que un día desaparecería el Estado, algo más que el partido. Todavía, por lo que se ve, está lejos el momento en que se acabe el Estado, y tendremos que seguir lidiando con este aparato, qué vamos a hacer. Está por decidir teóricamente, y, sobre todo, más que en la teoría, en la práctica, qué día y en qué mundo el Estado haya desaparecido. Entonces, de verdad, ya no será como alguien que se monte en un cohete para ir a otro planeta, sino que habremos cambiado este planeta (APLAUSOS).
    >
    > Carlos Marx dijo que ese día la humanidad habría salido de la prehistoria. Y lo creo, lo creí siempre y lo sigo creyendo, que el día que desaparezca la explotación del hombre por el hombre, el día que toda la humanidad se rija por principios socialistas o algo más, por principios comunistas, habría terminado la prehistoria."
    >
    > (Fidel Castro Ruz, "Discurso pronunciado por Fidel Castro Ruz, Presidente de la República de Cuba, en la clausura del XVI Congreso de la CTC, celebrado en el teatro 'Carlos Marx', el 28 de enero de 1990, Año 32 de la Revolución," http://www.cuba.cu/gobierno/discursos /1990/esp/f280190e.html)

44. "Desde Carlos V hata [sic] Talleyrand, nombres de clásica robustez o de demoniaca exigencia, han proclamado la extensión de su dominios en el cielo del paladar." José Lezama Lima, *Imagen y posibilidad* (Havana: Letras Cubanas, 1981), 135.
45. "Con el aprovechamiento cárnico de estas partes de la res pueden obtenerse subproductos que antes eran desechados por falta de experiencia. La iniciativa consiste en utilizar las orejas de las reses, la tráquea, esófago, bembo, recortes de tripas, cráneo y tendones para la fabricación de croquetas, morcillas caseras y hamburguesas." Victor Medero et al., *Con nuestros propios esfuerzos: Algunas experiencias para enfrentar el periodo especial en tiempo de paz* (Havana: Verde Olivo, 1992), 50.
46. Quoted in William Luis, "Exhuming *Lunes de Revolución*," *CR: The New Centennial Review* 2 no. 2 (2002): 261.
47. "Como enfermos que ni siquiera en habitaciones muy caldeadas consiguen olvidar el frío, tenemos instalada el hambre bien adentro." Ponte, *Las comidas profundas*, 44–45.
48. "Chuletas de arroz con patatas fritas, calamares fritos sin calamares." Ponte, 38.
49. Latour, *We Have Never Been Modern*, 4–7; italicized in the original.
50. Latour, 15.
51. "Madejas muy largas han tejido esa carne que puede desbaratarse con los dientes." Ponte, *Las comidas profundas*, 21.

52. For reports on the actual archaeological excavations, see Santiago F. Silva García, Reynaldo Pérez Jiménez, Orlando Álvarez de la Paz, and Leonardo Rojas Pérez, "Algunas consideraciones sobre la dieta . . . (Tercera Parte)," *Arqueología Centrosur de Cuba*, September 1, 2007, http://cuba-arqueologia-centrosur.blogspot.com/2007_09_01_archive.html. See also Litzie Álvarez Santana, "Descubren en Abreus piezas arqueológicas," *Azurina: Portal de la cultura en Cienfuegos*, December 2, 2009, http://www.azurina.cult.cu/index.php/noticias/1499-descubren-en-abreus-piezas-arqueologicas.
53. Ponte, *Las comidas profundas*, 23.
54. Walter Benjamin, "Excavation and Memory," in *Selected Writings, 2: 1927–1934*, ed. Michael W. Jennings (Cambridge, Mass.: Belknap, 1999), 576.
55. "La costumbre de hacer comidas en palabras." Ponte, *Las comidas profundas*, xx.
56. "Al comer, el cubano se incorpora el bosque." Ponte, 24.
57. "No debía existir otra meta personal que la de convertirse en un grano del tazón donde vendrían a comer fuerzas mayores, sobrehumanas." Ponte, 26.
58. Bennett, *Vibrant Matter*, xvii, 120–21.
59. I adopt Latour's coinage of "politics of nature" with a grain of salt: "Conceptions of politics and conceptions of nature have always formed a pair as firmly united as the two seats on a seesaw, where one goes down when the other goes up, and vice versa. There has never been any other politics than the politics *of* nature, and there has never been any other nature than the nature *of* politics." Bruno Latour, *Politics of Nature: How to Bring the Sciences into Democracy*, trans. Catherine Porter (Cambridge, Mass.: Harvard University Press, 2004), 28. The shortcomings of this important study include the following: an unwarranted faith in description; the omission of cultural difference for the sake of grounding a "single collective"; the assumption that Western science, oblivious of its colonial baggage, can function as lingua franca; and a hasty dissolution of the facts/values divide, particularly in spaces of former colonial domination.
60. "El mismo sobrecogimiento de quienes vieron por primera vez cómo un hombre fumaba hojas de tabaco." Ponte, *Las comidas profundas*. 30.
61. Latour, *We Have Never Been Modern*, 3.
62. Ponte, *Las comidas profundas*, 30.
63. See Franz Kafka, *The Metamorphosis and Other Stories*, trans. Donna Freed (New York: Barnes & Noble, 1996). Thought-provokingly, the original title is a portmanteau with a quantifier: "Ein Hungerkünstler." How many are there?
64. See Louis Althusser, "Ideology and Ideological State Apparatuses (Notes Towards an Investigation)," trans. Ben Brewster, in *Lenin and Philosophy and Other Essays* (New York: NYU Press 2001), 85–126.
65. Ponte, *Las comidas profundas*, 40, 57.
66. Ponte, 35.
67. Ponte, 45–47.
68. Ponte, 47.
69. Ponte, 49.

70. "Fermentaciones gemelas." Ponte, 48.
71. Karl Marx, *Capital: A Critique of Political Economy*, trans. Ben Fowkes (New York: Penguin, 1990), 916.
72. Lezama Lima, *Imagen y posibilidad*, 136.
73. "Aguarda por la piña." Ponte, *Las comidas profundas*, 50–51.
74. A case in point:

> Quien está sentado a la mesa de escribir y de comer recuerda las verdaderas comidas, lo que toman al final de sus vidas los grandes taoístas: un poco de rocío, un pedazo de nube, algún celaje, arcoiris. Lo que está al final del comer cubano, supone, el final de todas las metáforas de las comidas cubanas, es la sombra. Por eso Lezama Lima habrá escrito que el cubano al comer se incorpora el bosque. Un pueblo tan solar está obligado a comer oscuridades por naturaleza.
>
> (Ponte, *Las comidas profundas*, 40)

I have consulted the valuable elucidation of the concept of oceanic feeling in William B. Parsons, *The Enigma of the Oceanic Feeling: Revisioning the Psychoanalytic Theory of Mysticism* (Oxford: Oxford University Press, 1999).

75. Ponte, *Las comidas profundas*, 54. In the first edition of Marré's book, there are no punctuation marks through the traveling enumeration until the resounding, very local end: "Ese pan fue amasado con harina de la URSS El arroz vino de la China Las lentejas granaron en la vieja España Las verduras fueron cortadas en el valle de Güines . . . Nosotros tomamos agua de pozo La halamos con ¼ de caballo (con un motorcito de) El pozo es de roca serpentina azul y está al pie de un limonero." Luis Marré, *Habaneras y otras letras* (Havana: Unión de Escritores y Artistas, 1970), 30. Compare with Marré, *Obra escogida: Poesía y narrativa* (Havana: Letras cubanas, 2012), 50–51. For the state-of-the-art collection on post-Soviet Cuba, see Jacqueline Loss and José Manuel Prieto González's *Caviar with Rum: Cuba-USSR and the Post-Soviet Experience* (New York: Palgrave Macmillan, 2012). Also of note is chap. 2 of Casamayor Cisneros's monographic study of post-Soviet Cuban authors, *Utopía, distopía e ingravidez: Reconfiguraciones cosmológicas en la narrativa postsoviética cubana* (Madrid: Iberoamericana Vervuert, 2013), 135–46. In that section, she focuses on Ponte's interest in ruins and compares him to Senel Paz, Leonardo Padura, and others.
76. "Una mesa en la Habana . . ." Ponte, *Las comidas profundas*, 55 (suspension points in original).
77. Wittgenstein, *Tractatus Logico-Philosophicus*, §7.
78. There are limits to the transferability of Ortiz to contemporary critical discourse. His marriage metaphors can be sexist, and his racialization of sugar and tobacco racist. We read that brown sugar, that seductress, passes as white to "travel all over the world, reach all mouths, and bring a better price, climbing to the top of the social ladder" (*Cuban Counterpoint*, 7). Similarly, cigarettes are "amaricados"

(prissy) when compared to virile cigars (9). As these examples suggest, Ortiz is a son of his time, despite the fundamentally progressive tenor of his intellectual pursuits.

79. Arturo Uslar Pietri, *Nuevo mundo, mundo nuevo* (Caracas: Biblioteca Ayacucho, 1998), 341.
80. Coronil, introduction to *Cuban Counterpoint*, xxvii. Coronil goes on to say, "By casting commodities as the main actors of his historical narrative, Ortiz at once displaces the conventional focus on human historical protagonists and revalorizes historical agency. Acting as both objects and subjects of history, commodities are shown to be not merely products of human activity, but active forces which constrain and empower it. Thus historical agency comes to include the generative conditions of agency itself" (xxix–xxx).
81. Ortiz, *Contrapunteo cubano*, 305.
82. Malinowski, introduction to *Contrapunteo cubano*, 13.
83. With a strategic use of name-dropping, Bennett offers a succinct characterization of the two materialisms at stake: "I pursue a materialism in the tradition of Democritus-Epicurus-Spinoza-Diderot-Deleuze more than Hegel-Marx-Adorno. It is important to follow the trail of human power to expose social hegemonies (as historical materialists do). But my contention is that there is also public value in following the scent of a nonhuman, thingly power, the material agency of natural bodies and technological artifacts." Bennett, *Vibrant Matter*, xiii. Although its origins go at least as far back as the Greeks, I have called the first option "new materialism," following the capacious grouping of recent trends in Diana Coole and Samantha Frost's edited collection, *New Materialisms: Ontology, Agency, and Politics* (Durham, N.C.: Duke University Press, 2010).
84. Bennett, *Vibrant Matter*, xx.
85. Bennett, 120.
86. For a compelling deployment of this theoretical framework within popular culture, see Frederick Aldama's *Your Brain on Latino Comics: From Gus Arriola to Los Bros Hernandez*, Cognitive Approaches to Literature and Culture (Austin: University of Texas Press, 2009).
87. Fredric Jameson, *The Political Unconscious: Narrative as a Socially Symbolic Act* (Ithaca, N.Y.: Cornell University Press, 1981), 9.
88. See Arjun Appadurai, ed., *The Social Life of Things: Commodities in Cultural Perspective* (Cambridge: Cambridge University Press, 1986).
89. Robert Doran notes, in a metahistorical essay that historicizes metahistory itself, that although "White's tropological grid appeared at first glance to be rigid and deterministic," this structure responds to the necessity of choice taught by Sartrean existentialism. Condemned to be free, the literary historiographical model put forward by the present volume would forcibly, according to White's schema, embrace internal contradiction. The "trope" that it more closely aligns with is synecdoche, for it builds on a part—human-nonhuman relations in fiction—to understand the whole; the "mode" would be integrative; and the "emplotment" would be comedic, as befits the playful legacy of Fernando Ortiz. But then the ideology that goes with these traits

would be "conservative," rather than "radical," which is closer to my explicit orientation. At the same time, several portions of this volume would naturally map onto a metonymic trope, reductionist mode, and tragic emplotment—staples of Marxism. I make a note of this unresolved, if productive, tension. See Robert Doran, "Choosing the Past: Hayden White and the Philosophy of History," in *Philosophy of History After Hayden White*, ed. Robert Doran (London: Bloomsbury, 2013), 19.

90. Ericka Beckman makes a kindred argument in *Capital Fictions: The Literature of Latin America's Export Age* (Minneapolis: University of Minnesota Press, 2013). From a Foucaultian-Marxist perspective, she concentrates on commodities qua commodities—that is, as export products. This allows her to characterize various works of literature, some of which I also study, as "capital fictions." While I agree with the overall thrust of Beckman's volume, my footing in a different materialist tradition leads me to regard such economic narratives as a moment within a broader material transformation. Consequently, my reading of primary materials does not merely highlight their thematization of economic conditions but regards texts as sites for a renegotiation of human-nonhuman relations.

91. See Manuel DeLanda, *A New Philosophy of Society: Assemblage Theory and Social Complexity* (London: Continuum, 2006).

92. Néstor García Canclini, *Culturas híbridas: Estrategias para entrar y salir de la modernidad* (Mexico City: Grijalbo, 1989). Available in English translation as *Hybrid Cultures: Strategies for Entering and Leaving Modernity*, trans. Christopher L. Chiappari and Silvia L. Lopez (Minneapolis: University of Minnesota Press, 2005).

93. Viktor Shklovsky, "From 'Art as Technique' 1917," in *Modernism: An Anthology of Sources and Documents*, ed. Vassiliki Kolocotroni, Jane Goldman, and Olga Taxidou (Chicago: University of Chicago Press, 1998), 219.

94. Nariman Skakov and Alice E. M. Underwood have been my interlocutors on this issue. Aleksei Gastev (1882–1939) imported Ford's methods to the USSR and also wrote poems. He died in the purges.

95. Shklovsky, "Art as Technique," 219; italicized in the original.

1. Raw Stuff Disavowed

1. Bruno Latour, "From Realpolitik to Dingpolitik—or How to Make Things Public," in *Making Things Public: Atmospheres of Democracy*, ed. Bruno Latour and Peter Weibel (Cambridge, Mass.: MIT Press, 2005), 14–44; Peter Singer, *Animal Liberation*, 4th ed. (New York: Harper Collins, 2009). An enthusiastic, if heterodox, reading of these sources inspires this chapter, particularly the shift described by Latour and the eye-opening notion of "speciesism" first formulated by Singer.

2. For an English-language overview of those debates, I consulted Peter Steiner, *Russian Formalism: A Metapoetics* (Ithaca, N.Y.: Cornell University Press, 1984).

3. See Ángel Rama, *Transculturación narrativa en América Latina* (Buenos Aires: Andariego, 1984).

4. José Eustasio Rivera, *La Vorágine*, ed. Flor María Rodríguez-Arenas (Doral, Fl.: Stockcero, 2013), 174. Until otherwise noted, English translations are taken from *The Vortex; La vorágine*, trans. Earle K. James (New York: Putnam, 1935).
5. Tulio Halperín Donghi, *The Contemporary History of Latin America*, ed. and trans. John Charles Chasteen (Durham, N.C.: Duke University Press, 1993), 176–77.
6. Rivera, *The Vortex*, 249. "La secreta voz de las cosas le llenó su alma." Rivera, *La Vorágine*, 181.
7. Scott DeVries, "Swallowed: Political Ecology and Environmentalism in the Spanish American *novela de la selva*," *Hispania: A Journal Devoted to the Teaching of Spanish and Portuguese* 93, no. 4 (2010): 539.
8. Jennifer L. French, *Nature, Neo-Colonialism, and the Spanish American Regional Writers* (Hanover, N.H.: Dartmouth College Press, 2005), 112–54.
9. Quoted in Luis Carlos Herrera Molina, S.J., introduction to *La Vorágine*, in *José Eustasio Rivera: Obra literaria*, ed. Luis Carlos Herrera Molina, S.J. (Bogotá: Pontificia Universidad Javeriana, 2009), 270.
10. William Bull, "Nature and Anthropomorphism in *La Vorágine*," *Romanic Review* 39, no. 4 (1948): 315–18.
11. David Viñas, "'La Vorágine': Crisis, populismo y mirada," *Hispamérica* 3, no. 8 (1974): 18.
12. Rivera, *The Vortex*, 158.

> Aquella tarde rendí mi ánimo a la tristeza y una emoción romántica me sorprendió con vagas caricias. ¿Por qué viviría siempre solo en el arte y en el amor? y pensaba con dolorida inconformidad: '¡Si tuviera ahora a quién ofrecerle este armiñado ramillete de plumajes, que parecen espigas blancas! ¡Si alguien quisiera abanicarse con este alón de codúa marina, donde va prisionero el iris! ¡Si hubiera hallado con quién contemplar el garcero nítido, primavera de aves y colores! Con humillada pena advertí luego que en el velo de mi ilusión se embozaba Alicia, y procuré manchar con realismo crudo el pensamiento donde la intrusa resurgía.
>
> (Rivera, *La Vorágine*, 98–99)

13. Sharon Magnarelli, "La mujer y la naturaleza," in *La vorágine: A imagen y semejanza del hombre*, ed. Sharon Magnarelli and Monserrat Ordóñez (Bogotá: Alianza Editorial Colombiana, 1987), 335–52; and Monserrat Ordóñez, "Nota preliminar," in *La vorágine: A imagen y semejanza del hombre*, ed. Sharon Magnarelli and Monserrat Ordóñez (Bogotá: Alianza Editorial Colombiana, 1987), 13–18. See also Sharon Magnarelli, *The Lost Rib: Female Characters in the Spanish-American Novel* (Lewisburg, Pa.: Bucknell University Press, 1985), 38–58.
14. Rivera, *La Vorágine*, 238.
15. Ericka Beckman, *Capital Fictions: The Literature of Latin America's Export Age* (Minneapolis: University of Minnesota Press, 2013), 158–88.

16. Michael Pollan, *The Botany of Desire: A Plant's-Eye View of the World* (New York: Random House, 2001), xvii–xix.
17. Rivera, *La Vorágine*, 118.
18. Rivera, *The Vortex*, 167. The distinguished historian John Charles Chasteen produced a scintillating new translation of *La vorágine* in 2018, a whopping sixty years after the standard translation. His take on the passage tips the balance of violence and beauty in favor of the latter: "underneath the swaying iris with petals the color of Mapiripana's butterfly." José Eustasio Rivera, *The Vortex: A Novel*, trans. John Charles Chasteen (Durham, N.C.: Duke University Press, 2018), 110. However, I shall nonetheless stay with James's translation—for its historical value, and also because the Chasteen edition came out while this book was already in production.
19. Seymour Menton, "*La vorágine*: Circling the Triangle," *Hispania* 59, no. 3 (1976): 434.
20. Rubén Darío, "Filosofía," in *Obras completas*, ed. Julio Ortega (Barcelona: Galaxia Gutenberg, 2007), 286. For a kindred depiction of butterflies in *modernismo*, look no further than José A. Silva's eponymous "Mariposas": "Parecen nácares / O pedazos de cielo, / Cielos de tarde, / O brillos opalinos / De alas suaves." *Obra completa* (Caracas: Ayacucho, 1977), 25.
21. Rivera, *La Vorágine*, 231.
22. Rivera, *The Vortex*, 48.
23. Rivera, *The Vortex*, 128; modified translation.
24. César Uribe Piedrahita, *Toá: Narraciones de caucherías* (Buenos Aires, México: Espasa-Calpe, 1942).
25. See Kalman Mezey, César Uribe Piedrahita, J. Pataki, and J. Huertas-Lozano, "Niaara; A Digitalis-Like Colombian Arrow Poison," *Journal of Pharmacology and Experimental Therapeutics* 93, no. 2 (June 1948): 223–29.
26. "Como alguien podría coleccionar caballos, o autos. O sea los tengo en el establo o en el [garaje] pero también . . ." Ariel Magnus, *Muñecas* (Buenos Aires: Emecé, 2008), 90.
27. Saul Friedländer, *The Years of Extermination: Nazi Germany and the Jews, 1939–1945* (New York: Harper Collins, 2007).
28. Magnus tackles the topic of extermination and its aftermath more straightforwardly, and in a nonfiction register, in *La abuela* (Buenos Aires: Planeta, 2006). There, Magnus recounts his travels and conversations with his Jewish grandmother, an extermination camp survivor who fled to Brazil and later Argentina, while always maintaining a German identity in national terms. Magnus (b. 1975) himself would migrate to Germany and study in Heidelberg. He is interviewed in *Der Spiegel*: "Argentinischer Autor Magnus: 'Alle Wollen, Dass Du Nicht Deutscher Bist,'" interview by Stefan Kuzmany, *Spiegel Online*, October 8, 2010, http://www.spiegel.de/kultur/literatur/argentinischer-autor-magnus-alle-wollen-dass-du-nicht-deutscher-bist-a-721615.html.
29. Walter E. Hardenburg, *The Putumayo, The Devil's Paradise; Travels in the Peruvian Amazon Region and an Account of the Atrocities Committed Upon the Indians*

Therein, ed. C. Reginald Enock (London: Fisher Unwin, 1912), 25. In his preface, C. Reginald Enock, the book's editor, invokes the Black Legend by way of explanation of the atrocities committed. His emphasis in salvaging the honor of his countrymen is conspicuous, given that London's stock exchange funded the Arana brothers:

> The sinister occurrences on the Putumayo are, to some extent, the result of a sinister human element—the Spanish and Portuguese character. The remarkable trait of callousness to human suffering which the Iberian people of Portugal and Spain—themselves a mixture of Moor, Goth, Semite, Vandal, and other peoples—introduced into the Latin American race is here shown in its intensity, and is augmented by a further Spanish quality. The Spaniard often regards the Indians as animals. Other European people may have abused the Indians of America, but none have that peculiar Spanish attitude towards them of frankly considering them as non-human ... There is yet a further trait of the Latin American which to the Anglo-Saxon mind is almost inexplicable. This is the pleasure in the torture of the Indian as a diversion, not merely as a vengeance or 'punishment.' As has been shown on the Putumayo, and as happened on other occasions elsewhere, the Indians have been abused, tortured, and killed *por motivos frívolos*—that is to say, for merely frivolous reasons, or for diversion.
>
> (Hardenburg, *The Putumayo*, 38)

"Anglo-Saxon" plantations in North America and the atrocities committed thereon, rendered into fiction in a work as important as Toni Morrison's *Beloved* (1987), would be a good point of comparison.

30. Renowned carioca writer Euclides da Cunha's 1909 collection of literary essays, *À Margem da História*, resulted, as with Rivera and Uribe Piedrahita, from a government commission to explore the recesses of the motherland. The title plays on marginal regions, but also on the place of Brazil itself in history, "a vast expanse rather than a country." Da Cunha has words of qualified praise for *seringueiros*, the relatively less exploitative Brazilian counterparts to Peruvian and Colombian *caucheros*. See Rex Nielson, "Amazonian El Dorados and the Nation: Euclides da Cunha's *À Margem da História* and José Eustasio Rivera's *La Vorágine*," *Ometeca*, no. 16 (2011): 16–31.
31. John Tully, *The Devil's Milk: A Social History of Rubber* (New York: Monthly Review Press, 2011), 190–93.
32. "La muñeca que ve ahí, por ejemplo, respira, le late el corazón, se le calienta el cuerpo, menstrúa cada 28 días. Y es un modelo relativamente viejo, lo compré hace un año. Las nuevas hablan y traen cámaras de video en los ojos." Magnus, *Muñecas*, 89.
33. "Más alemán que los alemanes." Magnus, 102.
34. "Me la meta como se la mete a Lais ... Su verga de látex en mi agujero de silicona." Magnus, 114.

35. "Eso de que las mujeres se implanten silicona por todos lados no les vendrá de las muñecas." Magnus, 115.
36. Mariano García, *Degeneraciones textuales: Los géneros en la obra de César Aira* (Rosario, Argentina: Viterbo, 2006), 142.
37. Magnus, *Muñecas*, 32–33.
38. "Una fábula moderna," "de esas que relegan la moraleja a la creatividad ética de sus oyentes." Magnus, *Muñecas*, 32.
39. A super artist meets a super critic in Mieke Bal's outstanding *Of What One Cannot Speak* (Chicago: University of Chicago Press, 2011).
40. Nunca termino de aprehender cabalmente qué es lo que se espera que uno espere con tanta impaciencia.

    –Al principio hay un cadáver y al final encuentran al asesino—razoné en voz alta.—Pero para mí el cadáver es el del suspenso y el asesino es el guionista, en el peor de los casos con la complicidad del director y los actores.
    –En cambio en las películas de amor—continuó Selin con mi razonamiento como si fuera ella quien lo venía exponiendo-, desde el principio uno quiere que se besen y sabe que se van a besar y así y todo uno no puede despegarse del televisor hasta que finalmente se besan; eso es lo que yo llamo suspenso.

    (Magnus, *Muñecas*, 33)

41. See Ariel Magnus, *Un chino en bicicleta* (Buenos Aires: Interzona, 2007).
42. Fredric Jameson, *The Political Unconscious: Narrative as a Socially Symbolic Act* (Ithaca, N.Y.: Cornell University Press, 1981).
43. See Héctor Hoyos, *Beyond Bolaño: The Global Latin American Novel* (New York: Columbia University Press, 2015), 33–64.
44. "La vida es una fiesta a la que uno está invitado y va y no hay nadie." Magnus, *Muñecas*, 92.
45. "De pronto el cuarto parece trinchera barrida por los faros del enemigo. ¿Estaremos debajo del nivel del mar?" Magnus, 104.
46. Magnus, 17.
47. Hayden White, "Historical Truth, Estrangement, and Disbelief," in *Probing the Ethics of Holocaust Culture*, ed. by Claudio Fogu, Wulf Kansteiner, and Todd Presner (Cambridge, Mass.: Harvard University Press, 2016), 55.
48. Hayden White, "The Modernist Event," in *Figural Realism: Studies in the Mimesis Effect* (Baltimore: Johns Hopkins University Press, 2000), 66–86.
49. "Testigo de una tragedia." Magnus, *Muñecas*, 43; "El único sobreviviente de una tragedia personal que de otra forma seguiría ocurriendo en el recuerdo de Selin, invisible para el resto y con el correr del tiempo también para ella." Magnus, 47.
50. For a thorough discussion of Levi's metalinguistic reflections on the representability of the Holocaust, see Michael Tager, "Primo Levi and the Language of Witness," *Criticism* 35, no. 2 (1993): 265–88.

51. See Dominick LaCapra, *Writing History, Writing Trauma* (Baltimore: Johns Hopkins University Press, 2001).
52. Hannah Arendt, *Eichmann in Jerusalem: A Report on the Banality of Evil*, 2nd ed. (New York: Penguin, 1977), 107. See the discussion of Arendt in LaCapra, *Writing History, Writing Trauma*, 127.
53. "Me pregunto si esto de que las mujeres se implanten siliconas por todos lados no les vendrá de las muñecas. La naturaleza imita al arte, Lais. Dame tu mano. Primero el arte a la naturaleza y después al revés. Así. Y cuando te puedas embarazar, de nuevo al revés. Ida yvuelta idayvuelta idayvueltaid." Magnus, *Muñecas*, 115.
54. The first episode of the Huffington Post's "Love + Sex" podcast discusses the future of sexual androids; reportedly, mermen are in the works. See Carina Kolodny, "Are You Ready to Have Sex with Robots?," *The Huffington Post*, January 29, 2015, http://www.huffingtonpost.com/2015/01/29/future-of-sex-podcast_n_6569838.html. For a state-of-the-discipline exploration of representations of digital technology in Latin America, and a rich analysis of their potential for thinking about human-nonhuman desire, see Anna Castillo, "Plastic Companions: Posthuman Intimacy in Twenty-First-Century Latin America" (PhD dissertation, Stanford University, 2017). Castillo considers other contemporary narratives of sex dolls, including João Paulo Cuenca's *O único final feliz para uma estória de amor é um acidente* (São Paulo: Companhia das Letras, 2010).
55. See Catherine Malabou, *Plasticity at the Dusk of Writing: Dialectic, Destruction, Deconstruction* (New York: Columbia University Press, 2010).
56. "Igual aquí en Alemania también estamos muy avanzados, no se crea." Magnus, *Muñecas*, 60.
57. Fernando Coronil, "Challenging Colonial Histories: *Cuban Counterpoint*/Ortiz's Counterfetishism," in *Critical Theory, Cultural Politics and Latin American Narrative*, ed. Steven M. Bell, Albert H. LeMay, and Leonard Orr (Notre Dame, Ind.: University of Notre Dame Press, 1993), 61–80.
58. "Algo en la pureza del aire y en la quietud sobreexcitada del mobiliario." Magnus has the librarian contemplate the empty library in the hours before the books are "manoseados." Magnus, *Muñecas*, 22.
59. Pablo Neruda, "The United Fruit Co.," in *Canto general*, trans. Jack Schmitt (Berkeley: University of California Press, 1993), 179.
60. One point of reference would be the successful "Object Lessons" series by Bloomsbury Press, which to date has featured titles on drones, golf balls, and driver's licenses, among other subjects. Upon lecturing at Universidad Javeriana in Bogotá, Jeffrey Cedeño directed me to kindred work by Erna von der Walde, "Cien años de soledad, historia en fábula," *Cuadernos de Literatura* 18, no. 36 (2014): 109–14. Von der Walde shares my interest in Coronil and Ortiz, but aligns more closely with Beckman's approach, circumscribed to the Colombian context: "Podría organizarse una historia de la narrativa colombiana a partir de las formas en que se representan las relaciones sociales que se han estructurado alrededor de los diferentes proyectos de exportación de mercancías." Von der Walde, 110. Interestingly, she posits *The Vortex* as an antipode to *One Hundred Years of Solitude*.

61. Karl Marx, *Capital: A Critique of Political Economy*, trans. Ben Fowkes (New York: Penguin, 1990), 284–85.
62. Marx, 289; translation modified.
63. Marx, 284.

2. Of Rocks and Particles

1. *Conquista del desierto* was part of a repopulation scheme by obliteration of original peoples, construed as nonsubjects in much the same way as the territory itself was understood. See Tulio Halperín Donghi, *Una nación para el desierto argentino* (Buenos Aires: Centro Editor de América Latina, 1982).
2. "Para efectos de la protección y tutela de sus derechos, la Madre Tierra adopta el carácter de sujeto colectivo de interés público." Constitución política del Estado Plurinacional de Bolivia, article 5.
3. "El sistema viviente dinámico conformado por la comunidad indivisible de todos los sistemas de vida y los seres vivos, interrelacionados, interdependientes y complementarios, que comparten un destino común." Constitución política del Estado Plurinacional de Bolivia, article 3.
4. "La Madre Tierra es considerada sagrada, desde las cosmovisiones de las naciones y pueblos indígena originario campesinos." Constitución política del Estado Plurinacional de Bolivia, article 3.
5. See Bruce Albert, "O ouro canibal e a queda do céu: Uma crítica xamânica da economia política da natureza (Yanomami)," in *Pacificando o branco: Cosmologias do contato norte-amazônico*, ed. Bruce Albert and Alcita Rita Ramos (São Paulo: Unesp, 2002), 239–70. I thank Romina Wainberg for this reference.
6. "Matar de pena" and "iba a dolerle el corazón." Blanca Wiethüchter, *El jardín de Nora* (La Paz: Mujercita Sentada, 1998), 7.
7. Wiethüchter, 8.
8. "Con infinito cuidado . . . como si se tratara de un regalo amoroso." Wiethüchter, 7–10.
9. Aún aguardó un poco antes de echar a andar, en espera de sentir el rumor en su pecho, ese rumor que la venía acosando desde hacía años . . . desde el día en el que decidió *forzar la tierra* a producir un jardín como si estuviera en Viena. *Retuvo en el olvido al jardinero*, metida en sí misma, se hizo otra vez de la plancha, introdujo el pulgar, el índice y el dedo medio en el agua fría para esparcirla mecánicamente sobre un ropaje inexistente, hasta que el chisporroteo del agua sobre la palma caliente de la plancha la despertó de sus divagaciones, pero sin el rumor en el pecho, . . . en *la huerta del pecho* '¿quién puede renegar de la autoridad de un médico, después de tantos análisis?' había regresado a casa, sabiendo que lo que sucedía no era a causa de sus nervios sino '*un modo de expresarse de las cosas, Franz, de las cosas de las que no se habla*.'

(Wiethüchter, 11; my emphasis)

10. Wiethüchter, 29.
11. "Siempre atento a los rasgos étnicos de los indígenas." Wiethüchter, 8.
12. Wiethüchter, 7.
13. "Manzana de la discordia." Wiethüchter, 29.
14. In a learned article, Mary Carmen E. Molina describes holes as "tensión neurálgica" and "centro de la paradoja en la escritura" in Wiethüchter's oeuvre (43). Usefully, the critic carries her analysis across poetry collections such as *Asistir al tiempo* (1975), *El rigor de la llama* (1994), and *Qantatai* (1997). See Molina, "'Aquí, digo, y doy un salto': Hueco y lenguaje en la obra de Blanca Wiethüchter," in *La crítica y el poeta: Blanca Wiethüchter* (La Paz: Plural, 2011), 41–78.
15. "Miró anonadada el no hay de la nada que ahora ocupaba el lugar del rosal." Wiethüchter, *El jardín de Nora*, 15.
16. Marcelo Villena Alvarado, "Requiem para un modelo: Hueco y experiencia en la obra de Blanca Wiethüchter," *América: Cahier du CRICCAL* 34 (2005): 157–65.
17. See Thomas Aquinas, *Summa Theologica* 1.49.1. *Sancti Thomae Aquinatis Doctoris Angelici Opera, omnia iussu edita Leonis XIII P.M, Tomus Decimus Sextus Indices: Summa Theologiae et summa contra gentiles* (Rome: Apud Sedem Commissionis Leoninae, 1948).
18. Timothy Morton, *Hyperobjects: Philosophy and Ecology after the End of the World* (Minneapolis: University of Minnesota Press, 2013), 1.
19. Morton, 21.
20. Morton, 5.
21. Wiethüchter, *El jardín de Nora*, 29.
22. "El hueco, más que un grito, le pareció una diabólica sonrisa torcida en la armónica y luminosa placidez de pasto, hojas verdes y variedad de flores." Wiethüchter, 20.
23. See Pedro Mamani Choque and Daysi Teresa Ramos Alcalá, *Cosmovisión andina* (Cochabamba: Verbo Divino, 2013); and Manuel M. Marzal and Krzysztof Makowski, eds., *Religiones andinas* (Madrid: Trotta, 2005).
24. Wiethüchter, *El jardín de Nora*, 54–55.
25. "La dimensión generadora, materna, de esa ausencia." Villena Alvarado, "Requiem para un modelo," 160.
26. Quoted in Mónica. M. Velásquez Guzmán, *Múltiples voces en la poesía de Francisco Hernández, Blanca Wiethüchter y Raúl Zurita* (Mexico City: Colegio de México, 2009), 125.
27. See Robert P. Harrison, *Gardens: An Essay on the Human Condition* (Chicago: University of Chicago Press, 2008).
28. Harrison, ix.
29. See a fascinating source that Monasterios cites: Patricia Seed, *Ceremonies of Possession in Europe's Conquest of the New World, 1492–1640* (Cambridge: Cambridge University Press, 1995).
30. See Molina, "'Aquí, digo, y doy un salto,'" 64–77; Elizabeth Monasterios, "Rethinking Transculturation and Hibridity: An Andean Perspective," *Latin American Narratives and Cultural Identity* 7 (2004): 103.

31. Monasterios, "Rethinking Transculturation and Hybridity," 99–100.
32. Monasterios, 106n5.
33. Monasterios makes her case against "cultural hybridity," which she calls García Canclini's "postmodern version of transculturation," as follows: "Even though for many critics this concept stills offers a strong analytical option due to its emphasis on the non-resolution of contradictions, the fact that it works within the logic of capitalism and economic globalization makes it incompatible with cultural productions formulated from different economic and cultural logistics." Monasterios, 108n12. García Canclini was writing at a time when, as the Cold War thawed, Jürgen Habermas's theory of communicative action had great purchase in many universities across Latin America.
34. Monasterios, 102.
35. Monasterios, 96.
36. Michel Foucault, *The Order of Things: An Archaeology of the Human Sciences* (New York: Vintage, 1994), xviii.
37. In this way, of the three cosmological principles of encounter of opposites (*taypi*) separation of opposites (*puruma*), and unresolvable tension (*awqa*), the third category would be the more appropriate for Wiethüchter (103–4). A viable line of research for future studies would be to examine these notions and learn from them not just in an abstract sense but as forms of inhabiting nature.
38. Short of de-Westernization, Walter Mignolo, paraphrasing Aníbal Quijano, speaks about escaping mental slavery: "Decoloniality means first to delink (to detach) from [the] overall structure of knowledge in order to engage in an epistemic reconstitution [of] ways of thinking, languages, ways of life and being in the world that the rhetoric of modernity disavowed and the logic of coloniality implement." Walter Mignolo, "Key Concepts," interview in *E-International Relations*, January 21, 2017, https://www.e-ir.info/2017/01/21/interview-walter-mignolopart-2-key-concepts/.
39. Molina, "'Aquí, digo, y doy un salto,'" 73–76.
40. Molina, 76.
41. "Se paró el mayor: un leve estertor, seguido por una especie de hipo que se tragaba el aire como para darse un impulso a tiempo de cerrar los labios y emitir un extraño soplo que sonaba bbbbbb. Tomó aliento y—Bbbbbaabbbá . . . Y cerrando los labios—Mmmmaammmá . . . Aplaudieron todos." Wiethüchter, *El jardín de Nora*, 64.
42. See Velásquez, *Múltiples voces*, 113.
43. ¡Bbbbuuuueeeecccccooooo! El que se abrió ahí mismo, abismal y profundo, que se abrió con el viento de voces como una garganta que al despeñarse hacia el fondo dejaba al descubierto los negados jugos de un jardín oculto, que se destapó con un tumulto de piedras como frutos resecos, que ahora despeñadas sobre Franz y Nora los hundían sin oportunidad de voz en aquel hueco negro, despejado por aquella decena de bocas desbocadas, diseñadas con seguridad para otra cosa.

(Wiethüchter, *El jardín de Nora*, 65)

44. See Carlos Alonso, *The Spanish American Regional Novel: Modernity and Autochthony* (Cambridge: Cambridge University Press, 1989), 38–78.
45. Viktor Shklovsky, "From 'Art as Technique' 1917," in *Modernism: An Anthology of Sources and Documents*, ed. Vassiliki Kolocotroni, Jane Goldman, and Olga Taxidou (Chicago: University of Chicago Press, 1998), 219. See the introduction to this volume, n. 90.
46. See Gregory L. Ulmer, "The Puncept in Grammatology," in *On Puns: The Foundation of Letters*, ed. Jonathan Culler (Oxford: Basil Blackwell, 1988), 164–90.
47. Wiethüchter, *El jardín de Nora*, 14.
48. "Al otro lado del hueco, no había nada. Phutunhuicu, pronunciaron correctamente cuando aprendieron a hablar los mudos, Phutunhuicu, que en buen aymara es phutunku y en buen castellano, hueco. Pero, nadie los entendió." Wiethüchter, *El jardín de Nora*, 65.
49. Concerned, like Monasterios, that "identity is always open to commodification by the cultural-ideologic apparatus of global capitalism," Moreiras proposes instead that

> The relationship between the tactical essentialism contained in subalternist theoretical fictions and the radicality of subalternism as a thinking of negativity (insofar as subalternism is the thinking of whatever is left outside of, that is, negated (and therefore also 'cathected') by a hegemonic relation at any given moment) is not to be thought dialectically, but through the notion of a double articulation or double register whereby the subalternist will be able to engage both radical negativity and tactical positivity simultaneously and distinctly.
>
> (Alberto Moreiras, "Hybridity and Double Consciousness," *Cultural Studies* 13, no. 3 [1999]: 373–407)

50. Eduardo Viveiros de Castro, *Cannibal Metaphysics* (Minneapolis: University of Minnesota Press, 2014), 6.
51. Gabriel Giorgi, *Formas comunes: Animalidad, cultura, biopolítica* (Buenos Aires: Eterna Cadencia, 2014), chap. 1.
52. At the "Legal and Literary Persons" special session of the 2016 convention of the MLA, Nicolette Bruner discussed Edith Wharton in light of Citizens United, and vice versa. The essential signposts to the current law and literature debates in the English-speaking context, and promising attempts of expanding such debates beyond it, can be found in Liz Anker and B. Meyler's *New Directions in Law and Literature* (Oxford: Oxford University Press, 2017).
53. For eye-opening documentation on the matter, see Penelope Anthias, "Indigenous Peoples and the New Extraction: From Territorial Rights to Hydrocarbon Citizenship in the Bolivian Chaco," *Latin American Perspectives* 45, no. 2 (2018): 136–53. Mounting evidence notwithstanding, leftist ecological criticism of Morales has been dismissed by none other than John Beverley as infantile. See Beverley, *The Failure of Latin America: Postcolonialism in Bad Times* (Pittsburgh, Pa.: University of Pittsburgh Press, 2019).

54. César Aira, *God's Tea Party*, in *The Musical Brain, and Other Stories*, trans. Chris Andrews (New York: New Directions, 2015), 75–90.
55. For Argentina, see Craig Epplin's *Late Book Culture in Argentina* (New York: Bloomsbury, 2017). One of the most thoughtful studies to date of so-called independent publishing in Latin America is Nicolás Rodríguez Galvis's dissertation, *De nouveaux éditeurs 'indépendants' en Amérique Du Sud: Émergence, modes d'action, enjeux. Le cas de l'Argentine, du Chili et de la Colombie* (doctoral thesis, Paris XIII, 2016).
56. Such is the angle explored in Jesús Montoya Juárez's *Narrativas del simulacro: Videocultura, tecnología y literatura en Argentina y Uruguay* (Murcia, Spain: Universidad de Murcia, 2013).
57. Aira, *God's Tea Party*, 75; César Aira, *El té de Dios* (Guatemala City: Mata-Mata, 2010), 9.
58. See Donna Haraway's now classic *Primate Visions: Gender, Race, and Nature in the World of Modern Science* (New York: Routledge, 1989).
59. See Philip Lutgendorf, *Hanuman's Tale: The Messages of a Divine Monkey* (Oxford: Oxford University Press, 2007). Thanks to ethnomusicologist and South Asian specialist Anna Schultz for her elucidation of these references.
60. In this sense, Aira's work, in Rebecca Walkowitz's felicitous coinage, is "born translated"—not, however, in the sense of anticipating its intelligibility, but rather the proliferation of meaning that results from translation. Aira sits in the antipodes of what Tim Parks has called, in another, equally adroit formulation, "the dull global novel." See Rebecca L. Walkowitz, *Born Translated: The Contemporary Novel in an Age of World Literature* (New York: Columbia University Press, 2015); and Tim Parks, "The Dull New Global Novel," *New York Review of Books* (blog), February 9, 2010, https://www.nybooks.com/daily/2010/02/09/the-dull-new-global-novel/.
61. Aira, *El té de Dios*, 19.
62. Aira draws the notion of "flight forward" from Lewis Carroll's Red Queen: "It takes all the running you can do, to keep in the same place. If you want to get somewhere else, you must run at least twice as fast as that!" Lewis Carroll, *Alice's Adventures in Wonderland and Through the Looking-Glass and What Alice Found There*, ed. Roger Lancelyn Green (Oxford: Oxford University Press, 1998), 145.
63. Aira, *God's Tea Party*, 82. "[El Rey de los Monos] les asperja los ojos con limón [a los más débiles], les hace meter la punta de los dedos en el té hirviendo, les tapona las orejas con confites, la nariz con mermelada, les mete cucharitas de plata en el ano . . . En las pausas, traga litros de té, para alimentar su furia sin causa. Ese té debe de tener algo." Aira, *El té de Dios*, 20.
64. Aira, *God's Tea Party*, 84. "Fluía a través de un meteorito de acero y níquel como un pájaro cruza el cielo celeste de una mañana de primavera. Atravesaba un planeta y ni se enteraba. Con la misma fluidez impasible atravesaba un átomo. O un papel, una flor, un barco, un perro, un cerebro, un pelo." Aira, *El té de Dios*, 23.
65. Haraway, *Primate Visions*, 260.

2. OF ROCKS AND PARTICLES ▪ 251

66. Latour seems to capture the spirit of this interreligious cover art. He recalls a medieval Spanish *disputatio* as an example of how literature can undo fundamentalisms and merge insights from different constructivisms: "A monk, a rabbi, and an imam were requested to debate about their creeds and to demonstrate in public the proofs they had of determining the 'true religion.' I see great literature as a way to reassemble and to renew those debates, so crucial for future peace. On condition that a fourth representative be brought in: the scientist and the engineer." Bruno Latour, "The Powers of the Facsimile: A Turing Test on Science and Literature," in *Intersections: Essays on Richard Powers*, ed. Stephen Burn and Peter Dempsey (Champaign, Ill: Dalkey Archive, 2008), 287.
67. Aira, *God's Tea Party*, 77. "Van cursadas 'a la evolución', y llegan automáticamente al instinto de los monos, como un timbrazo." Aira, *El té de Dios*, 11.
68. Aira, *God's Tea Party*, 79. "Llegaríamos a ese espectáculo inaudito, divino, de una asamblea de monos sentaditos alrededor de una mesa levantando la taza con una mano, el meñique apuntando a la nada que los rodea . . . modosos, formales." Aira, *El té de Dios*, 16.
69. Latour, "The Powers of the Facsimile," 19.
70. See Diego Vecchio, "Procedimientos y máquinas célibes: Roussel, Duchamp, Aira," in *César Aira, une révolution*, ed. Michel Lafon, Cristina Breuil, and Margarita Remón-Raillard (Grenoble, France: Université Stendhal-Grenoble 3, 2005), 95–105.
71. Aira, *El té de Dios*, 26. "The resemblance between the words is not mere coincidence." Aira, *God's Tea Party*, 86.
72. "Constructivism is made to be the exact opposite of deconstruction while, at the same time, using many of the same resources. But the way they are nested in one another is entirely different. 'Telescoped' is actually a good metaphor: the more elements nested the better the view, whereas in the logic of critical deconstruction the more elements the more *delayed* the grasp should be." Latour, "The Powers of Facsimile," 276.
73. Aira, *God's Tea Party*, 24. "Estaba y no estaba. . . . Era el prototipo del colado." Aira, *El té de Dios*, 22–24.
74. Aira, *God's Tea Party*, 83.
75. Lewis Carroll, *Alice's Adventures in Wonderland*, 63. Bold in the original.
76. Aira, *God's Tea Party*, 38.

> Su identificación con el punto geométrico, que era la coquetería de la partícula, hacía que su manifestación en la realidad fuera una línea, porque un punto en el tiempo siempre será una línea. Y como por una línea pasan infinitos planos en distinto grado de inclinación, a la entrada de ésta en el Té de Dios se formaba una especie de molino de biombos delgadísimos en ángulos distintos y cambiantes, por los que resbalaban los monos. . . . Al ser tantos los planos, casi nunca dos monos quedaban en el mismo, lo que no impedía las peleas, al contrario.
>
> (Aira, *El té de Dios*, 26)

77. Aira, 89. "No había cosas en realidad, sino palabras, las palabras que recortaban trocitos de mundo y les hacían creer a los hombres que eran cosas." Aira, *El té de Dios*, 32.
78. "I understand by this phrase the cutting up [découpage] of the perceptual world that anticipates, through its sensible evidence, the distribution of shares and social parties. . . . And this redistribution itself presupposes a cutting up of what is visible and what is not, of what can be heard and what cannot, of what is noise and what is speech." Jacques Rancière, *The Philosopher and His Poor*, trans. John Drury, Corinne Oster, and Andrew Parker, (Durham, N.C.: Duke University Press, 2004), 225.
79. Aira, *God's Tea Party*, 86. "Molino de biombos delgadísimos en ángulos distintos y cambiantes." Aira, *El té de Dios*, 26.
80. Aira, *God's Tea Party*, 90. "Su partida de nacimiento." Aira, *El té de Dios*, 32.
81. Aira, *God's Tea Party*, 85. "Un accidente sin contrapartida." Aira, *El té de Dios*, 25.
82. Aira, *God's Tea Party*, 89; Aira, *El té de Dios*, 32.
83. Aira, *God's Tea Party*, 89, 90. "[Dios] no tenía más remedio que entrar en el juego lingüístico"; "cada uno hacía un recorte distinto." Aira, *El té de Dios*, 32.
84. Geoff Brumfiel, "Physicists Declare Victory in Higgs Hunt," *Nature*, July 4, 2012, https://www.nature.com/news/physicists-declare-victory-in-higgs-hunt-1.10940.
85. Aira, *God's Tea Party*, 89. "Donde se abrían los caminos de la masa y la energía." Aira, *El té de Dios*, 31.
86. Aira, *God's Tea Party*, 83. "Recorría la nada y el todo por igual, en caída libre, sin oficio ni beneficio." Aira, *El té de Dios*, 21.
87. Rita Felski, "Latour and Literary Studies," *PMLA* 130, no. 3 (2015): 737.
88. While Felski's overall point is valid, it builds on false dichotomies: "Instead of engaging in a hermeneutics of suspicion, we conceive of interpretation as a form of mutual making or composing. Instead of stressing our analytic detachment, we own up to our attachments, shrugging of the tired dichotomy of vigilant critic versus naive reader. Instead of demystifying aesthetic absorption, we see that experience as a key to the distinctive ways in which art solicits our attention" (Felski, "Latour and Literary Studies," 741–42). She develops her views in *The Limits of Critique* (Chicago: University of Chicago Press, 2015).
89. Felski, "Latour and Literary Studies," 738.
90. The distinguished comparatist and videogame designer Ian Bogost convincingly questions several aspects of Latour's thinking in *Alien Phenomenology, or What It's Like to Be a Thing* (Minneapolis: University of Minnesota Press, 2012). For all the influence of Latour's work, rather than viewing him as a founding figure for contemporary anthropodecentric thinking, it would be more accurate to picture him as a lightning rod.
91. Felski, "Latour and Literary Studies," 738.
92. Aira, *God's Tea Party*, 89; Aira, *El té de Dios*, 31.
93. Latour, "The Powers of the Facsimile," 272.

94. If we demand of matter that it acts as though it has vitality, then we overlook or downgrade the possibility of it simply persisting in a rock-like or mineral condition. And that means that we foreclose on the challenge of thinking through or about a domain of existence that is devoid of any trace of thought, feeling, will, or any other quality we habitually recognize in ourselves. To take a lead from Harman, 'rather than anthropomorphizing the inanimate realm,' we need to start 'morphing the human realm into a variant of the inanimate.'

(Nigel Clark, *Inhuman Nature: Sociable Life on a Dynamic Planet* [Los Angeles: SAGE, 2011], 24. I owe this germane reference to David Stentiford.)

95. Elizabeth Povinelli, *Geontopower: A Requiem to Late Liberalism* (Durham, N.C.: Duke University Press, 2016), 33.
96. Ilan Stavans, *Gabriel García Márquez: The Early Years* (New York: Palgrave Macmillan, 2010), 168.
97. Marisol de la Cadena, *Earth Beings: Ecologies of Practice Across Andean Worlds* (Durham, N.C.: Duke University Press, 2015), 186.
98. Jeffrey Jerome Cohen, *Stone: An Ecology of the Inhuman* (Minneapolis: University of Minnesota Press, 2015), 22.
99. "Muy blanda es el agua e da en piedra dura, / muchas vegadas dando faze grand cavadura, / por grand uso el rudo sabe grand letura, / muger mucho seguida olvida la cordura." Paraphrased by Raymond Willis as "Water is extremely soft, and it strikes on a hard stone, but by striking it time after time it makes a large hollow; by much repetition an unschooled man can learn a long text; a woman who is long pursued ends up by losing her prudence." Juan Ruiz, *Libro de buen amor*, ed. Raymond Willis (Princeton, N.J.: Princeton University Press, 1972), 144–45.

3. Corpse Narratives as Literary History

1. In Derrida's succinct formulation, not quite a definition but an illustration, "deconstruction does not consist in passing from one concept to another, but in overturning and displacing a conceptual order, as well as the nonconceptual order with which the conceptual order is articulated." Jacques Derrida, *Margins of Philosophy*, trans. Alan Bass (Chicago: University of Chicago Press, 1982), 329.
2. Theo D'haen, *The Routledge Concise History of World Literature* (London: Routledge, 2011).
3. Mads Rosendahl Thomsen, *Mapping World Literature: International Canonization and Transnational Literatures* (New York: Continuum, 2008), 30–31.
4. Slavoj Žižek, *The Sublime Object of Ideology* (London: Verso, 1989), 142.

5. David Damrosch, "World Literature in Theory and Practice," in *World Literature in Theory*, ed. David Damrosch (London: Wiley, 2014), 3.
6. See David Damrosch's account of Goethe's "invisible church" as related to World Literature in the introduction to *World Literature in Theory* (London: Wiley, 2014), 17. For an overview of Goethe's complex religious views, I consulted Walter Naumann's "Goethe's Religion," *Journal of the History of Ideas* 13, no. 2 (1952): 188–99.
7. Carl Schmitt, *Roman Catholicism and Political Form*, trans. G. L. Ulmen (Westport, Conn.: Greenwood, 1996), 7.
8. Emily Apter, *Against World Literature: On the Politics of Untranslatability* (New York: Verso, 2013).
9. Gloria Fisk, "'Against World Literature': The Debate in Retrospect," *American Reader*, April 9, 2014, http://theamericanreader.com/against-world-literature-the-debate-in-retrospect/.
10. Amir Eshel, *Futurity: Contemporary Literature and the Quest for the Past* (Chicago: University of Chicago Press, 2013); David Damrosch, "Toward a History of World Literature," *New Literary History* 39 (2008): 483.
11. See the webpage of the publisher Brill, https://brill.com/view/journals/jwl/jwl-overview.xml.
12. Gerald Graff, "Taking Cover in Coverage," *Profession* 86 (1986): 41–45.
13. Graff, 41.
14. See Héctor Hoyos, *Beyond Bolaño: The Global Latin American Novel* (New York: Columbia University Press, 2015), 14–69; Jorge Luis Borges, "The Aleph," in *Collected Fictions*, trans. Andrew Hurley (New York: Viking, 1998).
15. Johann Peter Eckermann, *Gespräche mit Goethe in den letzten Jahren seines Lebens* (Frankfurt: Insel, 1981), 19–20.
16. Pheng Cheah, *What is a World? On Postcolonial Literature as World Literature* (Durham, N.C.: Duke University Press, 2016), 6.
17. Peter Uwe Hohendahl, *Prismatic Thought: Theodor W. Adorno* (Lincoln: University of Nebraska Press, 1995).
18. See Eckermann, *Gespräche mit Goethe*, 20.
19. Immanuel Kant, *Critique of Judgement*, trans. J. H. Bernard (New York: Hafner, 1951), § 17, 236–84.
20. Damrosch, introduction to *World Literature in Theory*, 11.
21. I consulted the expanded version of the prologue featured in Lois Parkinson Zamora and Wendy B. Faris's edited collection, *Magical Realism: Theory, History, Community*, trans. Tanya Huntington and Lois Parkinson Zamora (Durham, N.C.: Duke University Press, 1995), 76–88.
22. Umberto Eco, *The Infinity of Lists: An Illustrated Essay*, trans. Alastair McEwen (New York: Rizzoli, 2009). The quote is taken from an interview with *Spiegel Online* on the occasion of a new exhibition at the Louvre in Paris which Eco curated. Eco, "We Like Lists Because We Don't Want to Die," interview by Susanne Beyer and Lothar Gorris, *Spiegel Online*, November 11, 2009, http://www.spiegel.de

/international/zeitgeist/spiegel-interview-with-umberto-eco-we-like-lists-because-we-don-t-want-to-die-a-659577.html.
23. David Damrosch, *What Is World Literature?* (Princeton, N.J.: Princeton University Press, 2003), 112.
24. Julia Kristeva, *The Powers of Horror: An Essay on Abjection*, trans. Leon S. Rouidez (New York: Columbia University Press, 1982), 3.
25. Although Mariano Siskind has argued, with Lacan and other psychoanalytical referents, that a desire for worldliness has been a driving force in Latin American writers, the bodily is not central to his argument. Siskind, *Cosmopolitan Desires: Global Modernity and World Literature in Latin America* (Evanston, Ill.: Northwestern University Press), 9.
26. Kristeva, *The Powers of Horror*, 2.
27. Roberto Bolaño, *By Night in Chile*, trans. Chris Andrews (London: Harvill, 2003), 45. "Las cuencas vacías . . . la quijada abierta como si tras entrever la inmortalidad aún se estuviera riendo." Roberto Bolaño, *Nocturno de Chile* (Barcelona: Anagrama, 2000), 62.
28. "You won't believe this, but [Ulises Lima] used to shower with a book. I swear. He read in the shower. How do I know? Easy. All his books were wet." Roberto Bolaño, *The Savage Detectives*, trans. Natasha Wimmer (New York: Picador, 2007), 246.
29. "Kafka comprendía que los viajes, el sexo y los libros son caminos que no llevan a ninguna parte, y que sin embargo son caminos por los que hay que internarse y perderse." Roberto Bolaño, *El gaucho insufrible* (Barcelona: Anagrama, 2003), 158.
30. Roberto Bolaño, *Nazi Literature in the Americas*, trans. Chris Andrews (New York: New Directions, 2008), 145.
31. Sarah Pollack, "Latin America Translated (Again): Roberto Bolaño's 'The Savage Detectives' in the United States," *Comparative Literature* 61, no. 3 (2009): 346–65.
32. See Emily Apter, "Literary World-Systems," in *Teaching World Literature*, ed. David Damrosch, (New York: Modern Language Association, 2009), 44–60.
33. Immanuel Wallerstein, "1968, Revolution in the World-System: Theses and Queries," *Theory and Society* 18, no. 4 (1989): 431, 436.
34. Allende's speech is featured in *Memoria chilena*, the Chilean virtual repository of works of national relevance, and at http://www.abacq.net/imagineria/discur5.htm.
35. Roberto Bolaño, "El Ojo Silva," *Letras libres* (July 2000): 68–72; "Mauricio 'The Eye' Silva," in *Last Evenings on Earth*, trans. Chris Andrews (New York: New Directions, 2006), 106–20.
36. "Es más necesario el ojo del culo solo que los de la cara; por cuanto uno sin ojos en ella puede vivir, pero sin ojo del culo ni pasar ni vivir." Francisco de Quevedo, *Gracias y desgracias del ojo del culo, dirigidas a Doña Juana Mucha, Montón de Carne, Mujer gorda por arrobas / escribiolos Juan Lamas, el del camisón cagado* (Alicante: Biblioteca Virtual Miguel de Cervantes, 2003), 23.
37. Georges Bataille, "The Solar Anus," in *Visions of Excess: Selected Writings, 1927–1933*, ed. and trans. Alan Stoekl (Minneapolis: University of Minnesota Press, 1985), 7–8.
38. Bataille, 8.

39. Bataille, 9.
40. Benjamin Noys, *George Bataille: A Critical Introduction* (London: Pluto, 2000), 69.
41. Roberto Bolaño, *The Insufferable Gaucho*, trans. Chris Andrews (New York: New Directions, 2010), 123–46.
42. Roberto Bolaño, *By Night in Chile*, trans. Chris Andrews (New York: New Directions, 2003), 116. Originally published as *Nocturno de Chile* (Barcelona: Anagrama, 2000).
43. Roberto Bolaño, *Amulet*, trans. Chris Andrews (New York: New Directions, 2008), 33. Originally published as *Amuleto* (Barcelona: Anagrama, 1999).
44. Kristeva, *The Powers of Horror*, 108.
45. Roberto Bolaño, *The Return*, trans. Chris Andrews (New York: New Directions, 2010), 135.
46. Bolaño, *The Return*, 138, 145, 140.
47. Natalie Depraz, "Leib/Körper/Fleisch," in *The Dictionary of Untranslatables*, ed. Barbara Cassin, trans. Emily Apter, Jacques Lezra, and Michael Wood (Princeton, N.J.: Princeton University Press, 2014), 561.
48. Bolaño, *The Return*, 136.
49. Bolaño, *The Return*, 144.
50. Bolaño, *The Return*, 141.
51. See Hoyos, *Beyond Bolaño*, 12–20.
52. Good starting points to survey this literature include an article by Sergio Villalobos-Ruminott and a collection by Nicholas Birns and Juan E. de Castro: Villalobos-Ruminott, "A Kind of Hell: Roberto Bolaño and the Return of World Literature," *Journal of Latin American Cultural Studies* 18, no. 2–3 (2009): 193–205; Birns and de Castro, eds., *Roberto Bolaño as World Literature* (New York: Bloomsbury, 2017).
53. Roberto Bolaño, *2666*, trans. Natasha Wimmer (New York: Farrar, Straus and Giroux, 2008), 74. Originally published as *2666* (Barcelona: Anagrama, 2004).
54. Bolaño, *2666*, trans. Wimmer, 17. "Los organizadores, los mismos que dejaron afuera la literatura contemporánea española o polaca o sueca, por falta de tiempo o de dinero, en un penúltimo capricho destinaron la mayor parte de los fondos a invitar a cuerpo de rey a estrellas de la literatura inglesa, y con el dinero que quedó trajeron a tres novelistas franceses." Bolaño, *2666*, 15.
55. Bolaño, *2666*, trans. Wimmer, 109. "En la entrada del hotel los dos porteros le pegaban al taxista, que estaba en el suelo. No se trataba de patadas continuadas. Digamos que lo pateaban cuatro o seis veces y paraban y le daban oportunidad de hablar o de irse, pero el taxista, que estaba doblado sobre su estómago, movía la boca y los insultaba y entonces los porteros le daban otra tanda de patadas." Bolaño, *2666*, 94.
56. Bolaño, *2666*, trans. Wimmer, 109, 77.
57. Friedrich Nietzsche, *Thus Spoke Zarathustra: A Book for Everyone and No One*, trans. R. J. Hollingdale (Harmondsworth, UK: Penguin, 1969), 68.
58. Bolaño, *2666*, trans. Wimmer, 115.
59. Bolaño, *2666*, trans. Wimmer, 136.

3. CORPSE NARRATIVES AS LITERARY HISTORY   ■   257

60. Bolaño, *2666*, trans. Wimmer, 130.

> En el patio donde se celebraba la barbacoa contemplaron múltiples agujeros humeantes. Los profesores de la Universidad de Santa Teresa demostraron inusitadas dotes para las labores del campo . . . procedieron a desenterrar la barbacoa, y un olor a carne y a tierra caliente se extendió por el patio bajo la forma de una delgada cortina de humo que los envolvió a todos como la niebla que precede a los asesinatos y que se esfumó de manera misteriosa, mientras las mujeres llevaban los platos a la mesa, dejando impregnadas las vestimentas y las pieles con su aroma.
>
> (Bolaño, *2666*, 172–73)

61. Bolaño, *2666*, trans. Wimmer, 346. "Una sombra de frustración cruzó la cara del policía." Bolaño, *2666*, 436.
62. Bolaño, *2666*, trans. Wimmer; translation modified. "Gritos, como si en una de las salas de la cárcel estuvieran celebrando una despedida de soltero . . . risas lejanas. Mugidos." Bolaño, *2666*, 436.
63. Bolaño, *2666*, trans. Wimmer, 384–85. "Haas le arrebató el punzón al Guajolote y le dijo al Anillo que se pusiera a cuatro patas. Si no tiemblas, pendejo, nada te pasará. Si tiemblas o tienes miedo, vas a tener dos agujeros para cagar. . . . Disciplina, chingados, sólo pido un poco de disciplina y respeto, dijo Haas cuando a su vez entró en el pasillo de las duchas. Luego se arrodilló detrás del Anillo, le susurró a éste que se abriera bien de piernas, y le introdujo lentamente el punzón hasta el mango." Bolaño, *2666*, 606–7.
64. Bolaño, *2666*, trans. Wimmer, 345. "Estamos vivos porque no hemos visto ni sabemos nada." Bolaño, *2666*, 435.
65. Bolaño, *2666*, trans. Wimmer, 545.

> Según los forenses la muerte se debió a estrangulamiento, con rotura del hueso hioides. En el cadáver, pese a su estado de descomposición, era posible apreciar huellas de golpes producidos por un objeto contundente en la cabeza, manos y piernas. Probablemente hubo violación. La fauna cadavérica encontrada en el cuerpo indicaba como fecha de fallecimiento aproximadamente la primera o la segunda semana de febrero. No hay identificación, aunque sus datos coinciden con los de Guadalupe Guzmán Prieto, de once años de edad, desaparecida el ocho de febrero, al atardecer, en la colonia San Bartolomé.
>
> (Bolaño, *2666*, 682)

66. See Chris Andrews, *Roberto Bolaño: An Expanding Universe* (New York: Columbia University Press, 2014), 394.
67. As noted by Arnoldo Kraus in the Mexican newspaper *El Universal* on March 13, 2016: http://www.eluniversal.com.mx/entrada-de-opinion/articulo/arnoldo-kraus/nacion/2016/03/13/feminicidio-en-mexico.

68. Bolaño, *2666*, trans. Wimmer, 195. "La idea es de Duchamp, dejar un libro de geometría colgado a la intemperie para ver si aprende cuatro cosas de la vida real." Bolaño, *2666*, 251.
69. Bolaño, *2666*, trans. Wimmer, 188. "Recordaría el incidente que me hizo olvidar el *Testamento geométrico*." Bolaño, *2666*, 243.
70. Bolaño, *2666*, trans. Wimmer, 189. "El dolor de los otros en la memoria de uno." Bolaño, *2666*, 244.
71. Max Horkheimer and Theodor W. Adorno, *Dialectic of Enlightenment: Philosophical Fragments*, trans. Edmund Jephcott (Stanford, Calif.: Stanford University Press, 2002), 88.
72. For an elaboration of this discussion see the piece by New School historian Federico Finchelstein, "Fascism, History and Evil in Roberto Bolaño," in *Roberto Bolaño as World Literature*, ed. Nicholas Birns and Juan De Castro (New York: Bloomsbury, 2017), 23–40.
73. Bolaño, *2666*, trans. Wimmer, 790. "Jesús es la obra maestra. Los ladrones son las obras menores. ¿Por qué están allí? No para realzar la crucifixión, como algunas almas cándidas creen, sino para ocultarla." Bolaño, *2666*, 989.
74. Bolaño, *2666*, trans. Wimmer, 734. "'El que me violenta por el culo', es decir 'el caníbal que me folla por el culo y después se come mi cuerpo', aunque también podía significar 'el que me toca (o me viola) y me mira a los ojos (para comerse mi alma)'." Bolaño, *2666*, 917.
75. Bolaño, *2666*, trans. Wimmer, 734.

> El asado, un cuadro invertido que colgado de una manera es, efectivamente, un gran plato metálico de piezas asadas, entre las que se distingue un lechoncillo y un conejo, y unas manos, probablemente de mujer o de adolescente, que intentan tapar la carne para que no se enfríe, y que colgado al revés nos muestra el busto de un soldado, con casco y armadura, y una sonrisa satisfecha y temeraria a la que le faltan algunos dientes, la sonrisa atroz de un viejo mercenario que te mira, y su mirada es aún más atroz que su sonrisa, como si supiera cosas de ti ... Todo dentro de todo, escribe Ansky. Como si Arcimboldo hubiera aprendido una sola lección, pero ésta hubiera sido de la mayor importancia.
>
> (Bolaño, *2666*, 917–18)

76. Walter Benjamin, "Theses on the Philosophy of History," in *Illuminations*, ed. and introd. Hannah Arendt, trans. Harry Zohn (New York: Schocken, 1969), 256.
77. Bolaño, *2666*, trans. Wimmer, 348. "Nadie presta atención a estos asesinatos, pero en ellos se esconde el secreto del mundo." Bolaño, *2666*, 439.
78. See Chris Andrews, *Roberto Bolaño: An Expanding Universe* (New York: Columbia University Press, 2014); and Oswaldo Zavala, *La modernidad insufrible: Roberto Bolaño en los límites de la literatura latinoamericana contemporánea* (Chapel Hill: University of North Carolina, 2015).

79. Sergio González Ramírez, *Huesos en el desierto* (Barcelona: Anagrama, 2002).
80. Fisk, "'Against World Literature': The Debate in Retrospect."
81. Evelio Rosero, *The Armies*, trans. Anne McLean (New York: New Directions, 2009).
82. José Pablo Feinmann, "Dieguito," in *Cuentos de fútbol Argentino*, ed. Roberto Fontanarrosa (Buenos Aires: Alfaguara, 1997), 60–64.
83. Diamela Eltit, *Impuesto a la carne* (Santiago: Planeta, 2010).
84. Rodrigo Rey Rosa, *El material humano* (Barcelona: Anagrama, 2009); Eduardo Halfon, "Han vuelto las aves," in *Signor Hoffman* (Barcelona: Libros del Asteroide, 2015).
85. Guadalupe Nettel, *El cuerpo en que nací* (Barcelona: Anagrama, 2011); Valeria Luiselli, *The Story of My Teeth*, trans. Christina McSweeney (London: Granta, 2015), originally published as *La historia de mis dientes* (Madrid: Sexto Piso, 2014); Pedro Juan Gutiérrez, *Tropical Animal*, trans. Peter Lownds (London: Faber, 2003), originally published as *Animal tropical* (Barcelona: Anagrama, 2000).
86. Patti Smith, *Hecatomb: A Poem*, illustrated by José Antonio Suárez Londoño (Medellín: SML, 2013).
87. Karl Marx and Friedrich Engels, *Manifest der Kommunistischen Partei*, in *Werke*, vol. 4 (Berlin: Dietz, 1959), 466.
88. Gregory L. Ulmer, "The Puncept in Grammatology," in *On Puns: The Foundation of Letters*, ed. Jonathan Culler (Oxford: Blackwell, 1988), 14.
89. Mads Rosendahl Thomsen, *The New Human in Literature: Posthuman Visions of Changes in Body, Mind and Society after 1900* (London: Bloomsbury, 2014).
90. Vilashini Cooppan, "Codes for World Literature: Network Theory and the Field Imaginary," in *Approaches to World Literature*, ed. Joachim Küpper (Berlin: Akademie, 2013), 111–12.
91. Cheah, *What is a World?*, 58.
92. Bolaño, *2666*, 81. "The great cemeteries at lightspeed." Bolaño, *2666*, trans. Wimmer, 57.

4. Praxis and Politics of Hyperfetishism

1. Or has it? Teo, the seventy-eight-year old former taco salesman who is protagonist of the Mexican Juan Pablo Villalobos's highly idiosyncratic and Aira-influenced *Te vendo un perro* (2015), squashes cockroaches with Adorno's *Aesthetic Theory*. Wilhelm, his Mormon friend from Utah, obliges with the Bible. Juan Pablo Villalobos, *Te vendo un perro* (Barcelona: Anagrama, 2015), 65. The winner of the Herralde and Guardian First Book Awards, Villalobos has been successfully translated into English by Rosalind Harvey and published by And Other Stories, the scintillating British publisher.
2. Karl Marx, *Capital: A Critique of Political Economy*, trans. Ben Fowkes (New York: Penguin, 1990), 164.
3. See an influential revision of Marx's thought in Moishe Postone's *Time, Labor, and Social Domination: A Reinterpretation of Marx's Critical Theory* (Cambridge:

Cambridge University Press, 1993). Postone's discussion of commodity fetishism as catalyzer of abstract labor—an agent in its own right, per his account—could complement my findings. An important caveat is that the agentic properties of things themselves are, arguably, further downplayed in his argument than in Marx's.

4. Marx, *Capital*, 165.
5. Walter Benjamin, "Capitalism as Religion," in *Selected Writings, 1: 1913–1926*, ed. Marcus Bullock and Michael W. Jennings (Cambridge, Mass: Harvard/Belknap Press, 1996), 288.
6. Marx, *Capital*, 165; my emphasis.
7. Karl Marx, "Theses on Feuerbach," in *Marx-Engels Selected Works*, vol. 1 (Moscow: Progress, 1969), 15.
8. "Men do not therefore bring the products of their labour into relation with each other as values because they see these objects merely as the material integuments of homogeneous human labour. The reverse is true: by equating their different products to each other in exchange as values, they equate their different kinds of labour as human labour." Marx, *Capital*, 166.
9. Marx, *Capital*, 176–77.
10. See Gabriel Egan's elucidating *Shakespeare and Marx* (Oxford: Oxford University Press, 2004).
11. Marx, *Capital*, 178; my emphasis.
12. René Girard, *Deceit, Desire, and the Novel: Self and Other in Literary Structure* (Baltimore: Johns Hopkins University Press, 1965).
13. See "Machine-Learning Promises to Shake up Large Swathes of Finance," *The Economist*, May 25, 2017, https://www.economist.com/finance-and-economics/2017/05/25/machine-learning-promises-to-shake-up-large-swathes-of-finance.
14. On the dialectics of Spanish American autonomy, see chap. 1 of Ángel Rama, *Rubén Darío y el modernismo* (Caracas: Alfadil, 1985). For a continental-philosophy-inspired and thoroughly documented take on *modernismo*, see especially the third edition of Rafael Gutiérrez Girardot, *Modernismo: supuestos históricos y culturales*, (Bogotá: Fondo de Cultura Económica, 2004).
15. The preliminary studies to both the Ayacucho and the Norma editions of Silva's works provide good pointers for seasoned and new readers alike. For a state-of-the-art study of nineteenth-century Colombian literature, see Felipe Martínez Pinzón's *Una cultura de invernadero: Trópico y civilización en Colombia (1808–1928)* (Madrid: Iberoamericana, 2016).
16. José Asunción Silva, Guizado E. Camacho, and Gustavo Mejía, *Obra Completa* (Caracas: Biblioteca Ayacucho, 1977), 22.
17. ¡Si os encerrara yo en mis estrofas,
    frágiles cosas que sonreís
    pálido lirio que te deshojas
    rayo de luna sobre el tapiz
    de húmedas flores, y verdes hojas

4. PRAXIS AND POLITICS OF HYPERFETISHISM ■ 261

> que al tibio soplo de mayo abrís,
> si os encerrara yo en mis estrofas,
> pálidas cosas que sonreís!
>
> ¡Si aprisionaros pudiera el verso
> fantasmas grises, cuando pasáis,
> móviles formas del Universo,
> sueños confusos, seres que os vais,
> ósculo triste, suave y perverso
> que entre las sombras al alma dais,
> si aprisionaros pudiera el verso
> fantasmas grises cuando pasáis!
>
> <div align="right">(Silva, <i>Obra completa</i>, 22)</div>

18. Roca's self-defined "light essay" (liviano ensayo) relates Silva's poem to other of his works and points out the author's interest in animism (11). Kindred claims include highlighting the role of objects as external memories, framing the whole of Silva's work as a conversation with things (coloquio con las cosas, 13) and stagings of intimacy (17). See Juan Manuel Roca, *Cartógrafa memoria: ensayos en torno a la poesía* (Medellín: EAFIT, 2003), 9–22.
19. Roca, 17.
20. José Asunción Silva, *After-Dinner Conversation: The Diary of a Decadent*, trans. Kelly Washbourne (Austin: University of Texas Press, 2010).
21. Silva, 18.
22. Silva, 51.
23. Ericka Beckman, Capital *Fictions: The Literature of Latin America's Export Age* (Minneapolis: University of Minnesota Press, 2013), 42–79.
24. A thoughtful alternative appears in Andrade, who downplays the colonial subjectivity at work in Silva's purportedly admiring European collections. The critic shows instead how those collections affirm a vigorous eclecticism. They reinterpret, rather than imitate, dandyism and decadence. The periphery becomes metropolis through commerce with non-Hispanic capitals: "The fact that Spanish objects are included among many others in this new system of objects also represents a refusal to assign that tradition a privileged position in the formation of the Latin American subject." María Mercedes Andrade, *Ambivalent Desires: Representations of Modernity and Private Life in Colombia (1890s–1950s)* (Lewisburg, Pa.: Bucknell University Press, 2011), 47.
25. See Héctor Hoyos, "Re-discovering Ice: García Márquez, Aira, and Vallejo on Chilling Memories," in *Gabriel García Márquez in Retrospect*, ed. Gene H. Bell-Villada (Lanham, Md.: Lexington, 2016), 103–14; and Hoyos, "El último gramático: Ensayos críticos sobre Fernando Vallejo," in "El malditismo de Fernando Vallejo como espectáculo melodramático," ed. Juanita Aristizábal and Brantley Nichols, special issue, *Cuadernos de Literatura* 19, no. 37 (2015): 169–76. See also Hoyos,

"La racionalidad herética de Fernando Vallejo y el derecho a la felicidad," *Revista de Estudios Sociales* 35 (2010): 113–22.
26. Fernando Vallejo, *La Virgen de los sicarios* (Bogotá: Santillana, 1994).
27. Fernando Vallejo, *Almas en pena, chapolas negras* (Bogotá: Santillana, 1995).
28. The store was called "R. Silva e Hijo" (R. Silva and Son) and was located next to the church of Santo Domingo at "291 and 293, Carrera 7a, segunda Calle Real (Cervantes Virtual)." An 1889 ad mentions English, French, and Viennese shoes for ladies (Casa de Poesía Silva). A few years later, in Prague, Franz Kafka's domineering father, all shop owner and no poet, had his own writer son work at his fine-goods store (*Galanteriewarenladen*), unequivocally named "Hermann Kafka." It was located at the Palais Kinsky, Altstadterring 16 (see Peter-André Alt, *Franz Kafka: der ewige Sohn; eine Biographie* [Munich: Beck, 2005], 30). The Bogotá and Prague businesses would be today's Bloomingdale's—writing and the universal commerce of objects are of a piece.
29. Marx, *Capital*, 233.
30. Vallejo, *Almas en pena*, 273.
31. David Graeber, *Debt: The First 5000 Years* (New York: Melville, 2011), 330.
32. Vallejo, *Almas en pena*, 237.
33. Bertolt Brecht, "Die Dreigroschenoper," in *Ausgewählte Werke*, vol. 1: Stücke 1 (Frankfurt am Main: Suhrkamp, 1997), 267.
34. The most capacious English-language study on the cultural politics of the period is José María Rodríguez García's *The City of Translation: Poetry and Ideology in Nineteenth-Century Colombia* (New York: Palgrave MacMillan, 2010).
35. Houses lost, regained, and everything in between are a recurrent theme in Colombian literature. Draft manuscripts for the country's most famous book, *One Hundred Years of Solitude* (1967), bore the title *La casa*; García Márquez's eclipsed contemporary, Manuel Mejía Vallejo, won the Rómulo Gallegos prize for *La casa de las dos palmas* (1988). In a sense, both novels are about haunted houses. More recently, the theme of expatriate Colombians trying to find a pied-à-terre or restore a family estate in the motherland is present in Santiago Gamboa's polemical *Una casa en Bogotá* and in Héctor Abad Faciolince's bestselling *La oculta*, both from 2014.
36.   [Los sanitarios ahorradores de agua] definitivamente son los mejores: por el espacio que ocupan, que es poco; por el agua que ahorran, que es mucha; y por el flotador, que no falla: es una válvula . . . Miren qué preciosidad de espejo de agua o encharque. Acople del sanitario al piso en PVC, muy ligero pero firme. Dos botones de descarga: ocho litros para sólidos, y seis litros para líquidos. Estoy encantado con ellos. Da gusto usarlos. ¡Qué bueno que los compré!

    (Fernando Vallejo, *Casablanca la bella* [Madrid: Alfaguara, 2013], 181)

37. Meanwhile, in the skeletal autobiographical short story "Biografía fantasma" the Mexican-Peruvian writer Mario Bellatin hopes that the toilets of his grandmother's demolished house are still in use. With its vertiginous metonymic drift, the piece

4. PRAXIS AND POLITICS OF HYPERFETISHISM ⬛ 263

converses well with Vallejo's novel. Form meets content: it reads as rubble turned highway turned forgetfulness. See Mario Bellatin, "Biografía fantasma," *Letras libres* 9, no. 104 (2007): 48–49.

38. Juanita C. Aristizábal, "Fiel a su corriente: Las repeticiones de Vallejo en *Casablanca la bella*," *Cuadernos de Literatura* 19, no. 37 (2014): 204–18.
39. Sherry Turkle, "The Things that Matter," in *Evocative Objects: Things We Think With*, ed. Sherry Turkle (Cambridge, Mass.: MIT Press, 2014), 5.
40. "Hay que nombrar las cosas para que existan, pero usted las nombra para que se acaben." Vallejo, *Casablanca la bella*, 106.
41. Margo Glantz, *Historia de una mujer que caminó por la vida con zapatos de diseñador* (Barcelona: Anagrama, 2005).
42. See Suzanne Ferriss and Malloy Young's *Chick Lit: The New Woman's Fiction* (New York: Routledge, 2006), 54.
43. See Margo Glantz, "Palabras para una fábula," *Debate feminista* 13, no. 26 (2002): 144–64.
44. See Brigitte Sassen's scathing critique in "Heidegger on van Gogh's Old Shoes: The Use/Abuse of a Painting," *Journal of the British Society for Phenomenology* 32, no. 3 (2001): 160–73.
45. Me interesa mucho la vida de Ferragamo, pensé hoy por la tarde. Idea por lo menos curiosa en alguien que tiene los pies deformes y está tirada en la playa en traje de baño y con los pies descalzos, y en uno de los pies ostenta un juanete imposible de disimular cuando se está descalza, y me pregunto ¿cómo me puede interesar la vida de un señor gordo que se pasó la vida siempre inclinado, midiendo pies, estudiando su anatomía, su estructura y luego confeccionando hormas de madera y que además fue fascista?

    (Glantz, Historia de una mujer, 40)

    Elizabeth Rosa Horan translates an earlier, slightly shorter version of "andante," which omits Ferragamo's fascism, among other aspects, in *The House of Memory: Stories by Jewish Women Writers of Latin America*, ed. Marjorie Agosín (New York: Feminist Press at CUNY, 1999), 197–206.
46. Me detengo, esto es muy importante; la obsesión principal de Nora García proviene de una concepción especial de la idea de la fama, está relacionada con el honor del nombre. Convencida, regresa a Ferragamo, vuelve a probarse los zapatos, la empleada le comenta, usted ya estuvo aquí, Nora asiente, ruega que se los muestren de nuevo, los contempla, los acaricia, se los pone, verifica que no se le note demasiado el juanete, se decide, se los quita, se encamina a la caja y los paga, pero antes de hacerlo pronuncia un voto, una manda a Santa Teresa de Jesús: usarlos solamente cuando se siente a escribir, como ahora lo hace, con los zapatos puestos, los zapatos Ferragamo que ha comprado en una exclusiva boutique de la calle Bond en Londres, acompañando al calzado, unas medias de ese mismo, exacto color (se comprará luego varios pares de Fogal, pues son las únicas que calzan

> con los zapatos del gran artesano, mejor, del gran artista del calzado) y, por fin, con solemnidad, ¡ya era hora!, sentada como franciscano seráfico a la máquina de escribir o frente a la computadora, fumándose un cigarrillo, oyendo a Bach, comiendo turrón de yema y bebiendo un oporto, comienza el acto más heroico de su vida; escribir *la historia de la mujer que caminó por la vida con zapatos de diseñador*.
>
> (Glantz, *Historia de una mujer*, 24)

47. Erin Graff, *The Wandering Signifier: Rhetoric of Jewishness in the Latin American Imaginary* (Durham, N.C.: Duke University Press, 2008), 67–71.
48. Margo Glantz, *Las genealogías* (Mexico City: Casillas, 1981); trans. Susan Bassnett as *The Family Tree: An Illustrated Novel* (London: Serpent's Tail, 1991).
49. See Margo Glantz, *Zona de derrumbe* (Rosario, Argentina: Viterbo, 2001).
50. Thorstein Veblen, *The Theory of the Leisure Class: An Economic Study of Institutions* (New York: Macmillan, 1899), 75.
51. Rubén Gallo, *New Tendencies in Mexican Art: The 1990s* (New York: Palgrave Mac-Millan, 2004), 66.
52. See Bill Brown, *Other Things* (Chicago: University of Chicago Press, 2015), 31.
53. "Le spectacle est le *capital* à un tel degré d'accumulation qu'il devient image." Guy Debord, *La société du spectacle* (Paris: Gallimard, 1992), 32.
54. See Guy Debord and Gil J. Wolman, "Mode d'emploi du détournement," *Les lèvres nues* 8 (1956): 3.

5. Digitalia from the Margins

1. Three indispensable sources from this rich, sprawling scholarly terrain are Langdon Winner, "Do Artifacts Have a Politics?," *Daedalus* 109, no. 1 (1980): 121–36; Chellis Glendinning, "Notes Toward a Neo-Luddite Manifesto," *Utne Reader* 38 (1990): 50–53; and Richard Barbrook and Andy Cameron, "The Californian Ideology," *Science as Culture* 6, no. 1 (1996): 44–72.
2. Amy Chua, *World on Fire: How Exporting Free Market Democracy Breeds Ethnic Hatred and Global Instability* (New York: Anchor, 2004), 62.
3. Chase Peterson-Withorn, "Forbes Billionaires: Full List of the 500 Richest People in the World 2015," *Forbes*, March 2, 2015, http://www.forbes.com/sites/chasewithorn/2015/03/02/forbes-billionaires-full-list-of-the-500-richest-people-in-the-world-2015/.
4. Susan Buck-Morss, *The Dialectics of Seeing: Walter Benjamin and the Arcades Project* (Cambridge, Mass.: MIT Press, 1991), 111.
5. Alec Wilkinson, "Immigration Blues," *New Yorker*, May 24, 2010, http://www.newyorker.com/magazine/2010/05/24/immigration-blues. I thank José David Saldívar for bringing this song to my attention.

6. "Ya traigo mi celular." Los Tigres del Norte, "El celular," recorded 1992, track 7 on *Con sentimiento y sabor (Tan bonita)*, Fonovisa Records, compact disc.
7. "Parezco influyente." Los Tigres del Norte, "El celular."
8. " El patrón me lo dio en el trabajo / porque un ejecutivo yo soy / la verdad que ya mero me rajo / me controla donde quiera que yo voy." Los Tigres del Norte, "El celular."
9. "Mi mujer por poquito me cacha / me tiene fichado con mi celular." Los Tigres del Norte, "El celular."
10. "Así funciona el silencioso negocio del turismo sexual en Cali." *El País*, April 22, 2012, http://www.elpais.com.co/elpais/cali/noticias/turismo-sexual-practica-cada-vez-comun-en-cali; Chip Torres, "Te voy a dar un byte," YouTube video, June 15, 2011, https://youtu.be/pDVORKo8rYs; Daddy Yankee, "El celular," recorded 2006–7, track 10 on *El Cartel: The Big Boss*, El Cartel/Interscope, compact disc.
11. Andrés López, *La pelota de letras*, Universal Music Colombia, [2004] 2005, DVD.
12. Another source worth considering at length would be Álex Rivera's low-budget, fascinating sci-fi film *Sleep Dealer* (2008). A bilingual story set in a dystopian future with a fully militarized border, it follows a Chicano drone pilot in the U.S. Army and the son of one of his targets south of the border. As they discover, the two men are not that different from each other—the orphan works in construction by way of virtual reality, based in Mexico but "working in" the United States. Álex Rivera, *Sleep Dealer*, Los Angeles: Maya Entertainment, 2009, DVD. For a cogent discussion of the film, see Luis Martín-Cabrera, "The Potentiality of the Commons: A Materialist Critique of Cognitive Capitalism from the Cyberbracer@s to the Ley Sinde," *Hispanic Review* 80, no. 4 (2012): 583–605.
13. I develop my reading of Zambra alongside a discussion of his musical references in Héctor Hoyos, "The Tell-Tale Computer: Obsolescence and Nostalgia in Chile after Alejandro Zambra," in *Mediatized Sensibilities: Technology, Literature, and Latin America*, ed. Matthew Bush and Tania Gentic (New York: Routledge, 2015), 109–24.
14. Patricio Fernández, "La gran novela leve," *El País*, August 10, 2013, https://elpais.com/cultura/2013/08/07/actualidad/1375896436_498243.html.
15. Alejandro Zambra, *Mis documentos* (Barcelona: Anagrama, 2014), trans. Megan McDowell as *My Documents* (San Francisco: McSweeney's, 2015).
16. See Alberto Fuguet and Sergio Gómez, eds. *McOndo* (Barcelona: Mondadori, 1996).
17. Alejandro Zambra, "Historia de un computador," *Letras libres* (August 2008): 44–47.
18. "Una vez solo, Sebastián instaló el computador y comprobó lo que ya sospechaba: que era notablemente inferior, desde todo punto de vista, al que ya tenía. Se rieron mucho con el marido de su madre, después del almuerzo. Luego ambos hicieron espacio en el sótano para guardar el computador, que sigue ahí desde hace años, a la espera, como se dice, de tiempos mejores." Zambra, "Historia de un computador," 47.
19. Walter Benjamin, *The Writer of Modern Life: Essays on Charles Baudelaire* (Cambridge, Mass.: Harvard University Press, 2006).

20. Jane Bennett, *Vibrant Matter: A Political Ecology of Things* (Durham, N.C.: Duke University Press, 2010), xvii.
21. "Como si obedeciera a un impulso y no a una decisión responsable." Zambra, "Historia de un computador," 44.
22. "Breves líneas *que él llamaba* versos libres," Zambra, 44; my emphasis.
23. Zambra, 44.
24. "Le asignaron una habitación individual." Zambra, 45.
25. "como si correspondieran a viajes distintos." Zambra, 45.
26. Jaron Lanier, *You Are Not a Gadget: A Manifesto* (New York: Vintage, 2011).
27. Lanier, 11. The quintessential Chilean example would be the 2010 hit single "Los adolescentes," by Dënver. Its music video, widely popular on YouTube, eroticizes suburban teenage life to staccato sequences and electronic beats. See Dënver, "Los adolescentes," YouTube video, October 2, 2011, https://youtu.be/olhj7V1QtGE.
28. Lanier, *You Are Not a Gadget*, 12.
29. Lanier, 12.
30. Nicholas Carr, *The Shallows: What the Internet Is Doing to Our Brains* (New York: Norton, 2011).
31. Walter Benjamin, "On Some Motifs in Baudelaire," in *Selected Writings, 4: 1938–1940*, ed. Howard Eiland and Michael W. Jennings (Cambridge, Mass: Harvard/Belknap Press, 2006), 328.
32. Jonathan Crary, *24/7: Late Capitalism and the Ends of Sleep* (New York: Verso, 2013), 10.
33. Glendinning, "Notes Toward a Neo-Luddite Manifesto," 51.
34. Another forward-looking thinker is the Italian philosopher Franco "Bifo" Berardi. He suggests, provocatively, that we present-day humans are, vis-à-vis the rise of automation, in the situation that Malinche was regarding Hernán Cortés's conquest of Mexico: we can temper it, but in any case, we will facilitate it. Franco Berardi, "Malinche and the End of the World," in *The Internet Does Not Exist*, ed. Julieta Aranda, Brian Kuan Wood, and Anton Vidokle (Berlin: Sternberg, 2015), 100–109.
35. Alejandro Zambra, "Recuerdos de un computador personal," in *Mis documentos* (Barcelona: Anagrama, 2014), 62.
36. Zambra, "Recuerdos de un computador personal," 62.
37. Walter Benjamin, "Baudelaire," trans. Rodney Livingston, in *The Writer of Modern Life: Essays on Charles Baudelaire*, ed. Michael W. Jennings (Cambridge, Mass.: Harvard/Belknap Press, 2006), 27.
38. Zygmunt Bauman, *Liquid Love: On the Frailty of Human Bonds* (Cambridge: Polity, 2003), 45.
39. Alejandro Zambra, *Bonsái* (Barcelona: Anagrama, 2006), 15.
40. Alejandro Zambra, *Bonsai*, trans. Caroline De Robertis (New York: Melville, 2012), 10.
41. Giorgio Agamben, "What Is an Apparatus?," in *What Is an Apparatus? and Other Essays*, trans. David Kishik and Stefan Pedatella (Stanford, Calif: Stanford University Press, 2009), 44.
42. Valeria de los Ríos expands on the Agamben connection in her article "Mapa cognitivo, memoria (im)política y medialidad: Contemporaneidad en Alejandro Zambra y Pola Oloixarac," *Revista de Estudios Hispánicos* 48, no. 1 (2014): 145–60.

43. Martin Jay offers a lucid critical response to Bauman's recurrent use of the liquid metaphor in "Liquidity Crisis: Zygmunt Bauman and the Incredible Lightness of Modernity," *Theory, Culture, and Society* 27, no. 6 (2010): 95–106.
44. I expand on this issue in "Aftershock: Naomi Klein and the Southern Cone," *Third Text* 26, no. 2 (2012): 217–28.
45. Idelber Avelar, *The Untimely Present: Postdictatorial Latin American Fiction and the Task of Mourning* (Durham, N.C.: Duke University Press, 1999); Nelly Richard, *The Insubordination of Signs: Political Change, Cultural Transformation, and Poetics of the Crisis*, trans. Alice A. Nelson and Silvia Tandeciarz (Durham, N.C., Duke University Press: 2004); Alberto Moreiras, "Hybridity and Double Consciousness," *Cultural Studies* 13, no. 3 (1999): 373–407; Moreiras, *The Exhaustion of Difference: The Politics of Latin American Cultural Studies* (Durham, N.C.: Duke University Press, 2001).
46. Martin Heidegger, "The Question Concerning Technology," in *The Question Concerning Technology, and Other Essays*, trans. William Lovitt (New York: Harper, 1977), 4.
47. Karl Marx, *Capital: A Critique of Political Economy*, trans. Ben Fowkes (New York: Penguin, 1990), 874–75.
48. Michael Armbrust, Armando Fox, Rean Griffith, Anthony D. Joseph, Randy H. Katz, Andrew Konwinski, Gunho Lee, David A. Patterson, Ariel Rabkin, Ion Stoica, and Matei Zaharia, "Above the Clouds: A Berkeley View of Cloud Computing," *Department of Electrical Engineering and Computer Sciences, University of California, Berkeley, Rep. UCB/EECS* 28, no. 13 (2009): 3.
49. Jorge Baradit, *Synco* (Barcelona: Ediciones B, 2008).
50. Baradit, 81.
51. See Edén Medina, *Cybernetic Revolutionaries* (Boston: MIT Press, 2011); and Evgeny Morozov, "The Socialist Origins of Big Data," *New Yorker*, October 13, 2014, http://www.newyorker.com/magazine/2014/10/13/planning-machine.
52. On the development of ARPANET and its ultimate adoption in civilian life, see Niels Brügger, ed., *Web History* (New York: Lang, 2010).
53. Detrás de ellos [pasó] un escuadrón de flamantes Fiat 600 que contenían el microcomputador personal desarrollado por el Instituto Miguel Enríquez para los ejecutivos de terreno de Synco, una maravilla de la miniaturización que había causado asombro en la última feria tecnológica mundial en París. El último Fiat 600 tiraba de un pequeño [remolque] acoplado con el modelo 'Atacama X-12', un moderno computador completamente inalámbrico de apenas ochenta kilos de peso.

    (Baradit, *Synco*, 211)

54. Baradit, 229, 285.
55. Across the Andes, notable Argentine works similarly defamiliarize our technological present, including Daniel Link's *Exposiciones* (Buenos Aires: Blatt & Ríos, 2013); and Sebastián Robles's *Las redes invisibles* (Buenos Aires: Momofuku, 2017).

Conclusions: Extractivism Estranged

1. See chapter 1, note 21.
2. See Bruno Latour, "Why Has Critique Run Out of Steam?," *Critical Inquiry* 30, no. 2 (2004): 225–48.
3. See Ursula K. Heise, "Ecocriticism and the Transnational Turn in American Studies," *American Literary History* 20, no. 1–2 (March 1, 2008): 381–404; Pheng Cheah, *What Is a World? On Postcolonial Literature as World Literature* (Durham, N.C.: Duke University Press, 2016).
4. Jason Moore, *Capitalism in the Web of Life: Ecology and the Accumulation of Capital* (New York: Verso, 2015).
5. "¿Quiere Ud. saber cuál es nuestro destino?, los campos para cultivar el añil, la grana, el café, la caña, el cacao y el algodón, las llanuras solitarias para criar ganados, los desiertos para cazar las bestias feroces, las entrañas de la tierra para excavar el oro que no puede saciar a esa nación avarienta." Simón Bolívar, "Carta de Jamaica," in *Carta de Jamaica y otros textos* (Caracas: Fundación Biblioteca Ayacucho, 2015), 56.
6. The most thoughtful exposition of how neoliberalism has bred its own ethos even in Pink Tide (extractivist) governments, and moreover in everyday urban practices, is Verónica Gago's *Neoliberalism from Below: Popular Pragmatics and Baroque Economies*, trans. Liz Mason-Deese (Durham, N.C.: Duke University Press, 2017).
7. Bruno Bosteels, *The Actuality of Communism* (London: Verso, 2011).
8. Bosteels, 29; my emphasis.
9. A touchstone in this discussion is Slavoj Žižek, *The Ticklish Subject: The Absent Centre of Political Ontology* (London: Verso, 1999).
10. Sheila Jasanoff and Sang-Hyun Kim, eds., *Dreamscapes of Modernity: Sociotechnical Imaginaries and the Fabrication of Power* (Chicago: University of Chicago Press, 2015).
11. Michael Hardt and Antonio Negri, *Multitude: War and Democracy in the Age of Empire* (New York: Penguin, 2004), xiii, xv.
12. Rosi Braidotti, *The Posthuman* (Cambridge: Polity, 2013), 22. For a useful overview of recent leftist thinking that, salutarily, includes the work of Donna Haraway, see Razmig Keucheyan, *Left Hemisphere: Mapping Contemporary Theory* (New York: Verso, 2013).
13. This position has been articulated differently by McKenzie Wark, who sets out to select "from within the archive those strands of Marxist theory for which the Anthropocene already appears as an object of thought and action in all but name." Wark, *Molecular Red: Theory for the Anthropocene* (London: Verso, 2015), xx. While I find Wark's cyborg-internationalist agenda persuasive, and consistent with some of my findings, I find his derision of high theory rather troubling.
14. Vladimir Ilich Lenin, *Collected Works*, vol. 32 (Moscow: Progress, 1973), 93.
15. Lenin, 94. I first learned about this argument from an excerpt, thought-provokingly featured alongside a Brecht poem on Lenin's death, that serves as the inaugural

piece of Debord and Wolman's remarkable situationist magazine, *Les Lèvres nues* 1 (1954): 3–4. Other underexamined sources of new materialist intuitions already present in historical materialism include the Soviet philosopher Evald Ilyenkov, who committed suicide in his fifties in the year 1979. See, especially, Ilyenkov, "The Materialist Conception of Thought as the Subject Matter of Logic," in *Dialectical Logic: Essays on Its History and Theory* (Moscow: Progress, 1977), 251–88. Ilyenkov's Mexican contemporary, José Revueltas, reflects on similar matters in "Razón dialéctica y mercancía," in *Dialéctica de la conciencia* (Mexico City: Era, 1982), 168–72.

16. For a thoughtful piece on the "crisis of the humanities," see Eric Hayot, "The Humanities as We Know Them Are Doomed. Now What?," *Chronicle of Higher Education*, July 1, 2018, https://www.chronicle.com/article/The-Humanities-as-We-Know-Them/243769. A fiery debate on the politics of digital humanities was sparked by Daniel Allington, Sarah Brouillette, and David Golumbia in "Neoliberal Tools (and Archives): A Political History of Digital Humanities," *Los Angeles Review of Books*, May 5, 2016, https://lareviewofbooks.org/article/neoliberal-tools-archives-political-history-digital-humanities/.

17. Bruno Latour, *Politics of Nature: How to Bring the Sciences into Democracy*, trans. Catherine Porter (Cambridge, Mass.: Harvard University Press, 2004), 237.

18. See Henry Petroski, *The Pencil: A History of Design and Circumstance* (New York: Knopf, 1992); Council of Supply Chain Management Professionals, *SCM Definitions and Glossary of Terms*, updated August 2013.

19. See Alberto Acosta, "Extractivism and Neoextractivism: Two Sides of the Same Curse," *Beyond Development* 61 (2013): 61–86.

20. Karl Marx and Friedrich Engels, *Manifest der Kommunistischen Partei*, in *Werke*, vol. 4 (Berlin: Dietz, 1959), 466.

21. An die Stelle der alten lokalen und nationalen Selbstgenügsamkeit und Abgeschlossenheit tritt ein allseitiger Verkehr, eine allseitige Abhängigkeit der Nationen voneinander. Und wie in der materiellen, so auch in der geistigen Produktion. Die geistigen Erzeugnisse der einzelnen Nationen werden Gemeingut. Die nationale Einseitigkeit und Beschränktheit wird mehr und mehr unmöglich, und aus den vielen nationalen und lokalen Literaturen bildet sich eine Weltliteratur.

(Marx and Engels, 466)

22. See Maxim Gorky, *Mother* (New York: Citadel, 1947); George Orwell, *1984* (Boston: Houghton Mifflin Harcourt, 2017); and Roberto Arlt, *Mad Toy* (Durham, N.C.: Duke University Press, 2002).

23. Bolaño, *2666*, trans. Natasha Wimmer (New York: Farrar, Straus and Giroux, 2008), 469. "Estrella quería saber cosas de computadoras, quería aprender, quería progresar, dijo la muchacha. Tanta computadora, tanta computadora, no me trago una palabra de lo que me dices, tortita, dijo Epifanio. Yo no soy su pinche tortita, dijo la muchacha." Bolaño, *2666* (Barcelona: Anagrama, 2004), 588.

24. Bolaño, *2666*, trans. Wimmer, 484. "Un experto en informática que ha levantado su propio negocio." Bolaño, *2666*, 606.
25. Vicky Funari and Sergio de la Torre, *Maquilapolis*, (San Francisco: California Newsreel, 2006), DVD.
26. In a riposte to Facebook executive Sheryl Sandberg's neoliberal feminism, which encourages (mostly white) women professionals to assert themselves by "leaning in" during Silicon Valley board meetings, the cultural critic bell hooks notes that gender equality discourse is sometimes oblivious of intersectionality and class: "Privileged white women often experience a greater sense of solidarity with men of their same class than with poor white women or women of color." bell hooks, "Dig Deep: Beyond Lean In," *Feminist Wire*, October 28, 2013, https://www.thefeministwire.com/2013/10/17973/.
27. Glendinning, "Notes towards a Neo-Luddite Manifesto," in *Utne Reader* 38 (1990): 51.
28. Alberto Vásquez-Figueroa, *Coltán* (Barcelona: Ediciones B, 2008), 79.
29. Vásquez-Figueroa, 42.
30. Michael Nest, *Coltan* (Cambridge: Polity, 2011), 2.
31. See Michel Foucault, *Naissance de la biopolitique: Cours au Collège de France (1978–1979)* (Paris: Gallimard, 2004).
32. NPR Staff, "After Dump, What Happens to Electronic Waste?," *NPR.org*, 21 December, 2010. http://www.npr.org/2010/12/21/132204954/after-dump-what-happens-to-electronic-waste.
33. Eric Herhuth has explored this aspect, along with the movie's heteronormalizing thrust, in "Life, Love, and Programming: The Culture and Politics of *WALL-E* and Pixar Computer Animation," *Cinema Journal* 53, no. 4 (2014): 53–75.
34. Kim Hyesoon, *All the Garbage in the World, Unite!*, trans. Don Mee Choi (Notre Dame, Ind.: Action, 2011), 29–30.
35. Ellen Banda-Aaku, *E Is for E-Waste* (San Francisco: Worldreader, 2017); Annie Leonard, Jonah Sachs, and Louis Fox, "The Story of Electronics," *The Story of Stuff Project*, accessed July 21, 2017, http://storyofstuff.org/movies/story-of-electronics/.
36. Jorge Furtado, *Ilha das Flores* (Casa de Cinema de Porto Alegre, 1989), film.
37. Eduardo Coutinho, dir., *Boca Do Lixo*, (1993; Rio de Janeiro: VideoFilmes, 2004), DVD; Lucy Walker and Karen Harley, *Waste Land* (London: Almega Projects, 2010), 99 min. For a survey of Brazilian cinema on garbage, see Ernesto Livon-Grosman, "Thinking on Film and Trash: A Few Notes," *ReVista: Harvard Review of Latin America* 14, no. 2 (2015): 53–55.
38. "Livre é o estado daquele que tem liberdade. Liberdade é uma palavra que o sonho humano alimenta, que não há ninguém que explique e ninguém que não entenda." Cecília Meireles, "Romance XXIV ou DA BANDEIRA DA INCONFIDÊNCIA," in *Romanceiro da inconfidência* (São Paulo: Editora da Universidade de São Paulo, 2004), 82.
39. NPR Staff, "After Dump."
40. Jasanoff and Kim, *Dreamscapes of Modernity*.

41. Karl Ove Knausgård, *Autumn*, vol. 1 (New York: Penguin Random House, 2017), 92.
42. Don Juan nos dio la espalda y pareció meterse un poco entre la enorme y solitaria mata de café. Como escondiéndose entre las hojas verdes. Como buscando algo entre las hojas verdes. Como queriendo que la vieja mata lo protegiera. Aún de espaldas, estaba quitándole granos de café a la vieja mata, lentamente, tiernamente, sus manos de campesino dejando que los frutos rojos cayeran insonoros sobre la tierra seca. Se agachó un poco, y le quitó los granos más bajos. Se estiró hacia las ramas de arriba, las jaló hacia él, y sus manos expertas las dejaron sin grano alguno. El suelo, alrededor de sus pies, se fue tornando rojo. Su sombrero de petate crujía contra el ramaje. Parecía él ahora más encorvado, más pequeño. Siguió quitando y botando los frutos al suelo. Siguió adentrándose en el follaje de la vieja mata, adentrándose en el verdor de tantas hojas y ramas de la vieja mata, hasta que todo él desapareció por completo.

> (Eduardo Halfon, "Han vuelto las aves," in *Signor Hoffman*
> [Barcelona: Libros del Asteroide, 2015], 72)

43. Claude Lanzmann, *Shoah* (Hollywood, Calif.: New Yorker Video, 2003), DVD. A kindred intervention, pertaining to unspeakable horrors of a different scale, is Patricio Guzmán's *El botón de Nácar* [*The Pearl Button*] (2014). The film's centerpiece is a pearl button found at the bottom of the ocean, in the process of calcifying back into the rock, as if coming home. The button is in fact forensic evidence (but not only that): it belonged to the shirt of a *desaparecido* thrown to the ocean under Pinochet. Patricio Guzmán, *The Pearl Button* (New York: Kino Lorber, 2016), DVD.
44. Theodor W. Adorno, "The Idea of Natural-History," in *Things Beyond Resemblance: Collected Essays on Theodor W. Adorno*, ed. and trans. Robert Hullot-Kentor (New York: Columbia University Press, 2006), 111–24. For an up-to-date take on some of these ideas, see chap. 7 of Jane Bennett's *Vibrant Matter: A Political Ecology of Things* (Durham, N.C.: Duke University Press, 2010). While discussing Darwin, Bennett devotes fascinating pages to the "small agency" of worms in human history—without the accumulated effects of their exertions, there would be no culture to speak of.
45. These meanings are also elucidated, more explicitly and programmatically, in Teixeira Coelho's *História natural da ditadura* (São Paulo: Iluminuras 2006). Equal parts Sebald and Oswald de Andrade, this name-dropping, free-associating rumination of a book features black-and-white photographs and long paragraphs that seek to "anticonstruct" dictatorship. Here dictatorship is understood as a more or less latent worldwide condition epitomized by the Chinese wall, the unfortunate and greatest achievement of humanity (in that it is the sole construction visible from space), countered by such constructions as Walter Benjamin's memorial in Port Bou. Coelho, a professor emeritus of cultural agency (ação cultural), offers a prescient, materialist call to arms for the ongoing resistance to the country's sharp rightist turn: "Tudo aquilo que entra *em tensão* ou que *trabalha* em tensão, como

se diz, a exemplo de um cabo de aço que sustenta uma ponte, *se solidifica cada vez mais*" (277).
46. Rubén Darío, "El rey burgués," in *Obras completas*, ed. Julio Ortega, vol. 1 (Barcelona: Galaxia Gutenberg, 2007), 63–67.
47. Rosario Castellanos, *Oficio de tinieblas* (Mexico City: Mortiz, 1966); trans. Esther Allen as *The Book of Lamentations* (New York: Penguin, 1998); Julio Cortázar, *Rayuela* (Madrid: Catedra, 1963); trans. Gregory Rabassa as *Hopscotch* (New York: Penguin, 1966).
48. See Jorge Coronado and Ximena Briceño, eds., *Visiones de los Andes: Ensayos críticos sobre el concepto de paisaje y región* (La Paz: University of Pittsburgh Press and Plural, 2019), 184–86.
49. See Malcolm Quinn, *The Swastika: Constructing the Symbol* (New York: Routledge, 2005).
50. Theodor W. Adorno, *Aesthetic Theory* (London: Continuum, 1997), 5.
51. This speculative claim is inspired in equal parts by Sidney Mintz's historical-materialist history of sugar and by Michael Pollan's observations on the coevolution of crops and concepts (see chapter 1). See Mintz, *Sweetness and Power: The Place of Sugar in Modern History* (New York: Penguin, 1986). For a forgotten classic history of Cuban sugar—which Mintz omits—see Manuel Moreno Fraginals's *The Sugarmill: The Socioeconomic Complex of Sugar in Cuba, 1760–1860* (New York: Monthly Review Press, 1976). The Spanish first edition, from 1964, is dedicated to Ernesto Che Guevara. Roberto González Echevarría pointed out Mintz's omission to me at Yale.
52. See Peter Maass, "What Happened at the Macondo Well?," *New York Review of Books*, September 29, 2011, http://www.nybooks.com/articles/2011/09/29/what-happened-macondo-well/.
53. Neil Larsen, "Literature, Immanent Critique, and the Problem of Standpoint," in *Literary Materialisms*, ed. Mathias Nilges and Emilio Sauri (New York: Palgrave Macmillan, 2013), 76.
54. Raymond L. Williams, "An Eco-critical Reading of *One Hundred Years of Solitude*," in *The Cambridge Companion to Gabriel García Márquez*, ed. Philip Swanson (Cambridge: Cambridge University Press, 2010), 64–77.

Bibliography

80 Anos: Euclides da Cunha na Amazônia. Manaus: Centro Cultural Francisco Matarazzo Sobrinho, 1985.

Acosta, Alberto. "Extractivism and Neoextractivism: Two Sides of the Same Curse." *Beyond Development* 61 (2013): 61–86.

Adorno, Theodor W. "The Idea of Natural-History." In *Things Beyond Resemblance: Collected Essays on Theodor W. Adorno*, ed. and trans. Robert Hullot-Kentor, 111–24. New York: Columbia University Press, 2006.

———. *Prisms*. Trans. Samuel Weber and Shierry Weber. London: Spearman, 1967.

Agamben, Giorgio. *What Is an Apparatus? and Other Essays*. Trans. David Kishik and Stefan Pedatella. Stanford, Calif: Stanford University Press, 2009.

Aira, César. *God's Tea Party*. In *The Musical Brain, and Other Stories*, trans. Chris Andrews, 75–90. New York: New Directions, 2015.

———. *El té de Dios*. Guatemala City: Mata-Mata, 2010.

Albert, Bruce. "O ouro canibal e a queda do céu: Uma crítica xamânica da economia política da natureza (Yanomami)." In *Pacificando o branco: Cosmologias do contato norte-amazônico*, ed. Bruce Albert and Alcita Rita Ramos, 239–70. São Paulo: Unesp, 2002.

Alonso, Carlos J. "La escritura fetichizadora de Antonio José Ponte." *Revista de Estudios Hispánicos* 43, no. 1 (2009): 93–108.

Althusser, Louis. "Ideology and Ideological State Apparatuses (Notes Towards an Investigation)." Trans. Ben Brewster. In *Lenin and Philosophy and Other Essays*, 85–126. New York: NYU Press, 2001.

Álvarez-Borland, Isabel. "El silencio del hambre: Figuras de la carencia en Antonio José Ponte." *Hispania: A Journal Devoted to the Teaching of Spanish and Portuguese* 90, no. 3 (2007): 443–52.

Álvarez Santana, Litzie. "Descubren en Abreus piezas arqueológicas." *Azurina: Portal de la cultura en Cienfuegos*, December 2, 2009. http://www.azurina.cult.cu/index.php/noticias/1499-descubren-en-abreus-piezas-arqueologicas.

Amaya-Amador, Ramón. *Prisión verde*. Buenos Aires: Agepe, 1957.

Andrade, María Mercedes. *Ambivalent Desires: Representations of Modernity and Private Life in Colombia (1890s–1950s)*. Lewisburg, Pa.: Bucknell University Press, 2011.

Andrews, Chris. *Roberto Bolaño: An Expanding Universe*. New York: Columbia University Press, 2014.

Appadurai, Arjun, ed. *The Social Life of Things: Commodities in Cultural Perspective*. Cambridge: Cambridge University Press, 1986.

Apter, Emily. *Against World Literature: On the Politics of Untranslatability*. New York: Verso, 2013.

———. "Literary World-Systems." In *Teaching World Literature*, ed. David Damrosch, 44–60. New York: Modern Language Association, 2009.

Aquinas, Thomas. *Sancti Thomae Aquinatis Doctoris Angelici Opera. Omnia iussu edita Leonis XIII P.M. Tomus Decimus Sextus Indices: Summa Theologiae et summa contra gentiles*. Rome: Apud Sedem Commissions Leoninae, 1948.

Arendt, Hannah. *Eichmann in Jerusalem: A Report on the Banality of Evil*. 2nd ed. New York: Penguin, 1977.

Aristizábal, Juanita C. "Fiel a su corriente: Las repeticiones de Vallejo en *Casablanca la bella*." *Cuadernos de Literatura* 19, no. 37 (2014): 204–18.

Arroyo, Jossiana. "Transculturation, Syncretism, and Hybridity." In *Critical Terms in Caribbean and Latin American Thought: Historical and Institutional Trajectories*, ed. Yolanda Martínez-San Miguel, Ben Sifuentes-Jáuregui, and Marisa Belausteguigoitia, 133–44. New York: Palgrave, 2016.

Avelar, Idelber. *The Untimely Present: Postdictatorial Latin American Fiction and the Task of Mourning*. Durham, N.C.: Duke University Press, 1999.

Banda-Aaku, Ellen. *E Is for E-Waste*. San Francisco: Worldreader, 2017.

Baradit, Jorge. *Synco*. Barcelona: Ediciones B, 2018.

Bataille, Georges. *The Bataille Reader*. Ed. Fred Botting and Scott Wilson. Oxford: Blackwell, 1997.

———. "The Solar Anus." In *Visions of Excess: Selected Writings, 1927–1933*, ed. and trans. Alan Stoekl, 5–9. Minneapolis: University of Minnesota Press, 1985.

Baum, Vicki. *The Weeping Wood*. Garden City, N.Y.: Doubleday, Doran, 1943.

Bauman, Zygmunt. *Liquid Love: On the Frailty of Human Bonds*. Cambridge: Polity, 2003.

Beasley-Murray, Jon. *Posthegemony: Political Theory and Latin America*. Minneapolis: University of Minnesota Press, 2010.

Beauvoir, Simone de. "La mémoire de l'horreur." In *Claude Lanzmann: Shoah*, 5–9. Paris: Fayard, 1985.

Beckman, Ericka. *Capital Fictions: The Literature of Latin America's Export Age*. Minneapolis: University of Minnesota Press, 2013.

Benjamin, Walter. "Baudelaire." Trans. Rodney Livingston. In *The Writer of Modern Life: Essays on Charles Baudelaire*, ed. Michael W. Jennings, 27–29. Cambridge, Mass.: Harvard/Belknap Press, 2006.

———. "Capitalism as Religion." In *Selected Writings, 1: 1913–1926*, ed. Marcus Bullock and Michael W. Jennings, 259–60. Cambridge, Mass.: Harvard/Belknap Press, 1996.

———. "Excavation and Memory." In *Selected Writings, 2: 1927–1934*, ed. Michael W. Jennings, Howard Eiland, and Gary Smith, 576. Cambridge, Mass.: Harvard/Belknap Press, 1999.

———. "On Some Motifs in Baudelaire." In *Selected Writings, 4: 1938–1940*, ed. Howard Eiland and Michael W. Jennings, 313–55. Cambridge, Mass: Harvard/Belknap Press, 2006.

———. "Theses on the Philosophy of History." In *Illuminations*, ed. and introd. Hannah Arendt, trans. Harry Zohn, 253–64. New York: Schocken, 1969.

Benmiloud, Karim, and Raphaël Estève, eds. *Les astres noirs de Roberto Bolaño*. Bordeaux: Universitaire, 2007.

Bennett, Jane. *Vibrant Matter: A Political Ecology of Things*. Durham, N.C.: Duke University Press, 2010.

Bennett, Jill. *Living in the Anthropocene / Leben Im Anthropozän*. Ostfildern, Germany: Hatje Cantz, 2011.

Beverley, John. *The Failure of Latin America: Postcolonialism in Bad Times*. Pittsburgh, Pa.: University of Pittsburgh Press, 2019.

———. *Latinamericanism after 9/11*. Durham: Duke University Press, 2011.

Birns, Nicholas, and Juan E. de Castro, eds. *Roberto Bolaño as World Literature*. New York: Bloomsbury, 2017.

Bogost, Ian. *Alien Phenomenology, or What It's Like to Be a Thing*. Minneapolis: University of Minnesota Press, 2012.

Bolaño, Roberto. *2666*. Trans. Natasha Wimmer. New York: Farrar, Straus and Giroux, 2008. Originally published as *2666* (Barcelona: Anagrama, 2004).

———. *Amulet*. Trans. Chris Andrews. New York: New Directions, 2008. Originally published as *Amuleto* (Barcelona: Anagrama, 1999).

———. *By Night in Chile*. Trans. Chris Andrews. New York: New Directions, 2003. Originally published as *Nocturno de Chile* (Barcelona: Anagrama, 2000).

———. *The Insufferable Gaucho*. Trans. Chris Andrews. New York: New Directions, 2010. Originally published as *El gaucho insufrible* (Barcelona: Anagrama, 2003).

———. *Nazi Literature in the Americas*. Trans. Chris Andrews. New York: New Directions, 2008.

———. *The Return*. Trans. Chris Andrews. New York: New Directions, 2010.

———. *The Savage Detectives*. Trans. Natasha Wimmer. New York: Farrar, Straus and Giroux, 2007.

Borges, Jorge Luis. "The Aleph." In *Collected Fictions*, trans. Andrew Hurley, 274–86. New York: Viking, 1998.

Boscagli, Maurizia. *Stuff Theory: Everyday Objects, Radical Materialism*. New York: Bloomsbury, 2014.

Bosteels, Bruno. *Marx and Freud in Latin America: Politics, Psychoanalysis, and Religion in Times of Terror*. New York: Verso, 2012.

Boym, Svetlana. *The Future of Nostalgia*. New York: Basic, 2001.

———. "Nostalgia and Its Discontents." *The Hedgehog Review* 9, no. 2 (2007): 7–18.

Braidotti, Rosi. *The Posthuman*. Cambridge: Polity, 2013.

Brecht, Bertolt. "Die Dreigroschenoper." In *Ausgewählte Werke*, vol. 1: Stücke 1. Frankfurt am Main: Suhrkamp, 1997.

Brown, Bill. *Other Things*. Chicago: University of Chicago Press, 2015.

———. *A Sense of Things: The Object Matter of American Literature*. Chicago: University of Chicago Press, 2003.

Brügger, Niels, ed. *Web History*. New York: Lang, 2010.

Buck-Morss, Susan. *The Dialectics of Seeing: Walter Benjamin and the Arcades Project*. Cambridge, Mass.: MIT Press, 1991.

Cadena, Marisol de la. *Earth Beings: Ecologies of Practice Across Andean Worlds*. Durham, N.C.: Duke University Press, 2015.

Caro, Antonio. *Minería*. 2012. Artwork.

Carpentier, Alejo. *The Kingdom of This World*. New York: Noonday, 1989.

Carr, Nicholas. *The Shallows: What the Internet Is Doing to Our Brains*. New York: Norton, 2011.

Carroll, Lewis. *Alice's Adventures in Wonderland and Through the Looking-Glass and What Alice Found There*. Ed. Roger Lancelyn Green. Oxford: Oxford University Press, 1998.

Casamayor-Cisneros, Odette. *Utopía, distopía e ingravidez: Reconfiguraciones cosmológicas en la narrativa postsoviética cubana*. Madrid: Iberoamericana Vervuert, 2013.

Castellanos, Rosario. *Oficio de tinieblas*. Mexico City: Mortiz, 1966. Trans. Esther Allen as *The Book of Lamentations* (New York: Penguin, 1998).

Castro Ruz, Fidel. "Discurso pronunciado por Fidel Castro Ruz, Presidente de la República de Cuba, en la clausura del XVI Congreso de la CTC, celebrado en el teatro 'Carlos Marx', el 28 de enero de 1990, Año 32 de la Revolución." Accessed May 16, 2018. http://www.cuba.cu/gobierno/discursos/1990/esp/f280190e.html.

Caycedo, Carolina. *Yuma, or the Land of Friends*. 2014. Digital prints on acrylic glass, satellite images. 580 × 473 cm. Eighth Berlin Biennale for Contemporary Art, Museen Dahlem.

Chamberlain, Gethin. "'They're Killing Us': World's Most Endangered Tribe Cries for Help." *Guardian*, April 22, 2012. https://www.theguardian.com/world/2012/apr/22/brazil-rainforest-awa-endangered-tribe.

Cheah, Pheng. *What Is a World? On Postcolonial Literature as World Literature*. Durham, N.C.: Duke University Press, 2016.

Chua, Amy. *World on Fire: How Exporting Free Market Democracy Breeds Ethnic Hatred and Global Instability*. New York: Anchor, 2004.

Coole, Diana H., and Samantha Frost, eds. *New Materialisms: Ontology, Agency, and Politics*. Durham, N.C.: Duke University Press, 2010.

Cooppan, Vilashini. "Codes for World Literature: Network Theory and the Field Imaginary." In *Approaches to World Literature*, ed. Joachim Küpper, 103–19. Berlin: Akademie, 2013.

Cornejo-Polar, Antonio. "Mestizaje e hibridez: los riesgos de las metáforas. Apuntes." *Revista Iberoamericana* 63, no. 180 (1997): 341–44.

Coronil, Fernando. Introduction to *Cuban Counterpoint: Tobacco and Sugar*, by Fernando Ortiz, ix–lvi. Trans. Harriet de Onís. Durham, N.C.: Duke University Press, 1995.

Cortázar, Julio. *Rayuela*. Madrid: Catedra, 1963. Trans. Gregory Rabassa as *Hopscotch* (New York: Penguin, 1966).
Council of Supply Chain Management Professionals. *SCM Definitions and Glossary of Terms*. Accessed July 1, 2017. http://cscmp.org/CSCMP/Educate/SCM_Definitions_and_Glossary_of_Terms/CSCMP/Educate/SCM_Definitions_and_Glossary_of_Terms.aspx?hkey=60879588-f65f-4ab5-8c4b-6878815ef921.
Coutinho, Eduardo, dir. *Boca do lixo*. 1993; Rio de Janeiro: VideoFilmes, 2004. DVD.
Crary, Jonathan. *24/7: Late Capitalism and the Ends of Sleep*. New York: Verso, 2013.
Curry-Machado, Jonathan, ed. *Global Histories, Imperial Commodities, Local Interactions*. New York: Palgrave Macmillan, 2013.
da Cunha, Euclides. *The Amazon: Land without History*. Oxford: Oxford University Press, 2006.
———. *Antologia euclidiana*. São Paulo: Editôra Pioneira, 1967.
———. *Trabalhos esparsos*. Rio de Janeiro: Academia Brasileira de Letras, 2009.
Damrosch, David. *Teaching World Literature*. New York: Modern Language Association, 2009.
———. "Toward a History of World Literature." *New Literary History* 39 (2008): 481–95.
———. *What Is World Literature?* Princeton, N.J.: Princeton University Press, 2003.
———. "World Literature in Theory and Practice." In *World Literature in Theory*, ed. David Damrosch. London: Wiley, 2014.
Darío, Rubén. "Filosofía." In *Obras completas*, ed. Julio Ortega, 285. Barcelona: Galaxia Gutenberg, 2007.
———. "El rey burgués." In *Obras completas*, ed. Julio Ortega, vol. 1, 63–67. Barcelona: galaxia Gutenberg, 2007.
David, Jérôme. "The Four Genealogies of 'World Literature.'" In *Approaches to World Literature*, ed. Joachim Küpper, 13–26. Berlin: Akademie, 2013.
Debord, Guy, and Wolman, Gil J. "Mode d'emploi du détournement." *Les lèvres nues* 8 (1956): 2–9.
DeLanda, Manuel. *A New Philosophy of Society: Assemblage Theory and Social Complexity*. London, New York: Continuum, 2006.
———. *A Thousand Years of Nonlinear History*. New York: Zone, 1997.
DeLanda, Manuel, and Graham Harman. *The Rise of Realism*. Cambridge: Polity, 2017.
De los Ríos, Valeria. "Mapa cognitivo, memoria (im)política y medialidad: Contemporaneidad en Alejandro Zambra y Pola Oloixarac." In "Theories of the Contemporary in South America," ed. Héctor Hoyos and Marília Librandi-Rocha. Special dossier, *Revista de Estudios Hispánicos* 48, no. 1 (2014): 145–60.
Dënver. "Los adolescentes." *Música, gramática, gimnasia*. Cazador Records, 2010. CD.
Depraz, Natalie. "Leib/Körper/Fleisch." In *The Dictionary of Untranslatables*, ed. Barbara Cassin, trans. Emily Apter, Jacques Lezra, and Michael Wood, 561–64. Princeton, N.J: Princeton University Press, 2014.
Derrida, Jacques. *Limited Inc*. Trans. Jeffrey Mehlman and Samuel Weber. Evanston, Ill.: Northwestern University Press, 1988.
———. *Margins of Philosophy*. Trans. Alan Bass. Chicago: University of Chicago Press, 1982.

———. *Of Hospitality: Anne Dufourmantelle Invites Jacques Derrida to Respond*. Trans. Rachel Bowlby. Stanford: Stanford University Press, 2000.

———. *Parages*. Trans. Tom Conley. Stanford, Calif: Stanford University Press, 2010.

DeVries, Scott. "Swallowed: Political Ecology and Environmentalism in the Spanish American *novela de la selva*." *Hispania: A Journal Devoted to the Teaching of Spanish and Portuguese* 93, no. 4 (2010): 535–46.

D'haen, Theo. *The Routledge Concise History of World Literature*. London: Routledge, 2011.

Doran, Robert. "Choosing the Past: Hayden White and the Philosophy of History." In *Philosophy of History After Hayden White*, ed. Robert Doran, 1–33. London: Bloomsbury, 2013.

Duttlinger, Carolin. "Imaginary Encounters: Walter Benjamin and the Aura of Photography." *Poetics Today* 29, no. 1 (2008): 79–101.

Eagleton, Terry. *Materialism*. New Haven, Conn.: Yale University Press, 2016.

Eco, Umberto. *The Infinity of Lists: An Illustrated Essay*. Trans. Alastair McEwen. New York: Rizzoli, 2009.

———. "We Like Lists Because We Don't Want to Die." Interview by Susanne Beyer and Lothar Gorris. *Spiegel Online*, November 11, 2009. http://www.spiegel.de/international/zeitgeist/spiegel-interview-with-umberto-eco-we-like-lists-because-we-don-t-want-to-die-a-659577.html.

Eckermann, Johann Peter. *Gespräche mit Goethe in den letzten Jahren seines Lebens*. Frankfurt: Insel, 1981.

Eltit, Diamela. *Impuesto a la carne*. Santiago: Planeta, 2010.

Engels, Friedrich, and Karl Marx. *The Communist Manifesto*. New Haven, Conn.: Yale University Press, 2012.

———. *Manifest der Kommunistischen Partei*. In *Werke*, vol. 4, 459–574. Berlin: Dietz, 1959.

Eshel, Amir. *Futurity: Contemporary Literature and the Quest for the Past*. Chicago: University of Chicago Press, 2013.

Espinosa, Patricia, ed. *Territorios en fuga: Estudios críticos sobre la obra de Roberto Bolaño*. Santiago: Frasis, 2003.

Ette, Ottmar. *TransArea: Eine Literarische Globalisierungsgeschichte*. Berlin: De Gruyter, 2012.

Ette, Ottmar, and Gesine Müller, eds. *Worldwide: Archipels de la mondialisation, archipiélagos de la globalización*. Madrid: Iberoamericana, 2012.

Feinmann, José Pablo. "Dieguito." In *Cuentos de fútbol Argentino*, ed. Roberto Fontanarrosa, 47–50. Buenos Aires: Alfaguara, 1997.

Felski, Rita. "Latour and Literary Studies." *PMLA* 130, no. 3 (2015): 737–42.

———. *The Limits of Critique*. Chicago: University of Chicago Press, 2015.

Fernández, Patricio. "La gran novela leve." *El País*, August 10, 2013. https://elpais.com/cultura/2013/08/07/actualidad/1375896436_498243.html.

Finchelstein, Federico. "Fascism, History and Evil in Roberto Bolaño." In *Roberto Bolaño as World Literature*, ed. Nicholas Birns and Juan De Castro, 23–40. New York: Bloomsbury, 2017.

Fisk, Gloria. "'Against World Literature': The Debate in Retrospect." *American Reader*, April 9, 2014. http://theamericanreader.com/against-world-literature-the-debate-in-retrospect/.

Font, Mauricio Augusto, and Alfonso W. Quiroz, eds. *Cuban Counterpoints: The Legacy of Fernando Ortiz*. Lanham, Md.: Lexington, 2005.
Foucault, Michel. *Naissance de la biopolitique: Cours au Collège de France (1978–1979)*. Paris: Gallimard, 2004.
——. *The Order of Things: An Archaeology of the Human Sciences*. New York: Vintage, 1994.
French, Jennifer L. *Nature, Neo-Colonialism, and the Spanish American Regional Writers*. Hanover, N.H: Dartmouth College Press, 2005.
Friedländer, Saul. *The Years of Extermination: Nazi Germany and the Jews, 1939–1945*. New York: Harper Collins, 2007.
Fuguet, Alberto, and Sergio Gómez, eds. *McOndo*. Barcelona: Mondadori, 1996.
Fukuyama, Francis. "The End of History?" *National Interest* 16 (1989): 3–18.
Funari, Vicky, and Sergio de la Torre. *Maquilapolis*. California Newsreel, 2006. Film.
Furtado, Jorge. *Ilha das Flores*. Casa de Cinema de Porto Alegre, 1989. Film.
Gallo, Rubén. *New Tendencies in Mexican Art: The 1990s*. New York: Palgrave MacMillan, 2004.
Garcia, Tristan, Mark Allan Ohm, and Jon Cogburn. *Form and Object: A Treatise on Things*. Edinburgh: Edinburgh University Press, 2014.
García Márquez, Gabriel. *Doce cuentos peregrinos*. Bogotá: Oveja Negra, 1994.
——. *Cien años de soledad*. Buenos Aires: Sudamericana, 1967.
Gerrard, John. *Farm (Pryor Creek, Oklahoma)*. Thomas Dane Gallery, 2015.
——. *Solar Reserve (Tonopah, Nevada)*. Lincoln Center, New York, 2014.
Glantz, Margo. *Las Genealogías*. Mexico City: Casillas, 1981. Trans. Susan Bassnett as *The Family Tree: An Illustrated Novel* (London: Serpent's Tail, 1991).
——. *Historia de una mujer que caminó por la vida con zapatos de diseñador*. Barcelona: Anagrama, 2005.
——. "Palabras para una fábula." *Debate feminista* 13, no. 26 (2002): 144–64.
——. *Zona de derrumbe*. Rosario, Argentina: Viterbo, 2001.
Glendinning, Chellis. "Notes Toward a Neo-Luddite Manifesto." *Utne Reader* 38 (1990): 50–53.
González Ramírez, Sergio. *Huesos en el desierto*. Barcelona: Anagrama, 2002.
Gootenberg, Paul. *Andean Cocaine: The Making of a Global Drug*. Chapel Hill: University of North Carolina Press, 2008.
Gordy, Katherine. "Dollarization, Consumer Capitalism and Popular Response." In *Cuba Today: Continuity and Change since the 'Período Especial'*, ed. Mauricio A. Font, Scott Larsen, and Danielle Xuereb, 13–30. New York: Bildner Center for Western Hemisphere Studies, 2004.
——. "'Sales + Economy + Efficiency = Revolution'? Dollarization, Consumer Capitalism, and Popular Responses in Special Period Cuba." *Public Culture* 18, no. 2 (2006): 383–412.
Graeber, David. *Debt: The First 5000 Years*. New York: Melville, 2011.
Graff, Erin. *The Wandering Signifier: Rhetoric of Jewishness in the Latin American Imaginary*. Durham, N.C.: Duke University Press, 2008.
Graff, Gerald. "Taking Cover in Coverage." *Profession* 86 (1986): 41–45.
Gutiérrez, Pedro Juan. *Tropical Animal*. Trans. Peter Lownds. London: Faber, 2003. Originally published as *Animal tropical* (Barcelona: Anagrama, 2000).

Halfon, Eduardo. "Han vuelto las aves." In *Signor Hoffman*, 11–37. Barcelona: Libros del Asteroide, 2015.

Halperín Donghi, Tulio. *The Contemporary History of Latin America*. Ed. and trans. John Charles Chasteen. Durham, N.C.: Duke University Press, 1993.

Hansen, Miriam Bratu. "Benjamin's Aura." *Critical Inquiry* 34 (2008): 336–75.

Haraway, Donna Jeanne. "Anthropocene, Capitalocene, Plantationocene, Chthulucene: Making Kin." *Environmental Humanities* 6, no. 1 (2015): 159–65.

———. *The Haraway Reader*. New York: Routledge, 2004.

———. *Primate Visions: Gender, Race, and Nature in the World of Modern Science*. New York: Routledge, 2013.

Hardenburg, Walter E. *The Putumayo, The Devil's Paradise; Travels in the Peruvian Amazon Region and an Account of the Atrocities Committed upon the Indians therein*. Ed. C. Reginald Enock. London: Fisher Unwin, 1912.

Hardt, Michael, and Antonio Negri. *Multitude: War and Democracy in the Age of Empire*. New York: Penguin, 2004.

Harman, Graham. *The Quadruple Object*. Winchester: Zero, 2011.

Harrison, Robert P. *Gardens: An Essay on the Human Condition*. Chicago: University of Chicago Press, 2008.

Hayot, Eric. "The Humanities as We Know Them Are Doomed. Now What?" *Chronicle of Higher Education*, July 1, 2018. https://www.chronicle.com/article/The-Humanities-as-We-Know-Them/243769.

Hecht, Susanna B. *The Scramble for the Amazon and the "Lost Paradise" of Euclides Da Cunha*. University of Chicago Press, 2013.

Heidegger, Martin. *The Question Concerning Technology, and Other Essays*. Trans. William Lovitt, New York: Harper, 1977.

———. *What Is a Thing?* Trans. W. B. Barton, Jr., and Vera Deutsch. Chicago: Regnery, 1968.

Heise, Ursula K. "Ecocriticism and the Transnational Turn in American Studies," *American Literary History* 20, no. 1–2 (March 1, 2008): 381–404.

Herhuth, Eric. "Life, Love, and Programming: The Culture and Politics of *WALL-E* and Pixar Computer Animation." *Cinema Journal* 53, no. 4 (2014): 53–75.

Herrera Molina, S.J., Luis Carlos. Introduction to *La Vorágine*. In *José Eustasio Rivera: Obra literaria*, ed. Luis Carlos Herrera Molina, S.J. Bogotá: Pontificia Universidad Javeriana, 2009.

Hohendahl, Peter Uwe. *Prismatic Thought: Theodor W. Adorno*. Lincoln: University of Nebraska Press, 1995.

Holt, Douglas. How Brands Become Icons: The Principles of Cultural Branding. Boston, Mass.: Harvard Business School Press, 2004.

Horkheimer, Max, and Theodor W. Adorno. *Dialectic of Enlightenment: Philosophical Fragments*. Trans. Edmund Jephcott. Stanford, Calif.: Stanford University Press, 2002.

Hoyos, Héctor. "Aftershock: Naomi Klein and the Southern Cone." *Third Text* 26, no. 2 (2012): 217–28.

———. *Beyond Bolaño: The Global Latin American Novel*. New York: Columbia University Press, 2015.

———. "La poesía de los objetos y la trayectoria: una lectura comparada y política de *Doce cuentos peregrinos*." In *Ensayos críticos sobre cuento colombiano, siglo XX*, ed. María Luisa Ortega, María Betty Osorio, and Adolfo Caicedo, 231–48. Bogotá: Uniandes, 2011.
———. "La racionalidad herética de Fernando Vallejo y el derecho a la felicidad." *Revista de Estudios Sociales* 35 (2010): 113–22.
———."Re-discovering Ice: García Márquez, Aira, and Vallejo on Chilling Memories." In *Gabriel García Márquez in Retrospect*, ed. Gene H. Bell-Villada, 103–14. Lanham, Md.: Lexington, 2016.
———. "The Tell-Tale Computer: Obsolescence and Nostalgia in Chile after Alejandro Zambra." In *Technology, Literature, and Digital Culture in Latin America: Mediatized Sensibilities in a Globalized Era*, ed. Matthew Bush and Tania Gentic, 109–24. New York: Routledge, 2015.
———. "El último gramático: Ensayos críticos sobre Fernando Vallejo." In "El malditismo de Fernando Vallejo como espectáculo melodramático," ed. Juanita Aristizábal and Brantley Nichols. Special issue, *Cuadernos de Literatura* 19, no. 37 (2015): 169–76.
Iglesias, Iván. "Ecocriticism, Determinism and Imperialism in the Wilderness of Heart of Darkness and La Vorágine." *Céfiro* 11, no. 1–2 (2011): 72–83.
Jameson, Fredric. *The Political Unconscious: Narrative as a Socially Symbolic Act*. Ithaca, N.Y.: Cornell University Press, 1981.
Jasanoff, Sheila, and Sang-Hyun Kim, eds., *Dreamscape of Modernity: Sociotechnical Imaginaries and the Fabrication of Power*. Chicago: University of Chicago Press, 2015.
Jay, Martin. "Liquidity Crisis: Zygmunt Bauman and the Incredible Lightness of Modernity." *Theory, Culture, and Society* 27, no. 6 (2010): 95–106.
Kafka, Franz. *The Metamorphosis and Other Stories*. Trans. Donna Freed. New York: Barnes & Noble, 1996.
Kane, Adrian Taylor, ed. *The Natural World in Latin American Literatures: Ecocritical Essays on Twentieth Century Writings*. Jefferson, N.C.: McFarland, 2010.
Kant, Immanuel. *Critique of Judgement*. Trans. J. H. Bernard. New York: Hafner, 1951.
Kim, Hyesoon. "ALL THE GARBAGE OF THE WORLD, UNITE!" Trans. Don Mee Choi, 2010. Presented at the *Poetry International Foundation, Rotterdam*, 2017. Accessed July 24, 2018. http://www.poetryinternationalweb.net/pi/site/poem/item/17521/poem_org_video_left/poem_english/0.
———. *All the Garbage of the World, Unite!* = *Chŏn Segye Ŭi Ssŭregi Yŏ Tan'gyŏl Hara*. Notre Dame, Ind.: Action, 2011.
Knausgård, Karl Ove. *Autumn*. Vol. 1. New York: Penguin Random House, 2017.
Kristeva, Julia. *The Powers of Horror: An Essay on Abjection*. Trans. Leon S. Rouidez. New York: Columbia University Press, 1982.
LaCapra, Dominick. *Writing History, Writing Trauma*. Baltimore: Johns Hopkins University Press, 2001.
Lanier, Jaron. *You Are Not a Gadget: A Manifesto*. New York: Vintage, 2011.
Lanzmann, Claude. *Shoah*. Hollywood, Calif.: New Yorker Video, 2003. DVD.
Larsen, Neil. "Literature, Immanent Critique, and the Problem of Standpoint." In *Literary Materialisms*, ed. Mathias Nilges and Emilio Sauri, 63–77. New York: Palgrave Macmillan, 2013.

Latour, Bruno. "From Realpolitik to Dingpolitik—or How to Make Things Public." In *Making Things Public: Atmospheres of Democracy*, ed. Bruno Latour and Peter Weibel. Cambridge, Mass.: MIT Press, 2005.

———. *Politics of Nature: How to Bring the Sciences into Democracy*. Trans. Catherine Porter. Cambridge, Mass.: Harvard University Press, 2004.

———. "The Powers of the Facsimile: A Turing Test on Science and Literature." In *Intersections: Essays on Richard Powers* (1st ed.), ed. Stephen Burn and Peter Dempsey, 263–92. Champaign, Ill.: Dalkey Archive, 2008.

———. *We Have Never Been Modern*. Trans. Catherine Porter. Cambridge, Mass: Harvard University Press, 1993.

———. "When Things Strike Back—a Possible Contribution of Science Studies." *British Journal of Sociology* 51, no 1 (2000): 107–23.

———. "Why Has Critique Run Out of Steam? From Matters of Fact to Matters of Concern." *Critical Inquiry* 30, no. 2 (2004): 225–48.

Lenin, Vladimir Ilich. *Collected Works*. Vol. 32. Moscow: Progress, 1973.

Leonard, Annie, Jonah Sachs, and Louis Fox. "The Story of Electronics." *The Story of Stuff Project*. Accessed July 21, 2017. http://storyofstuff.org/movies/story-of-electronics/.

Lezama Lima, José. "Corona de las frutas." *Lunes de Revolución* 40 (1959): 22–23.

———. *Imagen y posibilidad*. Havana: Letras Cubanas, 1981.

Livon-Grosman, Ernesto. "Thinking on Film and Trash: A Few Notes." *ReVista: Harvard Review of Latin America* 14, no. 2 (2015): 53–55.

Loss, Jacqueline, and José Manuel Prieto González, eds. *Caviar with Rum: Cuba-USSR and the Post-Soviet Experience*. New York: Palgrave Macmillan, 2012.

Luis, William. "Exhuming *Lunes de Revolución*." *CR: The New Centennial Review* 2, no. 2 (2002): 253–83.

Luiselli, Valeria. *The Story of My Teeth*. Trans. Christina McSweeney. London: Granta, 2015. Originally published as *La historia de mis dientes* (Madrid: Sexto Piso, 2014).

Maass, Peter. "What Happened at the Macondo Well?" *New York Review of Books*, September 29, 2011. http://www.nybooks.com/articles/2011/09/29/what-happened-macondo-well/.

Maeseneer, Rita de. *Devorando a lo cubano: Una aproximación gastrocrítica a textos relacionados con el siglo XIX y el Período Especial*. Madrid: Iberoamericana, 2012.

Magnus, Ariel. *Un chino en bicicleta*. Buenos Aires: Interzona, 2007.

———. *Muñecas*. Buenos Aires: Emecé, 2008.

Malinowski, Bronislaw. Introduction to *Contrapunteo cubano del tabaco y azúcar: Advertencia de sus contrastes agrarios, económicos, históricos y sociales, su etnografía y su transculturación*, by Fernando Ortiz, xi–xix. Havana: Universidad Central de las Villas, 1963.

Marré, Luis. *Habaneras y otras letras*. Havana: Unión de Escritores y Artistas, 1970.

Marx, Karl. *Capital: A Critique of Political Economy*. Trans. Ben Fowkes. New York: Penguin, 1990.

———. *Selected Writings*. 2nd ed. Oxford: Oxford University Press, 2000.

———. "Theses on Feuerbach." In *Marx-Engels Selected Works*, vol. 1, 13–15. Moscow: Progress, 1969.

Medero, Victor, Magaly Garcia, Nerelys Hernández, Jorge Garcia, Luis Ruiz Martínez, Rubén Cuervo, Martín Viera et al. *Con nuestros propios esfuerzos: Algunas experiencias para enfrentar el período especial en tiempo de paz.* Havana: Verde Olivo, 1992.

Mezey, Kalman, César Uribe Piedrahita, J. Pataki, and J. Huertas-Lozano. "Niaara; A Digitalis-Like Colombian Arrow Poison." *Journal of Pharmacology and Experiential Therapeutics* 93, no. 2 (June 1948): 223–29.

Mintz, Sidney Wilfred. *Sweetness and Power: The Place of Sugar in Modern History.* New York: Penguin, 1986.

Molina, Mary Carmen E. " 'Aquí, digo, y doy un salto': Hueco y lenguaje en la obra de Blanca Wiethüchter." In *La crítica y el poeta: Blanca Wiethüchter*, 41–78. La Paz: Plural, 2011.

Monasterios, Elizabeth. "Rethinking Transculturation and Hibridity: An Andean Perspective." *Latin American Narratives and Cultural Identity* 7 (2004): 94–110.

Montoya Juárez, Jesús. *Narrativas del simulacro: Videocultura, tecnología y literatura en Argentina y Uruguay.* Murcia, Spain: Universidad de Murcia, 2013.

Moore, Jason W. *Capitalism in the Web of Life: Ecology and the Accumulation of Capital.* New York: Verso, 2015.

Moreiras, Alberto. *The Exhaustion of Difference: The Politics of Latin American Cultural Studies.* Durham, N.C.: Duke University Press, 2001.

——. "Hybridity and Double Consciousness." *Cultural Studies* 13, no. 3 (1999): 373–407.

Moreno Fraginals, Manuel. *The Sugarmill: The Socioeconomic Complex of Sugar in Cuba, 1760–1860.* New York: Monthly Review Press, 1976.

Moretti, Franco. *Signs Taken for Wonders: On the Sociology of Literary Forms.* London: Verso Books, 1983.

Morton, Timothy. *Hyperobjects: Philosophy and Ecology after the End of the World.* Minneapolis: University of Minnesota Press, 2013.

Muniz, Vik. *Vik Muniz: Obra Completa, 1987–2009: Catálogo Raisonné.* Rio de Janeiro: Capivara, 2009.

Neruda, Pablo. *Canto general.* México: Océano, 1950.

Nest, Michael. *Coltan.* Cambridge: Polity, 2011.

Nettel, Guadalupe. *El cuerpo en que nací.* Barcelona: Anagrama, 2011.

Nielson, Rex. "Amazonian El Dorados and the Nation: Euclides da Cunha's *À Margem da História* and José Eustasio Rivera's *La Vorágine*." *Ometeca* 16 (2011): 16–31.

Nietzsche, Friedrich. *Thus Spoke Zarathustra: A Book for Everyone and No One.* Trans. R. J. Hollingdale. Harmondsworth, UK: Penguin, 1969.

Nilges, Mathias, and Emilio Sauri, eds. *Literary Materialisms.* New York: Palgrave Macmillan, 2013.

Nixon, Rob. *Slow Violence and the Environmentalism of the Poor.* Cambridge, Mass: Harvard University Press, 2011.

Noys, Benjamin. *George Bataille: A Critical Introduction.* London: Pluto, 2000.

NPR Staff. "After Dump, What Happens to Electronic Waste?" *NPR.org*, December 21, 2010. http://www.npr.org/2010/12/21/132204954/after-dump-what-happens-to-electronic-waste.

Ortiz, Carlos Daniel. "La idealización del amor y la mujer en *La Vorágine*." *Folios* 10, no. 28 (2008): 3–12.

Ortiz, Fernando. *Contrapunteo cubano del tabaco y el azúcar*. Madrid: Cátedra, 2002.

———. *Contrapunteo cubano del tabaco y el azúcar: Advertencia de sus contrastes agrarios, económicos, históricos y sociales, su etnografía y su transculturación*. Havana: Montero, 1940.

———. *Cuban Counterpoint: Tobacco and Sugar*. Trans. Harriet de Onis. Durham, N.C.: Duke University Press, 1995.

———. "Los factores humanos de la cubanidad." In *Fernando Ortiz*, ed. Julio Le Riverend, 149–57. Havana: Unión de Escritores y Artistas, 1973.

Pacheco, Felix. *Dous egressos da farda, o sr. Euclydes da Cunha e o sr. Alberto Rangel: A proposito do* Inferno verde. Florianópolis, Brazil: Insular, 2002.

Padilla, Heberto. "La poesía en su lugar." *Lunes de Revolución* 38 (1959): 5–6.

Parkinson Zamora, Lois. "Swords and Silver Rings: Magical Objects in the Work of Jorge Luis Borges and Gabriel García Márquez." In *A Companion to Magical Realism*, ed. Stephen Hart and Wen-chin Ouyang, 28–45. Rochester, N.Y.: Tamesis, 2005.

Parkinson Zamora, Lois, and Wendy B. Faris, eds. *Magical Realism: Theory, History, Community*. Durham, N.C.: Duke University Press, 1995.

Parsons, William B. *The Enigma of the Oceanic Feeling: Revisioning the Psychoanalytic Theory of Mysticism*. Oxford: Oxford University Press, 1999.

Paz, Octavio. *Pequeña crónica de grandes días*. México: Fondo de Cultura Económica, 1990.

Pérez Firmat, Gustavo. *The Cuban Condition: Translation and Identity in Modern Cuban Literature*. Cambridge: Cambridge University Press, 1989.

Petroski, Henry. *The Pencil: A History of Design and Circumstance*. New York: Knopf, 1992.

Pierre, Nora. *Les lieux de mémoire*. Paris: Gallimard 3, 1984.

Pineda Camacho, Roberto. *Holocausto en el amazonas: Una historia social de la Casa Arana*. 1st ed. Bogotá: Planeta Colombiana, 2000.

Piñera, Virgilio. "La carne." In *Cuentos completos*. Madrid: Alfaguara, 1999.

Polit Dueñas, Gabriela. *Narrating Narcos: Stories from Culiacan and Medellin*. Pittsburgh, Pa.: University of Pittsburgh Press, 2013.

Pollack, Sarah. "Latin America Translated (Again): Roberto Bolaño's 'The Savage Detectives' in the United States." *Comparative Literature* 61, no. 3 (2009): 346–65.

Pollan, Michael. *The Botany of Desire: A Plant's-Eye View of the World*. New York: Random House, 2001.

Ponte, Antonio José. *Las comidas profundas*. Rosario, Argentina: Viterbo, 2010.

———. "Meaning to Eat." Trans. Mark Schafer. *BOMB Magazine* 78 (January 1, 2002). https://bombmagazine.org/articles/meaning-to-eat.

Povinelli, Elizabeth. *Geontopower: A Requiem to Late Liberalism*. Durham, N.C.: Duke University Press, 2016.

Pratt, Mary Louise. *Imperial Eyes: Travel Writing and Transculturation*. New York: Routledge, 1992.

Quercia, Boris, dir. *Los 80, más que una moda*. Santiago de Chile: Cine Color Films, 2008. DVD.

Quevedo, Francisco de. *Gracias y desgracias del ojo del culo, dirigidas a Doña Juana Mucha, Montón de Carne, Mujer gorda por arrobas / escribiolos Juan Lamas, el del camisón cagado*. Alicante: Biblioteca Virtual Miguel de Cervantes, 2003.
Rama, Ángel. *Transculturación narrativa en América Latina*. Buenos Aires: Andariego, 1984.
Rangel, Alberto. *Inferno verde: Scenas e scenarios do Amazonas*. Tours, France: Typographia Arrault, 1927.
Revueltas, José. *Dialéctica de la conciencia*. Mexico City: Era, 1982.
Rey Rosa, Rodrigo. *El material humano*. Barcelona: Anagrama, 2009.
Richard, Nelly. *The Insubordination of Signs: Political Change, Cultural Transformation, and Poetics of the Crisis*. Trans. Alice A. Nelson and Silvia Tandeciarz. Durham, N.C., Duke University Press: 2004.
Rivera, Diego, and Instituto Nacional de Bellas Artes (Mexico). *Diego Rivera: Catálogo general de obra mural y fotografía personal*. 1st ed. Mexico City: Consejo Nacional para la Cultura y las Artes and Instituto Nacional de Bellas Artes, 1988.
Rivera, José Eustasio. *La vorágine*. Madrid: Cátedra, 1990.
——. *The Vortex*. Trans. Earle K. James. New York: Putnam, 1935.
Roca, Juan Manuel. *Cartógrafa memoria: Ensayos en torno a la poesía*. Medellín: EAFIT, 2003.
Rosendahl Thomsen, Mads. *Mapping World Literature: International Canonization and Transnational Literatures*. New York: Continuum, 2008.
——. *The New Human in Literature: Posthuman Visions of Changes in Body, Mind and Society after 1900*. London: Bloomsbury, 2014.
Rosero, Evelio. *The Armies*. Trans. Anne McLean. New York: New Directions, 2009.
Ruiz, Juan. *Libro de buen amor*. Ed. Raymond Willis. Princeton, N.J.: Princeton University Press, 1972.
Santí, Enrico Mario. "Towards a Reading of Fernando Ortiz's *Cuban Counterpoint*." *Review: Literature and Arts of the Americas* 37, no. 1 (2004): 6–18.
Sassen, Brigitte. "Heidegger on van Gogh's Old Shoes: The Use/Abuse of a Painting." *Journal of the British Society for Phenomenology* 32, no. 3 (2001): 160–73.
Saussy, Haun, ed. *Comparative Literature in an Age of Globalization*. Baltimore: Johns Hopkins University Press, 2006.
Schmitt, Carl. *Roman Catholicism and Political Form*. Trans. G. L. Ulmen. Westport, Conn.: Greenwood, 1996.
Shaw, Donald L. "When Was Modernism in Spanish-American Fiction?" *Bulletin of Spanish Studies* 79, no. 2–3 (2002): 395–409.
Shklovsky, Victor. "From 'Art as Technique' 1917." In *Modernism: An Anthology of Sources and Documents*, ed. Vassiliki Kolocotroni, Jane Goldman, and Olga Taxidou, 217–21. Chicago: University of Chicago Press, 1998.
Sierra, Gina Paola. "La fiebre del caucho en Colombia." *Banrepcultural*. Accessed May 1, 2018. http://www. banrepcultural. org/blaavirtual/revistas/credencial/octubre2011/la-fiebre-del-caucho-en-colombia.
Silva, José A. *After-Dinner Conversation: The Diary of a Decadent*. Trans. Kelly Washbourne. Austin: University of Texas Press, 2010.

Silva, José A., Guizado E. Camacho, and Gustavo Mejía. *Obra Completa*. Caracas: Biblioteca Ayacucho, 1977.
Silva García, Santiago F., Reynaldo Pérez Jiménez, Orlando Álvarez de la Paz, and Leonardo Rojas Pérez. "Algunas consideraciones sobre la dieta . . . (Tercera Parte)." *Arqueología Centrosur de Cuba*, September 1, 2007. http://cuba-arqueologia-centrosur.blogspot.com/2007_09_01_archive.html.
Siskind, Mariano. *Cosmopolitan Desires: Global Modernity and World Literature in Latin America*. Evanston, Ill.: Northwestern University Press, 2014.
Sloterdijk, Peter. *Spheres*. Trans. Wieland Hoband. 3 Vols. Los Angeles: Semiotext(e), 2011–16.
Smith, Patti. *Hecatomb: A Poem*. Illustrated by José Antonio Suárez Londoño. Medellín: SML, 2013.
Spitta, Silvia. *Misplaced Objects: Migrating Collections and Recollections in Europe and the Americas*. Austin: University of Texas Press, 2009.
Stanton, Andrew, dir. *WALL-E*. Los Angeles: Walt Disney Pictures, Pixar Animations, 2008. Film.
Steele, Kim. *Facebook's Server Farm*. Prineville, Ore., 2013.
Stein, Susan Isabel. "La Vorágine: The Symbolics of Masculine Logic and the Open Vortex(t)." *Bulletin of Hispanic Studies* 72, no. 2 (1995): 195–211.
Stubbs, Jean. "Tobacco in the *Contrapunteo*: Ortiz and the Havana Cigar." In *Cuban Counterpoints: The Legacy of Fernando Ortiz*, ed. Mauricio A. Font and Alfonso W. Quiroz, 105–23. Lanham, Md.: Lexington, 2005.
Taussig, Michael T. *My Cocaine Museum*. Chicago: University of Chicago Press, 2004.
Thayer, Willy. "El Golpe como consumación de la vanguardia." In *El fragmento repetido: Escritos en estado de excepción*, 15–46. Santiago: Metales Pesados, 2006.
Thomson, Norman. *El libro rojo del Putumayo: Precedido de una introducción sobre el verdadero escándalo de las atrocidades del Putumayo*. Bogotá: Planeta, 1995.
Tigres del Norte, Los. "El celular." https://www.letras.com/los-tigres-del-norte/1735690/.
Tully, John. *The Devil's Milk: A Social History of Rubber*. New York: Monthly Review Press, 2011.
Turkle, Sherry. "The Things that Matter." In *Evocative Objects: Things We Think With*, ed. Sherry Turkle, 3–10. Cambridge, Mass.: MIT Press, 2014.
——. "What Makes an Object Evocative?" In *Evocative Objects: Things We Think With*, ed. Sherry Turkle, 307–26. Cambridge, Mass.: MIT Press, 2014.
Ulmer, Gregory L. "The Puncept in Grammatology." In *On Puns: The Foundation of Letters*, ed. Jonathan Culler, 164–90. Oxford: Blackwell, 1988.
Unruh, Vicky. "Arturo Cova y *La vorágine*: La crisis de un escritor." *Revista de Estudios Hispánicos* 21, no. 1 (1987): 49–60.
Uribe Piedrahita, César. *Toá: Narraciones de caucherías*. Buenos Aires, México: Espasa-Calpe, 1942.
Uslar Pietri, Arturo, *Nuevo mundo, mundo nuevo*. Caracas: Biblioteca Ayacucho, 1998.
Vallejo, Fernando. *Almas en pena, chapolas negras*. Bogotá: Santillana, 1995.
——. *Casablanca la bella*. Madrid: Alfaguara, 2013.
——. *La Virgen de los sicarios*. Bogotá: Santillana, 1994.
Vargas Llosa, Mario. *El sueño del celta*. 2nd ed. Madrid: Alfaguara, 2010.

Varichon, Anne. *Être caoutchouc*. Paris: Seuil, 2006.
Vásquez-Figueroa, Alberto. *Coltán*. Barcelona: Ediciones B, 2008.
Veblen, Thorstein. *The Theory of the Leisure Class: An Economic Study of Institutions*. New York: Macmillan, 1899.
Vecchio, Diego. "Procedimientos y máquinas célibes: Roussel, Duchamp, Aira." In *César Aira, une revolution*, ed. Michel Lafon, Cristina Breuil, and Margarita Remón-Raillard, 95–105. Grenoble, France: Université Stendhal-Grenoble 3, 2005.
Velasco, María Mercedes de. "El mito de la Mapiripana y su valor estructural en *La Vorágine*." *Texto Crítico* 1, no. 1 (1995): 35–56.
Velásquez Guzmán, Mónica. *Múltiples voces en la poesía de Francisco Hernández, Blanca Wiethüchter y Raúl Zurita*. Mexico City: Colegio de México, 2009.
Villena Alvarado, Marcelo. "Requiem para un modelo: Hueco y experiencia en la obra de Blanca Wiethüchter." *América: Cahier du CRICCAL* 34 (2005): 157–66.
Viveiros de Castro, Eduardo. *Cannibal Metaphysics*. Minneapolis: University of Minnesota Press, 2014.
Walker, Lucy, and Karen Harley. *Waste Land*. London: Almega Projects, 2010. 99 min.
Walkowitz, Rebecca L. *Born Translated: The Contemporary Novel in an Age of World Literature*. New York: Columbia University Press, 2015.
Wallerstein, Immanuel. "1968, Revolution in the World-System: Theses and Queries." *Theory and Society* 18, no. 4 (1989): 431–49.
White, Hayden. "Historical Truth, Estrangement, and Disbelief." In *Probing the Ethics of Holocaust Culture*, ed. Claudio Fogu, Wulf Kansteiner, and Todd Presner, 53–71. Cambridge: Harvard University Press, 2016.
——. "The Practical Past," *Storiografia* 15, no. 15 (2011): 9–26.
Wiethüchter, Blanca. *El jardín de Nora*. La Paz: Mujercita Sentada, 1998.
Williams, Gareth. "Sovereignty and Melancholic Paralysis in Roberto Bolaño." *Journal of Latin American Cultural Studies* 18, no. 2–3 (2009): 125–40.
Williams, Raymond L. "An Eco-critical Reading of *One Hundred Years of Solitude*." In *The Cambridge Companion to Gabriel García Márquez*, ed. Philip Swanson, 64–77. Cambridge: Cambridge University Press, 2010.
Wittgenstein, Ludwig. *Tractatus Logico-Philosophicus*. Trans. Charles Kay Ogden. Mineola, N.Y.: Dover, 1999.
"World Lite: What is Global Literature?" *n+1* no. 17 (Fall 2013).
Zambra, Alejandro. *Bonsai*. Trans. Caroline De Robertis. New York: Melville, 2012. Originally published as *Bonsái* (Barcelona: Anagrama, 2006).
——. *Formas de volver a casa*. Barcelona: Anagrama, 2011.
——. "Historia de un computador." *Letras libres* (August 2008): 44–47.
——. *My Documents*. Trans. Megan McDowell. San Francisco: McSweeney's, 2015. Originally published as *Mis documentos* (Barcelona: Anagrama, 2014).
Zavala, Oswaldo. *La modernidad insufrible: Roberto Bolaño en los límites de la literatura latinoamericana contemporánea*. Chapel Hill: University of North Carolina, 2015.
Žižek, Slavoj. *The Indivisible Remainder: An Essay on Schelling and Related Matters*. London: Verso, 1996.
——. *The Sublime Object of Ideology*. London: Verso, 1989.

Index

Page numbers in *italics* indicate figures.

abject, 139; Bolaño and, 119, 121–35, 201; corpses and, 105–6, 111–13, 118, 201; Kristeva on, 111–12, 118; in Latin American literature, post-1989, 135–36
abuela, La (Magnus), 242n28
actants, actors and, 207
Actor-Network-Theory (ANT), 28–29, 201
Actuality of Communism, The (Bosteels), 204
"adolescentes, Los" (song), 266n27
Adorno, Theodor, 110, 127, 227, 259n1; Bolaño compared with, 130–31; on natural history, 221–22
After-Dinner Conversation (De sobremesa) (Silva), 34–35, 145, 155–56
Against World Literature (Apter), 108
Agamben, Giorgio, 185
Aira, César, 50, 52, 102, 137; *God's Tea Party*, 33–34, 68, 88–101, *91*, 250n60, 250n62; *The Musical Brain*, 88; translation of, 88–89, 98, 250n60. *See also God's Tea Party*
ajiaco, 11–12, 24, 80
Albert, Bruce, 71
alga (seaweed), 132
algae, 132–33

Alice's Adventures in Wonderland and Through the Looking-Glass and What Alice Found There (Carroll), 92–93, 96, 250n62
aliñado (Cuban liqueur), 24, 28
Allende, Salvador, 114–15, 171, 195, 197
All the Garbage of the World (Kim), 216–17
Almas en pena, chapolas negras (Vallejo), 35, 145, 156–58, 262n28
Althusser, Louis, 23, 147
Amazon basin. *See* rubber
Amazon EC2 (Amazon Elastic Compute Cloud), 188
amodernity, 27, 29, 36, 65
Amulet (Amuleto) (Bolaño), 118
Andean epistemologies, 81, 248n37
Andrade, María Mercedes, 261n24
Andrews, Chris, 88–91, 97, 135
animism, 102–3, 155, 261n18
ANT. *See* Actor-Network-Theory
Anthropocene, 268n13
anthropocentrism, 4–5, 32, 42, 65
anthropodecentrism, 5, 31, 63, 204, 206, 252n90
anti-Semitism, 130–31

anus: Bolaño and, 117–18, 126–27, 132; corpses and, 118–19; solar, 115–18, 126, 212
apes: in *God's Tea Party*, 88–90, 93, 96–97; Haraway on, 90, 93–94, 96; India and, 93–94. *See also* monkeys
Apollinaire, Guillaume, 23
Appadurai, Arjun, 32
Apple, 178, 180, 189, 210
Apter, Emily, 108
Aquinas, Thomas, 74
archeology, 20–21
Arcimboldo, Giuseppe, 133, *134*
Arendt, Hannah, 55
Aristizábal, Juanita, 160
Armies, The (Los ejércitos) (Rosero), 136
assemblage, 19, 70–71, 207, 224; Bennett on, 22, 179; personal computer in, 179–80; rubber in, 45–46
Aufhebung (sublation), 4, 100
Australia, Indigenous people in, 102
Autumn (Knausgård), 220, 222
Aymara: in *El jardín de Nora*, 71, 73, 76, 78–80, 84–85, 95–96; *kiswaras* and *kantutas* of, 80; *phutunhuicu* and, 84–85

Badiou, Alain, 180, 205
Balboa, Silvestre de, 18
bananas, 60, 226, 228
Banda-Aaku, Ellen, 217
Baradit, Jorge, 35, 190, 195–97
Barbrook, Richard, 172, 197
Bataille, Georges, 115–17, 212
Batista, Fulgencio, 233n17
Baudelaire, Charles, 35, 184
Bauman, Zygmunt, 184–85
Beauty Salon (Bellatin), 136
Beauvoir, Simone de, 221–22
Beckman, Ericka, 47, 156, 240n90
Be Damned (art series), 215
beer, 20
Beer, Stafford, 195–96
bees, 65–66
beets, 12, 234n26
Bellatin, Mario, 136, 262n37
Benjamin, Walter, 6, 110, 135, 147, 173, 185; on archeology, 20; on Baudelaire, 35, 184; memorial to, 271n45; on worker, technology and, 182
Bennett, Jane, 29, 37, 239n83; on assemblage, 22, 179; on nonhuman agency, 28, 35, 271n44; vibrant materialism of, 13, 21
Berardi, Franco (Bifo), 266n34
Bertonio, Ludovico, 85
Beverley, John, 249n53
biopolitics, 210, 216, 218
biopower, 101–2
black flock *(rebaño negro)*, 44
Boca do lixo (film), 217
bodies: anus, 115–19, 126–27, 132, 212; Bataille on, 115–17; Bolaño and, 34, 105, 112–13, 119–33, 137; corpse as limit of, 119–20; corpse as Other of, 139; corpses and, 34, 105–6, 111–13, 118–21, 125–26, 128–32, 136–39, 188, 200–201; in Latin American literature, post-1989, 136–37; *vagina dentata*, 48, 83
Body Where I Was Born, The (Nettel), 136
Bogost, Ian, 100, 252n90
Bolaño, Roberto, 58, 139, 210; abject and, 119, 121–35, 201; *Amulet*, 118; anus and, 117–18, 126–27, 132; bodies and, 34, 105, 112–13, 119–33, 137; *By Night in Chile*, 112–13, 117, 165; corpses and, 105, 112–13, 119–21, 125–26, 128–32; on femicide, 34, 128, 130–32, 135, 137, 211–12; "Labyrinth," 115; "Mauricio 'The Eye' Silva," 115, 117; *Nazi Literature in the Americas*, 54, 113; Nazism and, 54, 113, 130; puns of, 117–18, 120; "The Return," 119–21; *The Savage Detectives*, 114, 117, 121–22, 132, 255n28; solar economy of, 117, 126, 128, 132; *2666*, 34, 115, 117–18, 121–25, 128–33, 135, 178, 211–12; World Literature and, 113–15, 117–19, 121–24, 127, 129–30, 135. *See also 2666*
Bolívar, Simón, 203–4
Bolivia: decolonialism in, 81; extractivism in, 87, 249n53; MAS in, 81–82; National Constitution of, 69–71, 75, 86–87; *reloj del sur* in, 69–70, *70*
Bonsái (Zambra), 177, 184–85
Book of Good Love, The (Archpriest of Hita), 103
Book of Lamentations, The (Castellanos), 223
books, 143, 144, 201, 259n1

Borges, Jorge Luis, 58, 96, 98; Aleph of, 109, 123; Foucault and, 81, 144
Boscagli, Maurizia, 12
Bosteels, Bruno, 204–6
botón de Nácar, El (The Pearl Button) (film), 271n43
"Bourgeois King, The" (Darío), 223
Brahmanism, 24–25
Braidotti, Rosi, 206
Brecht, Bertolt, 158, 268n15
British Petroleum, 227–29
Brown, Bill, 168
Buffett, Warren, 173
Bukharin, Nikolay Ivanovich, 206–7
Bull, William, 45–46
butterflies, 47–48, 226, 242n20
By Night in Chile (Nocturno de Chile) (Bolaño), 112–13, 117, 165

cacao, 60, 61
calibanismo, 82
Cameron, Andy, 172, 197
Capital (Marx). *See* Marx, Karl
Capitalism in the Web of Life (Moore), 201–2
Capitalocene, 227
Caro, Antonio, 214–15
Caro, Miguel Antonio, 158
Carpentier, Alejo, 111
Carr, Nicholas, 182
Carroll, Lewis, 92–93, 96, 250n62
Cartesianism, 37–38, 153, 224
Casablanca la bella (Vallejo), 35, 145, 159–60
casa de las dos palmas, La (Mejía Vallejo), 262n35
Castellanos, Rosario, 223
Castro, Fidel, 23, 233n17; *Deep Foods* and, 17–18; Special Period introduced by, 14–16
Caycedo, Carolina, 215, 215–16
Céline, Louis-Ferdinand, 51, 55, 138
cell phone, 173–76
"celular, El" (song), 174–76
Chaplin, Charlie, 212
Charles V (king), 14–18, 24
Chasteen, John Charles, 242n18
Cheah, Pheng, 110, 138, 201

Chile: Allende in, 114–15, 171, 195, 197; digital technologies in, 171–72; neoliberalism in, 185, 195; Pinochet in, 113, 186, 195, 197; Synco in, 171, 195–97; Zambra and, 182–83, 185–86
chino en bicicleta, Un (Magnus), 53
Chocolate Pictures (Muniz), 61, 62
Christian literature, medieval, 103
Christie, Agatha, 213
Clark, Nigel, 253n94
cloud, 172, 186–87; critiquing, 189–97; public and private, 188–89
Coelho, Teixeira, 271n45
coevolution, 47, 151; bees and, 65–66; with rubber, 48–49, 64. *See also* evolution
coffee, 220–21
Cohen, Jeffrey, 103
Cold War, 15, 23, 36, 68, 196, 248n33
collective subjectivity, 69–71
Colombia: M. A. Caro in, 158; in *Casablanca la bella*, 159–60; extractivism in, 213–16; houses and literature of, 159, 262n35; *modernismo* in, 151, 158
coltan, 213–14, 216
Coltán (Vásquez-Figueroa), 213–14
comidas profundas, Las (Deep Foods) (Ponte). *See Deep Foods*
commodities, 239n80, 240n90; bananas, 60, 226, 228; digital-age, 2; feathers as, 47; oil, 227–29; rubber, 32–33, 36, 43–53, 44, 56–58, 64, 182, 200, 213, 220, 222–23; sugar, 7–12, 27–28, 49, 59, 103, 227, 238n78, 272n51; tobacco, 7–12, 22, 27–28, 42, 49, 59, 67, 103, 238n78
commodity fetishism, 211; counterfetishism and, 7–8, 13, 58; Glantz on, 162; hyperfetishism compared with, 144–46, 151, 160, 164, 170; Marx on, 34, 146–51, 154, 160, 170, 204, 259n3, 260n8; in *modernismo*, 156–57; smartphone, 172; supply chains and, 208
communism: Cuban, 14–18, 23–26, 233n17; as endpoint of history, 16; historical materialism and, 23, 30–31, 37, 204–5; Marxism and, 16, 30, 137, 204–5, 209; midcentury international, 30; Soviet-style, 29

Communist Manifesto (Marx and Engels), 137, 209
computer: cloud, 172, 186–97; literary production with, 218–19; smartphone as, 173; in supply chains, 210, 213, 216, 218–19; in *Synco*, 195–97; in *2666*, 211–12; waste of, 216–18
computer, personal, 172, 189, 208; in assemblage, 179–80; love and, 179, 181, 183–84, 204; sleep and, 182–83; Zambra on, 35, 177–84, 186, 204, 210–11
conatus, 48–49
concentration camps, 50, 242n28
Conquest of the Desert *(Conquista del desierto)*, 67–68, 246n1
Con sentimiento y sabor (Tan bonita) (album), 174
conspicuous consumption, 164–65, 202
constructivism, 95, 251n72
Contrapunteo cubano del tabaco y del azúcar (Cuban Counterpoint) (Ortiz). See Ortiz, Fernando
Cooppan, Vilashini, 138
Coronil, Fernando, 234n22; on commodities, Ortiz and, 7–8, 13, 27, 58, 239n80; on counterfetishism, Ortiz and, 7–8, 58
corpses: abject and, 105–6, 111–13, 188, 201; anus and, 118–19; Bolaño and, 105, 112–13, 119–21, 125–26, 128–32; language and, 119–20; in Latin American literature, post-1989, 136–37; orientation toward, 34, 105–6, 111–12, 138–39, 200–201
correlationism, 74–77
corrido, 35, 174–76, 189
Cortázar, Julio, 121, 223
Cortés, Hernán, 266n34
Cosmopolitan Desires (Siskind), 127
counterfetishism, 7–8, 13, 58
Courbet, Gustave, 17
Coutinho, Eduardo, 217
Crary, Jonathan, 35, 183
credit, 157–58
creolization, 6, 203
critical theory, 201, 204–5
Cuba, 37, 135; *ajiaco* of, 11–12, 24, 80; *aliñado* of, 24; hunger in, 17–18, 23–24; Ortiz and politics of, 233n17; Ponte and, 14–25; Special Period of, 14–18, 23, 25; sugar in, 7–12, 27–28, 49, 59, 103, 238n78; tobacco in, 7–12, 27–28, 42, 49, 59, 67, 103, 233n14
Cuban Counterpoint (Contrapunteo cubano del tabaco y del azúcar) (Ortiz). See Ortiz, Fernando
Cybersyn (Synco), 171, 195–97

Daddy Yankee, 176
Dali, Salvador, 229
dam, 83, 193, 215, 215–16
Damrosch, David, 107, 109, 111
Darío, Rubén, 48, 151, 223
Darwinism, 94–95
Debord, Guy, 168–69, 217, 268n15
debt, 157–58
decolonialism, 81–82, 248n38
deconstruction, 6, 8, 98, 106, 201; constructivism and, 95, 251n72; Derrida and, 95, 253n1; puns and, 95, 139
Deep Foods (Las comidas profundas) (Ponte), 99; *aliñado* in, 24; archeology and, 20–21; beer in, 20; Charles V in, 14–18, 24; eroticism in, 17, 23–25; as fruit, history in, 17; history, end of, and, 15–17; hunger in, 17–19, 23–24; incorporation in, 21–22, 24; nonhuman agency in, 27–28; Ortiz and, 22, 24, 26; pineapple in, 14–15, 17–18, 21, 24; Russell in, 19–20; tobacco in, 22
Deepwater Horizon oil spill, 227–29
DeLanda, Manuel, 36
de la Torre, Sergio, 212
Deleuze, Gilles, 205–6, 239n83
Democritus, 99
Dënver, 266n27
Depraz, Natalie, 120
De Robertis, Carolina, 184–85
Derrida, Jacques, 95, 115, 119, 253n1
desert, 67–68, 86, 246n1
De sobremesa (After-Dinner Conversation) (Silva). See *After-Dinner Conversation*
destorifying, 55, 222
detectives salvajes, Los (The Savage Detectives) (Bolaño). See *Savage Detectives, The*

détournement, 168–69, 193
device, 37
Devil's Paradise, The (Hardenburg), 50–51, 242n29
Devil Wears Prada, The (Weisberger), 161
DeVries, Scott, 45
D'haen, Theo, 106–7, 110
Dialectic of Enlightenment (Adorno and Horkheimer), 130–31
dialectics, 65, 68, 86, 92, 146, 231n4
dictatorship, 271n45
Dictionary of Untranslatables, The (Depraz), 120
"Dieguito" (Feinmann), 136
Dieste, Rafael, 130
digital technologies, 183, 266n34; artworks critiquing, 189–97; cell phone, 173–76; in Chile, 171–72; estrangement of, 172, 174, 186, 197, 211; extractivism and, 68, 172, 182, 187–89, 193–95, 197–98, 203–4, 211–13; ideologies of, 35, 172, 189, 197–98, 212; Internet of Things, 2, 186–87, 196; Lanier on, 181–82; lock-in effect of, 181; neoliberalism and, 173, 177; obsolescence of, Zambra on, 177–79, 186, 211; primitive accumulation and, 187–89, 193–95, 197–98; privatization of, 173–74, 177–78; Synco, 171, 195–97; waste of, 216–18. *See also* computer
disposal, artifact, 213, 216–18
divinity. *See God's Tea Party*
Don Quixote (fictional character), 137
Doran, Robert, 239n89

e-books, 144
Eco, Umberto, 111, 128
eco-criticism, 45–46, 201–2, 228–29
ecology, political, 228–29, 231n4
economicism, 30–31, 170
ejércitos, Los (The Armies) (Rosero), 136
Eltit, Diamela, 136
emplotment, 7, 32, 53, 119, 200, 239n89
Engels, Friedrich, 30–31, 137, 209
Enock, C. Reginald, 242n29
eroticism, 17, 23–25
Escobar, Pablo, 156, 160

Eshel, Amir, 108–9
Espejo de paciencia (Balboa), 18
estrangement: of digital technologies, 172, 174, 186, 197, 211; extractivism and, 35–36, 224; of human-nonhuman assemblages, 224; of Shklovsky, 37–38; of Zambra, 185–86
evolution, 94–95
extermination: Guatemalan genocide, 221; of indigenous Patagonians, 67–68, 246n1; Magnus on, 50, 52–58, 63, 242n28; rubber and, 50–51; White on, 7, 54–55, 222, 232n10
Extractive Zone, The (Gómez-Barris), 231n2
extractivism, 102, 209, 219, 231n2; Bolívar on, 203–4; in Bolivia, 87, 249n53; in Colombia, 213–16, *215*; desert, 68; digital, 68, 172, 182, 187–89, 193–95, 197–98, 203–4, 211–13; estranged, 35–36, 224; Glantz and, 164; in Guatemala, 220–22; in language, 226; Latin American configuration of, 203; Magnus on, 50–51, 56–58; mineral, 213–15; mining, 68, 87, 213–14; oil, 227–29; rubber, 32–33, 43–52, 44, 57–58, 182, 200, 213, 223; transcultural materialism as critique of, 3, 22, 87–88, 199, 202, 208, 212, 222–24, 227–29; Zambra and, 181–82, 210, 216. *See also* supply chains

Facebook, 193, *194*
Facebook's Server Farm (photograph), *194*
Family Tree, The (Las genealogías) (Glantz), 163
Farm (Pryor Creek, Oklahoma) (artwork), 191–93, *192*
feathers, 46–47
Feinmann, José Pablo, 136
Felski, Rita, 100, 144, 252n88
femicide, 129; feminicide, 115, 131; Juárez, Holocaust and, 130–31; in *2666*, 34, 128, 130–32, 135, 137, 211–12
feminism, 270n26
Fernández, Patricio (Pato), 177
Ferragamo, 162–64
Fisk, Gloria, 135
Flores, Fernando, 195–96

food, 2; *ajiaco*, 11–12, 24, 80; bananas, 60, 226, 228; beets, 12, 234n26; meat, 41–42, 224; Ortiz on, 11–12, 27, 80, 234n26; pineapple, 14–15, 17–18, 21, 24; Ponte on, 14–27, 38, 63, 67, 99; tomato, 217–18
Fortunes and Misfortunes of the Asshole (Gracias y desgracias del ojo del culo) (Quevedo), 115–16
Foucault, Michel, 81, 101–2, 144, 216–17
French, Jennifer, 45, 231n4
Freud, Sigmund, 25, 53, 56, 123, 175; commodity fetish and, 164; Muniz portrait of, 61
Friedländer, Saul, 50, 54–55
fruit: bananas, 60, 226, 228; in *Deep Foods*, as history, 17; pineapple, 14–15, 17–18, 21, 24; tomato, 217–18; United Fruit Company, 194, 228
Fuguet, Alberto, 178
Fukuyama, Francis, 15, 114
Funari, Vicky, 212
Furtado, Jorge, 217

Gallo, Rubén, 165–66, 168–69
García, Daniel, 17
García Canclini, Néstor, 36, 80–81, 248n33
García Linera, Álvaro, 82
García Márquez, Gabriel: bananas and, 60, 226, 228; on Macondo, 178, 227–29; *One Hundred Years of Solitude*, 60, 103, 178, 226–29, 262n35
Gardens (Harrison), 78–79
Gastev, Aleksei, 240n94
Gates, Bill, 173
gender, 119; Glantz on, 161; machismo, 176, 183–84; neoliberal feminism, 270n26
genealogías, Las (The Family Tree) (Glantz), 163
genocide, 221
genre, 119
geological time, 86–88
geology: in *God's Tea Party*, 33–34, 88, 93; in *El jardín de Nora*, 33–34, 77, 79, 84, 86–87. See also mountains
geontopower, 101–2
Germany, 50–51, 56–58, 242n28

Gerrard, John, 195; *Farm (Pryor Creek, Oklahoma)*, 191–93, *192*; *Solar Reserve (Tonopah, Nevada)*, 190, 190–91, *191*
Ghost (film), 120
Giorgi, Gabriel, 87
Glantz, Margo: *The Family Tree*, 163; on Ferragamo, 162–64; *Historia de una mujer que caminó por la vida con zapatos de diseñador*, 35, 145, 161–65; hyperfetishism of, 35, 145, 161–65, 202
Glendinning, Chellis, 183, 213
God's Tea Party (El té de Dios) (Aira), 33–34, 68; apes, monkeys in, 88–90, 93–97; Carroll and, 92–93, 96, 250n62; divinity in, 90–91, *91*, 92–94, 98–99; evolution in, 94–95; Hindu iconography and, 90–91, *91*, 93; hyperobject in, 99, 101; nonhuman agency in, 93, 95–100; puns of, 90, 95; subatomic particle in, 88–89, 93, 95–101; World Literature and, 90–91, 94, 250n60
Goethe, Johann Wolfgang von, 106, 108–10, 139
gold, 171–72, 214–15
Gómez-Barris, Macarena, 231n2
González Ramírez, Sergio, 135
González Segura, Ricardo, 85
Google, 192–93
Gracias y desgracias del ojo del culo (Fortunes and Misfortunes of the Asshole) (Quevedo), 115–16
Graeber, David, 158
Graff, Gerald, 109
Guatemala, 136; extractivism in, 220–22; genocide in, 221; *God's Tea Party* published in, 88, 90, *91*, 94
Gutiérrez, Pedro Juan, 136
Guzmán, Patricio, 271n43

Habermas, Jürgen, 248n33
Halfon, Eduardo, 136, 220–22
ham *(jamón)*, 42
Hanuman (Hindu deity), 90–91, *91*, 93
"Han vuelto las aves" (Halfon), 136, 220–22
Haraway, Donna, 90, 93–94, 96
Hardenburg, Walter E., 50–51, 242n29
Hardt, Michael, 205–6
Harman, Graham, 234n19

Harrison, Robert, 78–79
"Hecatomb" (Smith, P.), 137
Hegel, Georg Wilhelm Friedrich, 30, 64, 138, 157, 239n83
Heidegger, Martin, 162, 170, 187, 193, 216
Higgs boson, 95, 97–99
Hinduism, 90–91, *91*, 93
historia (history, story), 223
Historia de una mujer que caminó por la vida con zapatos de diseñador (Glantz). *See* Glantz, Margo
"Historia de un computador" (Zambra). *See* Zambra, Alejandro
História natural da ditadura (Coelho), 271n45
historical materialism. *See* materialism
historicism, 30–32, 63
history, end of, 15–17
history, natural, 221–22
Hita, Archpriest of, 103
holes. *See* Wiethüchter, Blanca
Holocaust, 7, 217, 221–22, 232n10; Juárez femicides and, 130–31; Magnus and, 50, 53–55, 242n28
Holocausto del Palacio de Justicia, 52
Holt, Douglas, 162
hooks, bell, 270n26
Hopscotch (Cortázar), 121, 223
Horkheimer, 130–31
houses, 159, 262n35
"Human Factors of Cubanity, The" (Ortiz), 7, 11–12
hunger, 17–19, 23–24
hybridity, 81, 85–86, 248n33, 249n9
hydropower, 193, *215*, 215–16
hyperfetishism, 208; commodity fetishism compared with, 144–46, 151, 160, 164, 170; of Glantz, 35, 145, 161–65, 202; of Magnus, 58; in *Ricas y famosas*, 35, 145, *165*, 165–69, *166*, *167*; of Silva, 34–35, 145, 152–60, 261n18; of Vallejo, 145, 156–60, 202
hyperobject: correlationism rejected by, 74–76; in *God's Tea Party*, 99, 101; *El jardín de Nora* and, 33, 68, 74–77, 82, 86, 101; Morton on, 33–34, 68, 74–77, 99; pachamama as, 76–77

idealism: Marx and, 147–48; materialism countering, 30, 34, 116–17
ideological state apparatuses, 23, 147
ideology: digital, 35, 172, 189, 197–98, 212; transcultural materialism critiquing, 31
Ilha das Flores (documentary), 217
Ilyenkov, Evald, 268n15
Impuesto a la carne (Eltit), 136
incorporation, 21–22, 24
India, 93–94
Institutional Revolutionary Party (Partido Revolucionario Institucional) (PRI). *See* Partido Revolucionario Institucional
Internet of Things, 2, 186–87, 196

James, Earl K., 48
Jameson, Fredric, 31, 53
jamón (ham), 42
jardín de Nora, El (Wiethüchter), 93, 100, 248n37; Aymara in, 71, 73, 76, 78–80, 84–85, 95–96; Bolivian National Constitution and, 69; decolonialism and, 81–82; geology in, 33–34, 77, 79, 84, 86–87; hybridity and, 85–86; hyperobject and, 33, 68, 74–77, 82, 86, 101; language and, 71–73, 76–78, 82–83, 86; Molina on, 81–82; Monasterios on, 79–81; muteness in, 80, 82–86; nature-culture and, 76–79, 99, 200; of nonhuman agency, verisimilitude in, 74–76, 84; as *novela de la tierra*, 83–84; pachamama in, 71, 75–77; paradise and, 73–74, 82–83
Jasanoff, Sheila, 205, 218
Journal of World Literature, 109–10
Juana Inés de la Cruz, 161
Juárez, Mexico, femicide in. *See* femicide

Kafka, Franz, 23, 28, 262n28
Kant, Immanuel, 110
kantutas, 80
Kanzepolsky, Adriana, 23
Kim Hyesoon, 216–17
Kingdom of This World, The (Carpentier), 111
kiswaras, 80
Kittler, Friedrich, 138, 210, 219
Klein, Naomi, 185

Knausgård, Karl Ove, 36, 220, 222
Kristeva, Julia, 111–13, 118

labor: exploitation of, Marx on, 64–66; Zambra and, 182–83
"Labyrinth" (Bolaño), 115
Lacanian psychoanalysis, 82–83, 112, 255n25; corpses, bodily excretions in, 119; hyperfetishism and, 164; *objet petit a* in, 121; suture in, 118
LaCapra, Dominick, 55, 226
language, 6–7; corpses and, 119–20; extractivism in, 226; *El jardín de Nora* and, 71–73, 76–78, 82–83, 86; nonhuman agency of, 138
Lanier, Jaron, 181–82
Lanzmann, Claude, 221
Larsen, Neil, 229
latex. *See* rubber
Latin Americanism: nature-culture in, 102–3; new materialism and, 5–6, 202; transcultural materialism and, 224–25; World Literature and, 5–6, 201
Latin American literature, post-1989, 135–37
Latour, Bruno, 37, 98, 144; amodernity of, 27, 29, 36, 65; anthropodecentrism and, 252n90; ANT of, 28–29; Constitution of, 19, 49, 86; on constructivism, 95, 251n72; on critique, 201; Cuban writers and, 13–14, 19, 22–23; on human, nonhuman and, 19, 22–23, 27, 41, 53–54, 100; on literature, 99–101, 251n66; on nature-culture, 19, 48, 59; on nonhuman agency, 28–29, 100; *Politics of Nature*, 237n59; *We Have Never Been Modern*, 65
Lenin, Vladimir Ilich, 206–7, 268n15
"Letter from Jamaica" (Bolívar), 203
Levi, Primo, 55
Lezama Lima, José, 17–18, 21–22, 24
lists, 111, 128
literary studies, 226; anthropocentrism of, 32; materialism and, 29, 100, 156, 201, 223, 227
literatura nazi en América, La (Nazi Literature in the Americas) (Bolaño). *See Nazi Literature in the Americas*

lock-in effect, technological, 181
López, Andrés, 176–77
love: liquid, Bauman on, 184–85; Zambra on, 35, 177–79, 181, 183–85, 204
Luiselli, Valeria, 136
Lukács, Georg, 97, 205

Machado de Assis, Joaquim Maria, 119
machismo, 176, 183–84
Macondo (fictional town), 178, 227–29
Macondo oil spill, 227–29
Mad Hatter (fictional character), 92, 96
magical realism *(lo real maravilloso)*, 74, 111
Magnarelli, Sharon, 46–47
Magnus, Ariel: *La abuela*, 242n28; *Un chino en bicicleta*, 53; on extractivism, 50–51, 56–58; Germany and, 50–51, 56–58, 242n28; historicism, anthropodecentric, of, 63; Holocaust and, 50, 53–55, 242n28; hyperfetishism of, 58; *Muñecas*, 33, 49–59, 63; Nazism and, 50–55, 57, 63, 242n28; on rubber, 33, 49–52, 56–57; sex dolls and, 33, 50–51, 56–59; transcultural materialism of, 49, 58–60, 62–63. *See also Muñecas*
Malabou, Catherine, 57
Malinche, 266n34
Malinowski, Bronisław, 7, 9, 28
Mapping World Literature (Rosendahl Thomsen), 107
maquiladoras, 211–13, 216
Maquilápolis (documentary), 212–13
"Mariposas" (Silva), 242n20
Marré, Luis, 24–25, 37
Martí, José, 233n14
Marvell, Andrew, 111
Marx, Karl, 175, 188; *Capital*, 64, 146, 149, 157, 168, 187, 260n8; on commodity fetishism, 34, 146–51, 154, 160, 170, 204, 259n3, 260n8; communism and, 204; *Communist Manifesto*, 137, 209; on credit, 157; Cuba and, 16, 24; economicism of, 30–31; on exchange and use value, 148–51, 168, 260n8; on fetishism, hyperfetishism compared with, 145; Hegel and, 30, 64, 157, 239n83; on labor, exploitation of, 64–66; nonhuman agency and, 149–52, 182;

Ortiz and, 13; primitive accumulation and, 145–46, 156, 187, 204; on raw material, 63–66, 201–2; on surplus value, 64; on World Literature, 137, 209

Marxism, 10, 213, 219, 268n13; ecology compared with, 228–29, 231n4; metonymic trope and, 239n89; new materialism and, 4, 232n5; transcultural materialism and, 65–66, 86

MAS (Movimiento al Socialismo), 81–82

material humano, El (Rey Rosa), 136

materialism, 2–3; base, 115, 131; of Bataille, 115; of Bolaño, 113–14, 131; of *God's Tea Party*, 88, 93; idealism countered by, 30, 34, 116–17; language and, 6–7; literary studies and, 29, 100, 156, 201, 223, 227; nonhuman agency in, 30–31, 225; of Ortiz, 7, 9–14, 19, 26–27, 103; of Ponte, 21–23, 25–26, 67; vibrant, 13, 21

materialism, historical, 23, 28; new materialism and, 4, 37, 64, 100, 144, 204, 206–7, 225, 232n5; nonhuman agency in, 30–31

materialism, new, 29, 143; of Bennett, 13, 21–22, 37, 239n83; critical theory with, 204–5; historical materialism and, 4, 37, 64, 100, 144, 204, 206–7, 225, 232n5; Latin Americanism and, 5–6, 202; Marxism and, 4, 232n5; nature-culture and, 19, 28, 48, 59; Ortiz as precursor to, 7, 9–14, 19, 27; realism and, 10, 234n19; speculative leftism and, 206; transcultural materialism and, 4, 36–37, 100

materialism, transcultural, 2; bounds of, 225–26; commodity fetishism and, 34; extractivism critiqued by, 3, 22, 87–88, 199, 202, 208, 212, 222–24, 227–29; as historicism, 30–31; human and nonhuman critiqued by, 199–200, 224–25; hyperfetishism in, 144–45; ideology critiqued by, 31; of *El jardín de Nora*, 69, 74, 76–79, 81–82, 86–87; on Latin Americanism, impact of, 224–25; Latour and, 13–14, 37; literary studies and, 100, 223; of Magnus, 49, 58–60, 62–63; Marxism and, 65–66, 86;

materialisms, historical and new, in, 4, 37, 100; narrative and method converging in, 84; nature-culture in, 13, 79, 201–2, 224–25; new materialism and, 4, 36–37, 100; nonhuman agency in, 30–31, 225; as postanthropocentric, 42, 65; raw material in, 43; of J. E. Rivera, 60, 62–63, 65, 67; for World Literature, 37, 105, 137–39, 201

materia prima (raw material). *See* raw material

"Mauricio 'The Eye' Silva" ("Ojo Silva, El") (Bolaño), 115, 117

McOndo, 178

meat, 41–42, 206, 224

medieval Christian literature, 103

Meireles, Cecília, 217

Mejía Vallejo, Manuel, 262n35

Memórias Póstumas de Brás Cubas (Machado de Assis), 119

Menton, Seymour, 48

Mentz, Steve, 232n8

metonymic trope, 239n89

Mexico: corrido in, history of, 174; femicide in, 34, 128–32, 135, 137, 211–12; PRI in, 165–66; in *Ricas y famosas*, 145, 165, 165–69, 166, 167; telecommunications in, Slim and, 173–74, 203; Tlatelolco massacre in, 118

Mexico, Gulf of, 227–28

Microsoft Windows, 176, 178, 182

Microsoft Word, 212

MIDI (Musical Instrument Digital Interface), 181

Mignolo, Walter, 248n38

minerals, 213–15

Minería (artwork), 214

mining, 68, 87, 213–14

Mintz, Sidney, 272n51

Mis documentos (My Documents) (Zambra), 177–78

modernismo, 151, 156–58

modernity, 27, 29, 36, 65

Modern Times (film), 212

Molina, Mary Carmen E., 81–82, 247n14

Monasterios, Elizabeth, 79–82, 85, 248n33

monkeys, 91, 93–94

Moore, Jason, 201–2
Morales, Evo, 82, 203, 249n53
Moreiras, Alberto, 8, 86, 249n49
Morrison, Toni, 55, 242n29
Morton, Tim, 97; on hyperobject, 33–34, 68, 74–77, 99; posthumanism of, 77
mountains, 68, 76, 79, 103, 225
Movimiento al Socialismo. *See* MAS
Muñecas (Magnus): extermination in, 50, 52–58, 63; rubber, silicone in, 33, 49–52, 56–57; rubber precedents of, 33, 49; sex dolls in, 33, 50–51, 56–59
Muniz, Vik, 60, *61*, 62, 217
Musical Brain, The (Aira), 88
Musical Instrument Digital Interface. *See* MIDI
My Bloody Valentine, 75
My Documents (Mis documentos) (Zambra), 177–78
My Struggle (Knausgård), 220

National Union of Writers and Artists of Cuba (UNEAC), 24–25
nature: historical and, 221–22, 271n44; politics of, Latour and, 22–23, 237n59
nature-culture, 65, 228; *El jardín de Nora* and, 76–79, 99, 200; in Latin Americanism, 102–3; new materialism and, 19, 28, 48, 59; in transcultural materialism, 13, 79, 201–2, 224–25
Nazi Literature in the Americas (La literatura nazi en América) (Bolaño), 54, 113
Nazism, 7, 162, 197, 217, 222, 232n10; Adorno and Horkheimer on, 130–31; Bolaño and, 54, 113, 130; cultural inspirations for, 195, 226; Magnus and, 50–55, 57, 63, 242n28; rubber and, 51, 53, 57–58
negativity, 85–87, 249n49
Negri, Antonio, 205–6
neoliberalism, 270n26; biopolitics of, 216; in Chile, 185, 195; digital technologies and, 173, 177
neo-Luddism, 182–83
neo-Spinozism, 205–7
Neruda, Pablo, 60, 195
Nest, Michael, 214

Nettel, Guadalupe, 136
New Human in Literature, The (Rosendahl Thomsen), 138
Nietzsche, Friedrich, 124
1968, 114–15
1989, Latin American literature after, 135–37
Nixon, Rob, 222
Nocturno de Chile (By Night in Chile) (Bolaño). *See By Night in Chile*
nonhuman, human and, 228, 253n94; abject communicating, 201; actant and actor in, 207; assemblage of, 19, 22, 70–71, 179–80, 207, 224; coevolution of, 47–49, 64–66, 151; Latour on, 19, 22–23, 27, 41, 53–54, 100; magnitude and scale in, 79; in rubber, 44–46; storifying, 222–23; transcultural materialism critiquing, 199–200, 224–25; in *2666*, 132–33
nonhuman agency, 207, 229; animism and, 102–3, 155, 261n18; Bennett on, 28, 35, 271n44; communism and, 204; of computer, Zambra on, 179–80; in *Deep Foods*, 27–28; in *God's Tea Party*, 93, 95–100; in historical materialism, 30–31; in *El jardín de Nora*, verisimilitude of, 74–76, 84; of language and matter, 138; Latour on, 28–29, 100; Marx and, 149–52, 182; Ortiz on, 27–28, 59; in transcultural materialism, 30–31, 225; in *The Vortex*, 45; of worms, 271n44
Nora, Pierre, 58
nostalgia, 159–60, 182, 186, 210
novela de la tierra, 83–84
Noys, Benjamin, 116
nudging, 143

objet petit a, 121
oceanic feeling, 25
oil, 227–29
"Ojo Silva, El" ("Mauricio 'The Eye' Silva") (Bolaño), 115, 117
One Hundred Years of Solitude (García Márquez). *See* García Márquez, Gabriel
ontological turn, political, 205–7
Ordóñez, Monserrat, 46–47
origenismo, 17, 235n38

Ortiz, Fernando: on *ajiaco*, 11–12, 80; on beets, 12, 234n26; Coronil on, 7–8, 13, 27, 58, 239n80; *Cuban Counterpoint*, 7–12, 26–28, 59, 103, 233n17, 234n22, 238n78, 239n80; Cuban politics and, 233n17; "The Human Factors of Cubanity," 7, 11–12; Latour and, 13–14, 19, 22–23; Magnus compared with, 63; materialism of, 7, 9–14, 19, 26–27, 43, 103; as new materialist precursor, 7, 9–14, 19, 27; on nonhuman agency, 27–28, 59; Ponte and, 22, 24, 26; on radio, 233n14; on sugar, 7–12, 27–28, 49, 59, 103, 238n78; on tobacco, 7–12, 27–28, 42, 49, 59, 67, 103, 238n78; on *transculturación*, 3, 7–12, 49, 80–81, 199, 224–26
Our Lady of the Assassins (La Virgen de los sicarios) (Vallejo), 156
Ovid, 56

pachamama, 71, 75–77, 87, 101
Padilla, Heberto, 17–18
paradise, 73–74, 82–83
Parks, Tim, 250n60
Partido Revolucionario Institucional (Institutional Revolutionary Party) (PRI), 165–66
Patagonia, indigenous exterminationin, 67–68, 246n1
Paz, Octavio, 15–16, 161
Pearl Button, The (El botón de Nácar) (film), 271n43
Pelota de letras (stand-up act), 176–77
Peluffo, Ana, 183
pencil, 208–9
Pérez Firmat, Gustavo, 11
personhood, juridical, 69–70, 86–87, 249n52
Peru, 103
phutunhuicu, 84–85
pineapple, 14–15, 17–18, 21, 24
Piñera, Virgilio, 22
Pink Tide, 203, 268n6
Pinochet, Augusto, 113, 186, 195, 197, 271n43
plasticity, 57, 80
Polar, Cornejo, 8, 82, 224–25
Politics of Nature (Latour), 237n59

Pollack, Sarah, 114
Pollan, Michael, 47, 64–65
Ponte, Antonio José, 38, 63; Cuban Special Period and, 14–18, 23, 25; *Deep Foods*, 14–27, 99; exile of, 14–15; Lezama Lima and, 17, 21–22, 24; Marré and, 24–25; materialism of, 21–23, 25–26, 67; *origenismo* and, 17, 235n38; Ortiz and, 22, 24, 26. *See also Deep Foods*
posthumanism, 77–78, 84, 138
Postone, Moishe, 259n3
potatoes, 47
Povinelli, Elizabeth, 101–2
Powers, Richard, 99–100
Powers of Horror, The (Kristeva), 118
Pratt, Mary Louise, 7, 9
PRI. *See* Partido Revolucionario Institucional
primitive accumulation: digital technologies and, 187–89, 193–95, 197–98; Gerrard and, 191; Marx and, 145–46, 156, 187, 204
privatization, 69, 87, 173–74, 177–78
production, literary, 218–19
projection, 175
prú. *See aliñado*
puncept, 137
puns, 136, 139; of Bolaño, 117–18, 120; in *God's Tea Party*, 90, 95
Putas asesinas (Bolaño), 119

quantum physics, 68, 88, 93, 95
Quevedo, Francisco de, 115–16
Quijano, Aníbal, 248n38

radio, 233n14
Rama, Ángel, 7, 9, 43, 80, 224–25
Rancière, Jacques, 97, 252n78
raw material, 43, 224; Bolívar on, 203; labor, exploitation of, and, 64–65; Latin American literary turn to, 57, 60; Marx on, 63–66, 201–2; in supply chains, 208–9
realism, 10, 209, 234n19
real maravilloso (magical realism), 74, 111
rebaño negro (black flock), 44
"Recuerdos de un computador personal" (Zambra), 178, 183–84
Red Queen (fictional character), 250n62

reification, digital, 181
reloj del sur, 69–70, *70*
"Return, The " ("El retorno")(Bolaño), 119–21
Rey Rosa, Rodrigo, 136
Ricas y famosas (photographic essay). *See* Rossell, Daniela
Rivera, Álex, 265n12
Rivera, Diego, 60, *61*
Rivera, José Eustasio, 59; transcultural materialism of, 60, 62–63, 65, 67; *The Vortex*, 33, 44–50, 83, 151, 182, 200, 242n18. *See also Vortex, The*
Roca, Juan Manuel, 153, 261n18
Roman law, 69–70
Rosendahl Thomsen, Mads, 107, 138
Rosero, Evelio, 136
Rosler, Martha, 165
Rossell, Daniela: criticism of, 165–66; *Ricas y famosas*, 35, 145, 165–69, *166*, *167*
Routledge Concise History of World Literature, The (D'haen), 106–7
rubber: in Amazon basin, extraction of, 32–33, 43–45, *44*, 57–58, 200, 213, 223; in assemblage, 45–46; balls of, 43–44, *44*, 52, 64; as black flock, 44; coevolution with, 48–49, 64; Knausgård on, 36, 220, 222; Magnus on, 33, 49–52, 56–57; native extermination, exploitation, and, 50–51; Nazism and, 51, 53, 57–58; potatoes compared with, 47; in *The Vortex*, 44–46, 48–49, 182, 200. *See also* raw material
Ruiz, Juan, 10
Russell, Bertrand, 19–20
Russian formalism, 37–38, 42

Salcedo, Doris, 52
Sancho Panza (fictional character), 137
Sandberg, Sheryl, 270n26
San Jose, California, 174
Santí, Enrico Mario, 234n22
Santiago, Chile, 185, 195
Saussure, Ferdinand de, 43
Savage Detectives, The (Bolaño), 114, 117, 121–22, 132, 255n28
Schmitt, Carl, 108

science and technology studies (STS), 205
seaweed *(alga)*, 132
sediment, 227
sex dolls, 66; industry of, 57, 245n54; in *Muñecas*, 33, 50–51, 56–59
Shakespeare, William, 85
Shallows, The (Carr), 182
Shatapatha Brahmana, 24–25
Shklovsky, Viktor, 37–38, 84
Shoah (documentary), 221
shoes, 161–62
silicone. *See* rubber
Silicon Valley, 186, 197–98, 218, 270n26
Silva, José Asunción, 165, 261n24; *After-Dinner Conversation*, 34–35, 145, 155–56; in *Almas en pena, chapolas negras*, 35, 145, 156–58, 262n28; animism of, 155, 261n18; credit, debt, and, 157–58; hyperfetishism of, 34–35, 145, 152–60, 261n18; "Mariposas," 242n20; *modernismo* and, 151, 157–58; sister of, 153, *154*; "The Voice of Things," 152–55, 261n18
Sinaloa, Mexico, 174
Singer, Peter, 41, 240n1
Siskind, Mariano, 127, 255n25
sleep, 182–83
Sleep Dealer (film), 265n12
Slim, Carlos, 173–74, 203
Sloterdijk, Peter, 14
smartphone, 68, 144, 171–74
Smith, Adam, 187
Smith, Patti, 137
Social History of Rubber, A (Tully), 51
socialism, 29–30
socialist realism, 209
sociotechnical imaginaries, 205, 218
software, 37, 188, 198, 213, 218–19; iPhoto, 180; lock-in of, 181; Microsoft Windows, 176, 178, 182; Microsoft Word, 212
solar anus, 115–18, 126, 212
solar economy, 117, 126, 128, 132
Solar Reserve (Tonopah, Nevada) (artwork), 190, 190–91, *191*
Sollers, Philippe, 115
Soviet Union, 14, 25, 37, 45, 240n94
Special Period, Cuban, 14–18, 23, 25

speciesism, 94, 199, 240n1
speculative leftism, 205–7
Spheres (Sloterdijk), 14
Spinoza, Baruch, 48, 205–7, 239n83
Steele, Kim, 193–95, *194*
storifying, 222–23. *See also* destorifying
"Story of Electronics, The" (video), 217
Story of My Teeth, The (Luiselli), 136
STS. *See* science and technology studies
Suárez, José Antonio, 137
subalternism, 85–86, 249n49
subatomic particle: in *God's Tea Party*, 88–89, 93, 95–101; Higgs boson, 95, 97–99
sublation *(Aufhebung)*, 4, 100
sugar, 272n51; Ortiz on, 7–12, 27–28, 49, 59, 103, 238n78; sediment and, 227
supply chains, 222; computer in, 210, 213, 216, 218–19; disposal in, 213, 216–18; *Maquilápolis* and critique of, 212–13; raw material in, 208–9
suspicion, 100–101, 225, 252n88
Synco (Baradit), 195–97
Synco (Cybersyn), 171, 195–97

Tea Party (political movement), 89, 94, 98
techno-utopianism, 35, 172, 212
té de Dios, El (Aira). *See God's Tea Party*
telecommunications, 173–74, 177
Telmex, 173
Tempest, The (Shakespeare), 85
Ten Little Indians (Christie), 213
Testamento geométrico (Dieste), 130
Te vendo un perro (Villalobos), 259n1
Thoreau, Henry David, 28
Tigres del Norte, Los, 35, 174–76, 189
Time, Labor, and Social Domination (Postone), 259n3
Tlatelolco massacre, 118
Toá (Uribe Piedrahita), 33, 49
tobacco: in *Deep Foods*, 22; Ortiz on, 7–12, 27–28, 42, 49, 59, 67, 103, 238n78
toilet, 159–60, 262n37
Toledo, Alejandro, 103
tomato, 217–18
Tractatus Logico-Philosophicus (Wittgenstein), 25–26

transculturación (transculturation), 222; Monasterios on, 79–81, 248n33; Ortiz on, 3, 7–12, 49, 80–81, 199, 224–26; Pratt on, 7, 9; tobacco, sugar, and, 7–8
transcultural materialism. *See* materialism, transcultural
translation, 137; of Aira, 88–89, 98, 250n60; of *The Vortex*, 45, 242n18
Trilling, Lionel, 103
Tropical Animal (Gutiérrez), 136
Tully, John, 51
Turkle, Sherry, 160
2666 (Bolaño), 117, 178; bodies and, 121–25, 132–33; computers in, 211–12; corpses in, 125, 128–29, 132; femicide in, 34, 115, 128, 130–32, 135, 137, 211–12; nonhuman allusions in, 132–33

Ulmer, Gregory L., 137
UNEAC. *See* National Union of Writers and Artists of Cuba
United Fruit Company, 194, 228
"United Fruit Company, The" (Neruda), 60
University of California, Berkeley, 188
Uribe Piedrahita, César, 33, 49, 51
Uslar Pietri, Arturo, 27
USSR. *See* Soviet Union

vagina dentata, 48, 83
Valderrama, Patricia, 42
Vallejo, Fernando, 165, 202; *Almas en pena, chapolas negras*, 35, 145, 156–58, 262n28; *Casablanca la bella*, 35, 145, 159–60; *Our Lady of the Assassins*, 156
value: exchange and use, 144, 148–51, 164, 168, 260n8; misuse, 168–69; surplus, 64, 172, 208, 210, 218
Van Gogh, Vincent, 162
Vásquez-Figueroa, Alberto, 213–14, 216
Veblen, Thorstein, 164
Vecchio, Diego, 95
Venus of Willendorf, 1
Vibrant Matter (Bennett), 22
Villalobos, Juan Pablo, 259n1
Villena Alvarado, Marcelo, 74, 77, 81
Viñas, David, 46

Virgen de los sicarios, La (Our Lady of the Assassins) (Vallejo), 156
Viveiros de Castro, Eduardo, 86–87
"Voice of Things, The" ("La voz de las cosas") (Silva), 152–55, 261n18
von der Walde, Erna, 245n60
Vortex, The (La vorágine) (J. E. Rivera), 33, 83, 151; black flock in, 44; eco-critical readings of, 45–46; feathers in, 46–48; rubber in, 44–46, 48–49, 182, 200; socio-critical readings of, 45–46; translations of, 45, 242n18
"voz de las cosas, La" ("The Voice of Things") (Silva), 152–55, 261n18

Walkowitz, Rebecca, 250n60
Wall-E (film), 216
Wallerstein, Immanuel, 114
Wark, McKenzie, 268n13
Washbourne, Kelly, 155
waste, 213, 216–18
Waste Land (documentary), 217
We Have Never Been Modern (Latour), 65
Weisberger, Lauren, 161
Weltliteratur (World Literature). *See* World Literature
White, Hayden, 31, 226, 239n89; on extermination, 7, 54–55, 222, 232n10; typologies of, 32
Whitehead, Alfred North, 101
Wiethüchter, Blanca, 88, 102; holes and, 73–76, 84–85, 247n14; *El jardín de Nora*, 33–34, 68–69, 71–87, 93, 95–96, 99–101, 200, 248n37. *See also* jardín de Nora, El
Williams, Raymond L., 229

Wittgenstein, Ludwig, 4, 25–26
work. *See* labor
World Literature: as autotelic, 106–10; Bolaño and, 113–15, 117–19, 121–24, 127, 129–30, 135; corpse, orientation toward, for, 34, 105–6, 111–12, 138–39, 200–201; extractivism and, 36, 219; *God's Tea Party* and, 90–91, 94, 250n60; idealism in, materialism countering, 34, 116–17; Latin Americanism and, 5–6, 201; Marx and Engels on, 137, 209; sociotechnical imaginaries and, 205, 218; transcultural materialism for, 37, 105, 137–39, 201; Wallerstein and, 114
worldliteraturism, 5, 34, 106–7
worms, 271n44

You Are Not a Gadget (Lanier), 181–82
YUMA, or the Land of Friends (artwork), 215, 215–16

Zambra, Alejandro, 189; *Bonsái*, 177, 184–85; as Chilean, 182–83, 185–86; digital lock-in and, 181; digital obsolescence and, 177–79, 186, 211; extractivism and, 181–82, 210, 216; "Historia de un computador," 178–83, 186, 210, 216; love and, 35, 177–79, 181, 183–85, 204; *Mis documentos*, 177–78; nonhuman agency and, 179–80; oeuvre of, 177; on personal computer, 35, 177–84, 186, 210–11; "Recuerdos de un computador personal," 178, 183–84; on sleep, 182–83
Zapata, Emiliano, 167–68
Žižek, Slavoj, 107, 204

GPSR Authorized Representative: Easy Access System Europe, Mustamäe tee 50, 10621 Tallinn, Estonia, gpsr.requests@easproject.com

www.ingramcontent.com/pod-product-compliance
Lightning Source LLC
Chambersburg PA
CBHW021935290426
44108CB00012B/848